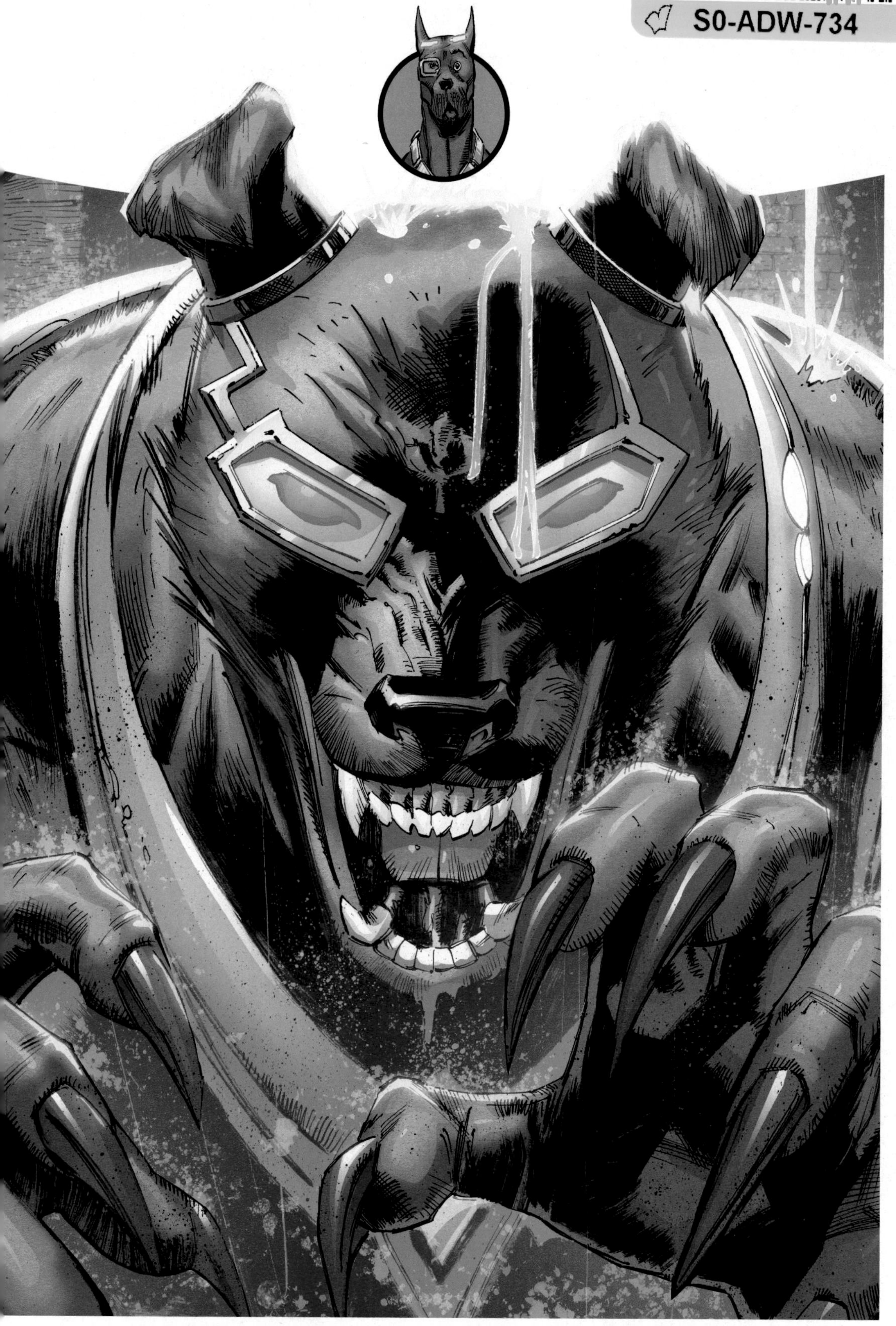

SCOOBY APOCALYPSE

VOL.5

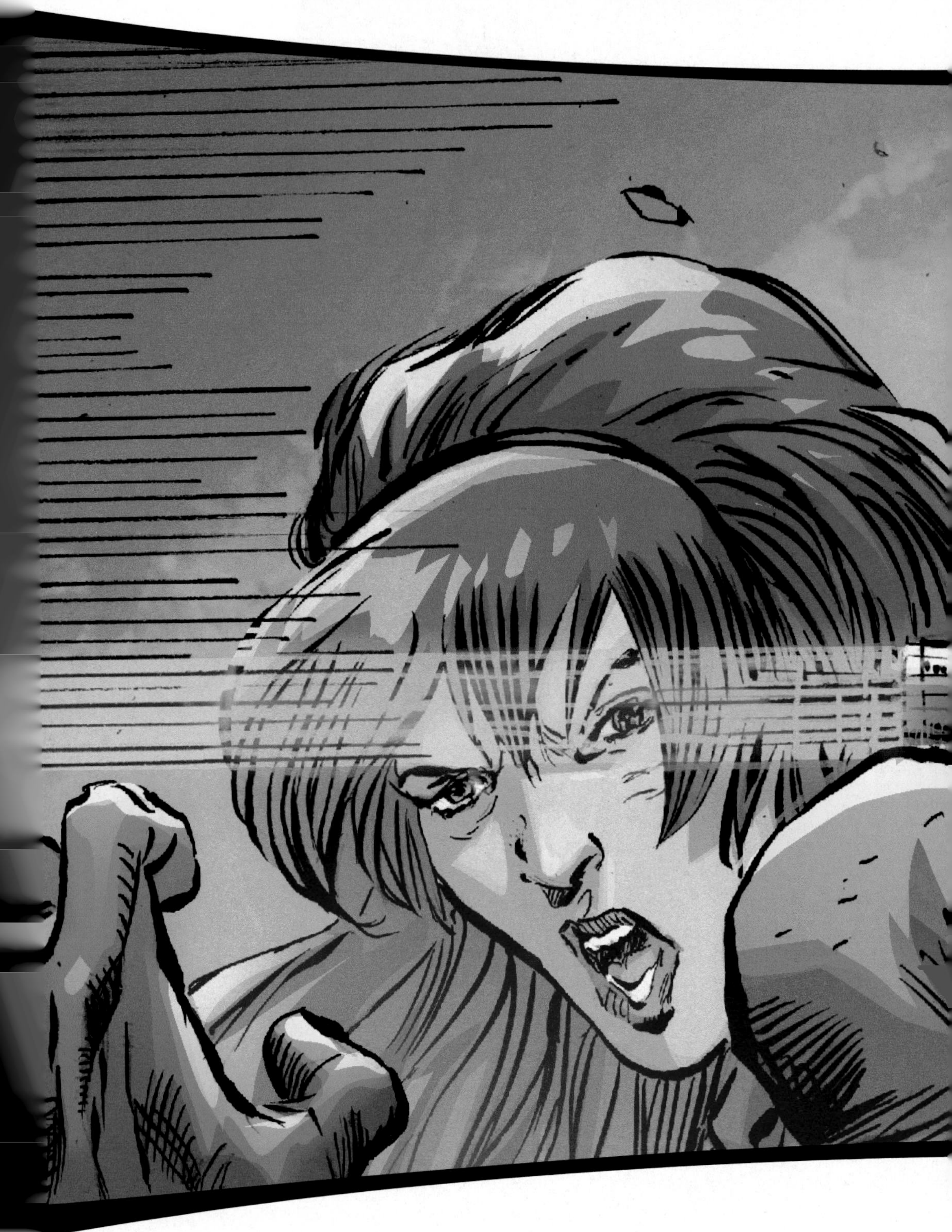

SCOOBY APOCALYPSE

VOL. 5

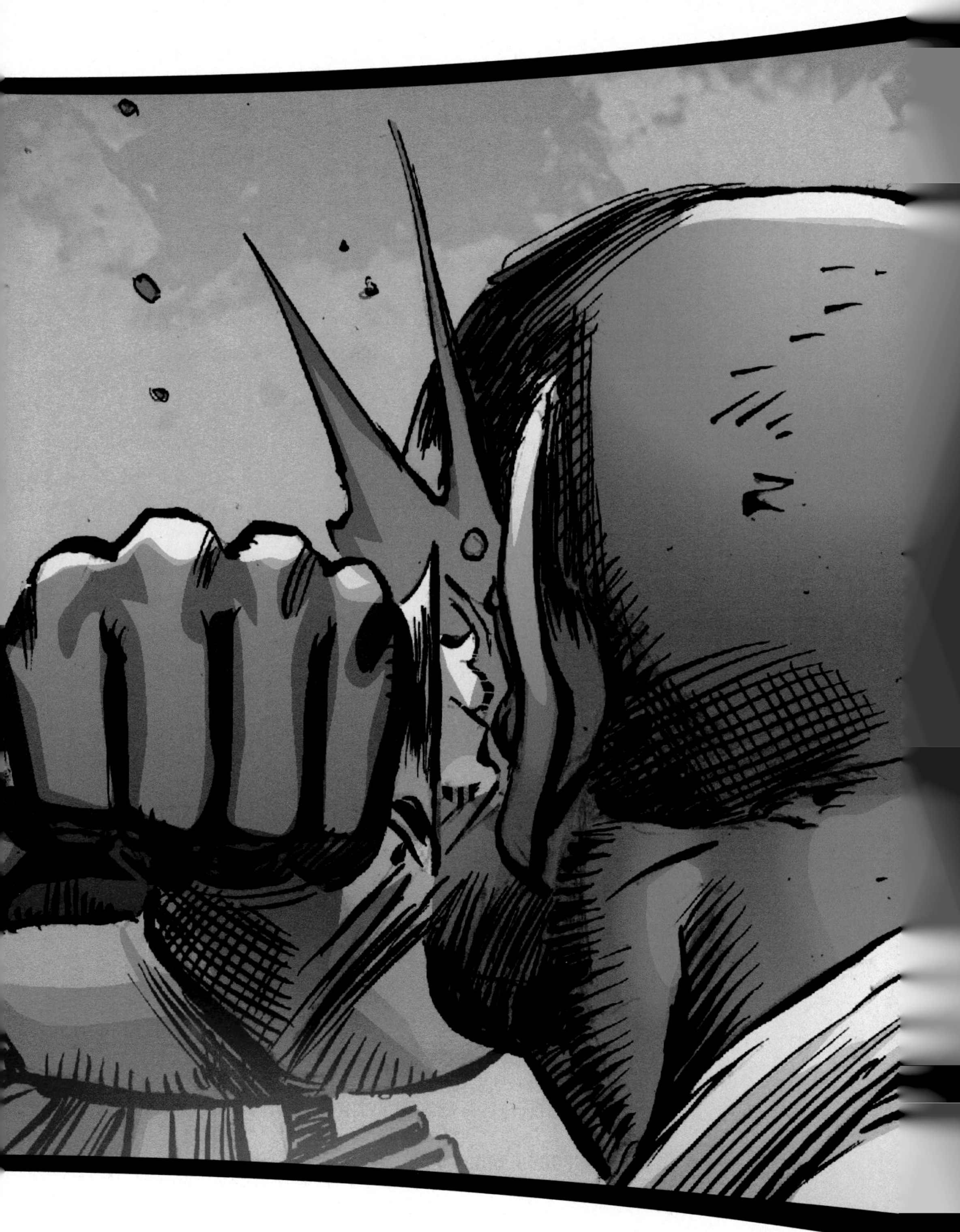

KEITH GIFFEN J.M. DeMATTEIS writers
PAT OLLIFFE RON WAGNER TOM MANDRAKE
SAM LOTFI YVEL GUICHET CHRIS BATISTA pencillers
TOM PALMER TOM MANDRAKE ANDY OWENS SCOTT HANNA
SAM LOTFI YVEL GUICHET inkers HI-FI JOHN RAUCH colorists
TRAVIS LANHAM letterer JUAN FERREYRA collection cover artis
Based on a concept by JIM LE

HARVEY RICHARDS Editor - Original Series LIZ ERICKSON Assistant Editor - Original Series
JEB WOODARD Group Editor - Collected Editions ERIKA ROTHBERG Editor - Collected Edition
STEVE COOK Design Director - Books MEGEN BELLERSEN Publication Design

BOB HARRAS Senior VP - Editor-in-Chief, DC Comics
PAT McCALLUM Executive Editor, DC Comics

DAN DiDIO Publisher JIM LEE Publisher & Chief Creative Officer
AMIT DESAI Executive VP - Business & Marketing Strategy, Direct to Consumer & Global Franchise Management
BOBBIE CHASE VP & Executive Editor, Young Reader & Talent Development MARK CHIARELLO Senior VP - Art, Design & Collected Editions
JOHN CUNNINGHAM Senior VP - Sales & Trade Marketing BRIAR DARDEN VP - Business Affairs
ANNE DePIES Senior VP - Business Strategy, Finance & Administration DON FALLETTI VP - Manufacturing Operations
LAWRENCE GANEM VP - Editorial Administration & Talent Relations ALISON GILL Senior VP - Manufacturing & Operations
JASON GREENBERG VP - Business Strategy & Finance HANK KANALZ Senior VP - Editorial Strategy & Administration
JAY KOGAN Senior VP - Legal Affairs NICK J. NAPOLITANO VP - Manufacturing Administration
LISETTE OSTERLOH VP - Digital Marketing & Events EDDIE SCANNELL VP - Consumer Marketing
COURTNEY SIMMONS Senior VP - Publicity & Communications JIM (SKI) SOKOLOWSKI VP - Comic Book Specialty Sales & Trade Marketing
NANCY SPEARS VP - Mass, Book, Digital Sales & Trade Marketing MICHELE R. WELLS VP - Content Strategy

SCOOBY APOCALYPSE VOL. 5

Published by DC Comics. All new material Copyright © 2019 Hanna-Barbera. All Rights Reserved.
Originally published in single magazine form in SCOOBY APOCALYPSE 25-30. Copyright © 2018 Hanna-Barbera. All Rights Reserved.
The stories, characters and incidents featured in this publication are entirely fictional. DC Comics does not read or accept unsolicited submissions of ideas, stories or artwork.

DC Comics, 2900 West Alameda Ave., Burbank, CA 91505
Printed by LSC Communications, Kendallville, IN, USA. 4/19/19. First Printing.
ISBN: 978-1-4012-8957-7

Library of Congress Cataloging-in-Publication Data is available.

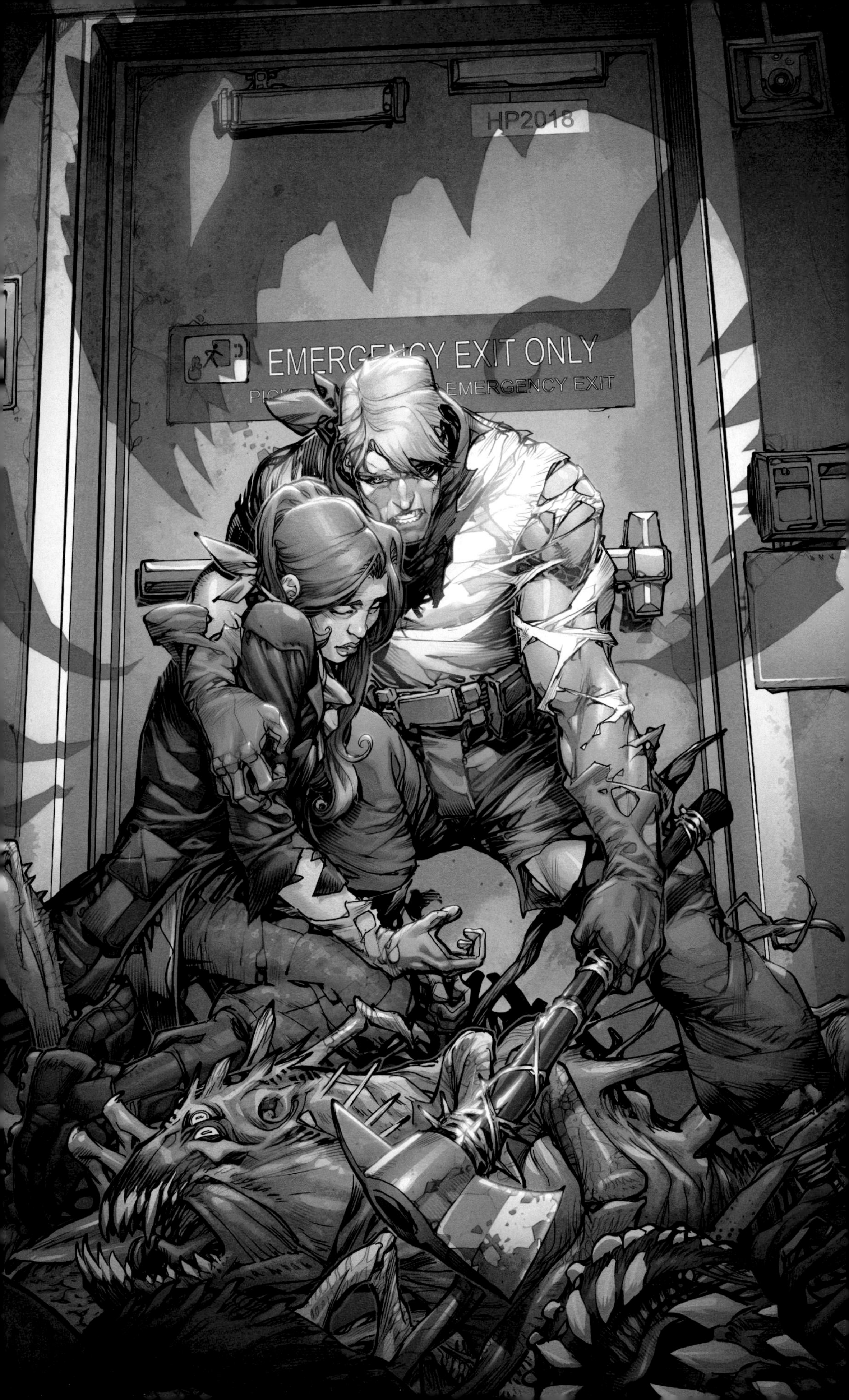
HP2018
EMERGENCY EXIT ONLY
EMERGENCY EXIT

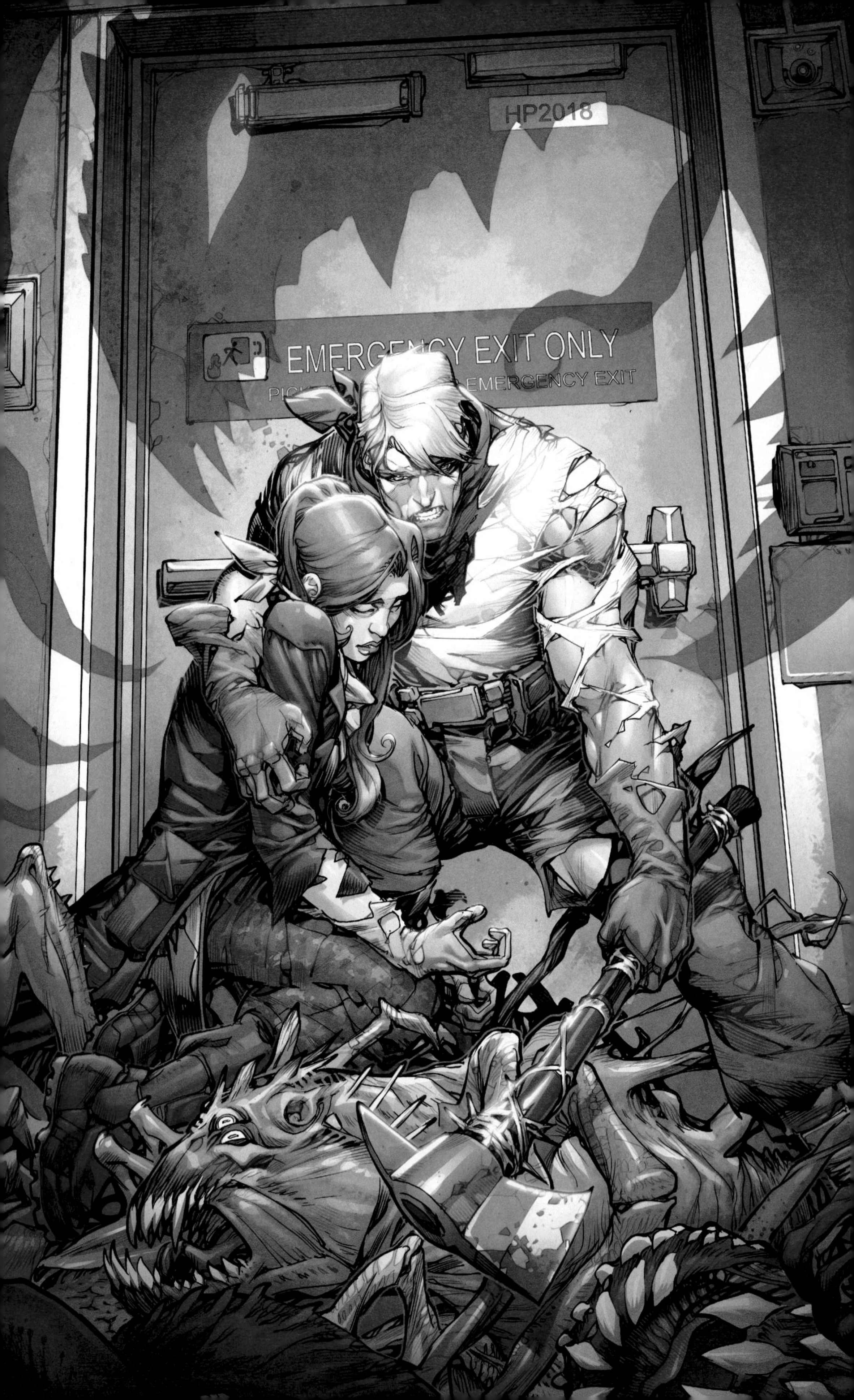
HP2018
EMERGENCY EXIT ONLY
EMERGENCY EXIT

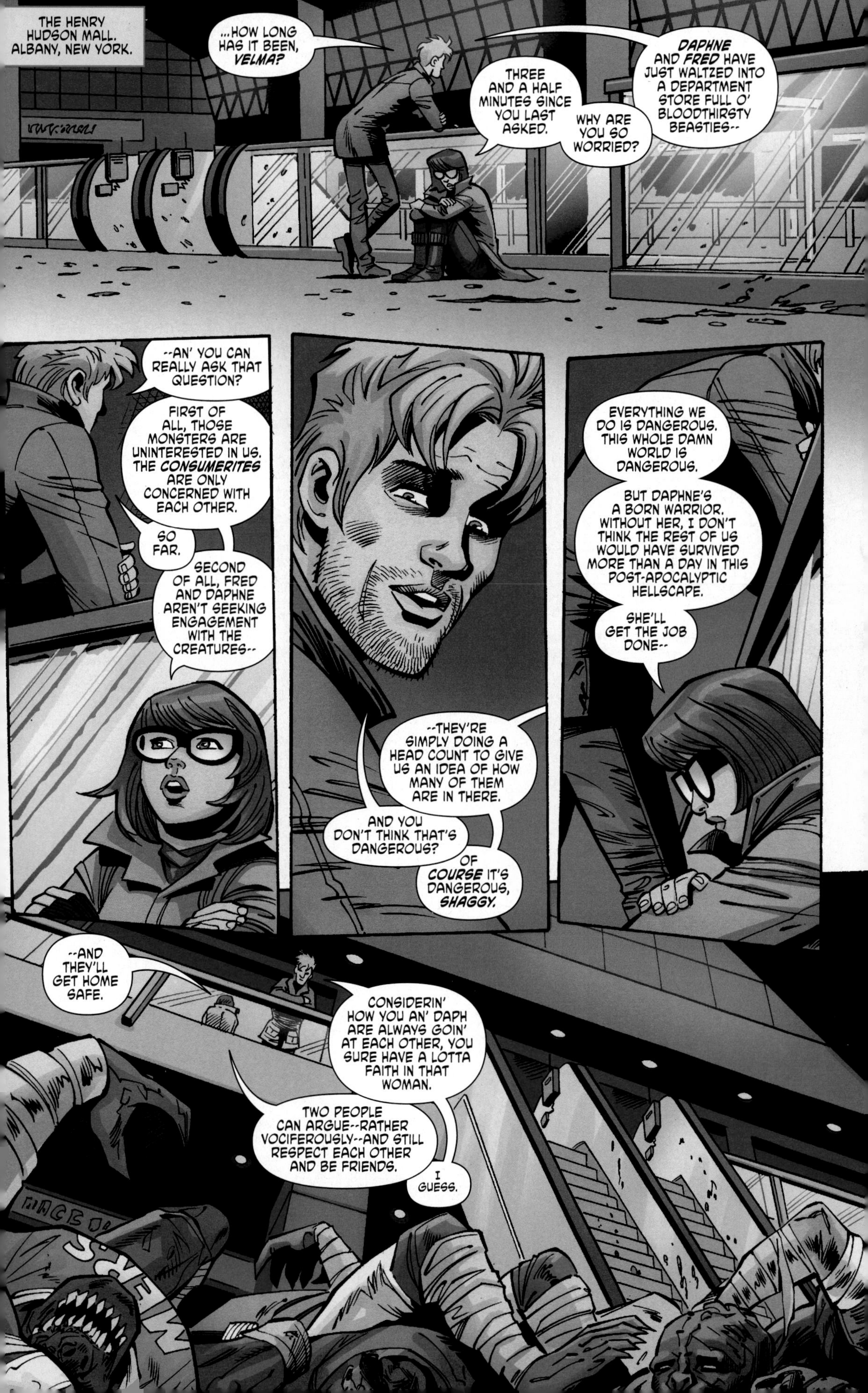
THE HENRY HUDSON MALL. ALBANY, NEW YORK.
...HOW LONG HAS IT BEEN, VELMA?
THREE AND A HALF MINUTES SINCE YOU LAST ASKED.
WHY ARE YOU SO WORRIED?
DAPHNE AND FRED HAVE JUST WALTZED INTO A DEPARTMENT STORE FULL O' BLOODTHIRSTY BEASTIES--
--AN' YOU CAN REALLY ASK THAT QUESTION?
FIRST OF ALL, THOSE MONSTERS ARE UNINTERESTED IN US. THE CONSUMERITES ARE ONLY CONCERNED WITH EACH OTHER.
SO FAR.
SECOND OF ALL, FRED AND DAPHNE AREN'T SEEKING ENGAGEMENT WITH THE CREATURES--
--THEY'RE SIMPLY DOING A HEAD COUNT TO GIVE US AN IDEA OF HOW MANY OF THEM ARE IN THERE.
AND YOU DON'T THINK THAT'S DANGEROUS?
OF COURSE IT'S DANGEROUS, SHAGGY.
EVERYTHING WE DO IS DANGEROUS. THIS WHOLE DAMN WORLD IS DANGEROUS.
BUT DAPHNE'S A BORN WARRIOR. WITHOUT HER, I DON'T THINK THE REST OF US WOULD HAVE SURVIVED MORE THAN A DAY IN THIS POST-APOCALYPTIC HELLSCAPE.
SHE'LL GET THE JOB DONE--
--AND THEY'LL GET HOME SAFE.
CONSIDERIN' HOW YOU AN' DAPH ARE ALWAYS GOIN' AT EACH OTHER, YOU SURE HAVE A LOTTA FAITH IN THAT WOMAN.
TWO PEOPLE CAN ARGUE--RATHER VOCIFEROUSLY--AND STILL RESPECT EACH OTHER AND BE FRIENDS.
I GUESS.

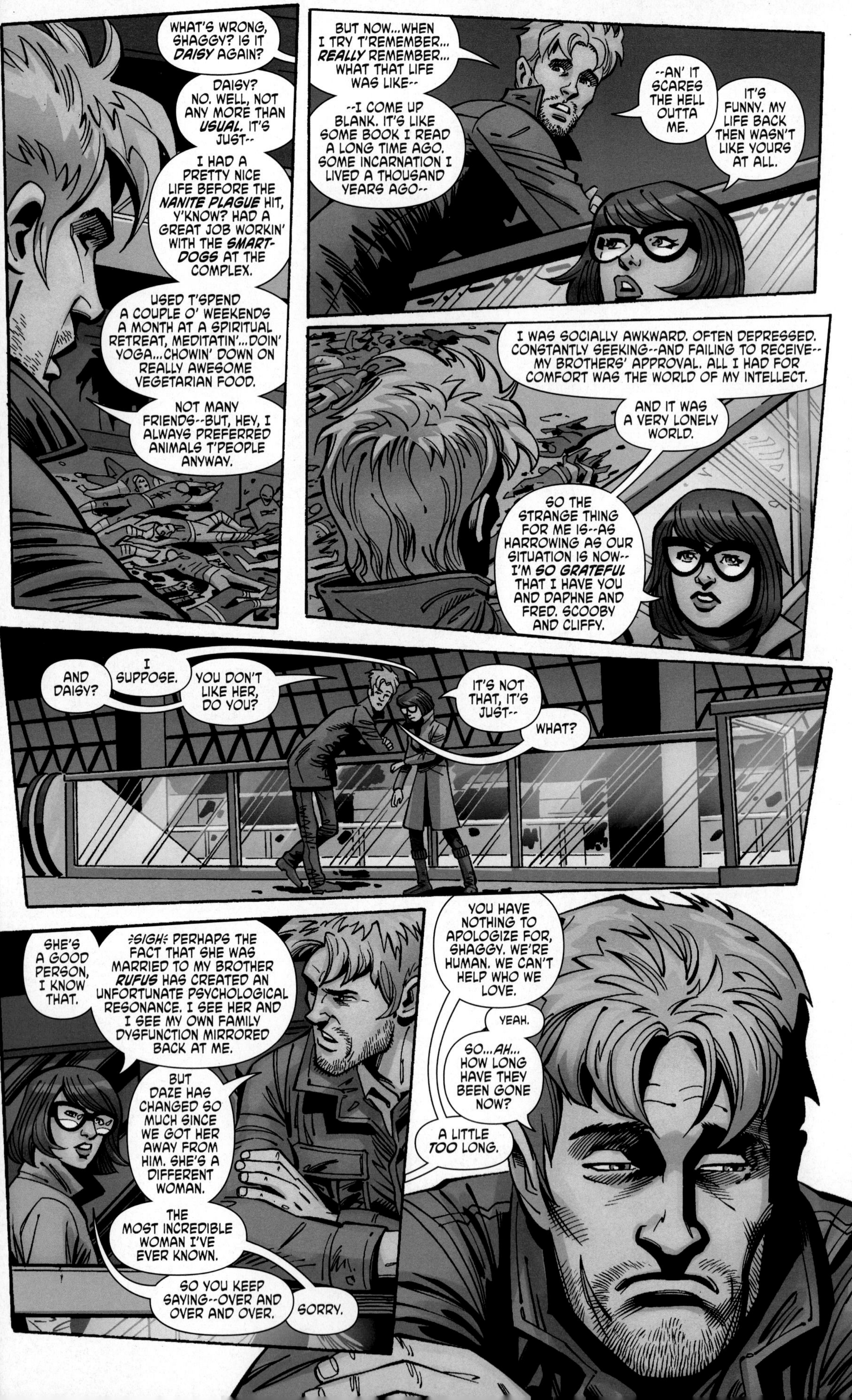
WHAT'S WRONG, SHAGGY? IS IT DAISY AGAIN?
DAISY? NO. WELL, NOT ANY MORE THAN USUAL. IT'S JUST--
I HAD A PRETTY NICE LIFE BEFORE THE NANITE PLAGUE HIT, Y'KNOW? HAD A GREAT JOB WORKIN' WITH THE SMART-DOGS AT THE COMPLEX.
USED T'SPEND A COUPLE O' WEEKENDS A MONTH AT A SPIRITUAL RETREAT, MEDITATIN'...DOIN' YOGA...CHOWIN' DOWN ON REALLY AWESOME VEGETARIAN FOOD.
NOT MANY FRIENDS--BUT, HEY, I ALWAYS PREFERRED ANIMALS T'PEOPLE ANYWAY.
BUT NOW...WHEN I TRY T'REMEMBER... REALLY REMEMBER... WHAT THAT LIFE WAS LIKE--
--I COME UP BLANK. IT'S LIKE SOME BOOK I READ A LONG TIME AGO. SOME INCARNATION I LIVED A THOUSAND YEARS AGO--
--AN' IT SCARES THE HELL OUTTA ME.
IT'S FUNNY. MY LIFE BACK THEN WASN'T LIKE YOURS AT ALL.
I WAS SOCIALLY AWKWARD. OFTEN DEPRESSED. CONSTANTLY SEEKING--AND FAILING TO RECEIVE--MY BROTHERS' APPROVAL. ALL I HAD FOR COMFORT WAS THE WORLD OF MY INTELLECT.
AND IT WAS A VERY LONELY WORLD.
SO THE STRANGE THING FOR ME IS--AS HARROWING AS OUR SITUATION IS NOW--I'M SO GRATEFUL THAT I HAVE YOU AND DAPHNE AND FRED. SCOOBY AND CLIFFY.
AND DAISY?
I SUPPOSE.
YOU DON'T LIKE HER, DO YOU?
IT'S NOT THAT, IT'S JUST--
WHAT?
SHE'S A GOOD PERSON, I KNOW THAT.
≷SIGH≶ PERHAPS THE FACT THAT SHE WAS MARRIED TO MY BROTHER RUFUS HAS CREATED AN UNFORTUNATE PSYCHOLOGICAL RESONANCE. I SEE HER AND I SEE MY OWN FAMILY DYSFUNCTION MIRRORED BACK AT ME.
BUT DAZE HAS CHANGED SO MUCH SINCE WE GOT HER AWAY FROM HIM. SHE'S A DIFFERENT WOMAN.
THE MOST INCREDIBLE WOMAN I'VE EVER KNOWN.
SO YOU KEEP SAYING--OVER AND OVER AND OVER.
SORRY.
YOU HAVE NOTHING TO APOLOGIZE FOR, SHAGGY. WE'RE HUMAN. WE CAN'T HELP WHO WE LOVE.
YEAH.
SO...AH... HOW LONG HAVE THEY BEEN GONE NOW?
A LITTLE TOO LONG.

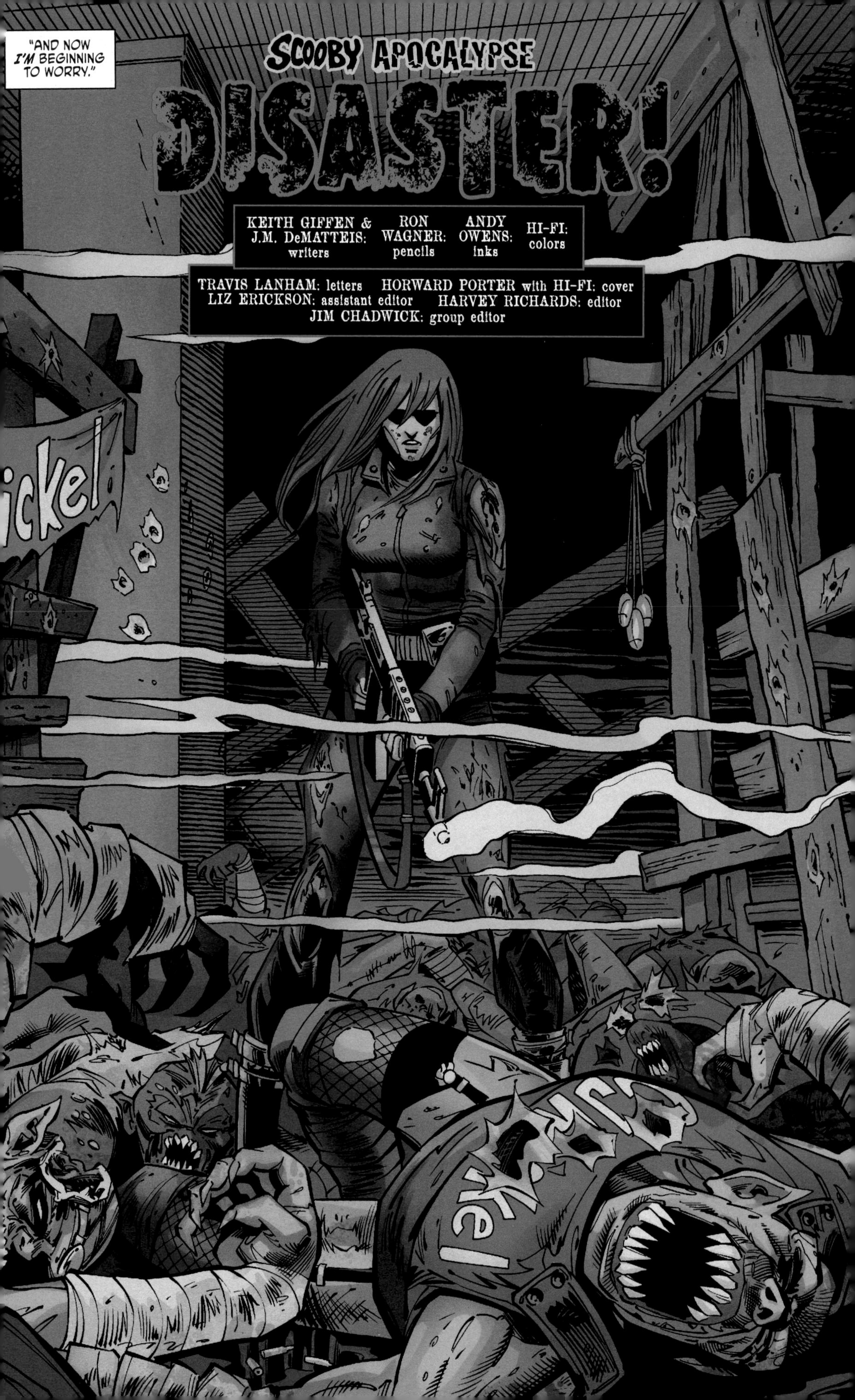

"AND NOW I'M BEGINNING TO WORRY."
SCOOBY APOCALYPSE
DISASTER!
KEITH GIFFEN & J.M. DeMATTEIS: writers
RON WAGNER: pencils
ANDY OWENS: inks
HI-FI: colors
TRAVIS LANHAM: letters HORWARD PORTER with HI-FI: cover
LIZ ERICKSON: assistant editor HARVEY RICHARDS: editor
JIM CHADWICK: group editor
ickel

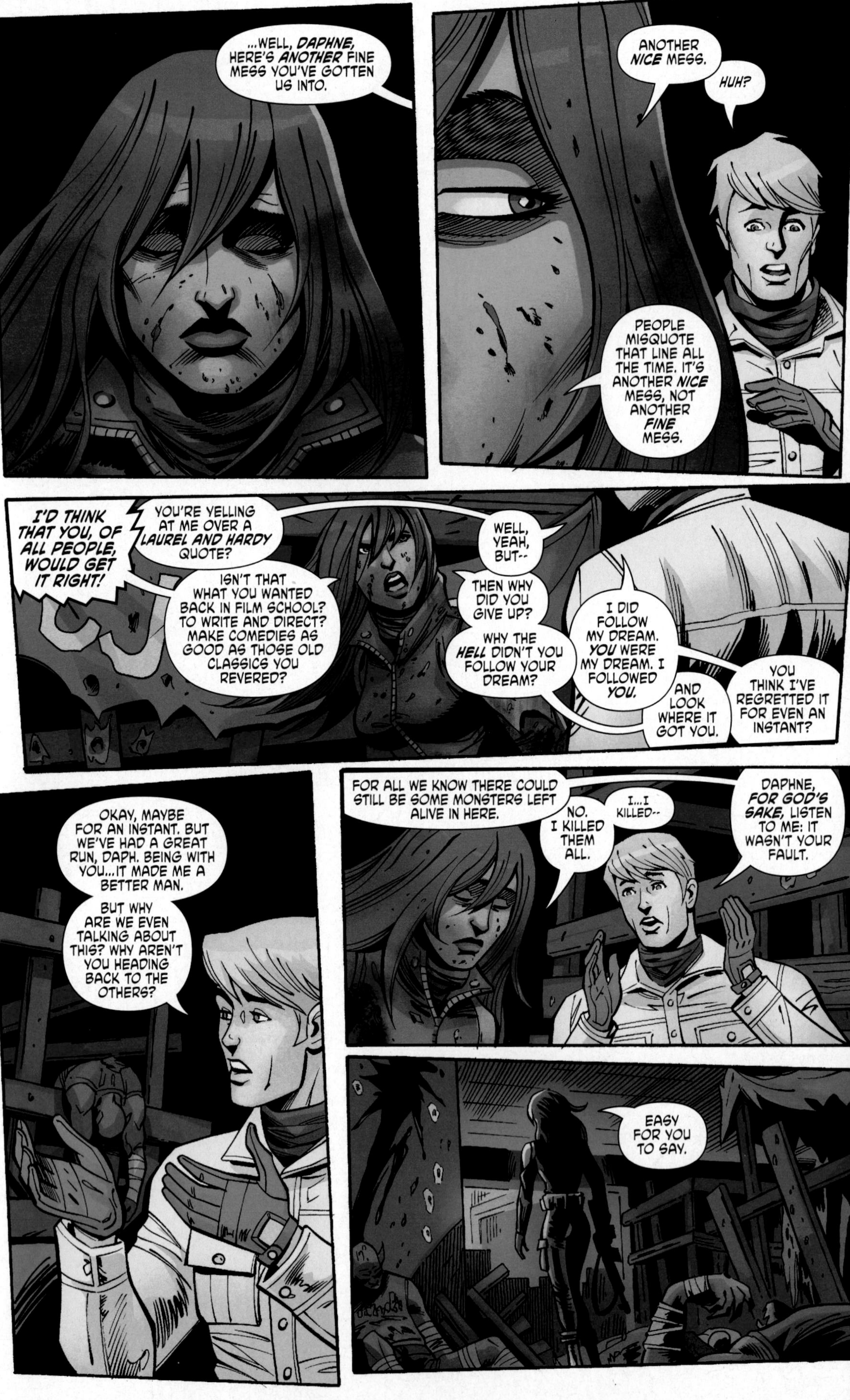
...WELL, DAPHNE, HERE'S ANOTHER FINE MESS YOU'VE GOTTEN US INTO.
ANOTHER NICE MESS.
HUH?
PEOPLE MISQUOTE THAT LINE ALL THE TIME. IT'S ANOTHER NICE MESS, NOT ANOTHER FINE MESS.
YOU'RE YELLING AT ME OVER A LAUREL AND HARDY QUOTE?
I'D THINK THAT YOU, OF ALL PEOPLE, WOULD GET IT RIGHT!
WELL, YEAH, BUT--
ISN'T THAT WHAT YOU WANTED BACK IN FILM SCHOOL? TO WRITE AND DIRECT? MAKE COMEDIES AS GOOD AS THOSE OLD CLASSICS YOU REVERED?
THEN WHY DID YOU GIVE UP?
WHY THE HELL DIDN'T YOU FOLLOW YOUR DREAM?
I DID FOLLOW MY DREAM. YOU WERE MY DREAM. I FOLLOWED YOU.
AND LOOK WHERE IT GOT YOU.
YOU THINK I'VE REGRETTED IT FOR EVEN AN INSTANT?
OKAY, MAYBE FOR AN INSTANT. BUT WE'VE HAD A GREAT RUN, DAPH. BEING WITH YOU...IT MADE ME A BETTER MAN.
BUT WHY ARE WE EVEN TALKING ABOUT THIS? WHY AREN'T YOU HEADING BACK TO THE OTHERS?
FOR ALL WE KNOW THERE COULD STILL BE SOME MONSTERS LEFT ALIVE IN HERE.
I...I KILLED--
NO. I KILLED THEM ALL.
DAPHNE, FOR GOD'S SAKE, LISTEN TO ME: IT WASN'T YOUR FAULT.
EASY FOR YOU TO SAY.

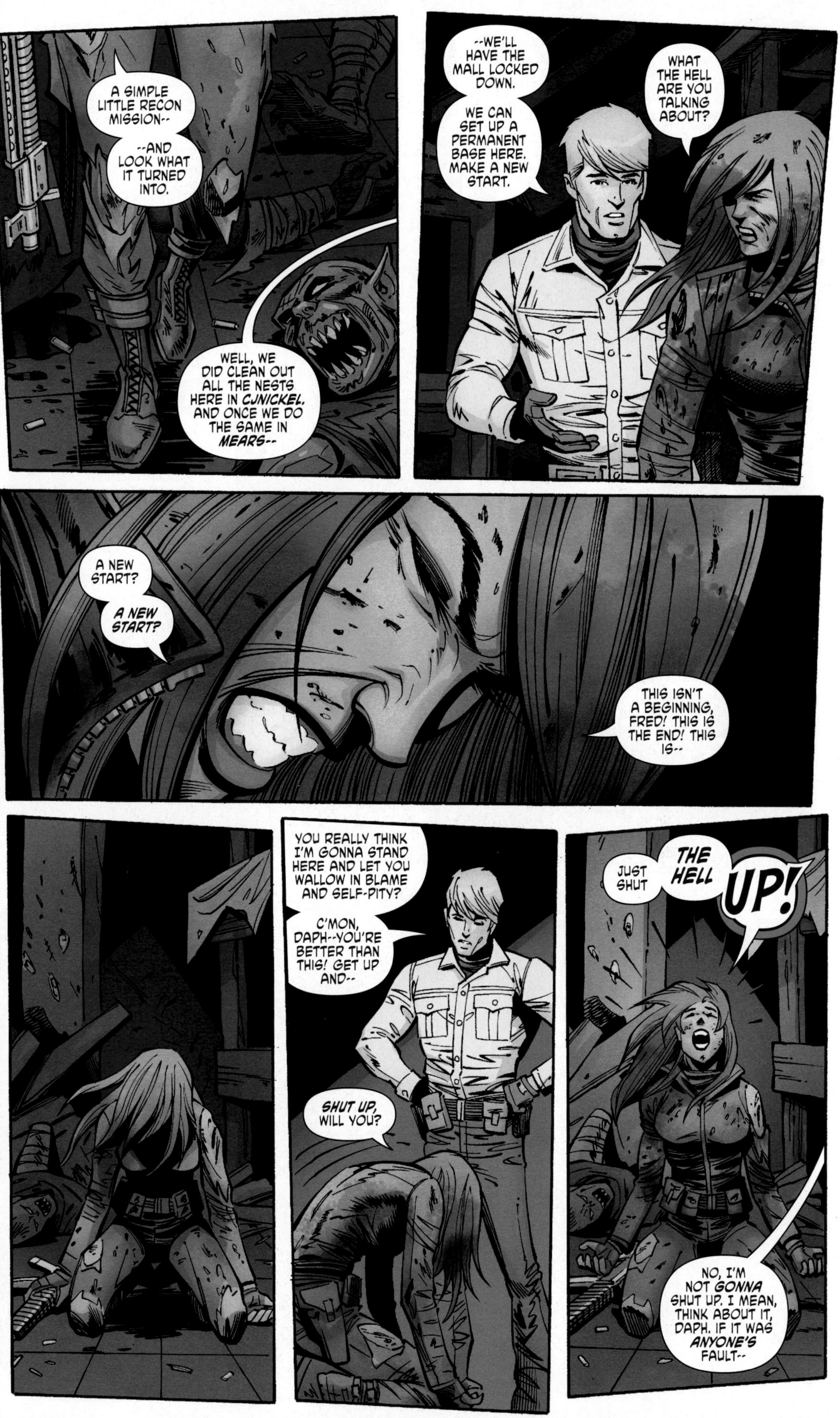
A SIMPLE LITTLE RECON MISSION--
--AND LOOK WHAT IT TURNED INTO.
WELL, WE DID CLEAN OUT ALL THE NESTS HERE IN CJNICKEL. AND ONCE WE DO THE SAME IN MEARS--
--WE'LL HAVE THE MALL LOCKED DOWN.
WE CAN SET UP A PERMANENT BASE HERE. MAKE A NEW START.
WHAT THE HELL ARE YOU TALKING ABOUT?
A NEW START?
A NEW START?
THIS ISN'T A BEGINNING, FRED! THIS IS THE END! THIS IS--
YOU REALLY THINK I'M GONNA STAND HERE AND LET YOU WALLOW IN BLAME AND SELF-PITY?
C'MON, DAPH--YOU'RE BETTER THAN THIS! GET UP AND--
SHUT UP, WILL YOU?
JUST SHUT
THE HELL
UP!
NO, I'M NOT GONNA SHUT UP. I MEAN, THINK ABOUT IT, DAPH. IF IT WAS ANYONE'S FAULT--

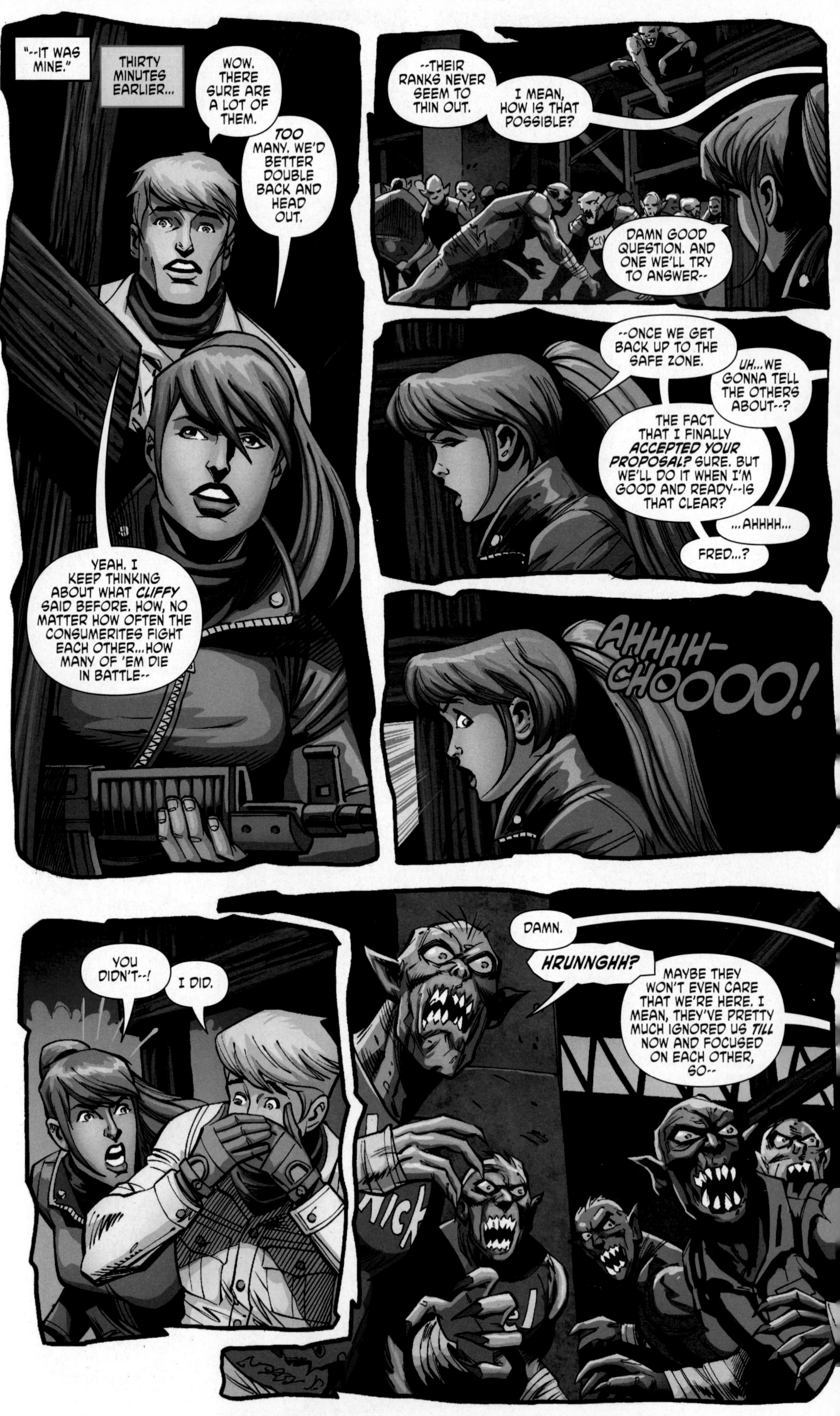
"--IT WAS MINE."
THIRTY MINUTES EARLIER...
WOW. THERE SURE ARE A LOT OF THEM.
TOO MANY. WE'D BETTER DOUBLE BACK AND HEAD OUT.
YEAH. I KEEP THINKING ABOUT WHAT CLIFFY SAID BEFORE. HOW, NO MATTER HOW OFTEN THE CONSUMERITES FIGHT EACH OTHER...HOW MANY OF 'EM DIE IN BATTLE--
--THEIR RANKS NEVER SEEM TO THIN OUT.
I MEAN, HOW IS THAT POSSIBLE?
DAMN GOOD QUESTION. AND ONE WE'LL TRY TO ANSWER--
--ONCE WE GET BACK UP TO THE SAFE ZONE.
UH...WE GONNA TELL THE OTHERS ABOUT--?
THE FACT THAT I FINALLY ACCEPTED YOUR PROPOSAL? SURE. BUT WE'LL DO IT WHEN I'M GOOD AND READY--IS THAT CLEAR?
...AHHHH...
FRED...?
AHHHH-CHOOOOO!
YOU DIDN'T--!
I DID.
DAMN.
HRUNNGHH?
MAYBE THEY WON'T EVEN CARE THAT WE'RE HERE. I MEAN, THEY'VE PRETTY MUCH IGNORED US TILL NOW AND FOCUSED ON EACH OTHER, SO--

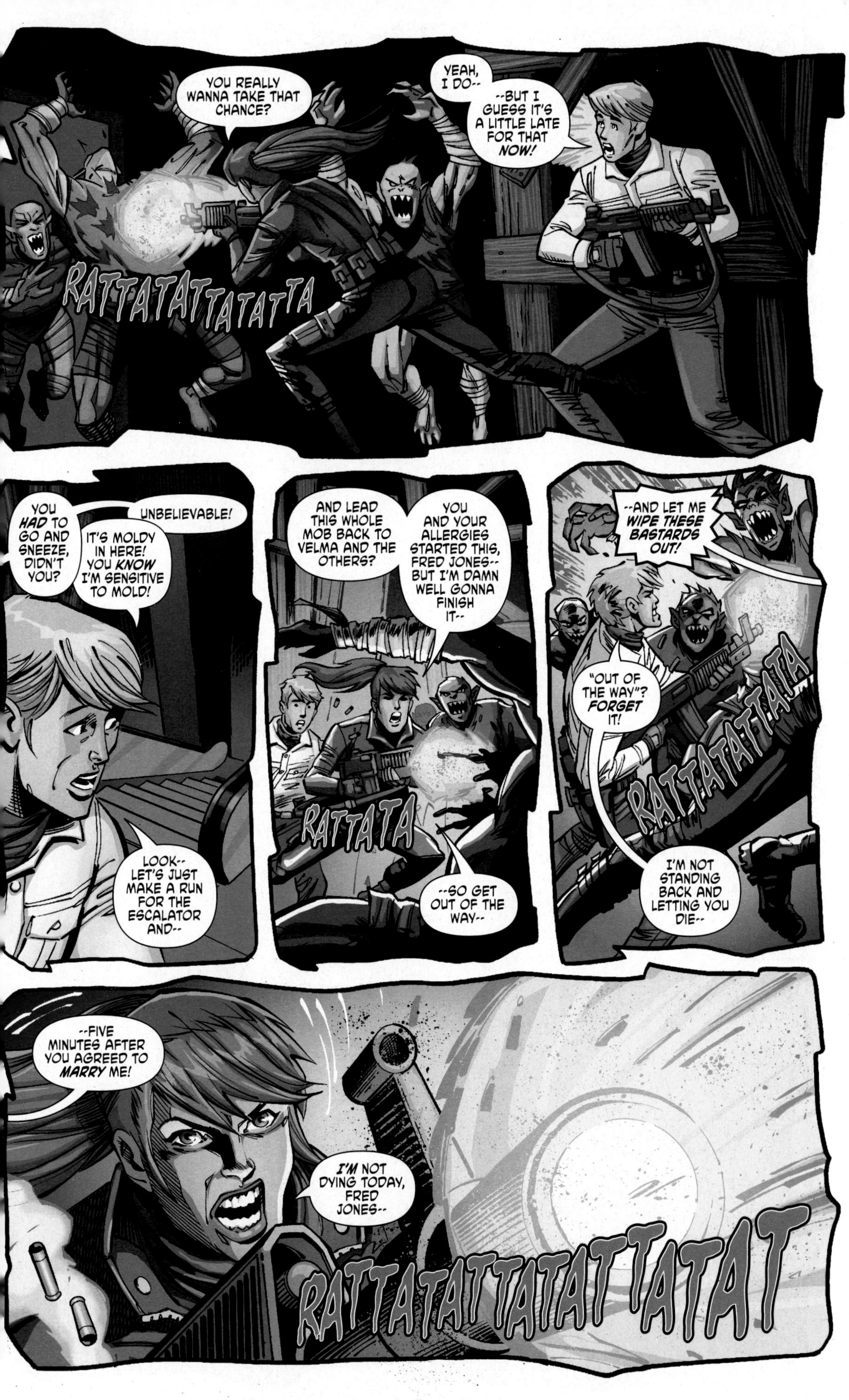

YOU REALLY WANNA TAKE THAT CHANCE?
YEAH, I DO--
--BUT I GUESS IT'S A LITTLE LATE FOR THAT NOW!
RATTATATTATATTA
YOU HAD TO GO AND SNEEZE, DIDN'T YOU?
UNBELIEVABLE!
IT'S MOLDY IN HERE! YOU KNOW I'M SENSITIVE TO MOLD!
LOOK-- LET'S JUST MAKE A RUN FOR THE ESCALATOR AND--
AND LEAD THIS WHOLE MOB BACK TO VELMA AND THE OTHERS?
YOU AND YOUR ALLERGIES STARTED THIS, FRED JONES-- BUT I'M DAMN WELL GONNA FINISH IT--
RATTATA
--SO GET OUT OF THE WAY--
--AND LET ME WIPE THESE BASTARDS OUT!
"OUT OF THE WAY"? FORGET IT!
RATTATATTATA
I'M NOT STANDING BACK AND LETTING YOU DIE--
--FIVE MINUTES AFTER YOU AGREED TO MARRY ME!
I'M NOT DYING TODAY, FRED JONES--
RATTATATTATATTATAT

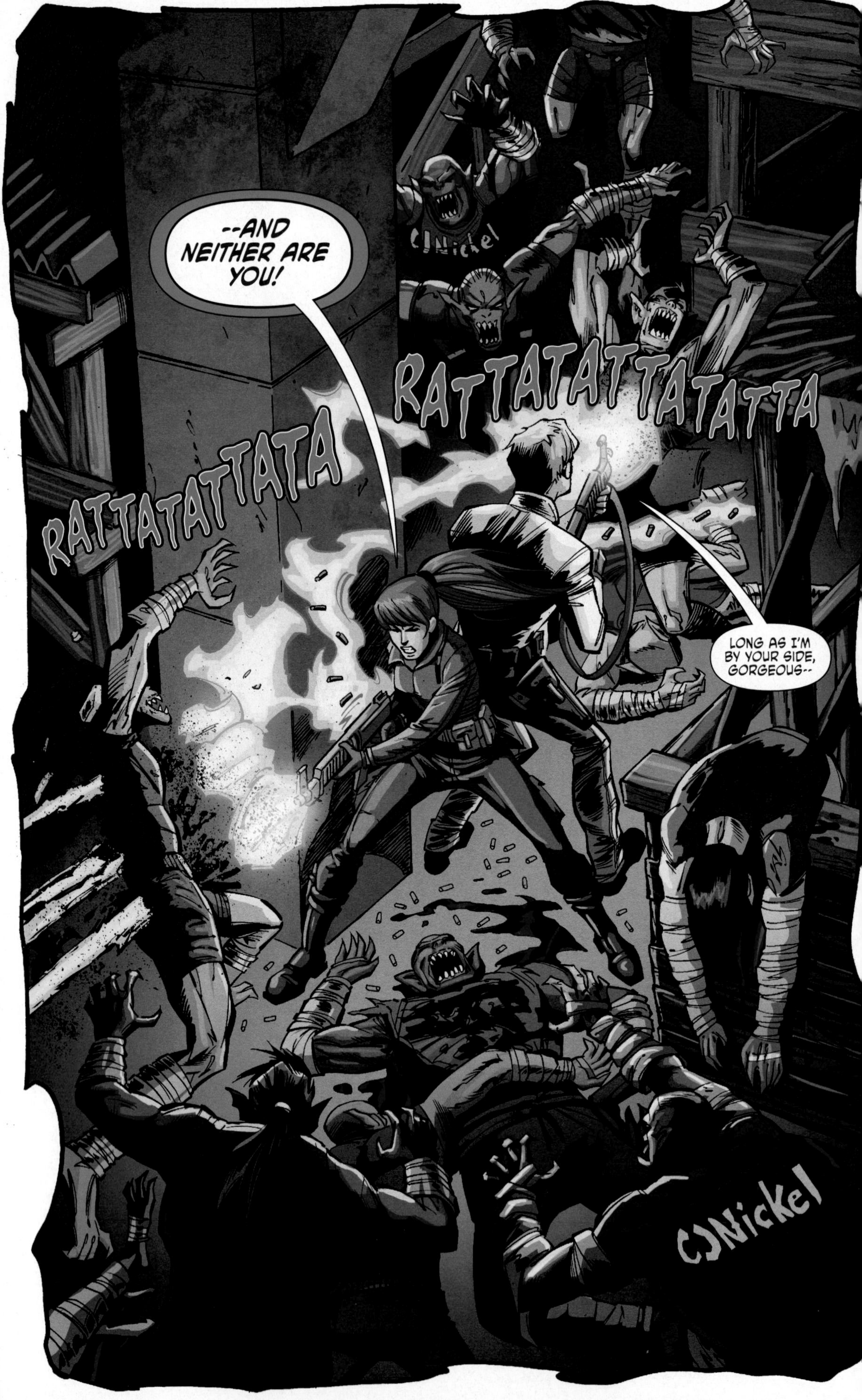
--AND NEITHER ARE YOU!
RATTATATTATA
RATTATATTATATTA
LONG AS I'M BY YOUR SIDE, GORGEOUS--
CJNickel

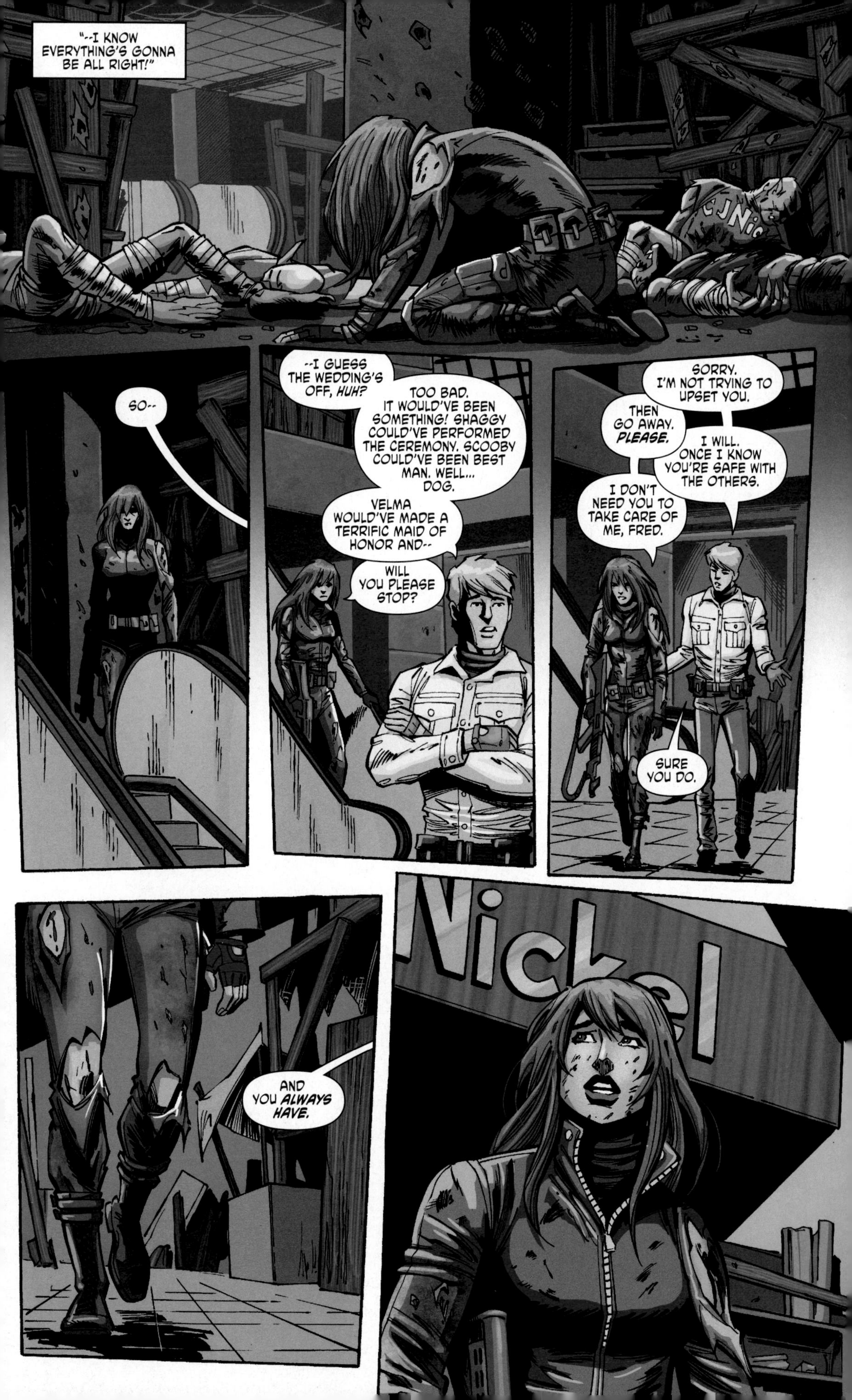

"--I KNOW EVERYTHING'S GONNA BE ALL RIGHT!"
CJNic
SO--
--I GUESS THE WEDDING'S OFF, *HUH?*
TOO BAD. IT WOULD'VE BEEN SOMETHING! SHAGGY COULD'VE PERFORMED THE CEREMONY. SCOOBY COULD'VE BEEN BEST MAN. WELL... DOG.
VELMA WOULD'VE MADE A TERRIFIC MAID OF HONOR AND--
WILL YOU PLEASE STOP?
SORRY. I'M NOT TRYING TO UPSET YOU.
THEN GO AWAY. ***PLEASE.***
I WILL. ONCE I KNOW YOU'RE SAFE WITH THE OTHERS.
I DON'T NEED YOU TO TAKE CARE OF ME, FRED.
SURE YOU DO.
AND YOU ***ALWAYS HAVE.***
Nick l

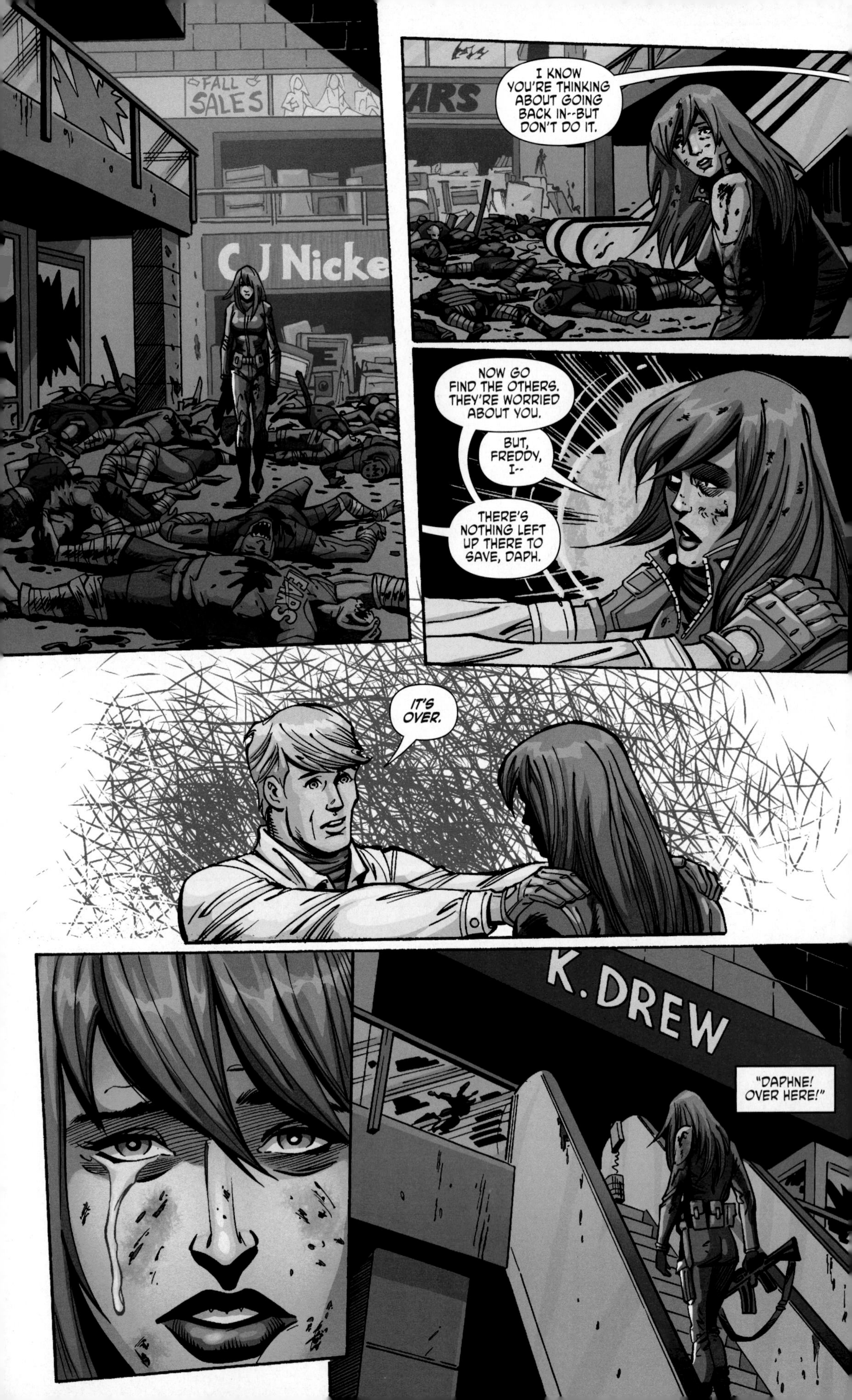
FALL SALES
C J Nicke
I KNOW YOU'RE THINKING ABOUT GOING BACK IN--BUT DON'T DO IT.
NOW GO FIND THE OTHERS. THEY'RE WORRIED ABOUT YOU.
BUT, FREDDY, I--
THERE'S NOTHING LEFT UP THERE TO SAVE, DAPH.
IT'S OVER.
K. DREW
"DAPHNE! OVER HERE!"

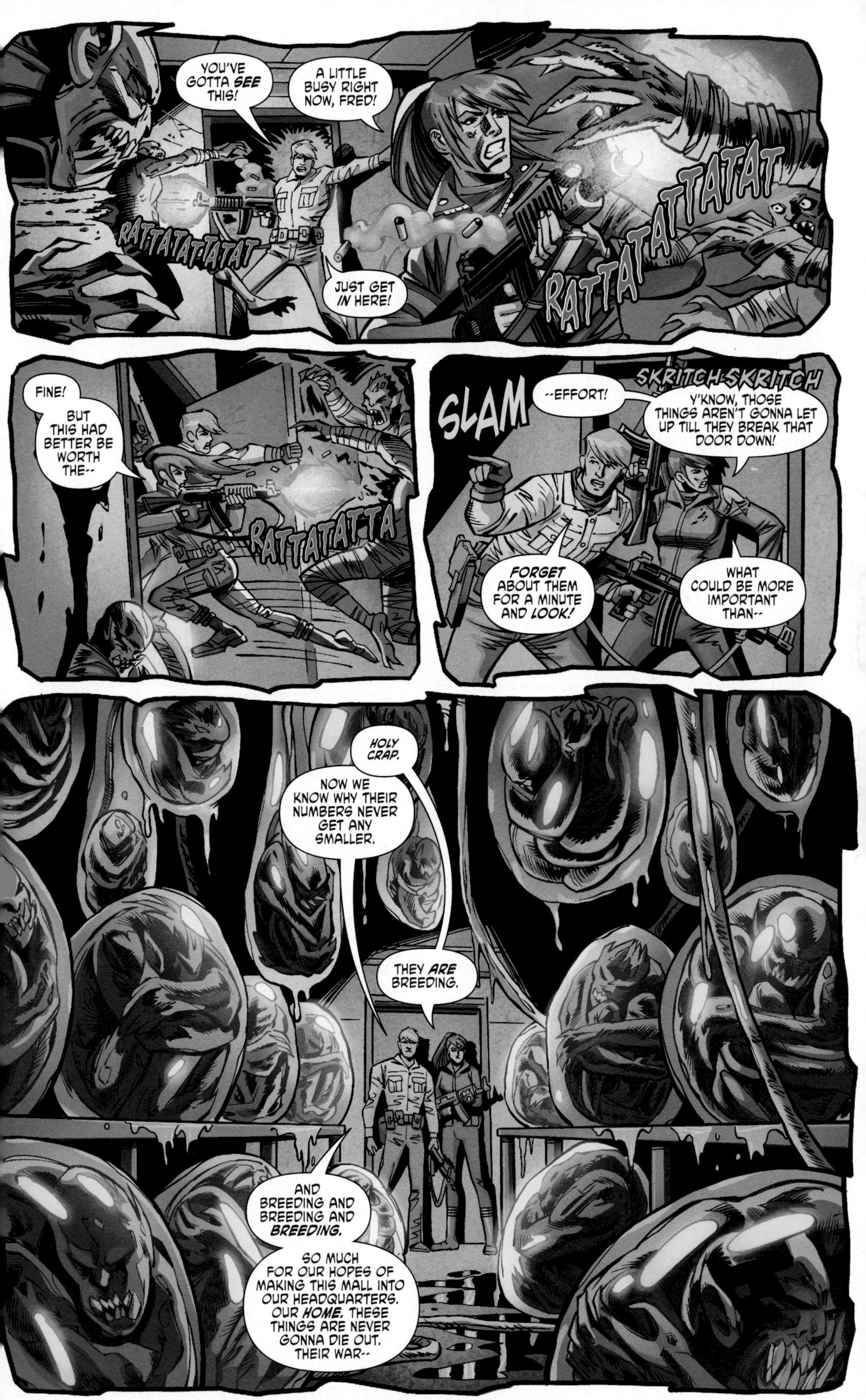
YOU'VE GOTTA SEE THIS!
A LITTLE BUSY RIGHT NOW, FRED!
RATTATATTATAT
RATTATATTATAT
JUST GET IN HERE!
RATTATAT
FINE!
BUT THIS HAD BETTER BE WORTH THE--
RATTATATTA
SLAM
--EFFORT!
SKRITCH SKRITCH
Y'KNOW, THOSE THINGS AREN'T GONNA LET UP TILL THEY BREAK THAT DOOR DOWN!
FORGET ABOUT THEM FOR A MINUTE AND LOOK!
WHAT COULD BE MORE IMPORTANT THAN--
HOLY CRAP.
NOW WE KNOW WHY THEIR NUMBERS NEVER GET ANY SMALLER.
THEY ARE BREEDING.
AND BREEDING AND BREEDING AND BREEDING.
SO MUCH FOR OUR HOPES OF MAKING THIS MALL INTO OUR HEADQUARTERS. OUR HOME. THESE THINGS ARE NEVER GONNA DIE OUT. THEIR WAR--

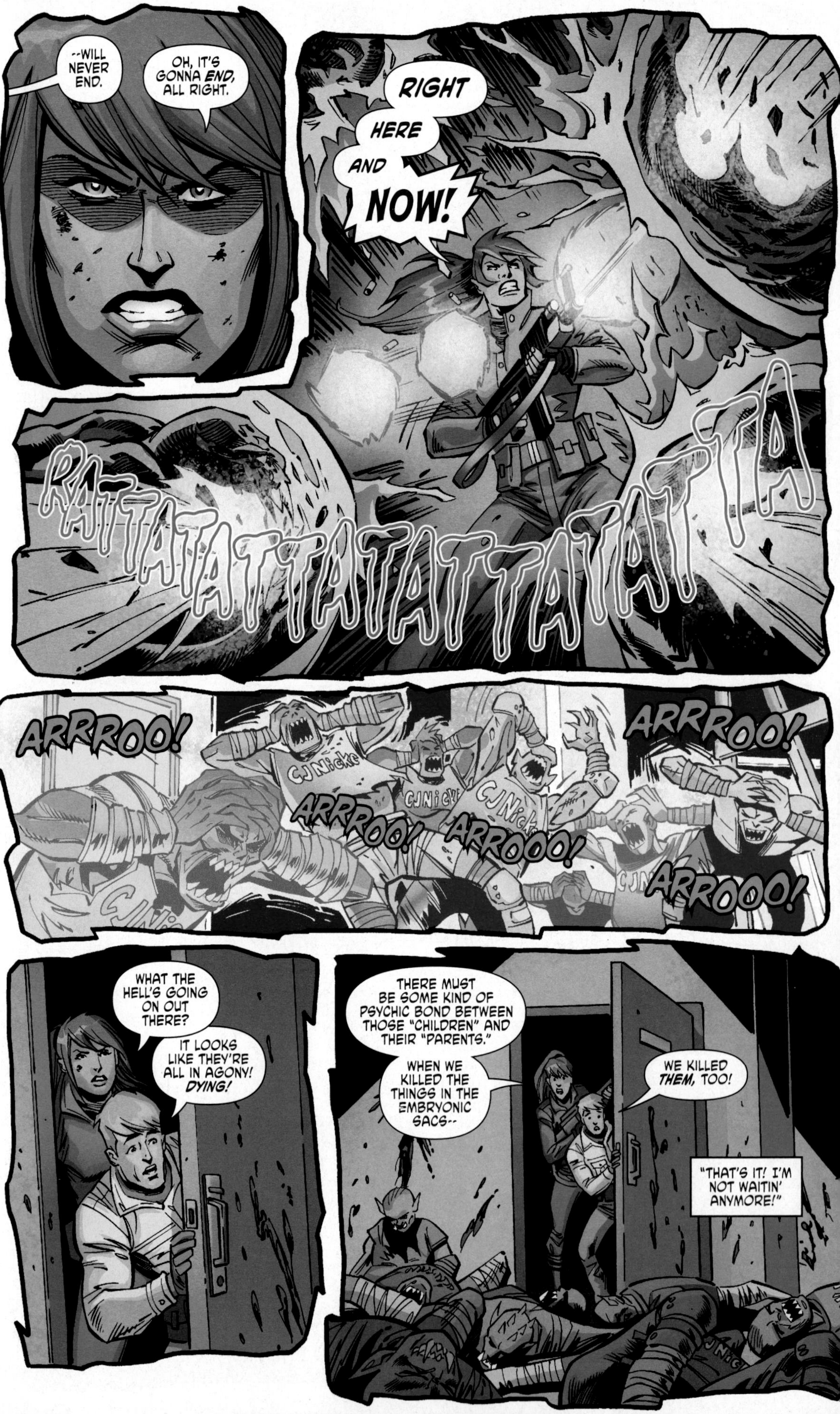
--WILL NEVER END.
OH, IT'S GONNA END, ALL RIGHT.
RIGHT HERE AND NOW!
RATTATATTATATTATATTA
ARRROO!
ARRROO!
ARRROO!
ARROOO!
ARROOO!
WHAT THE HELL'S GOING ON OUT THERE?
IT LOOKS LIKE THEY'RE ALL IN AGONY! DYING!
THERE MUST BE SOME KIND OF PSYCHIC BOND BETWEEN THOSE "CHILDREN" AND THEIR "PARENTS."
WHEN WE KILLED THE THINGS IN THE EMBRYONIC SACS--
WE KILLED THEM, TOO!
"THAT'S IT! I'M NOT WAITIN' ANYMORE!"

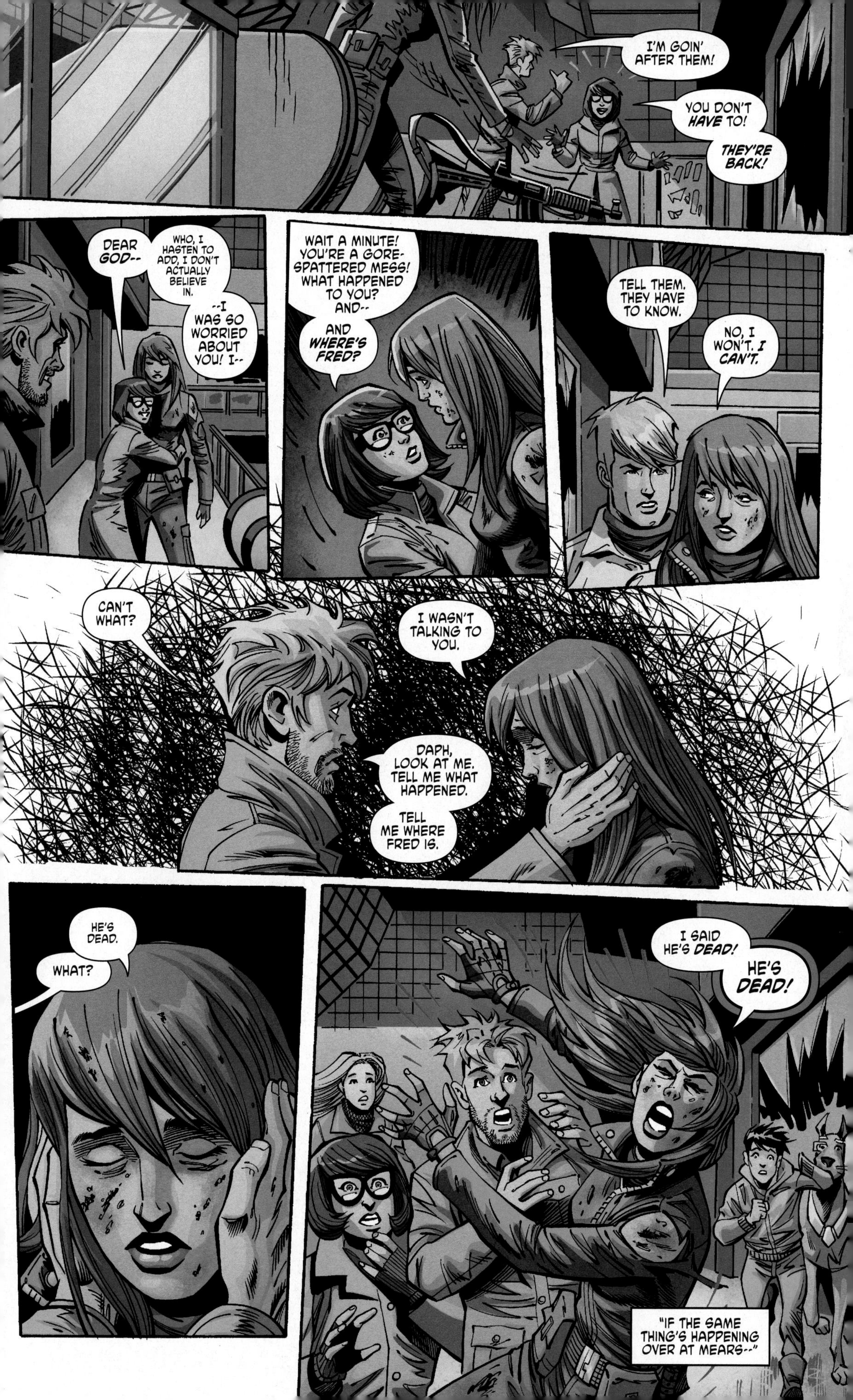
I'M GOIN' AFTER THEM!
YOU DON'T HAVE TO!
THEY'RE BACK!
DEAR GOD--
WHO, I HASTEN TO ADD, I DON'T ACTUALLY BELIEVE IN.
--I WAS SO WORRIED ABOUT YOU! I--
WAIT A MINUTE! YOU'RE A GORE-SPATTERED MESS! WHAT HAPPENED TO YOU? AND--
AND WHERE'S FRED?
TELL THEM. THEY HAVE TO KNOW.
NO, I WON'T. I CAN'T.
CAN'T WHAT?
I WASN'T TALKING TO YOU.
DAPH, LOOK AT ME. TELL ME WHAT HAPPENED.
TELL ME WHERE FRED IS.
HE'S DEAD.
WHAT?
I SAID HE'S DEAD!
HE'S DEAD!
"IF THE SAME THING'S HAPPENING OVER AT MEARS--"

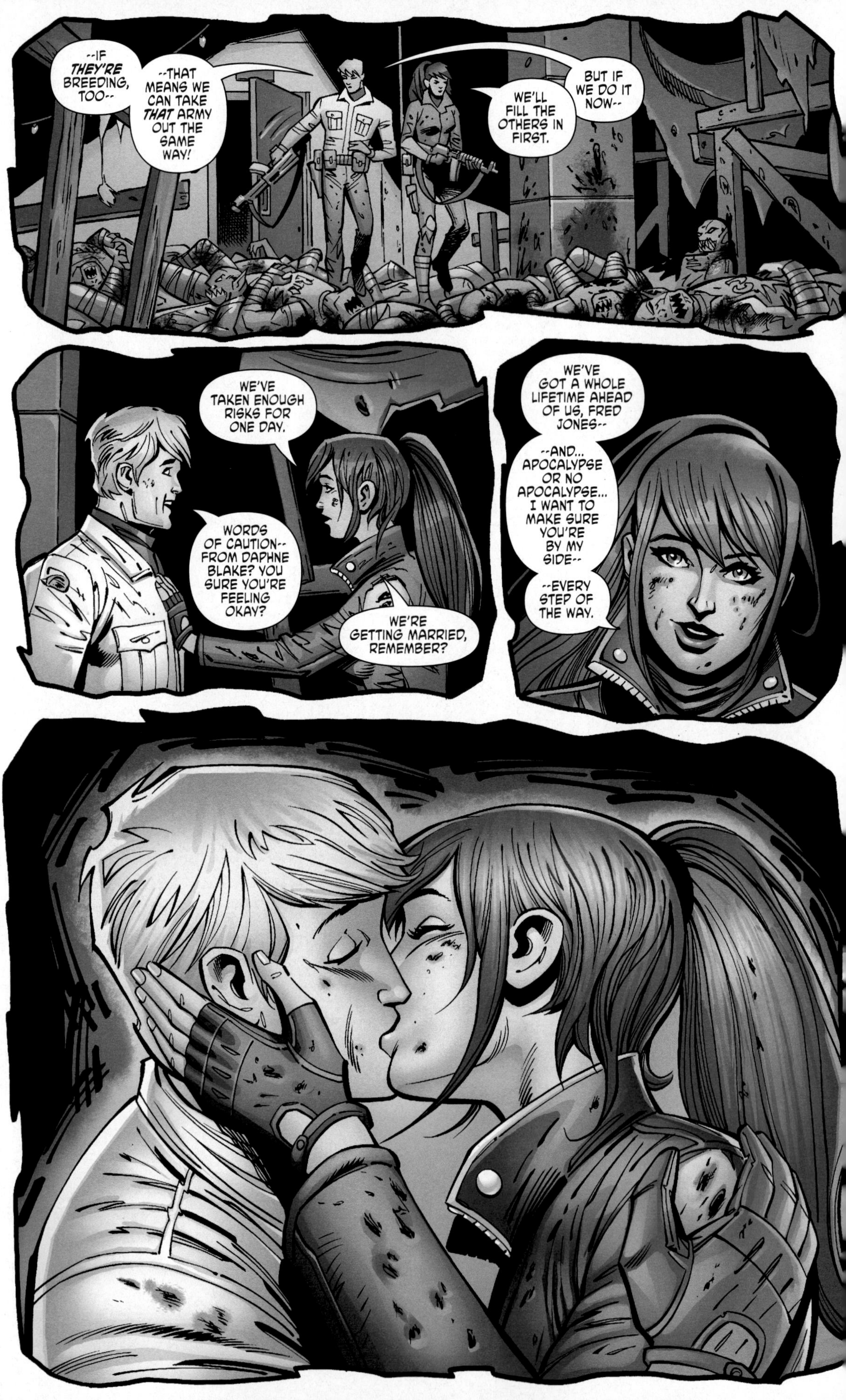
--IF *THEY'RE* BREEDING, TOO--
--THAT MEANS WE CAN TAKE *THAT* ARMY OUT THE SAME WAY!
BUT IF WE DO IT NOW--
WE'LL FILL THE OTHERS IN FIRST.
WE'VE TAKEN ENOUGH RISKS FOR ONE DAY.
WORDS OF CAUTION--FROM DAPHNE BLAKE? YOU SURE YOU'RE FEELING OKAY?
WE'RE GETTING MARRIED, REMEMBER?
WE'VE GOT A WHOLE LIFETIME AHEAD OF US, FRED JONES--
--AND... APOCALYPSE OR NO APOCALYPSE... I WANT TO MAKE SURE YOU'RE BY MY SIDE--
--EVERY STEP OF THE WAY.

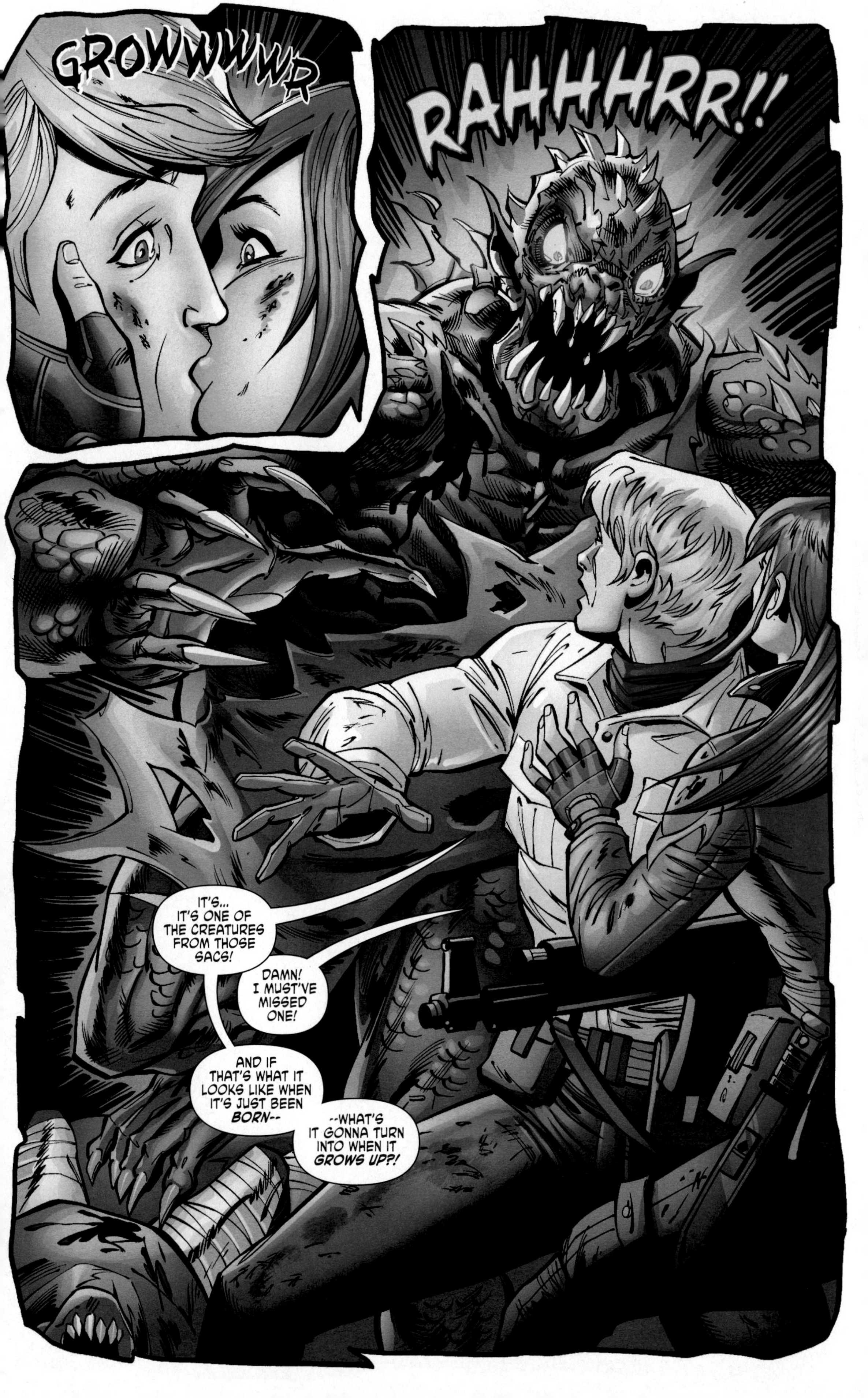
GROWWWWR
RAHHHRR!!
IT'S... IT'S ONE OF THE CREATURES FROM THOSE SACS!
DAMN! I MUST'VE MISSED ONE!
AND IF THAT'S WHAT IT LOOKS LIKE WHEN IT'S JUST BEEN *BORN*--
--WHAT'S IT GONNA TURN INTO WHEN IT *GROWS UP*?!

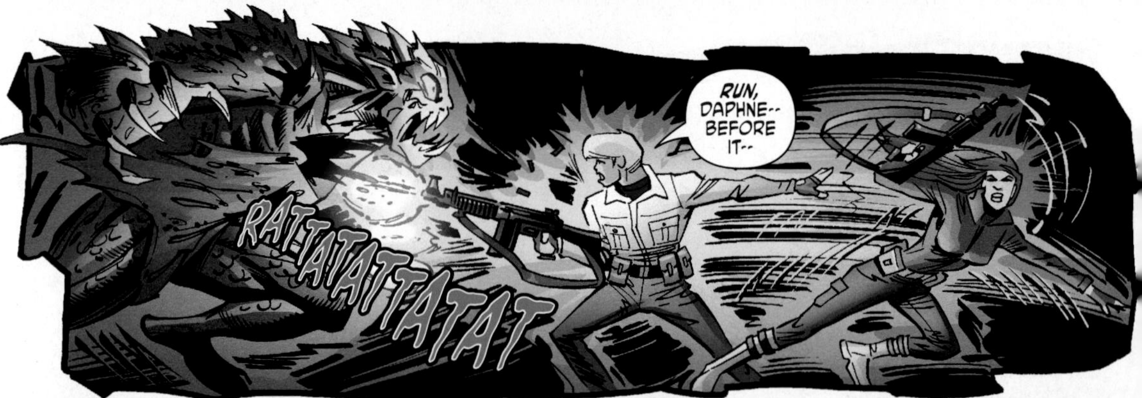
RUN, DAPHNE-- BEFORE IT--
RATTATATTATATAT

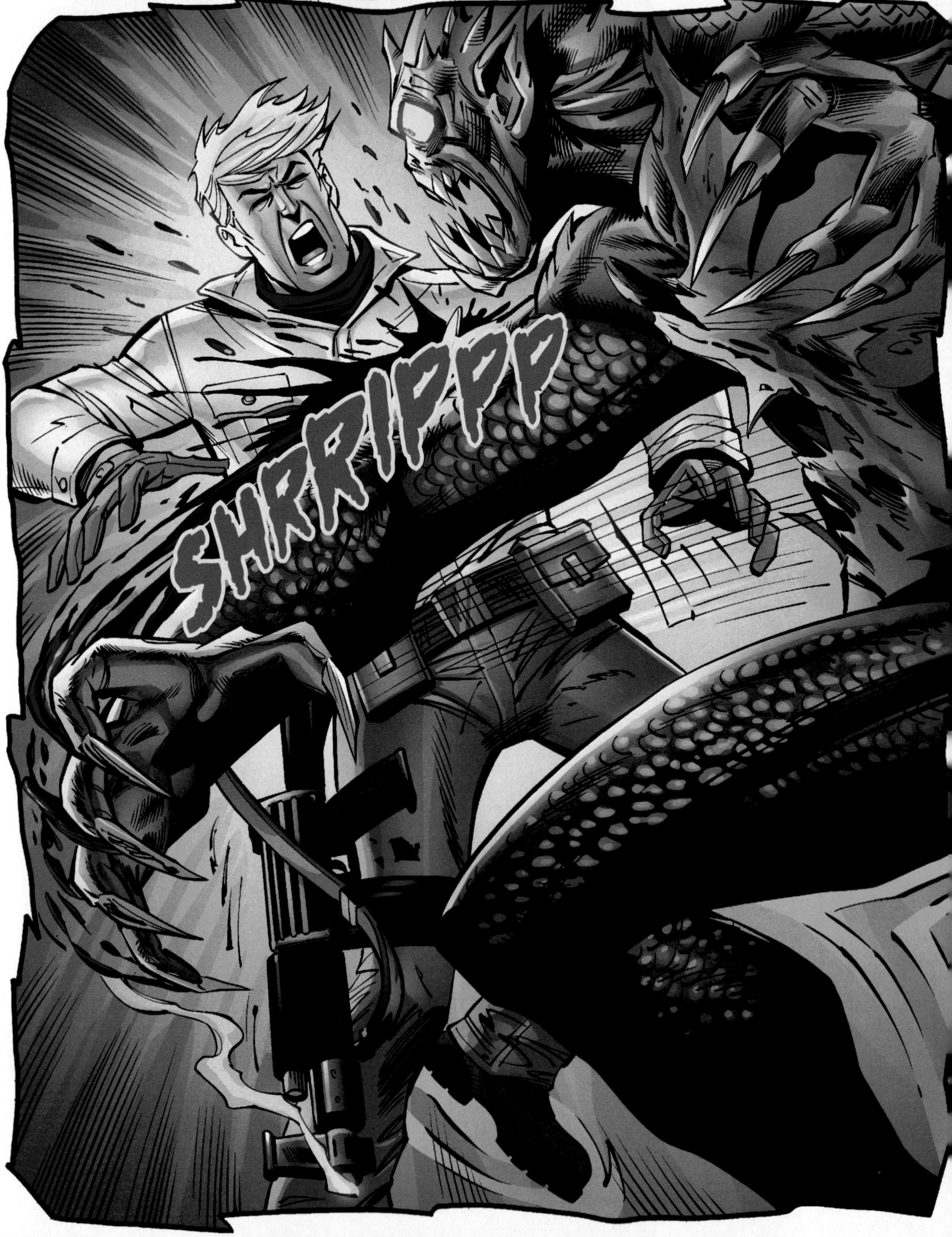
SHRRIPPP

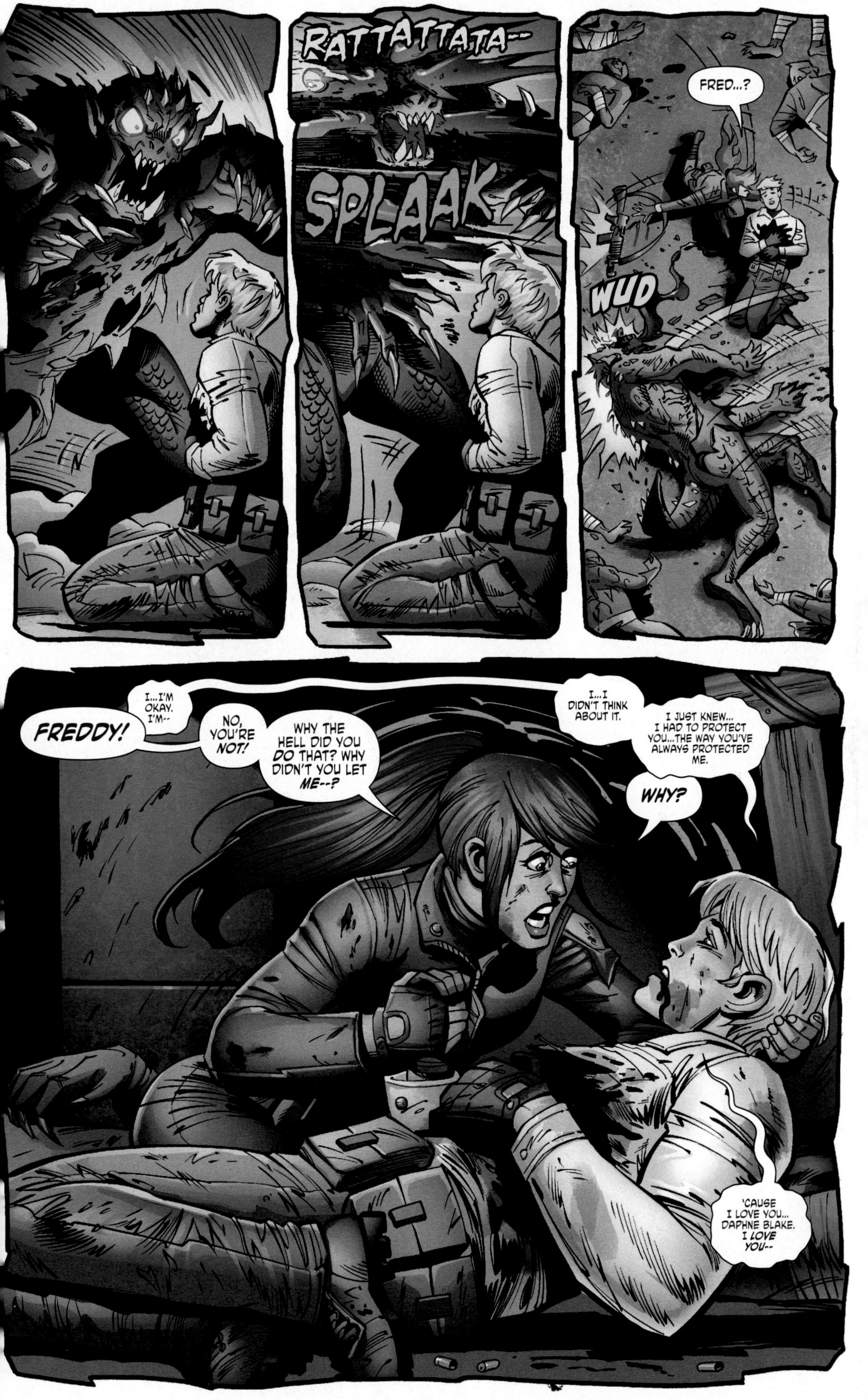
RATTATTATA--
SPLAAK
FRED...?
WUD
FREDDY!
I...I'M OKAY. I'M--
NO, YOU'RE NOT!
WHY THE HELL DID YOU DO THAT? WHY DIDN'T YOU LET ME--?
I...I DIDN'T THINK ABOUT IT.
I JUST KNEW... I HAD TO PROTECT YOU...THE WAY YOU'VE ALWAYS PROTECTED ME.
WHY?
'CAUSE I LOVE YOU... DAPHNE BLAKE. I LOVE YOU--

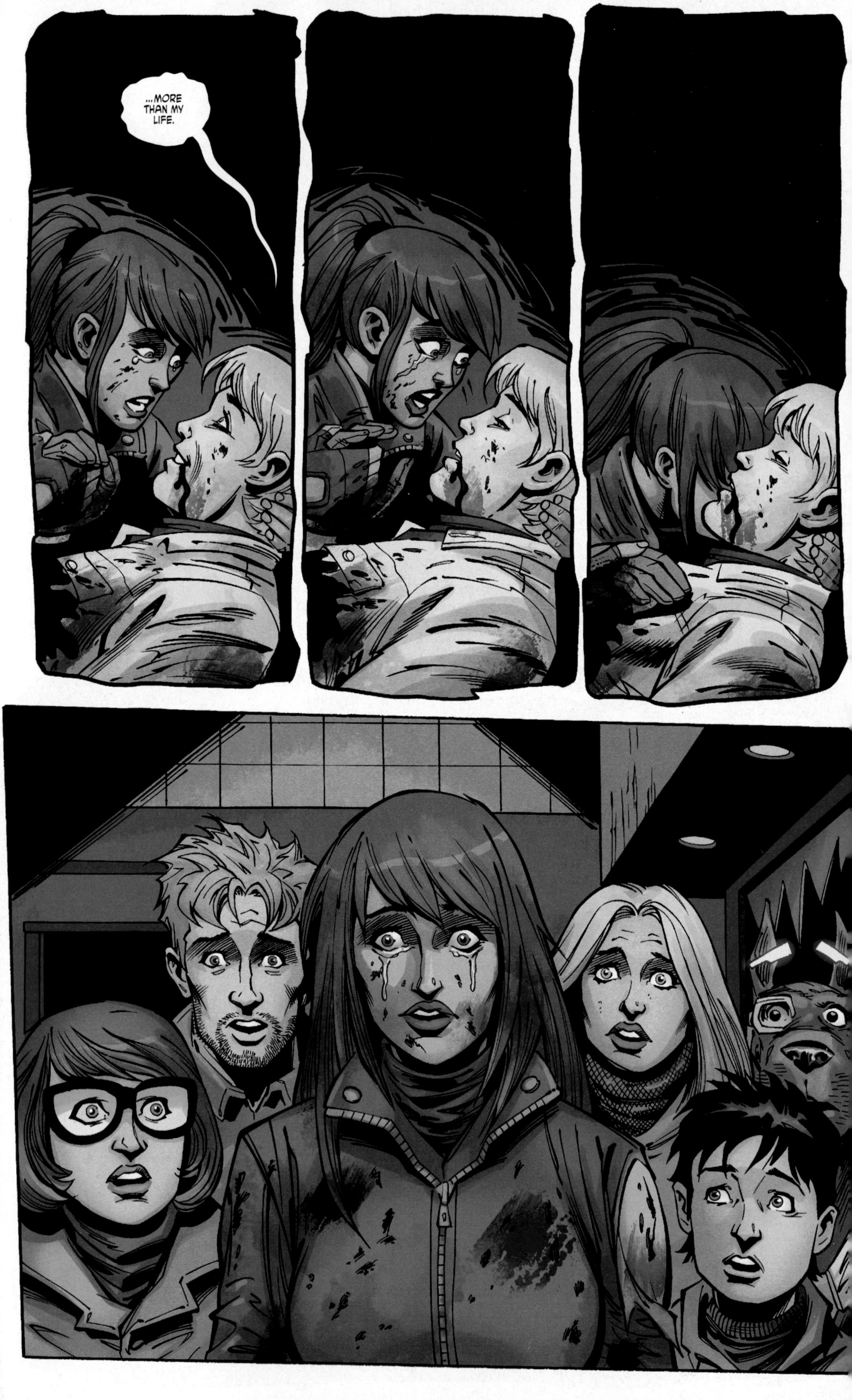
...MORE THAN MY LIFE.

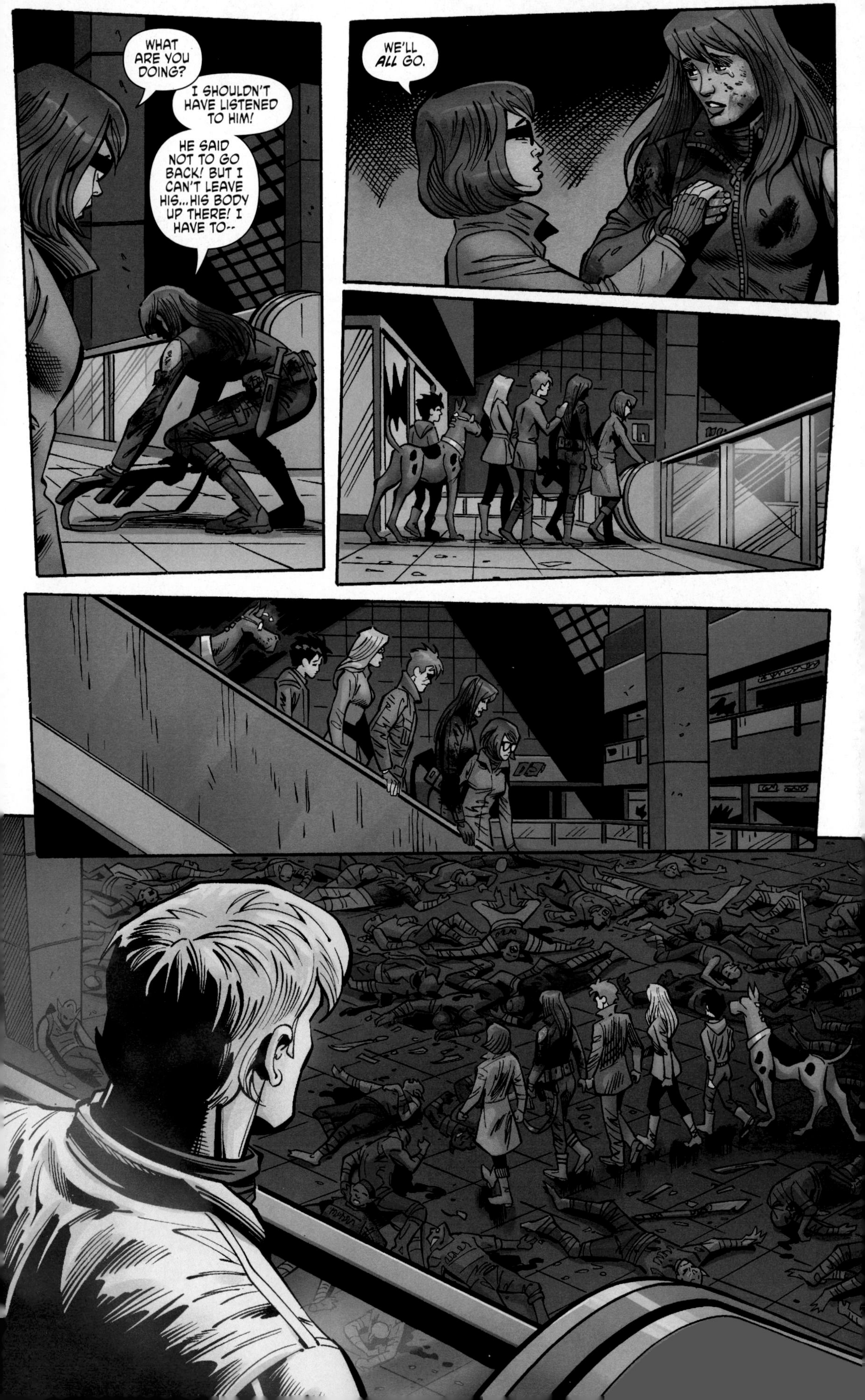
WHAT ARE YOU DOING?
I SHOULDN'T HAVE LISTENED TO HIM!
HE SAID NOT TO GO BACK! BUT I CAN'T LEAVE HIS...HIS BODY UP THERE! I HAVE TO--
WE'LL *ALL* GO.

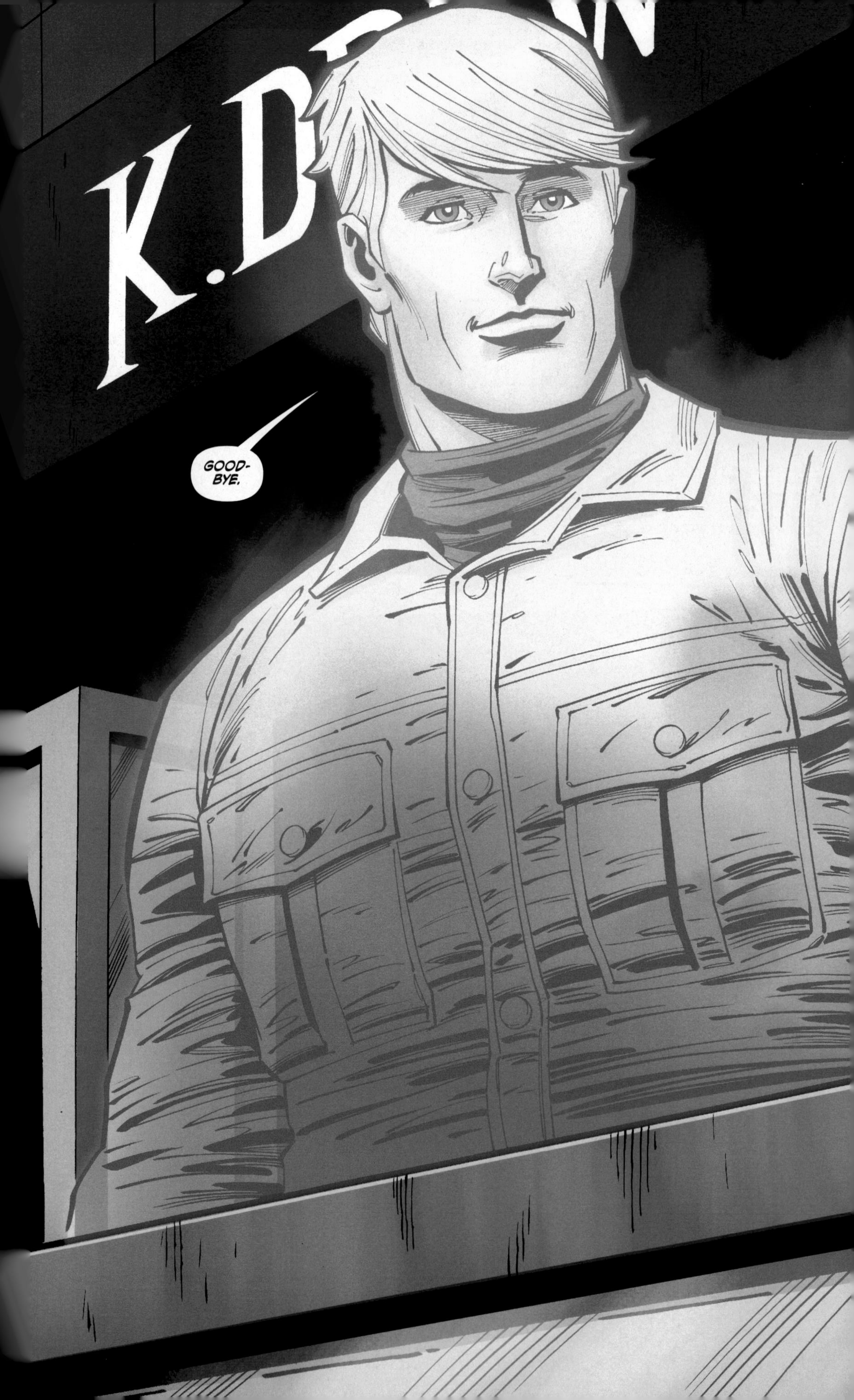
K.D
GOOD-BYE.

THE SWISS ALPS...

...YOU TRAITOROUS #$@!!

WHY, *AGENT BEA*-- I FIND YOUR LANGUAGE SHOCKING!

YOU THINK THIS IS FUNNY, *DOUBLE-Q?*

WELL, IT *IS* MILDLY AMUSING.

SEE HOW AMUSED YOU ARE WHEN I KICK YOUR SORRY ASS FROM HERE BACK T'LANGLEY!

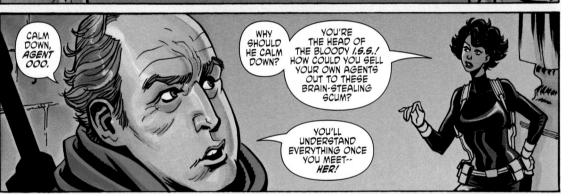

CALM DOWN, *AGENT 000.*

WHY SHOULD HE CALM DOWN?

YOU'RE THE HEAD OF THE BLOODY *I.S.S.!* HOW COULD YOU SELL YOUR OWN AGENTS OUT TO THESE BRAIN-STEALING SCUM?

YOU'LL UNDERSTAND EVERYTHING ONCE YOU MEET-- *HER!*

"HER" WHO?

THE VISIONARY BEHIND OUR ORGANIZATION! THE WOMAN WHO SHOWED ME THE ERROR OF MY WAYS!

I PRESENT TO YOU THE ONE, THE ONLY--

I....I CAN'T *BELIEVE* IT!

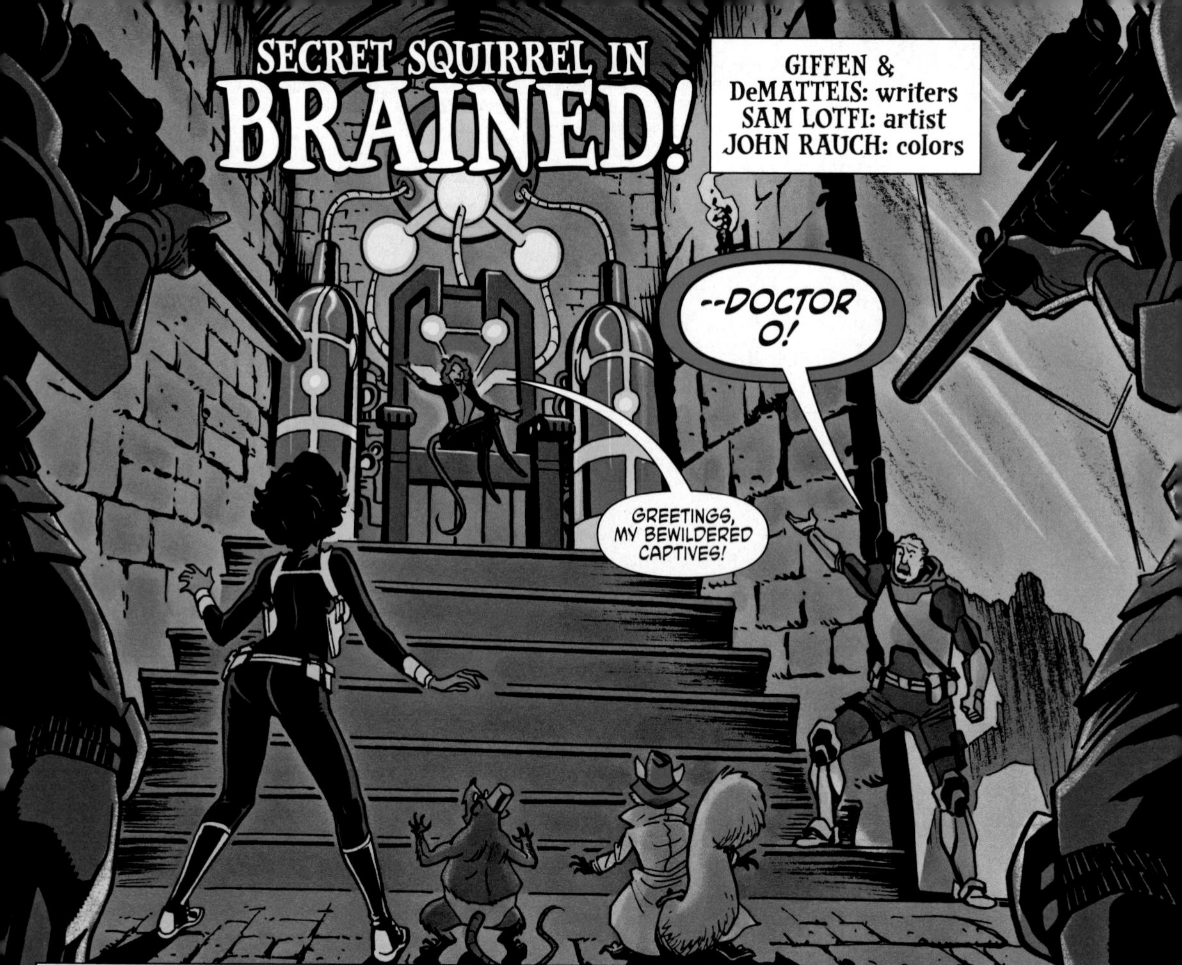
SECRET SQUIRREL IN
BRAINED!
GIFFEN & DeMATTEIS: writers
SAM LOTFI: artist
JOHN RAUCH: colors
--DOCTOR O!
GREETINGS, MY BEWILDERED CAPTIVES!

TRAVIS LANHAM: letters LIZ ERICKSON: asst. editor HARVEY RICHARDS: editor JIM CHADWICK: is often mistaken for Daniel Craig

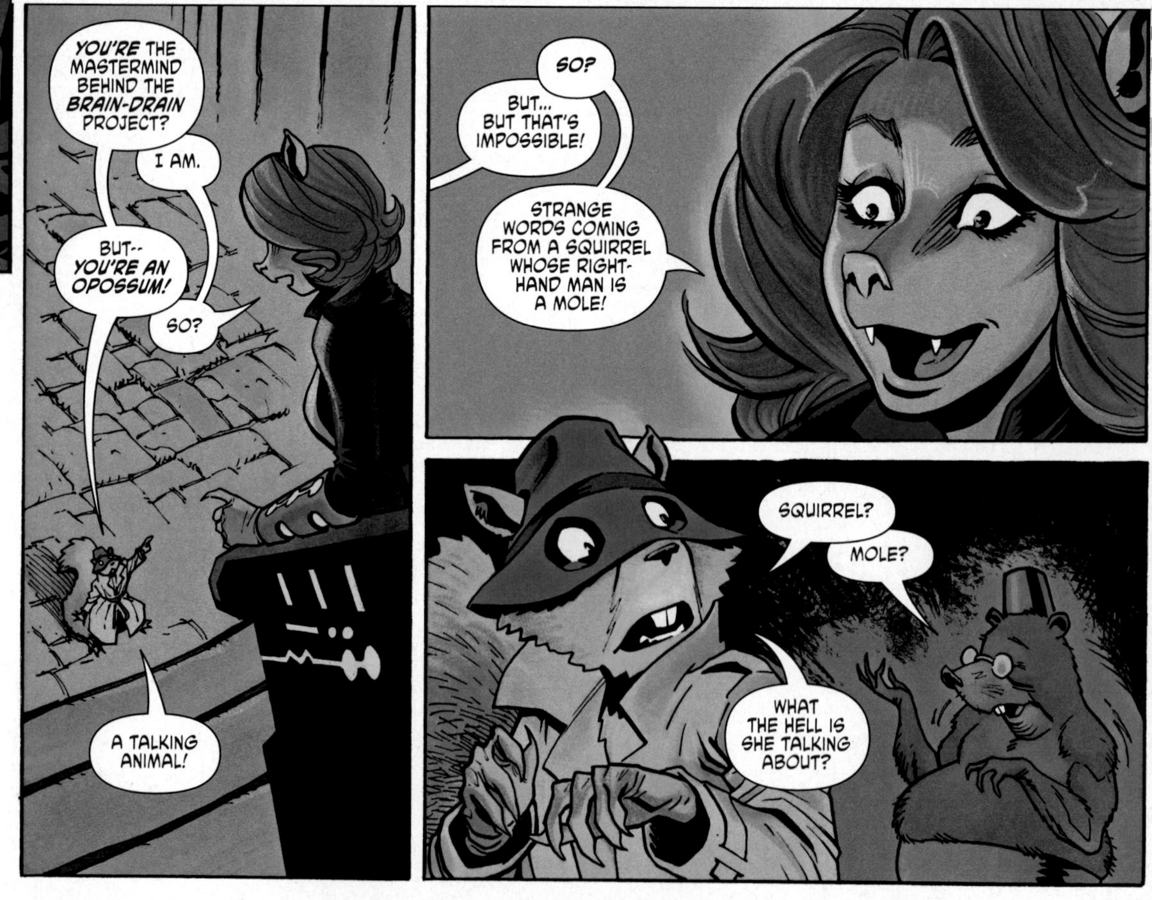
YOU'RE THE MASTERMIND BEHIND THE *BRAIN-DRAIN* PROJECT?
I AM.
BUT-- *YOU'RE AN OPOSSUM!*
SO?
A TALKING ANIMAL!
SO?
BUT... BUT THAT'S IMPOSSIBLE!
STRANGE WORDS COMING FROM A SQUIRREL WHOSE RIGHT-HAND MAN IS A MOLE!
SQUIRREL?
MOLE?
WHAT THE HELL IS SHE TALKING ABOUT?

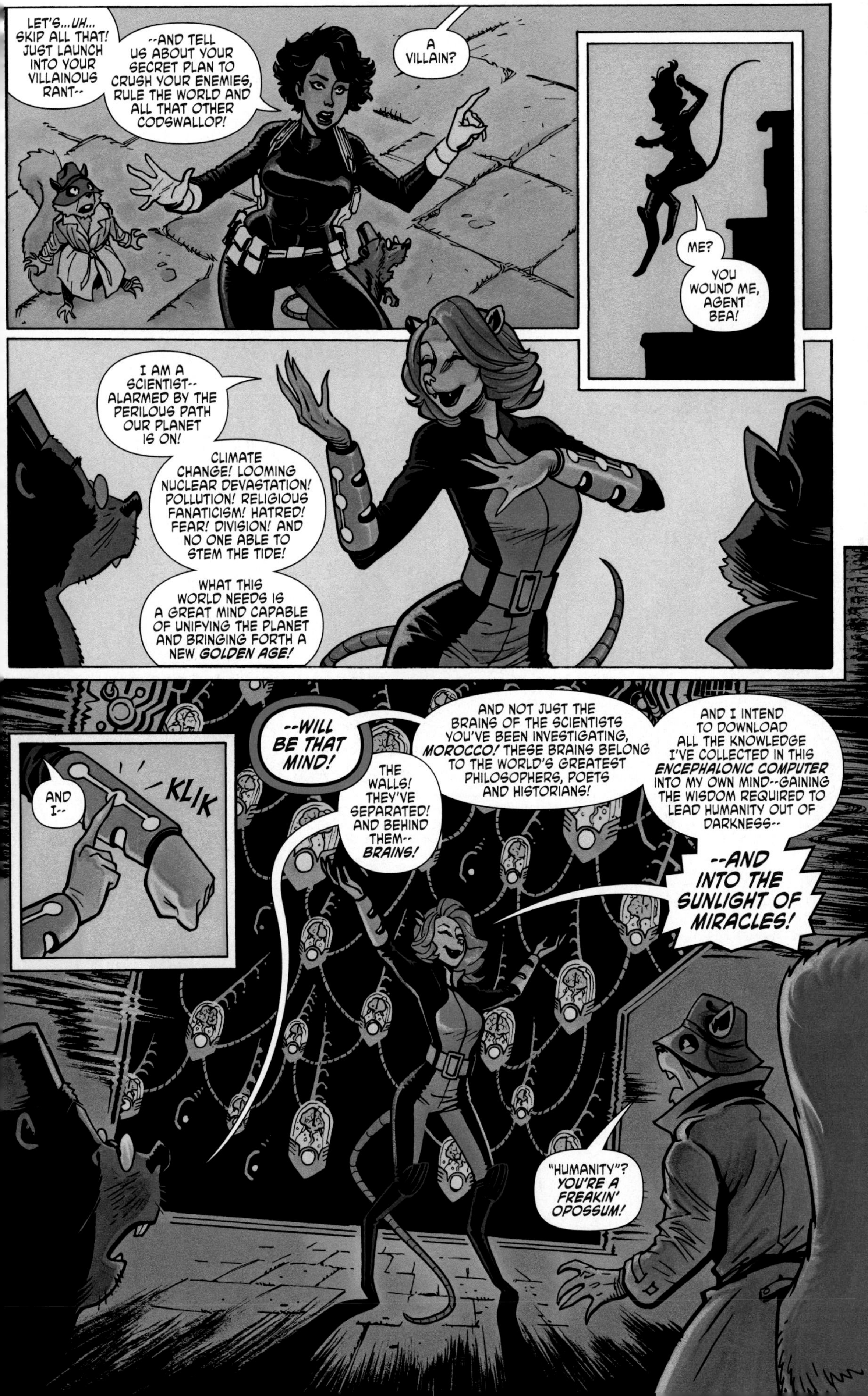
LET'S...UH... SKIP ALL THAT! JUST LAUNCH INTO YOUR VILLAINOUS RANT--
--AND TELL US ABOUT YOUR SECRET PLAN TO CRUSH YOUR ENEMIES, RULE THE WORLD AND ALL THAT OTHER CODSWALLOP!
A VILLAIN?
ME?
YOU WOUND ME, AGENT BEA!
I AM A SCIENTIST-- ALARMED BY THE PERILOUS PATH OUR PLANET IS ON!
CLIMATE CHANGE! LOOMING NUCLEAR DEVASTATION! POLLUTION! RELIGIOUS FANATICISM! HATRED! FEAR! DIVISION! AND NO ONE ABLE TO STEM THE TIDE!
WHAT THIS WORLD NEEDS IS A GREAT MIND CAPABLE OF UNIFYING THE PLANET AND BRINGING FORTH A NEW GOLDEN AGE!
AND I--
KLIK
--WILL BE THAT MIND!
THE WALLS! THEY'VE SEPARATED! AND BEHIND THEM-- BRAINS!
AND NOT JUST THE BRAINS OF THE SCIENTISTS YOU'VE BEEN INVESTIGATING, MOROCCO! THESE BRAINS BELONG TO THE WORLD'S GREATEST PHILOSOPHERS, POETS AND HISTORIANS!
AND I INTEND TO DOWNLOAD ALL THE KNOWLEDGE I'VE COLLECTED IN THIS ENCEPHALONIC COMPUTER INTO MY OWN MIND--GAINING THE WISDOM REQUIRED TO LEAD HUMANITY OUT OF DARKNESS--
--AND INTO THE SUNLIGHT OF MIRACLES!
"HUMANITY"? YOU'RE A FREAKIN' OPOSSUM!

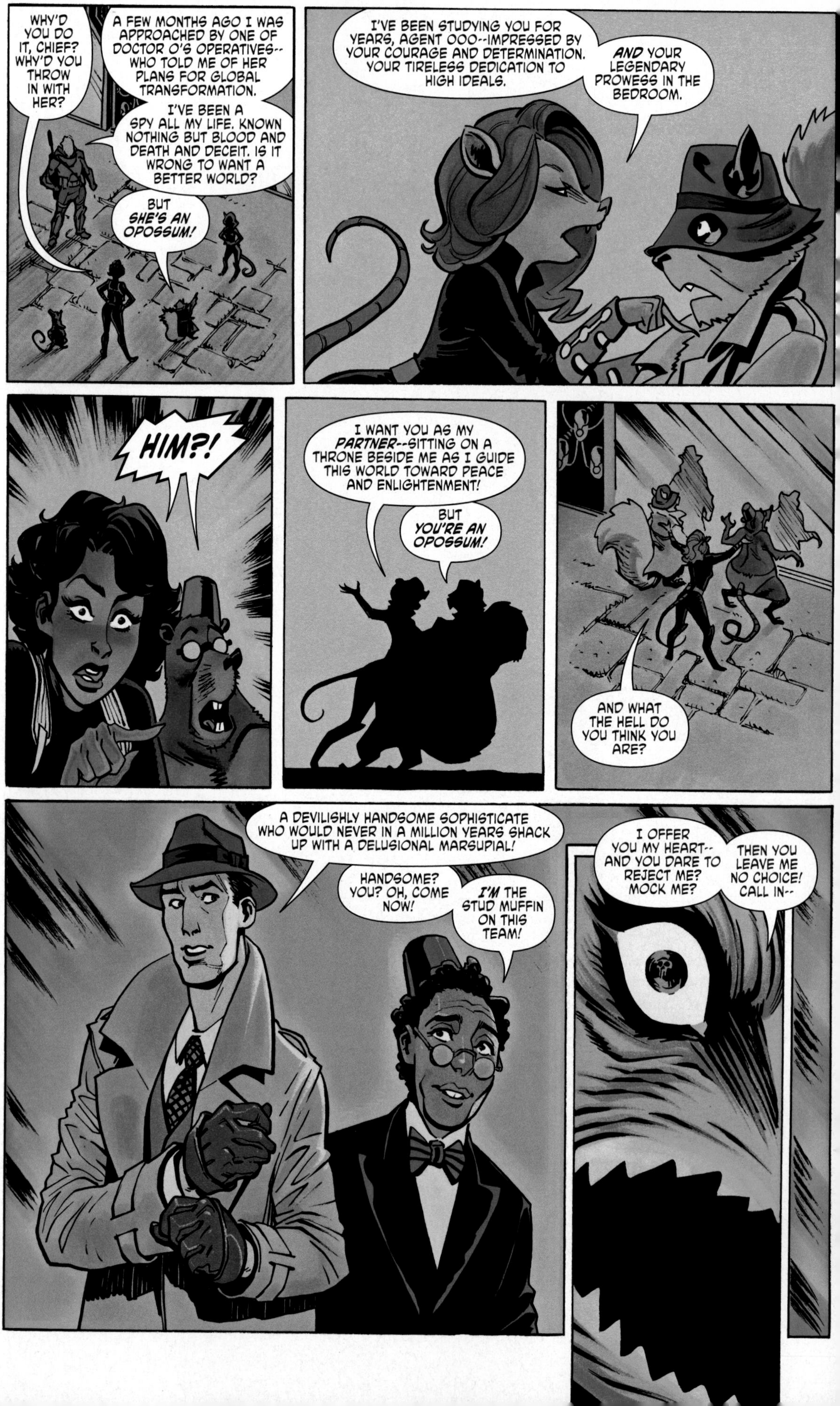
WHY'D YOU DO IT, CHIEF? WHY'D YOU THROW IN WITH HER?
A FEW MONTHS AGO I WAS APPROACHED BY ONE OF DOCTOR O'S OPERATIVES-- WHO TOLD ME OF HER PLANS FOR GLOBAL TRANSFORMATION.
I'VE BEEN A SPY ALL MY LIFE. KNOWN NOTHING BUT BLOOD AND DEATH AND DECEIT. IS IT WRONG TO WANT A BETTER WORLD?
BUT SHE'S AN OPOSSUM!
I'VE BEEN STUDYING YOU FOR YEARS, AGENT OOO--IMPRESSED BY YOUR COURAGE AND DETERMINATION. YOUR TIRELESS DEDICATION TO HIGH IDEALS.
AND YOUR LEGENDARY PROWESS IN THE BEDROOM.
HIM?!
I WANT YOU AS MY PARTNER--SITTING ON A THRONE BESIDE ME AS I GUIDE THIS WORLD TOWARD PEACE AND ENLIGHTENMENT!
BUT YOU'RE AN OPOSSUM!
AND WHAT THE HELL DO YOU THINK YOU ARE?
A DEVILISHLY HANDSOME SOPHISTICATE WHO WOULD NEVER IN A MILLION YEARS SHACK UP WITH A DELUSIONAL MARSUPIAL!
HANDSOME? YOU? OH, COME NOW!
I'M THE STUD MUFFIN ON THIS TEAM!
I OFFER YOU MY HEART-- AND YOU DARE TO REJECT ME? MOCK ME?
THEN YOU LEAVE ME NO CHOICE! CALL IN--

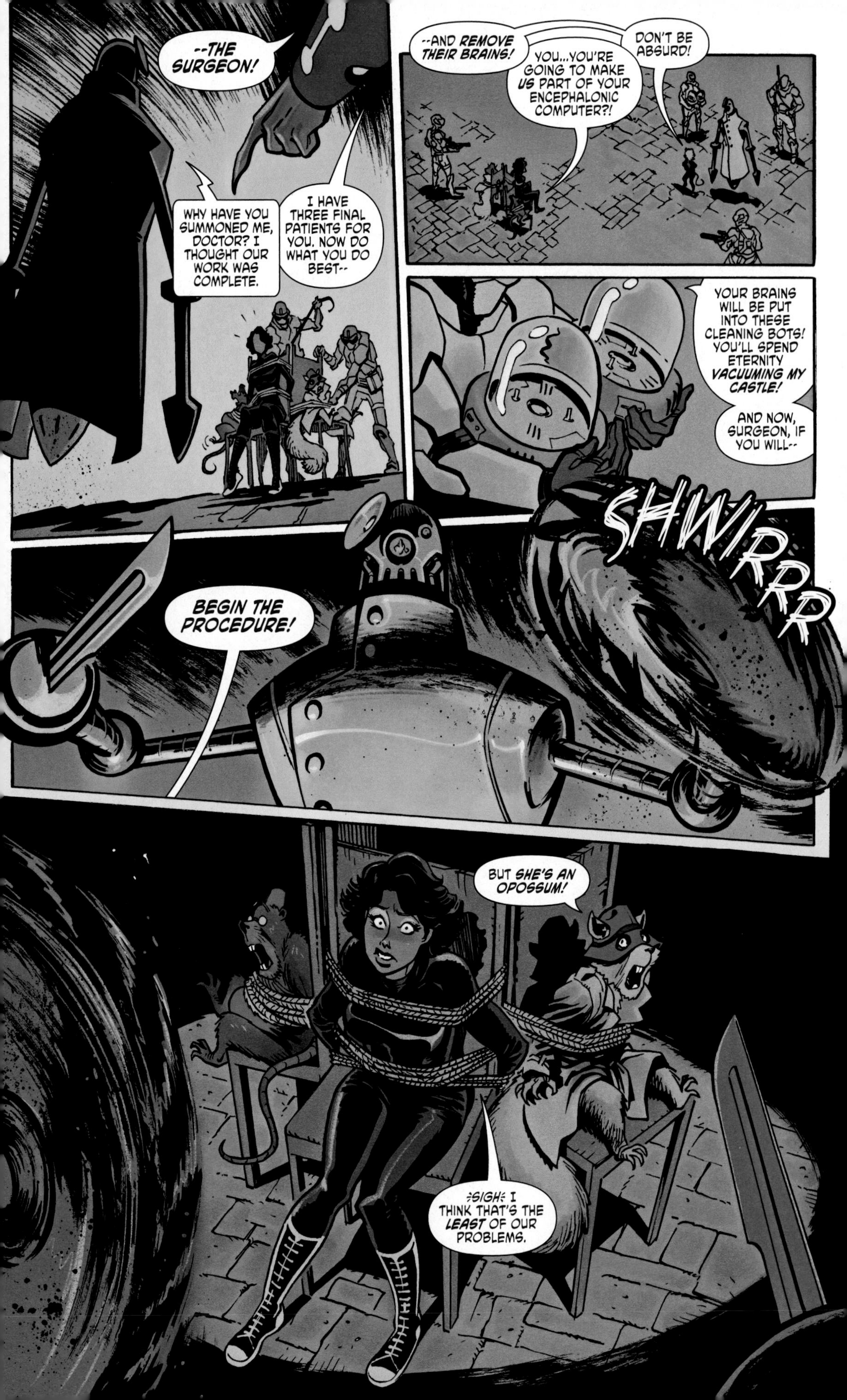
--THE SURGEON!
WHY HAVE YOU SUMMONED ME, DOCTOR? I THOUGHT OUR WORK WAS COMPLETE.
I HAVE THREE FINAL PATIENTS FOR YOU. NOW DO WHAT YOU DO BEST--
--AND REMOVE THEIR BRAINS!
YOU...YOU'RE GOING TO MAKE US PART OF YOUR ENCEPHALONIC COMPUTER?!
DON'T BE ABSURD!
YOUR BRAINS WILL BE PUT INTO THESE CLEANING BOTS! YOU'LL SPEND ETERNITY VACUUMING MY CASTLE!
AND NOW, SURGEON, IF YOU WILL--
BEGIN THE PROCEDURE!
SHWIRRR
BUT SHE'S AN OPOSSUM!
SIGH I THINK THAT'S THE LEAST OF OUR PROBLEMS.

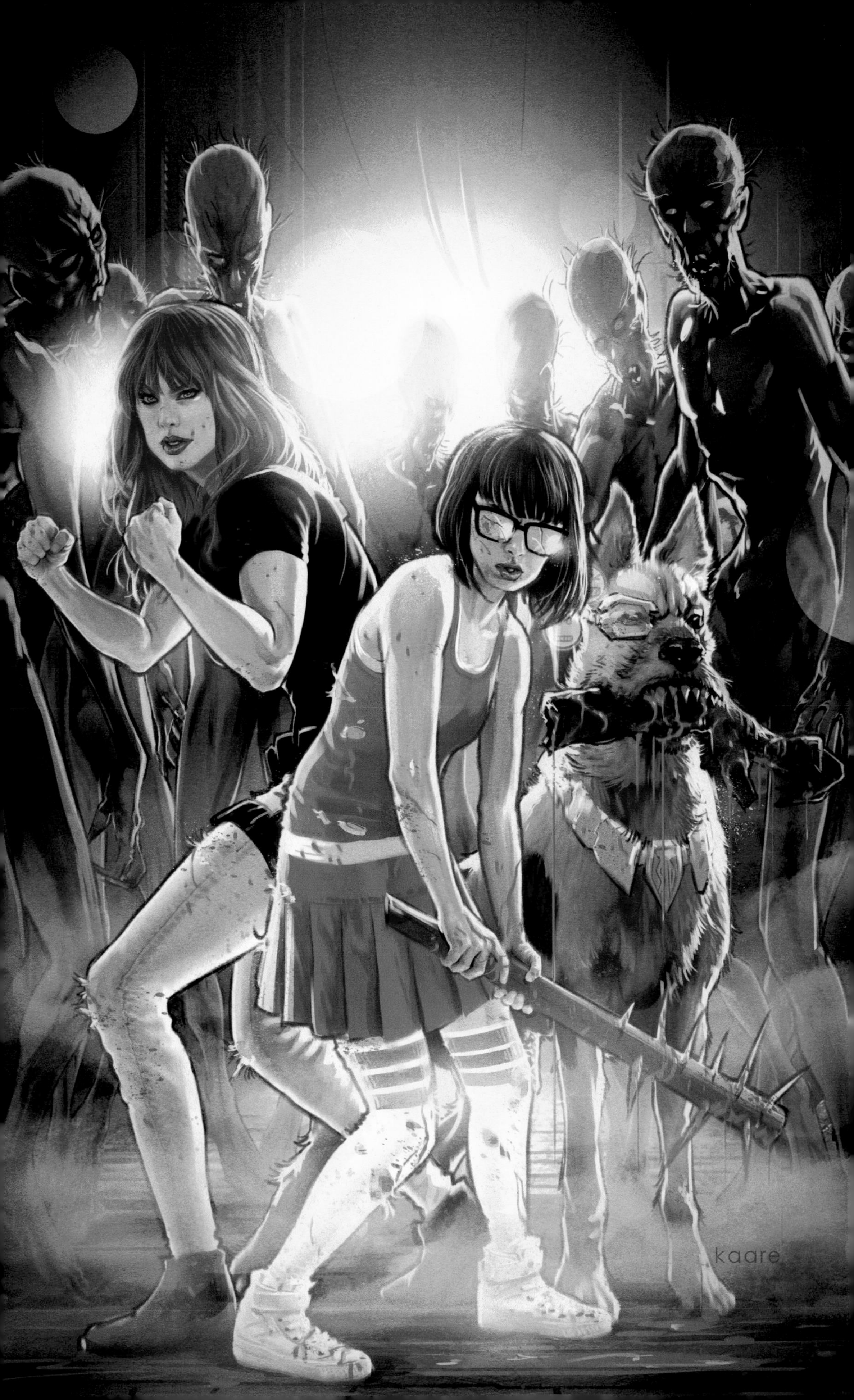
kaare

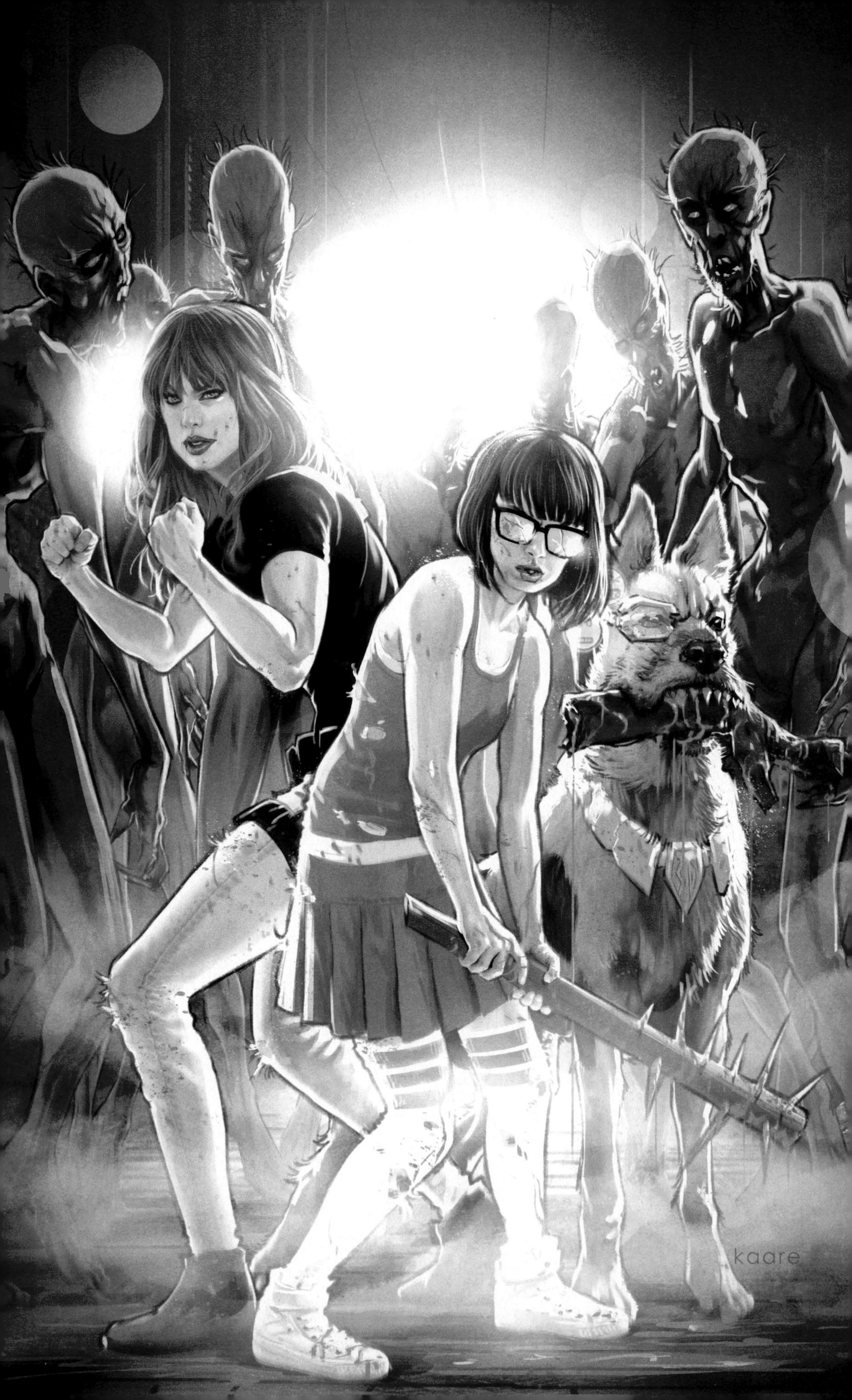
kaare

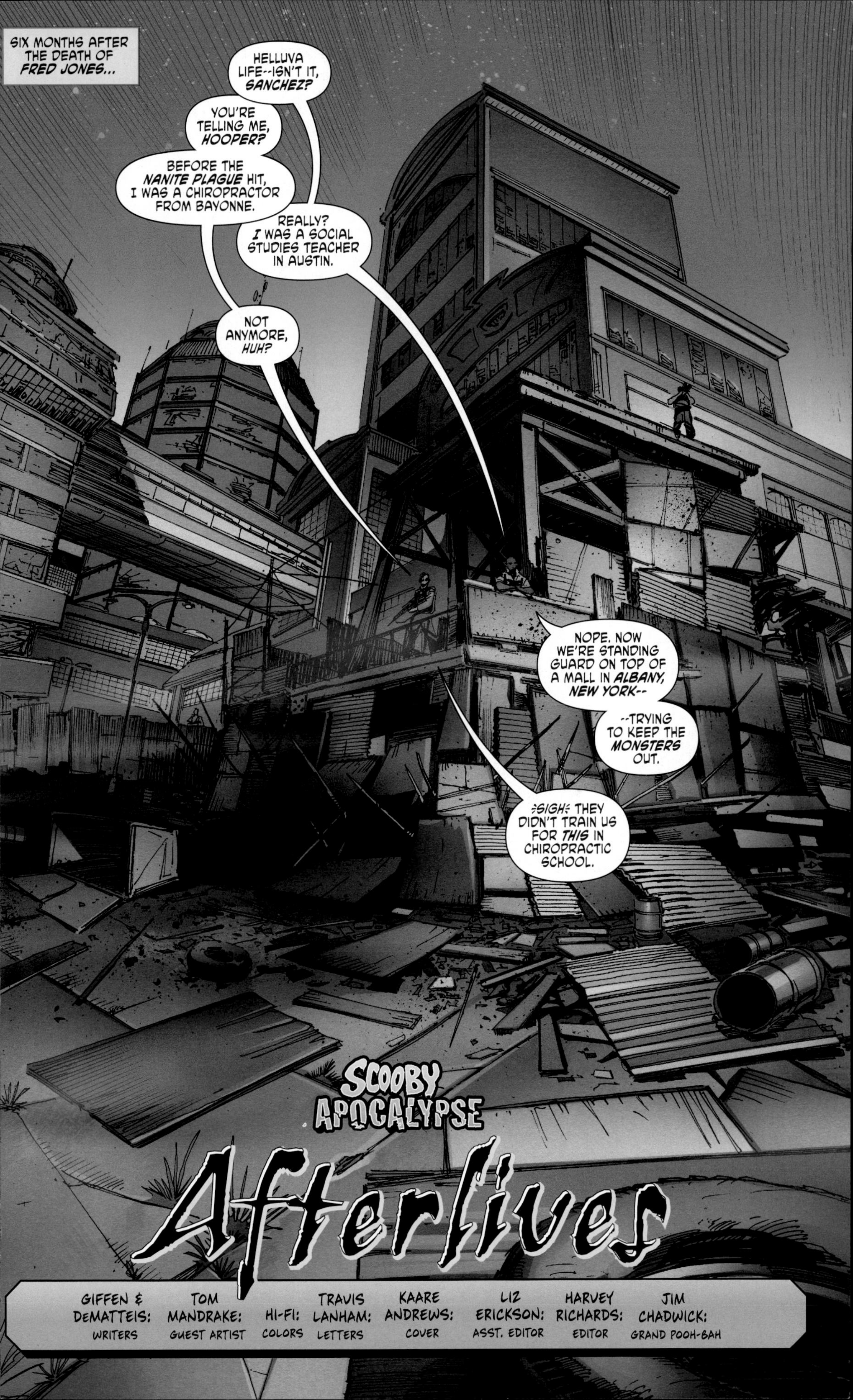
SIX MONTHS AFTER THE DEATH OF *FRED JONES...*
HELLUVA LIFE--ISN'T IT, *SANCHEZ?*
YOU'RE TELLING ME, *HOOPER?*
BEFORE THE *NANITE PLAGUE* HIT, I WAS A CHIROPRACTOR FROM BAYONNE.
REALLY? *I* WAS A SOCIAL STUDIES TEACHER IN AUSTIN.
NOT ANYMORE, *HUH?*
NOPE. NOW WE'RE STANDING GUARD ON TOP OF A MALL IN *ALBANY, NEW YORK--*
--TRYING TO KEEP THE *MONSTERS* OUT.
=SIGH= THEY DIDN'T TRAIN US FOR *THIS* IN CHIROPRACTIC SCHOOL.
SCOOBY APOCALYPSE
Afterlives
GIFFEN & DeMATTEIS: WRITERS
TOM MANDRAKE: GUEST ARTIST
HI-FI: COLORS
TRAVIS LANHAM: LETTERS
KAARE ANDREWS: COVER
LIZ ERICKSON: ASST. EDITOR
HARVEY RICHARDS: EDITOR
JIM CHADWICK: GRAND POOH-BAH

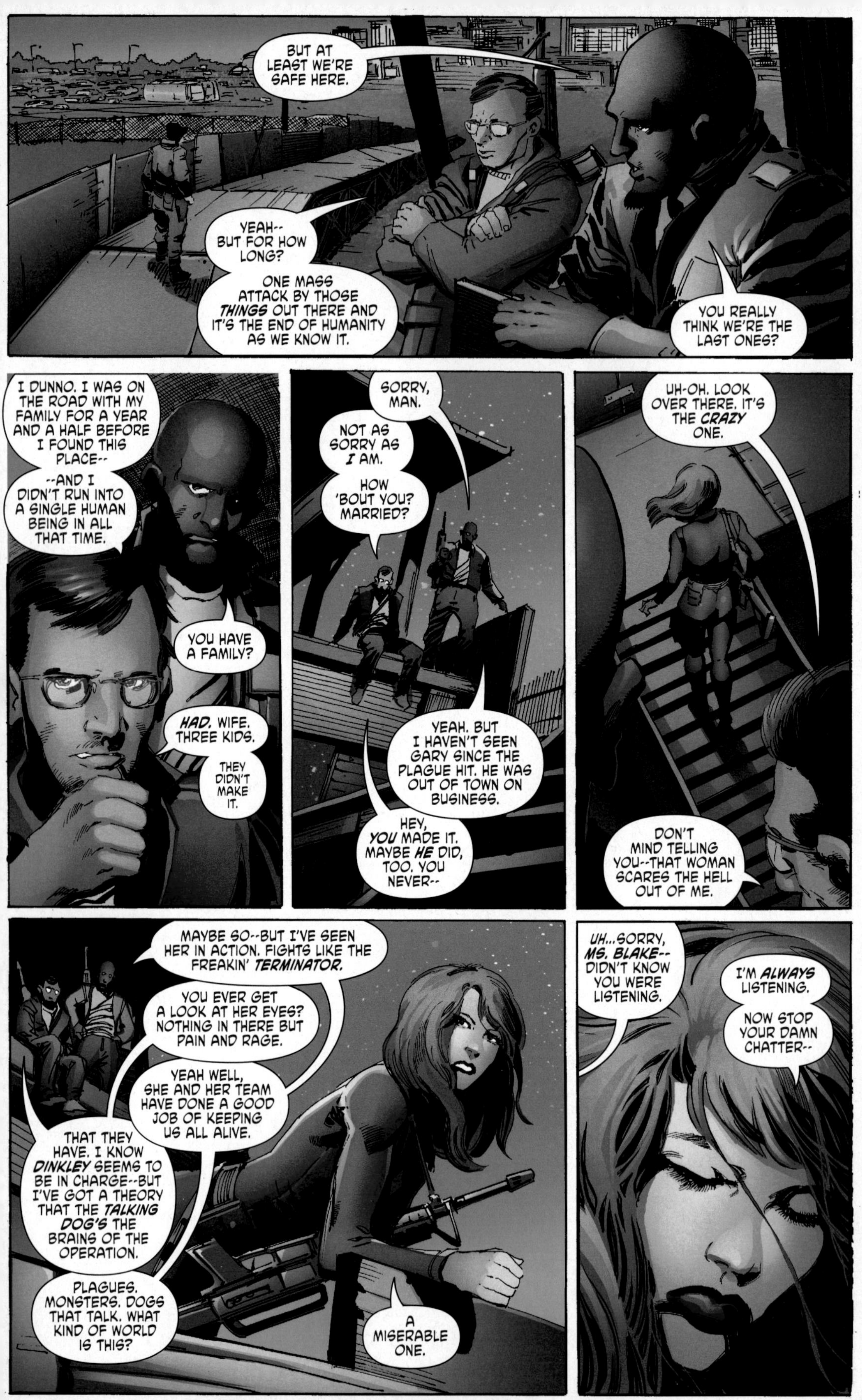
BUT AT LEAST WE'RE SAFE HERE.
YEAH-- BUT FOR HOW LONG?
ONE MASS ATTACK BY THOSE *THINGS* OUT THERE AND IT'S THE END OF HUMANITY AS WE KNOW IT.
YOU REALLY THINK WE'RE THE LAST ONES?
I DUNNO. I WAS ON THE ROAD WITH MY FAMILY FOR A YEAR AND A HALF BEFORE I FOUND THIS PLACE--
--AND I DIDN'T RUN INTO A SINGLE HUMAN BEING IN ALL THAT TIME.
YOU HAVE A FAMILY?
HAD. WIFE. THREE KIDS.
THEY DIDN'T MAKE IT.
SORRY, MAN.
NOT AS SORRY AS *I* AM.
HOW 'BOUT YOU? MARRIED?
YEAH. BUT I HAVEN'T SEEN GARY SINCE THE PLAGUE HIT. HE WAS OUT OF TOWN ON BUSINESS.
HEY, *YOU* MADE IT. MAYBE *HE* DID, TOO. YOU NEVER--
UH-OH. LOOK OVER THERE. IT'S THE *CRAZY* ONE.
DON'T MIND TELLING YOU--THAT WOMAN SCARES THE HELL OUT OF ME.
MAYBE SO--BUT I'VE SEEN HER IN ACTION. FIGHTS LIKE THE FREAKIN' *TERMINATOR.*
YOU EVER GET A LOOK AT HER EYES? NOTHING IN THERE BUT PAIN AND RAGE.
YEAH WELL, SHE AND HER TEAM HAVE DONE A GOOD JOB OF KEEPING US ALL ALIVE.
THAT THEY HAVE. I KNOW *DINKLEY* SEEMS TO BE IN CHARGE--BUT I'VE GOT A THEORY THAT THE *TALKING DOG'S* THE BRAINS OF THE OPERATION.
PLAGUES. MONSTERS. DOGS THAT TALK. WHAT KIND OF WORLD IS THIS?
A MISERABLE ONE.
UH...SORRY, *MS. BLAKE--* DIDN'T KNOW YOU WERE LISTENING.
I'M *ALWAYS* LISTENING.
NOW STOP YOUR DAMN CHATTER--

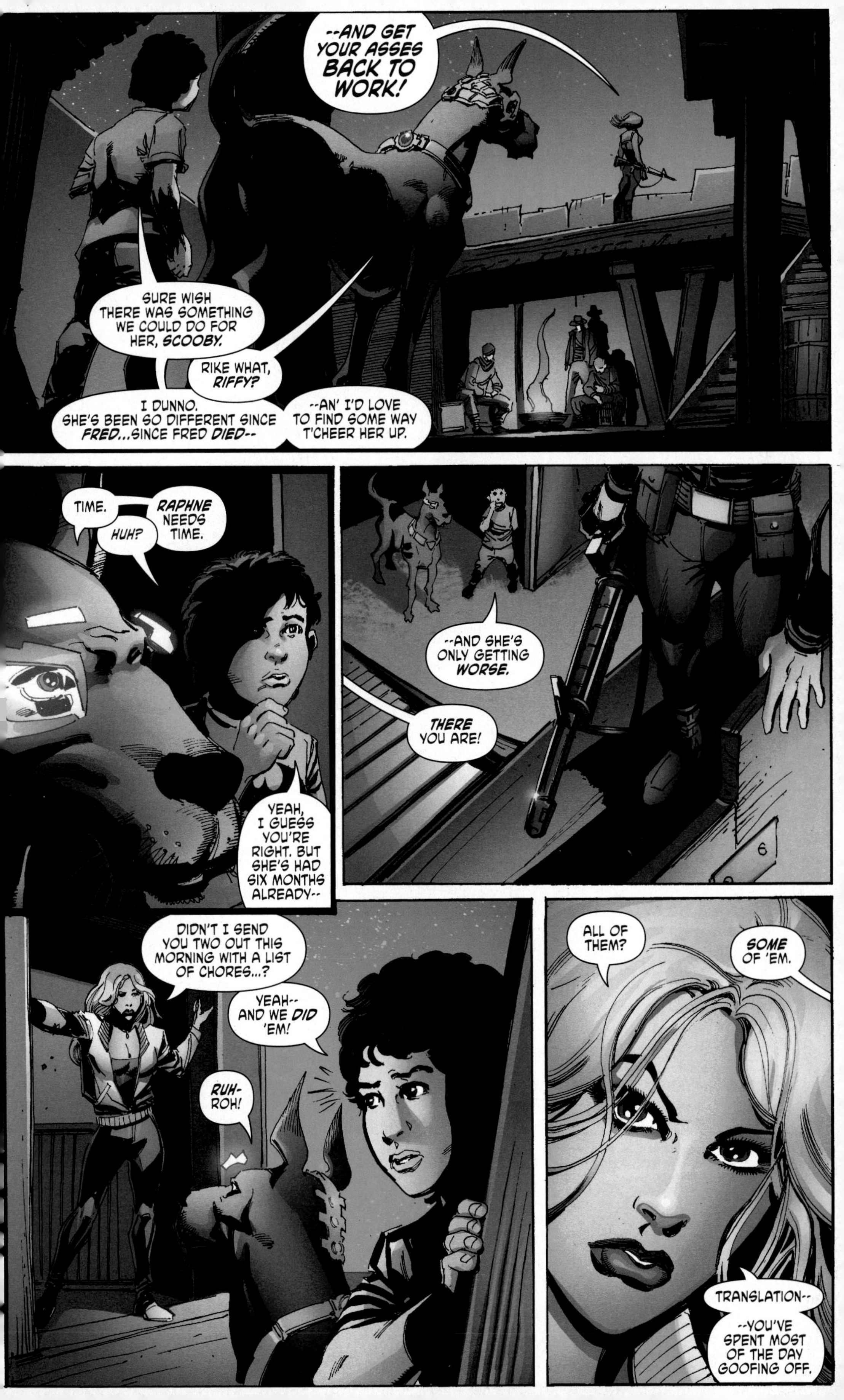
--AND GET YOUR ASSES BACK TO WORK!
SURE WISH THERE WAS SOMETHING WE COULD DO FOR HER, SCOOBY.
RIKE WHAT, RIFFY?
I DUNNO. SHE'S BEEN SO DIFFERENT SINCE FRED...SINCE FRED DIED--
--AN' I'D LOVE TO FIND SOME WAY T'CHEER HER UP.
TIME.
HUH?
RAPHNE NEEDS TIME.
YEAH, I GUESS YOU'RE RIGHT. BUT SHE'S HAD SIX MONTHS ALREADY--
--AND SHE'S ONLY GETTING WORSE.
THERE YOU ARE!
DIDN'T I SEND YOU TWO OUT THIS MORNING WITH A LIST OF CHORES...?
YEAH-- AND WE DID 'EM!
RUH-ROH!
ALL OF THEM?
SOME OF 'EM.
TRANSLATION--
--YOU'VE SPENT MOST OF THE DAY GOOFING OFF.

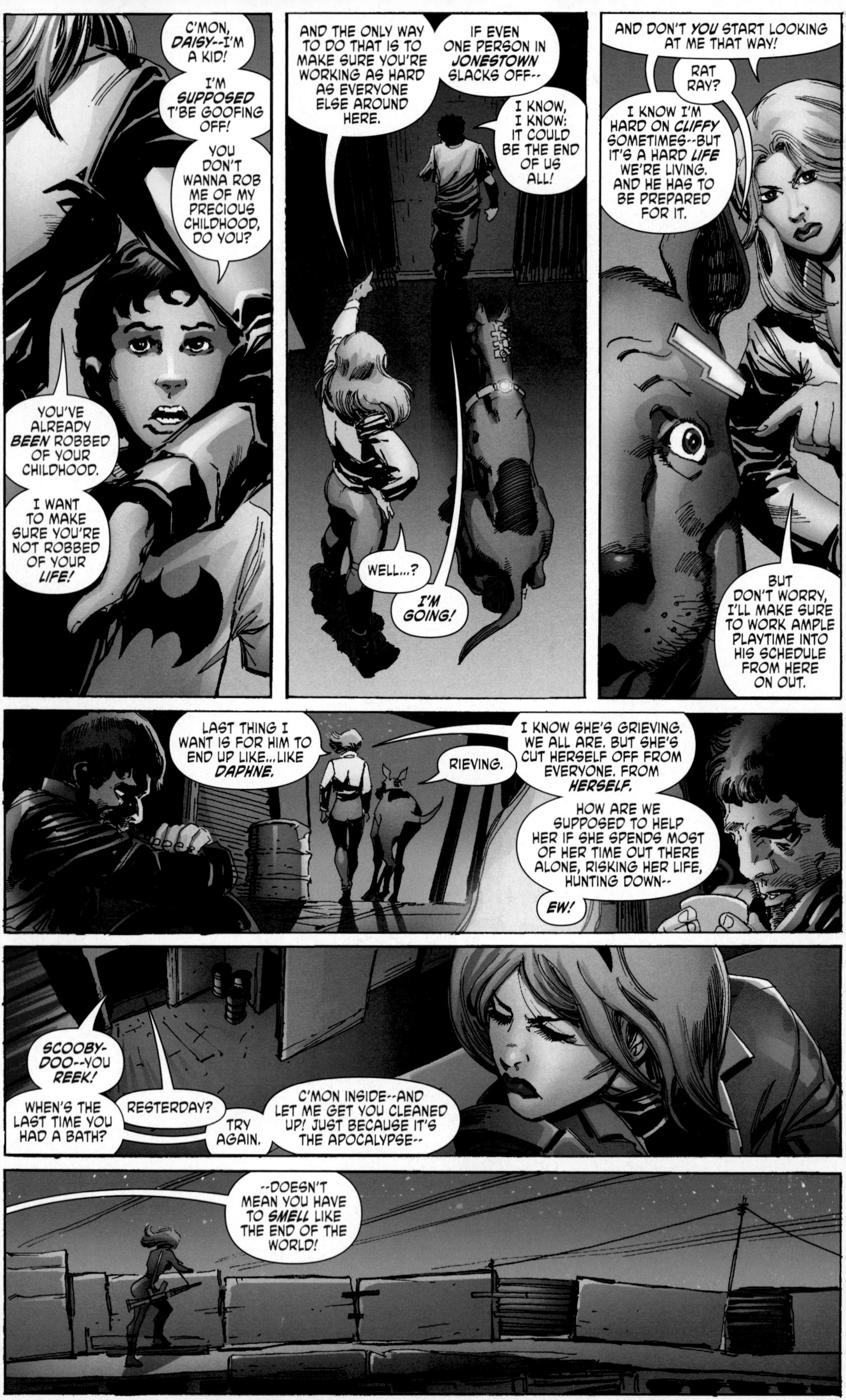
C'MON, DAISY--I'M A KID!
I'M SUPPOSED T'BE GOOFING OFF!
YOU DON'T WANNA ROB ME OF MY PRECIOUS CHILDHOOD, DO YOU?
YOU'VE ALREADY BEEN ROBBED OF YOUR CHILDHOOD.
I WANT TO MAKE SURE YOU'RE NOT ROBBED OF YOUR LIFE!
AND THE ONLY WAY TO DO THAT IS TO MAKE SURE YOU'RE WORKING AS HARD AS EVERYONE ELSE AROUND HERE.
IF EVEN ONE PERSON IN JONESTOWN SLACKS OFF--
I KNOW, I KNOW: IT COULD BE THE END OF US ALL!
WELL...?
I'M GOING!
AND DON'T YOU START LOOKING AT ME THAT WAY!
RAT RAY?
I KNOW I'M HARD ON CLIFFY SOMETIMES--BUT IT'S A HARD LIFE WE'RE LIVING. AND HE HAS TO BE PREPARED FOR IT.
BUT DON'T WORRY, I'LL MAKE SURE TO WORK AMPLE PLAYTIME INTO HIS SCHEDULE FROM HERE ON OUT.
LAST THING I WANT IS FOR HIM TO END UP LIKE...LIKE DAPHNE.
RIEVING.
I KNOW SHE'S GRIEVING. WE ALL ARE. BUT SHE'S CUT HERSELF OFF FROM EVERYONE. FROM HERSELF.
HOW ARE WE SUPPOSED TO HELP HER IF SHE SPENDS MOST OF HER TIME OUT THERE ALONE, RISKING HER LIFE, HUNTING DOWN--
EW!
SCOOBY-DOO--YOU REEK!
WHEN'S THE LAST TIME YOU HAD A BATH?
RESTERDAY?
TRY AGAIN.
C'MON INSIDE--AND LET ME GET YOU CLEANED UP! JUST BECAUSE IT'S THE APOCALYPSE--
--DOESN'T MEAN YOU HAVE TO SMELL LIKE THE END OF THE WORLD!

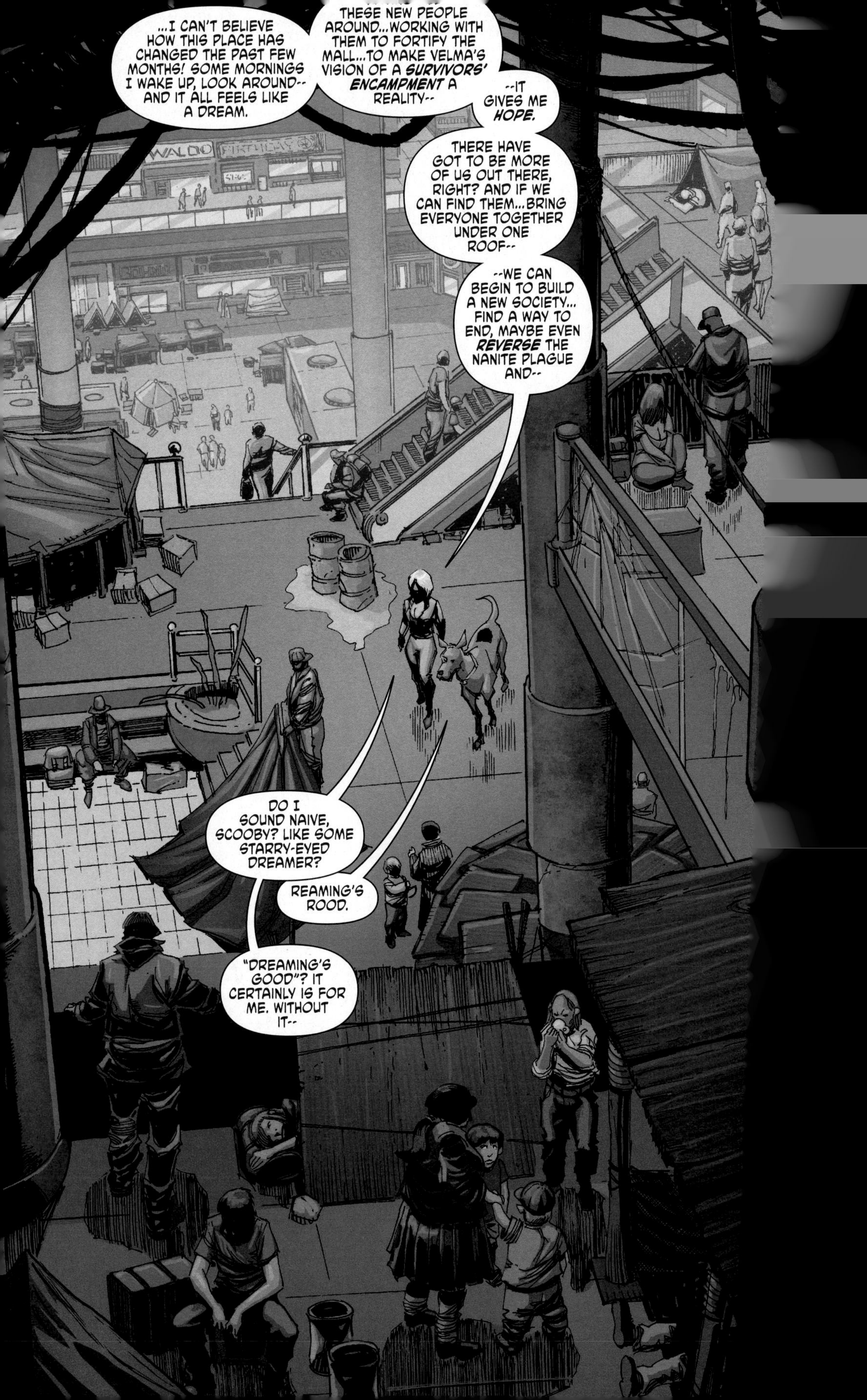
...I CAN'T BELIEVE HOW THIS PLACE HAS CHANGED THE PAST FEW MONTHS! SOME MORNINGS I WAKE UP, LOOK AROUND-- AND IT ALL FEELS LIKE A DREAM.
THESE NEW PEOPLE AROUND...WORKING WITH THEM TO FORTIFY THE MALL...TO MAKE VELMA'S VISION OF A SURVIVORS' ENCAMPMENT A REALITY--
--IT GIVES ME HOPE.
THERE HAVE GOT TO BE MORE OF US OUT THERE, RIGHT? AND IF WE CAN FIND THEM...BRING EVERYONE TOGETHER UNDER ONE ROOF--
--WE CAN BEGIN TO BUILD A NEW SOCIETY... FIND A WAY TO END, MAYBE EVEN REVERSE THE NANITE PLAGUE AND--
DO I SOUND NAIVE, SCOOBY? LIKE SOME STARRY-EYED DREAMER?
REAMING'S ROOD.
"DREAMING'S GOOD"? IT CERTAINLY IS FOR ME. WITHOUT IT--
WALDO

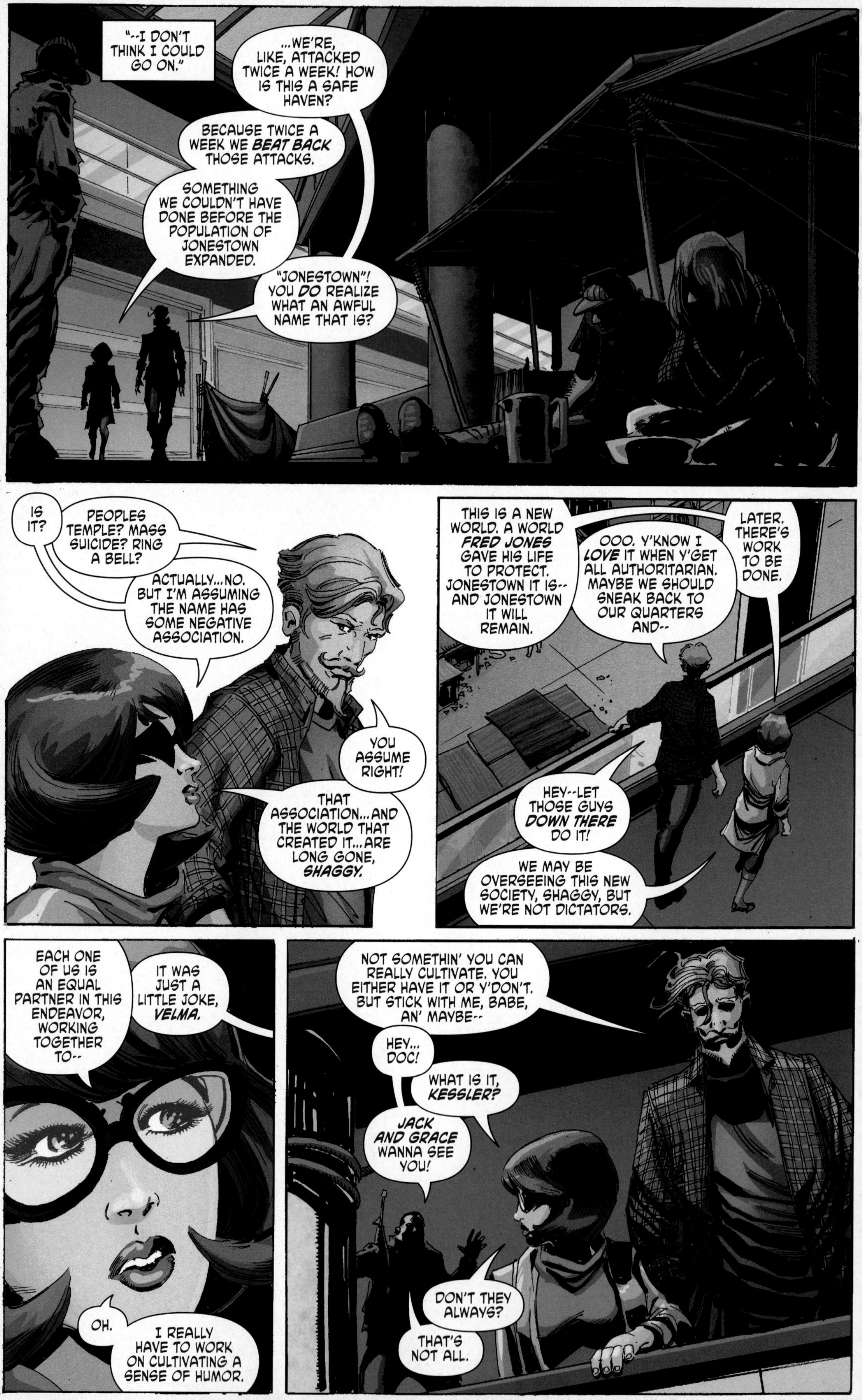
"--I DON'T THINK I COULD GO ON."
...WE'RE, LIKE, ATTACKED TWICE A WEEK! HOW IS THIS A SAFE HAVEN?
BECAUSE TWICE A WEEK WE BEAT BACK THOSE ATTACKS.
SOMETHING WE COULDN'T HAVE DONE BEFORE THE POPULATION OF JONESTOWN EXPANDED.
"JONESTOWN"! YOU DO REALIZE WHAT AN AWFUL NAME THAT IS?
IS IT?
PEOPLES TEMPLE? MASS SUICIDE? RING A BELL?
ACTUALLY...NO. BUT I'M ASSUMING THE NAME HAS SOME NEGATIVE ASSOCIATION.
YOU ASSUME RIGHT!
THAT ASSOCIATION...AND THE WORLD THAT CREATED IT...ARE LONG GONE, SHAGGY.
THIS IS A NEW WORLD. A WORLD FRED JONES GAVE HIS LIFE TO PROTECT. JONESTOWN IT IS--AND JONESTOWN IT WILL REMAIN.
OOO. Y'KNOW I LOVE IT WHEN Y'GET ALL AUTHORITARIAN. MAYBE WE SHOULD SNEAK BACK TO OUR QUARTERS AND--
LATER. THERE'S WORK TO BE DONE.
HEY--LET THOSE GUYS DOWN THERE DO IT!
WE MAY BE OVERSEEING THIS NEW SOCIETY, SHAGGY, BUT WE'RE NOT DICTATORS.
EACH ONE OF US IS AN EQUAL PARTNER IN THIS ENDEAVOR, WORKING TOGETHER TO--
IT WAS JUST A LITTLE JOKE, VELMA.
OH.
I REALLY HAVE TO WORK ON CULTIVATING A SENSE OF HUMOR.
NOT SOMETHIN' YOU CAN REALLY CULTIVATE. YOU EITHER HAVE IT OR Y'DON'T. BUT STICK WITH ME, BABE, AN' MAYBE--
HEY... DOC!
WHAT IS IT, KESSLER?
JACK AND GRACE WANNA SEE YOU!
DON'T THEY ALWAYS?
THAT'S NOT ALL.

SOUTHSIDE SEWER ACCESS IS SHOWING SIGNS OF ACTIVITY.

AGAIN? I THOUGHT DAPHNE, LIKE, SCARED 'EM ALL AWAY!

HEY, IF THERE'S ONE THING WE'VE LEARNED--

--IT'S THAT THOSE BASTARDS ARE PERSISTENT.

YEAH. AN' DEADLY.

SOMETIMES I THINK WE'D BE BETTER OFF BACK ON THE ROAD, LOCKED UP TIGHT IN THE *MYSTERY MACHINE.*

YOU CAN'T POSSIBLY MEAN THAT.

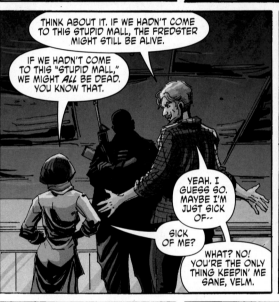

THINK ABOUT IT. IF WE HADN'T COME TO THIS STUPID MALL, THE FREDSTER MIGHT STILL BE ALIVE.

IF WE HADN'T COME TO THIS "STUPID MALL," WE MIGHT *ALL* BE DEAD. YOU KNOW THAT.

YEAH. I GUESS SO. MAYBE I'M JUST SICK OF--

SICK OF ME?

WHAT? NO! YOU'RE THE ONLY THING KEEPIN' ME SANE, VELM.

I'D BE LOST WITHOUT YOU.

I KNOW. I JUST WANTED TO HEAR YOU SAY IT.

NOW YOU AND KESSLER GO MUCK AROUND IN THE SEWER WHILE I DEAL WITH JACK AND GRACE.

AND BELIEVE ME--

EA

--*YOU TWO* HAVE GOT THE LESS ODIOUS ASSIGNMENT.

WHEN *THE KUBELSKYS* ARRIVED HERE AND TOLD ME THAT THEY'D OWNED A CHAIN OF RESTAURANTS IN THE MIDWEST--

--I THOUGHT THEY'D BE THE PERFECT CANDIDATES TO HELP ME RUN DAY-TO-DAY OPERATIONS.

BUT THEY SEEM INCAPABLE OF MAKING DECISIONS ON THEIR OWN.

I UNDERSTAND THAT THEY'RE A LITTLE IN AWE OF ME--

--IT'S IMPOSSIBLE TO ENCOUNTER A BRILLIANT MIND LIKE MINE AND *NOT* BE--

--BUT THERE'S A THIN LINE BETWEEN AWE AND INCOMPETENCE--

EAS

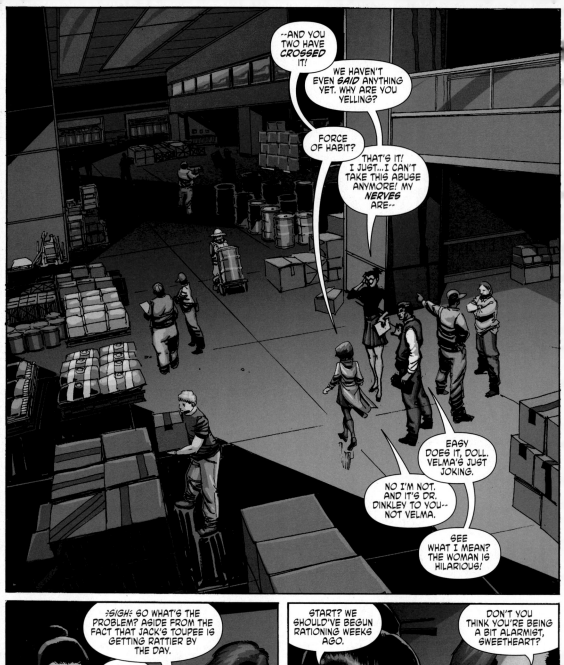

--AND YOU TWO HAVE *CROSSED* IT!

WE HAVEN'T EVEN *SAID* ANYTHING YET. WHY ARE YOU YELLING?

FORCE OF HABIT?

THAT'S IT! I JUST...I CAN'T TAKE THIS ABUSE ANYMORE! MY *NERVES* ARE--

EASY DOES IT, DOLL. VELMA'S JUST JOKING.

NO I'M NOT. AND IT'S DR. DINKLEY TO YOU-- NOT VELMA.

SEE WHAT I MEAN? THE WOMAN IS HILARIOUS!

⟨SIGH⟩ SO WHAT'S THE PROBLEM? ASIDE FROM THE FACT THAT JACK'S TOUPEE IS GETTING RATTIER BY THE DAY.

IT *IS*, DARLING.

THE PROBLEM IS THE *FOOD SUPPLY*, VEL...UH...DR. DINKLEY. IF THE JONESTOWN POPULATION KEEPS EXPANDING AT THE CURRENT RATE--

--WE MAY HAVE TO START RATIONING.

START? WE SHOULD'VE BEGUN RATIONING WEEKS AGO.

DON'T YOU THINK YOU'RE BEING A BIT ALARMIST, SWEETHEART?

ALARMIST? WE'RE ALL GOING TO BE SKELETONS, LIVING OFF STYROFOAM AND CARDBOARD, IF WE DON'T FIND ANOTHER FOOD SOURCE.

NOW, NOW, DEAR ONE. WE STILL HAVE ENOUGH PACKAGED AND CANNED GOODS TO LAST TILL--

REALLY, JACK?

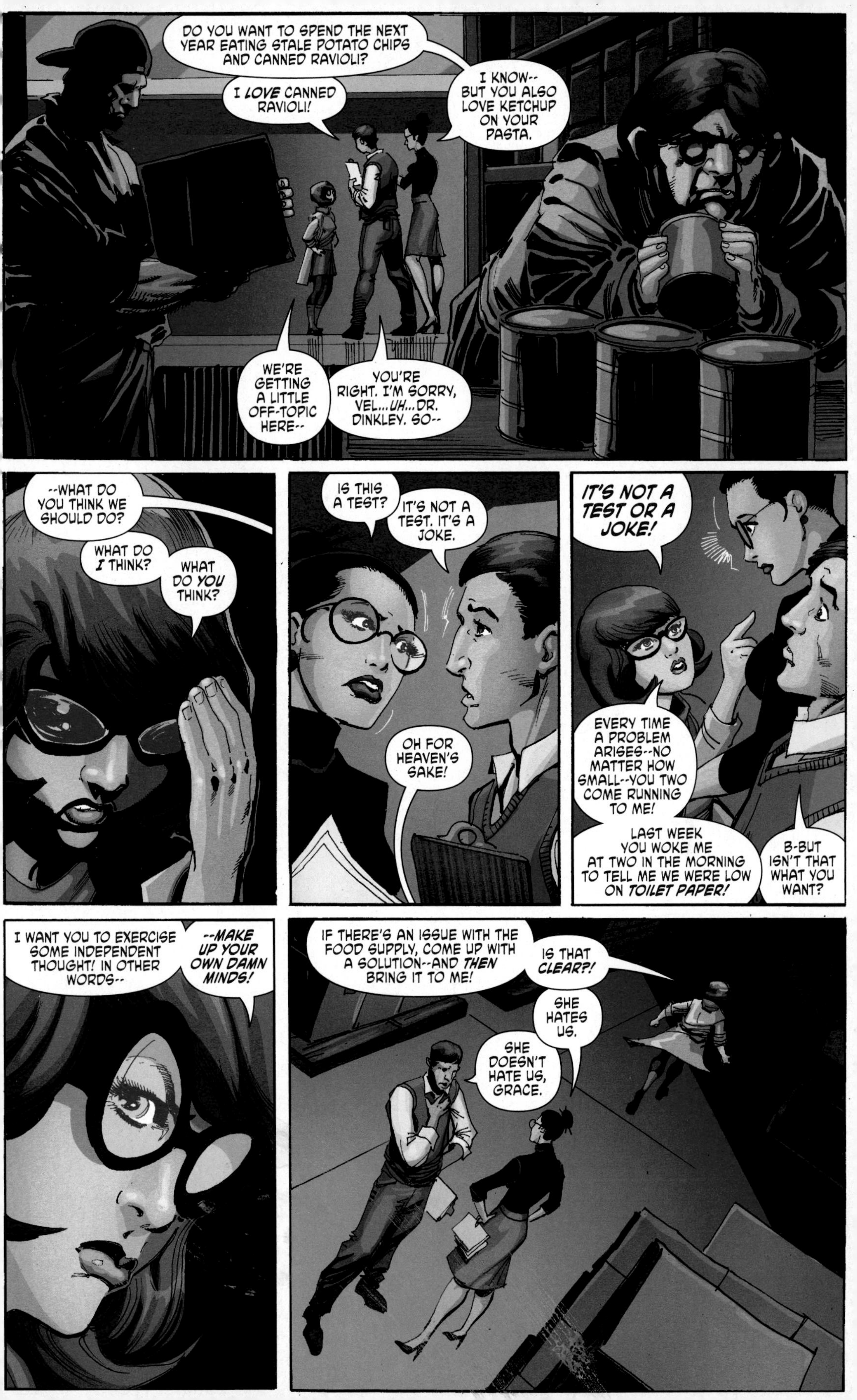
DO YOU WANT TO SPEND THE NEXT YEAR EATING STALE POTATO CHIPS AND CANNED RAVIOLI?
I *LOVE* CANNED RAVIOLI!
I KNOW-- BUT YOU ALSO LOVE KETCHUP ON YOUR PASTA.
WE'RE GETTING A LITTLE OFF-TOPIC HERE--
YOU'RE RIGHT. I'M SORRY, VEL...*UH*...DR. DINKLEY. SO--
--WHAT DO YOU THINK WE SHOULD DO?
WHAT DO *I* THINK?
WHAT DO *YOU* THINK?
IS THIS A TEST?
IT'S NOT A TEST. IT'S A JOKE.
OH FOR HEAVEN'S SAKE!
IT'S NOT A TEST OR A JOKE!
EVERY TIME A PROBLEM ARISES--NO MATTER HOW SMALL--YOU TWO COME RUNNING TO ME!
LAST WEEK YOU WOKE ME AT TWO IN THE MORNING TO TELL ME WE WERE LOW ON *TOILET PAPER!*
B-BUT ISN'T THAT WHAT YOU WANT?
I WANT YOU TO EXERCISE SOME INDEPENDENT THOUGHT! IN OTHER WORDS--
--MAKE UP YOUR OWN DAMN MINDS!
IF THERE'S AN ISSUE WITH THE FOOD SUPPLY, COME UP WITH A SOLUTION--AND *THEN* BRING IT TO ME!
IS THAT *CLEAR?!*
SHE HATES US.
SHE DOESN'T HATE US, GRACE.

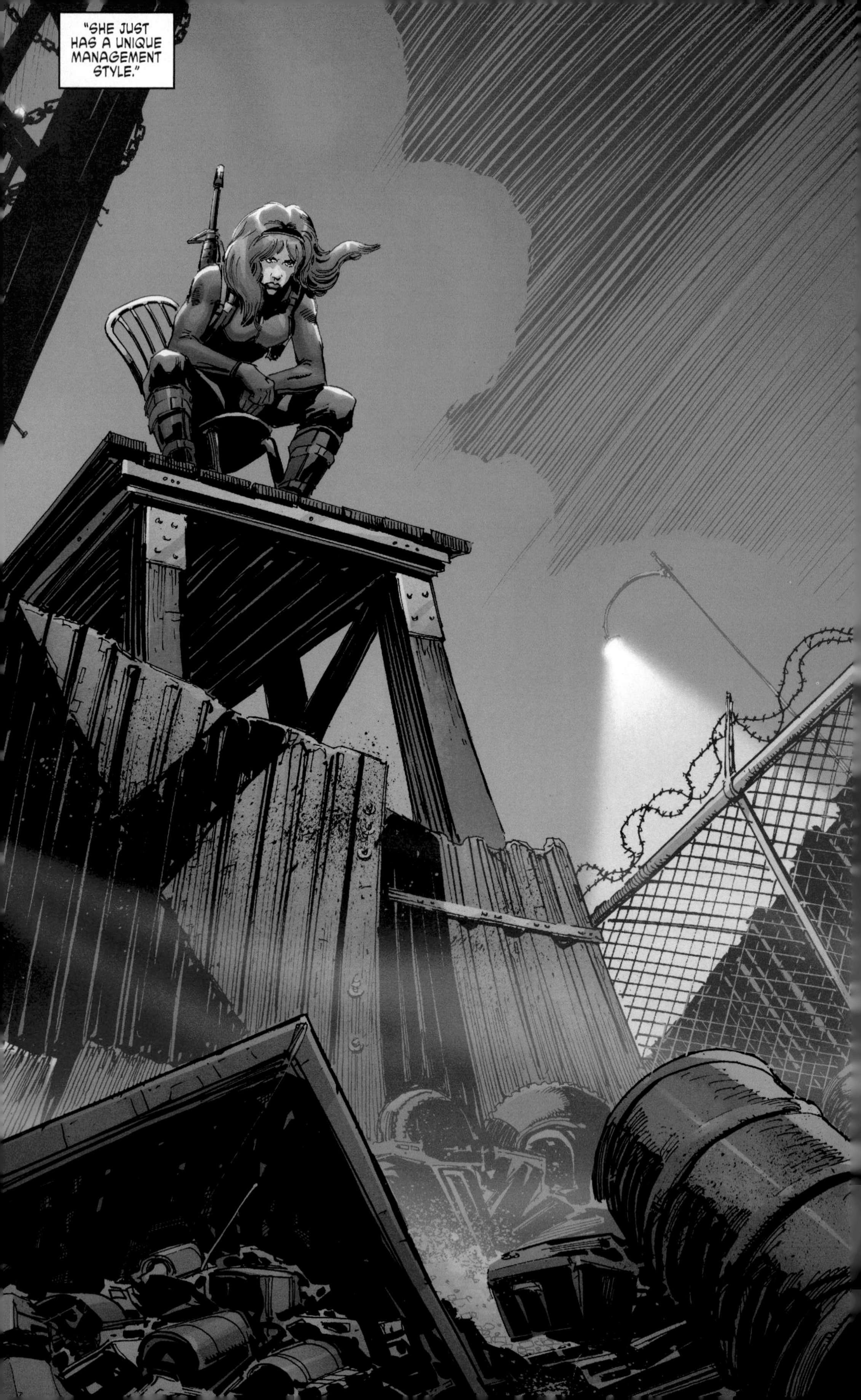
"SHE JUST HAS A UNIQUE MANAGEMENT STYLE."

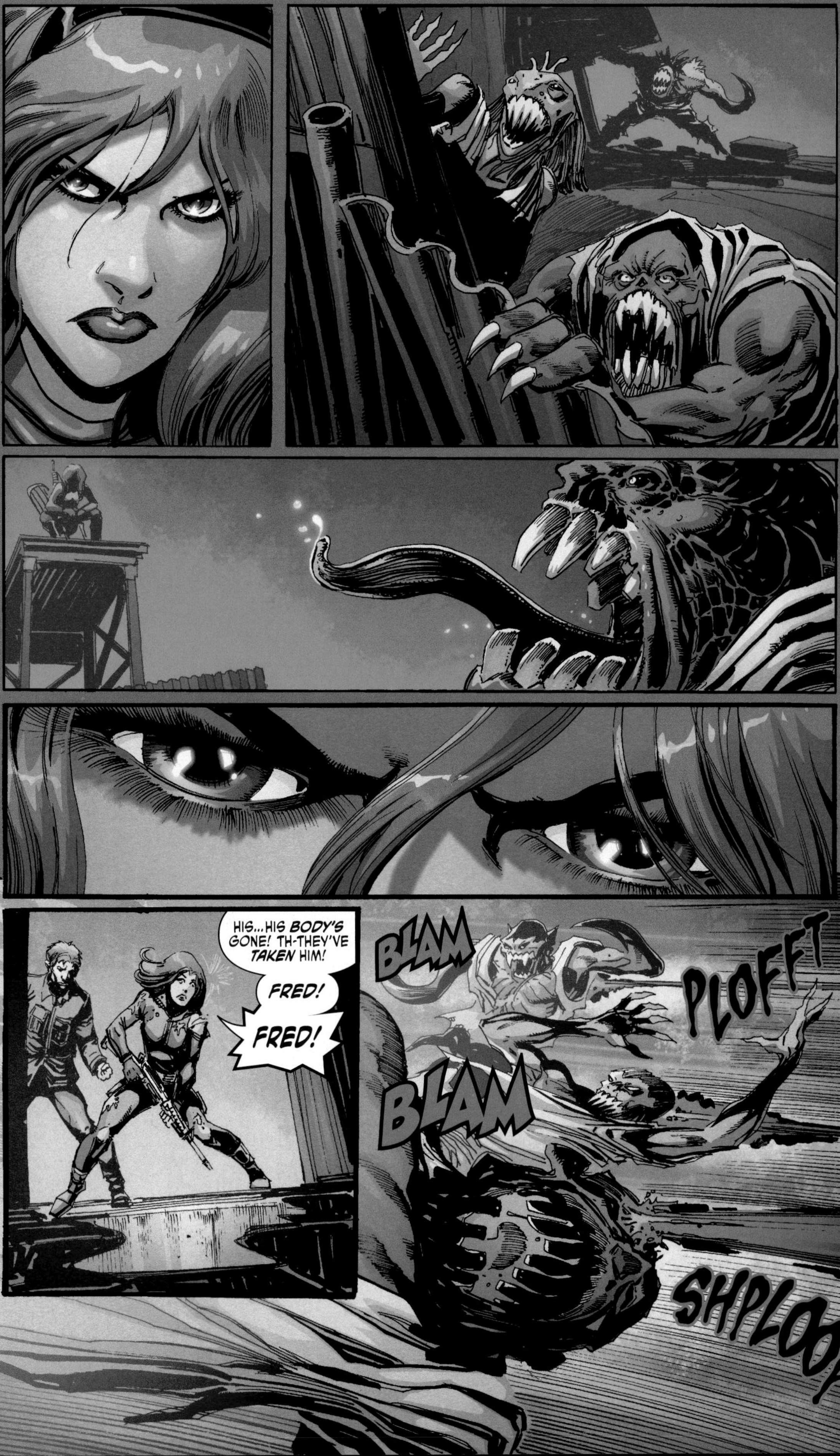
HIS...HIS BODY'S GONE! TH-THEY'VE TAKEN HIM!
FRED!
FRED!
BLAM
PLOFFT
BLAM
SHPLOOP

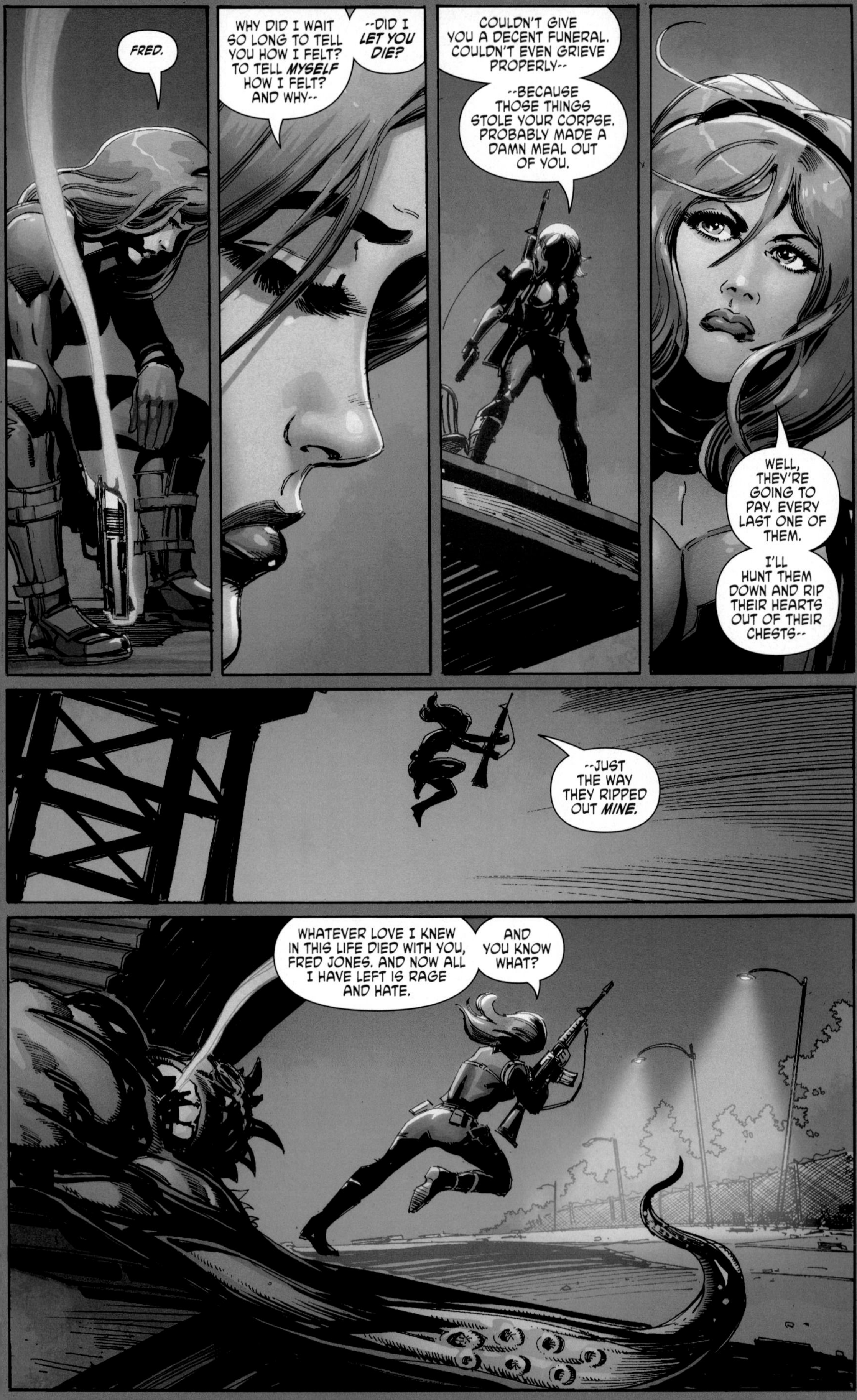
FRED.
WHY DID I WAIT SO LONG TO TELL YOU HOW I FELT? TO TELL *MYSELF* HOW I FELT? AND WHY--
--DID I *LET YOU DIE?*
COULDN'T GIVE YOU A DECENT FUNERAL. COULDN'T EVEN GRIEVE PROPERLY--
--BECAUSE THOSE THINGS STOLE YOUR CORPSE. PROBABLY MADE A DAMN MEAL OUT OF YOU.
WELL, THEY'RE GOING TO PAY. EVERY LAST ONE OF THEM.
I'LL HUNT THEM DOWN AND RIP THEIR HEARTS OUT OF THEIR CHESTS--
--JUST THE WAY THEY RIPPED OUT *MINE.*
WHATEVER LOVE I KNEW IN THIS LIFE DIED WITH YOU, FRED JONES. AND NOW ALL I HAVE LEFT IS RAGE AND HATE.
AND YOU KNOW WHAT?

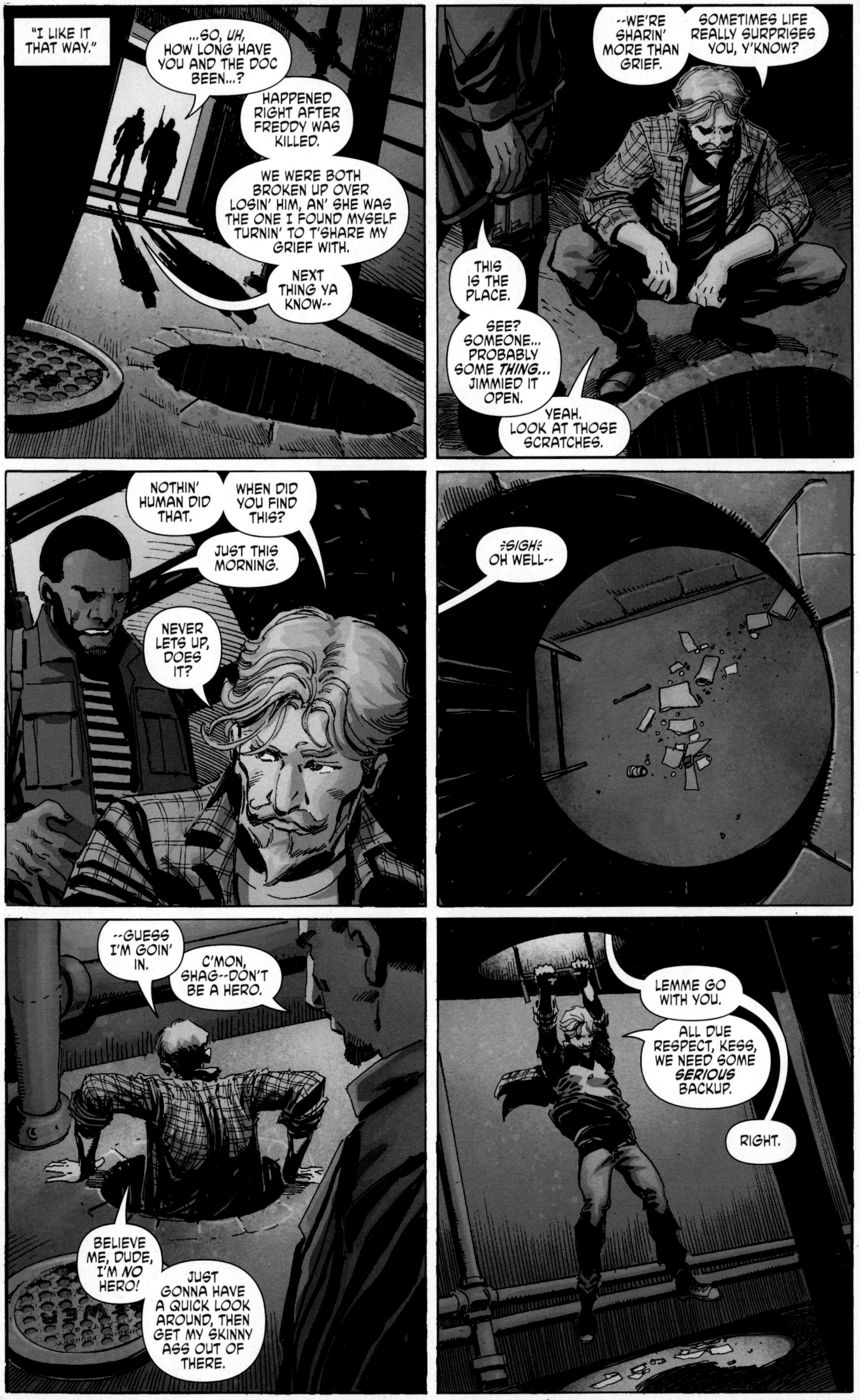
"I LIKE IT THAT WAY."
...SO, UH, HOW LONG HAVE YOU AND THE DOC BEEN...?
HAPPENED RIGHT AFTER FREDDY WAS KILLED.
WE WERE BOTH BROKEN UP OVER LOSIN' HIM, AN' SHE WAS THE ONE I FOUND MYSELF TURNIN' TO T'SHARE MY GRIEF WITH.
NEXT THING YA KNOW--
--WE'RE SHARIN' MORE THAN GRIEF.
SOMETIMES LIFE REALLY SURPRISES YOU, Y'KNOW?
THIS IS THE PLACE.
SEE? SOMEONE... PROBABLY SOME THING... JIMMIED IT OPEN.
YEAH. LOOK AT THOSE SCRATCHES.
NOTHIN' HUMAN DID THAT.
WHEN DID YOU FIND THIS?
JUST THIS MORNING.
NEVER LETS UP, DOES IT?
SIGH OH WELL--
--GUESS I'M GOIN' IN.
C'MON, SHAG--DON'T BE A HERO.
BELIEVE ME, DUDE, I'M NO HERO!
JUST GONNA HAVE A QUICK LOOK AROUND, THEN GET MY SKINNY ASS OUT OF THERE.
LEMME GO WITH YOU.
ALL DUE RESPECT, KESS, WE NEED SOME SERIOUS BACKUP.
RIGHT.

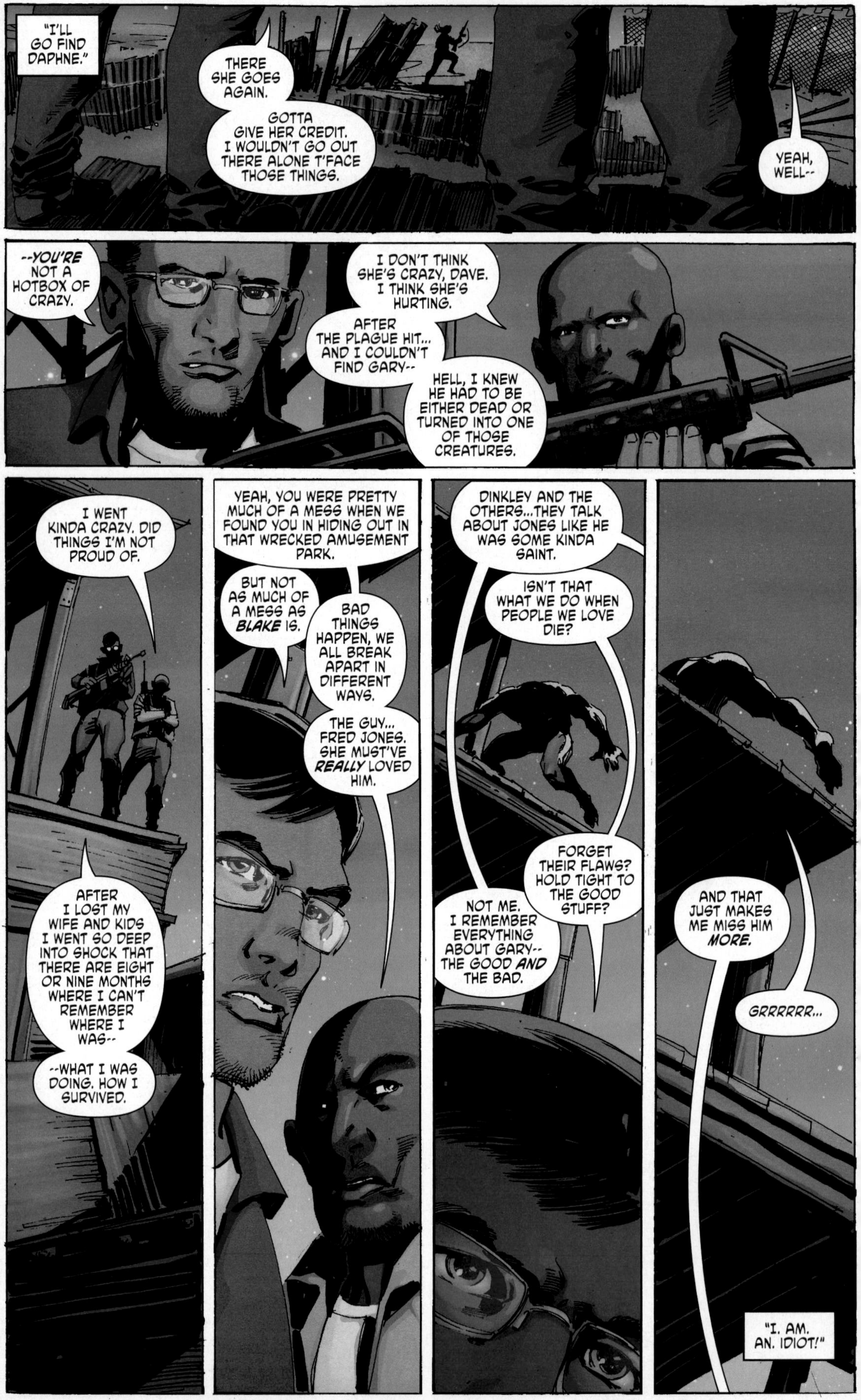
"I'LL GO FIND DAPHNE."
THERE SHE GOES AGAIN.
GOTTA GIVE HER CREDIT. I WOULDN'T GO OUT THERE ALONE T'FACE THOSE THINGS.
YEAH, WELL--
--YOU'RE NOT A HOTBOX OF CRAZY.
I DON'T THINK SHE'S CRAZY, DAVE. I THINK SHE'S HURTING.
AFTER THE PLAGUE HIT... AND I COULDN'T FIND GARY--
HELL, I KNEW HE HAD TO BE EITHER DEAD OR TURNED INTO ONE OF THOSE CREATURES.
I WENT KINDA CRAZY. DID THINGS I'M NOT PROUD OF.
AFTER I LOST MY WIFE AND KIDS I WENT SO DEEP INTO SHOCK THAT THERE ARE EIGHT OR NINE MONTHS WHERE I CAN'T REMEMBER WHERE I WAS--
--WHAT I WAS DOING. HOW I SURVIVED.
YEAH, YOU WERE PRETTY MUCH OF A MESS WHEN WE FOUND YOU IN HIDING OUT IN THAT WRECKED AMUSEMENT PARK.
BUT NOT AS MUCH OF A MESS AS BLAKE IS.
BAD THINGS HAPPEN, WE ALL BREAK APART IN DIFFERENT WAYS.
THE GUY... FRED JONES. SHE MUST'VE REALLY LOVED HIM.
DINKLEY AND THE OTHERS...THEY TALK ABOUT JONES LIKE HE WAS SOME KINDA SAINT.
ISN'T THAT WHAT WE DO WHEN PEOPLE WE LOVE DIE?
FORGET THEIR FLAWS? HOLD TIGHT TO THE GOOD STUFF?
NOT ME. I REMEMBER EVERYTHING ABOUT GARY-- THE GOOD AND THE BAD.
AND THAT JUST MAKES ME MISS HIM MORE.
GRRRRRR...
"I. AM. AN. IDIOT!"

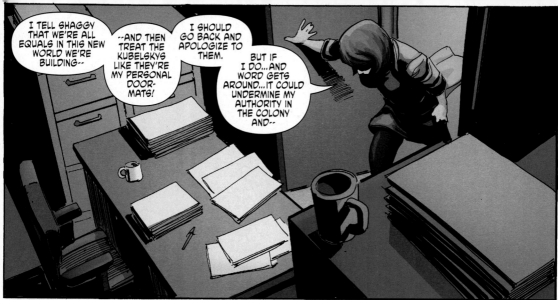

I TELL SHAGGY THAT WE'RE ALL EQUALS IN THIS NEW WORLD WE'RE BUILDING--

--AND THEN TREAT THE KUBELSKYS LIKE THEY'RE MY PERSONAL DOORMATS!

I SHOULD GO BACK AND APOLOGIZE TO THEM.

BUT IF I DO...AND WORD GETS AROUND...IT COULD UNDERMINE MY AUTHORITY IN THE COLONY AND--

WHAT MADE ME THINK I COULD BE A LEADER?

MY BROTHERS WERE RIGHT. I'M AN INSECURE, SOCIALLY AWKWARD, INCOMPETENT FAILURE. AND THERE'S NO WAY I CAN--

NO. DON'T DEMEAN YOURSELF LIKE THIS, VELMA.

MAYBE YOU WERE THAT PERSON ONCE-- BUT THESE PAST TWO YEARS HAVE CHANGED YOU. MADE YOU A BETTER PERSON. A *STRONGER* PERSON.

IT'S ALSO MADE YOU SOMEONE WHO TALKS OUT LOUD TO HERSELF ENTIRELY TOO MUCH!

ALL RIGHT. TAKE A DEEP BREATH AND START OVER.

GO BACK AND TALK TO JACK AND GRACE. YOU CAN BEGIN A NEW RELATIONSHIP.

MAINTAIN AUTHORITY WITHOUT HARANGUING AND HUMILIATING THEM. IN FACT, YOU--

DR. DINKLEY!

WHAT?

W-WE DID WHAT YOU SAID: TOOK THE INITIATIVE! MADE OUR OWN DECISIONS!

AND?

WELL, WE THOUGHT WE COULD SLOW DOWN FOOD CONSUMPTION IF WE STARTED *CHARGING* FOR MEALS. THAT... UH...DIDN'T REALLY GO OVER WELL.

THERE'S A *RIOT* IN THE CAFETERIA AND SECURITY'S THREATENING TO *SHOOT* PEOPLE!

YAAAAHH!

ALL THINGS CONSIDERED--

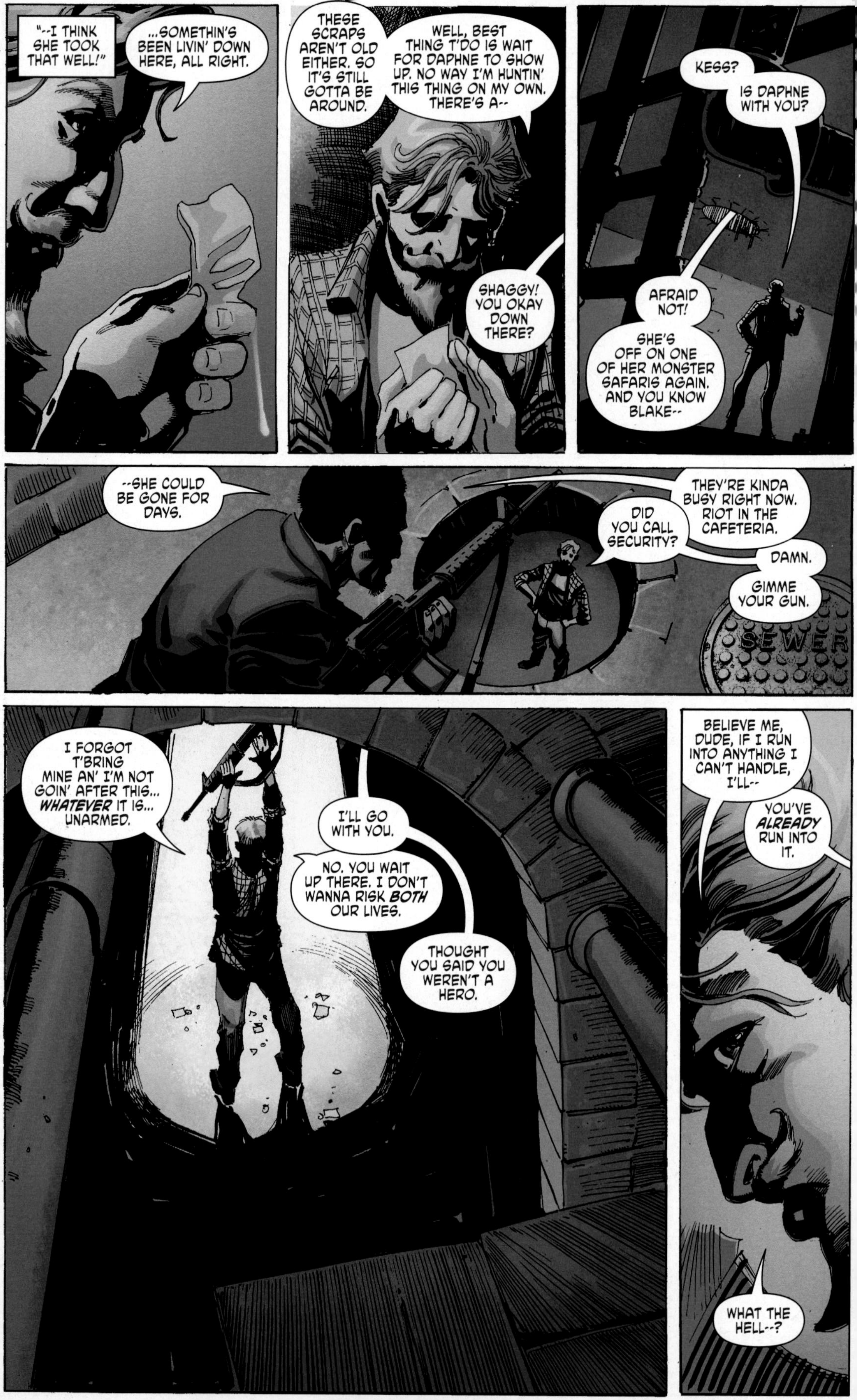
"--I THINK SHE TOOK THAT WELL!"
...SOMETHIN'S BEEN LIVIN' DOWN HERE, ALL RIGHT.
THESE SCRAPS AREN'T OLD EITHER. SO IT'S STILL GOTTA BE AROUND.
WELL, BEST THING T'DO IS WAIT FOR DAPHNE TO SHOW UP. NO WAY I'M HUNTIN' THIS THING ON MY OWN. THERE'S A--
SHAGGY! YOU OKAY DOWN THERE?
KESS?
IS DAPHNE WITH YOU?
AFRAID NOT!
SHE'S OFF ON ONE OF HER MONSTER SAFARIS AGAIN. AND YOU KNOW BLAKE--
--SHE COULD BE GONE FOR DAYS.
DID YOU CALL SECURITY?
THEY'RE KINDA BUSY RIGHT NOW. RIOT IN THE CAFETERIA.
DAMN.
GIMME YOUR GUN.
SEWER
I FORGOT T'BRING MINE AN' I'M NOT GOIN' AFTER THIS... *WHATEVER* IT IS... UNARMED.
I'LL GO WITH YOU.
NO. YOU WAIT UP THERE. I DON'T WANNA RISK *BOTH* OUR LIVES.
THOUGHT YOU SAID YOU WEREN'T A HERO.
BELIEVE ME, DUDE, IF I RUN INTO ANYTHING I CAN'T HANDLE, I'LL--
YOU'VE *ALREADY* RUN INTO IT.
WHAT THE HELL--?

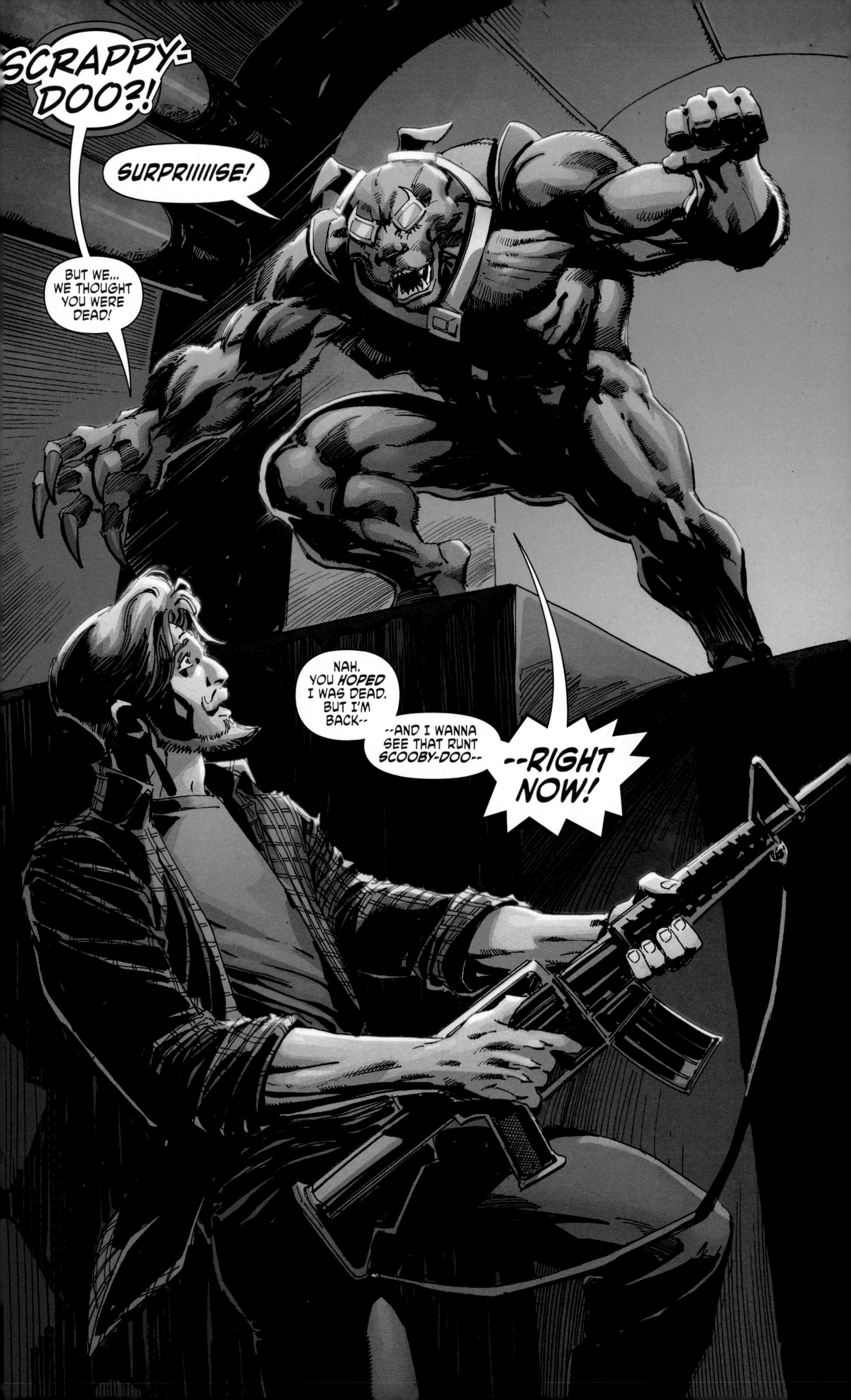
SCRAPPY-DOO?!
SURPRIIIIISE!
BUT WE... WE THOUGHT YOU WERE DEAD!
NAH. YOU *HOPED* I WAS DEAD. BUT I'M BACK--
--AND I WANNA SEE THAT RUNT SCOOBY-DOO--
--RIGHT NOW!

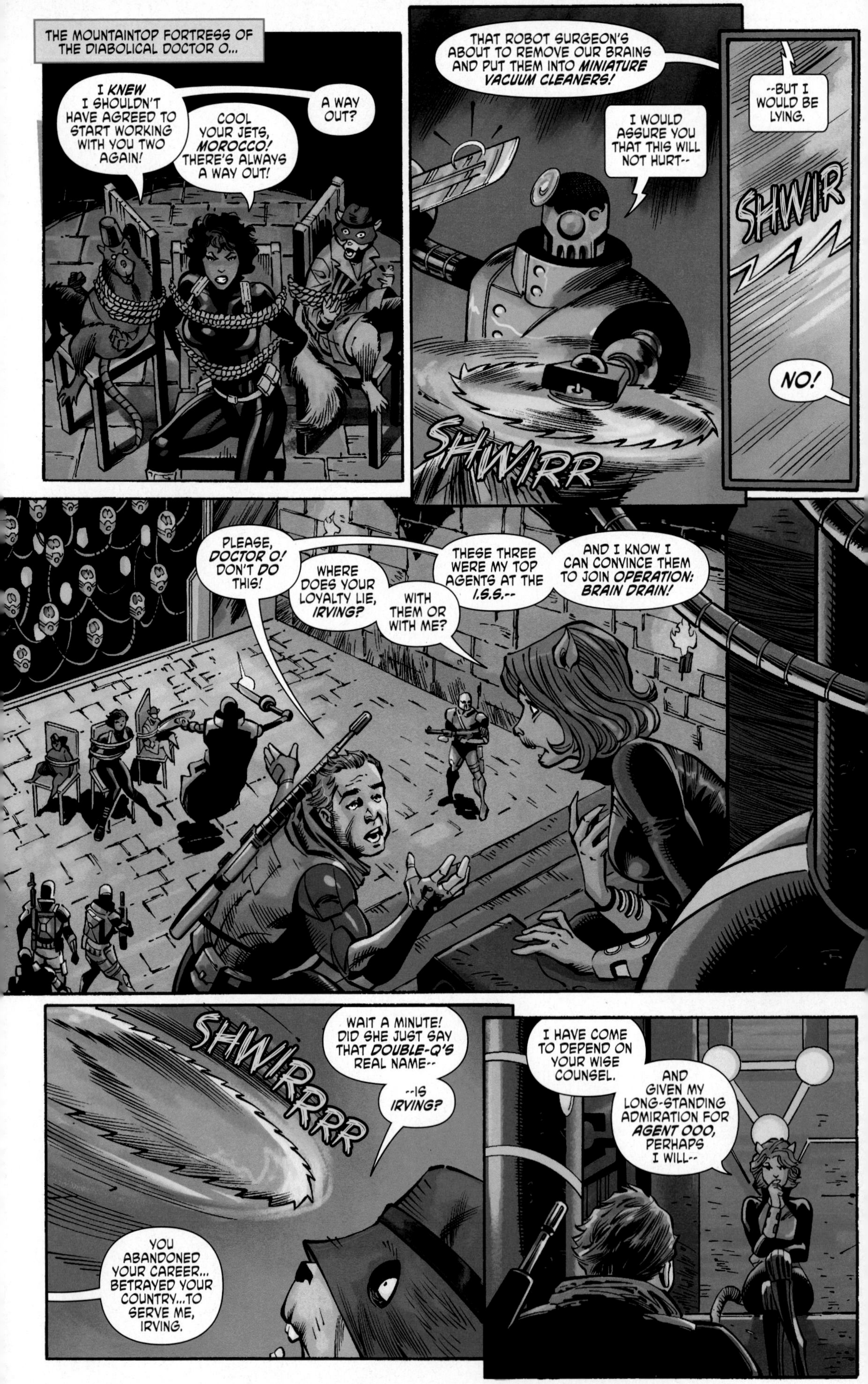
THE MOUNTAINTOP FORTRESS OF THE DIABOLICAL DOCTOR O...
I KNEW I SHOULDN'T HAVE AGREED TO START WORKING WITH YOU TWO AGAIN!
COOL YOUR JETS, MOROCCO! THERE'S ALWAYS A WAY OUT!
A WAY OUT?
THAT ROBOT SURGEON'S ABOUT TO REMOVE OUR BRAINS AND PUT THEM INTO MINIATURE VACUUM CLEANERS!
I WOULD ASSURE YOU THAT THIS WILL NOT HURT--
--BUT I WOULD BE LYING.
SHWIR
SHWIRR
NO!
PLEASE, DOCTOR O! DON'T DO THIS!
WHERE DOES YOUR LOYALTY LIE, IRVING?
WITH THEM OR WITH ME?
THESE THREE WERE MY TOP AGENTS AT THE I.S.S.--
AND I KNOW I CAN CONVINCE THEM TO JOIN OPERATION: BRAIN DRAIN!
SHWIRRRR
WAIT A MINUTE! DID SHE JUST SAY THAT DOUBLE-Q'S REAL NAME--
--IS IRVING?
YOU ABANDONED YOUR CAREER... BETRAYED YOUR COUNTRY...TO SERVE ME, IRVING.
I HAVE COME TO DEPEND ON YOUR WISE COUNSEL.
AND GIVEN MY LONG-STANDING ADMIRATION FOR AGENT OOO, PERHAPS I WILL--

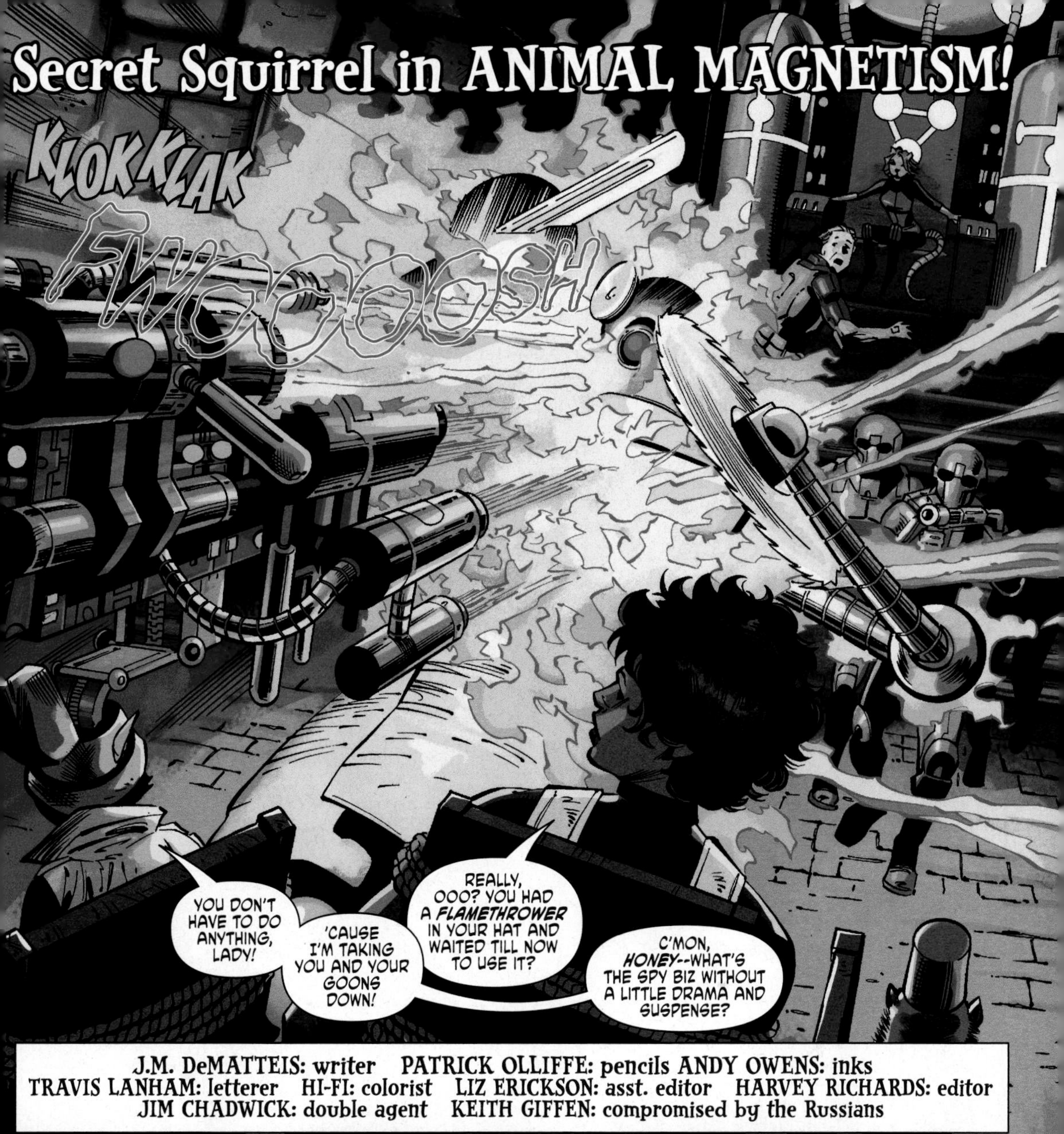
Secret Squirrel in ANIMAL MAGNETISM!
KLOKKLAK
FWOOOOOSH
YOU DON'T HAVE TO DO ANYTHING, LADY!
'CAUSE I'M TAKING YOU AND YOUR GOONS DOWN!
REALLY, OOO? YOU HAD A *FLAMETHROWER* IN YOUR HAT AND WAITED TILL NOW TO USE IT?
C'MON, *HONEY*--WHAT'S THE SPY BIZ WITHOUT A LITTLE DRAMA AND SUSPENSE?

J.M. DeMATTEIS: writer PATRICK OLLIFFE: pencils ANDY OWENS: inks
TRAVIS LANHAM: letterer HI-FI: colorist LIZ ERICKSON: asst. editor HARVEY RICHARDS: editor
JIM CHADWICK: double agent KEITH GIFFEN: compromised by the Russians

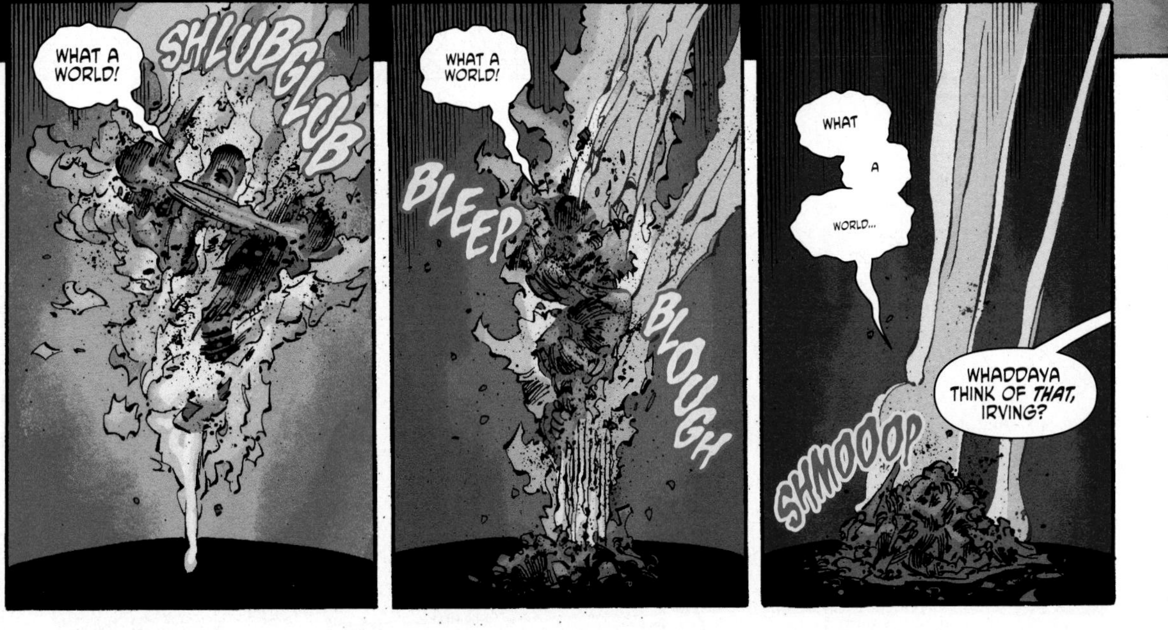
WHAT A WORLD!
SHLUBGLUB
WHAT A WORLD!
BLEEP
BLOUGH
WHAT A WORLD...
WHADDAYA THINK OF *THAT*, IRVING?
SHMOOOP

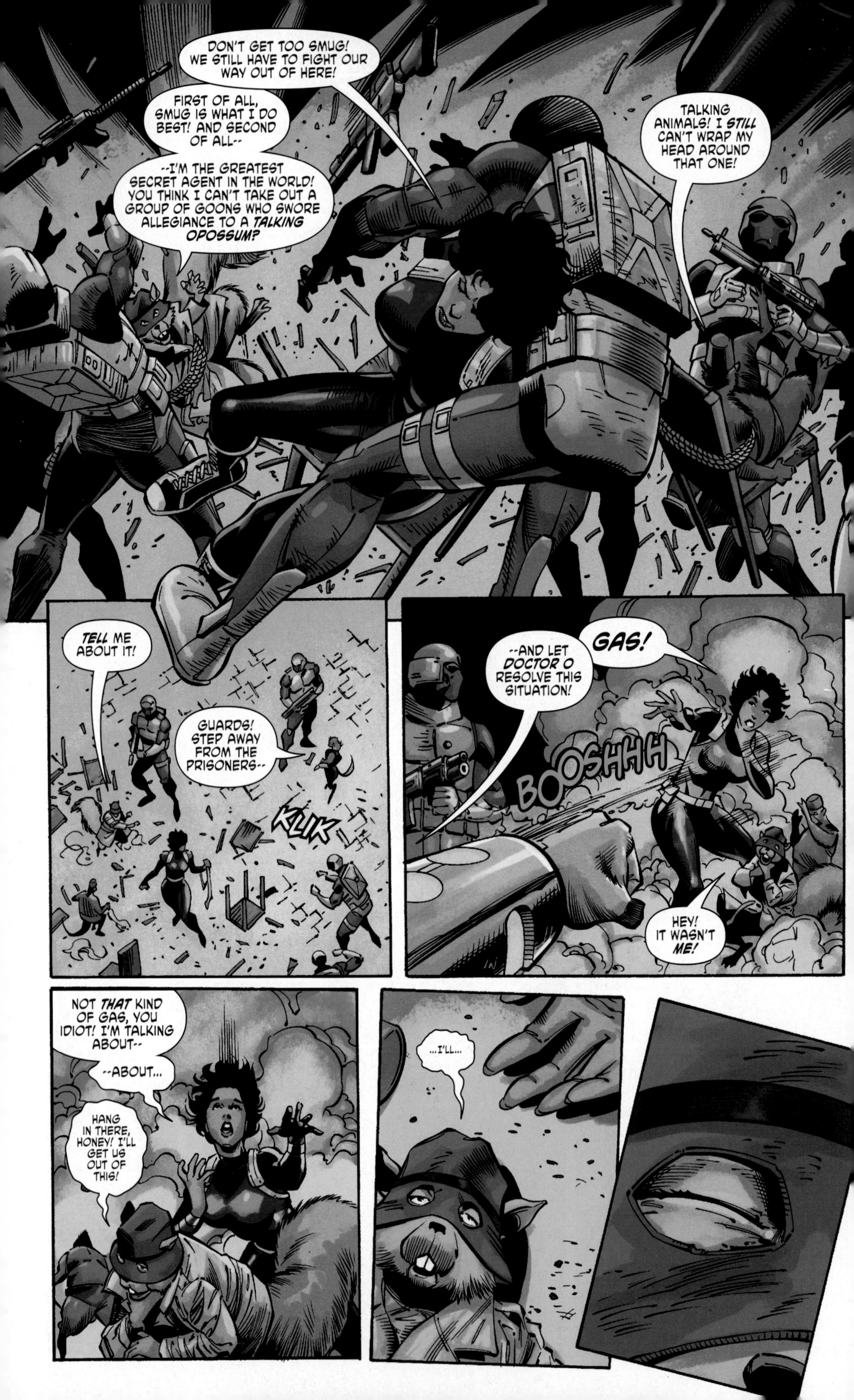
DON'T GET TOO SMUG! WE STILL HAVE TO FIGHT OUR WAY OUT OF HERE!
FIRST OF ALL, SMUG IS WHAT I DO BEST! AND SECOND OF ALL--
--I'M THE GREATEST SECRET AGENT IN THE WORLD! YOU THINK I CAN'T TAKE OUT A GROUP OF GOONS WHO SWORE ALLEGIANCE TO A TALKING OPOSSUM?
TALKING ANIMALS! I STILL CAN'T WRAP MY HEAD AROUND THAT ONE!
TELL ME ABOUT IT!
GUARDS! STEP AWAY FROM THE PRISONERS--
KLIK
--AND LET DOCTOR O RESOLVE THIS SITUATION!
GAS!
BOOSHHH
HEY! IT WASN'T ME!
NOT THAT KIND OF GAS, YOU IDIOT! I'M TALKING ABOUT--
--ABOUT...
HANG IN THERE, HONEY! I'LL GET US OUT OF THIS!
...I'LL...

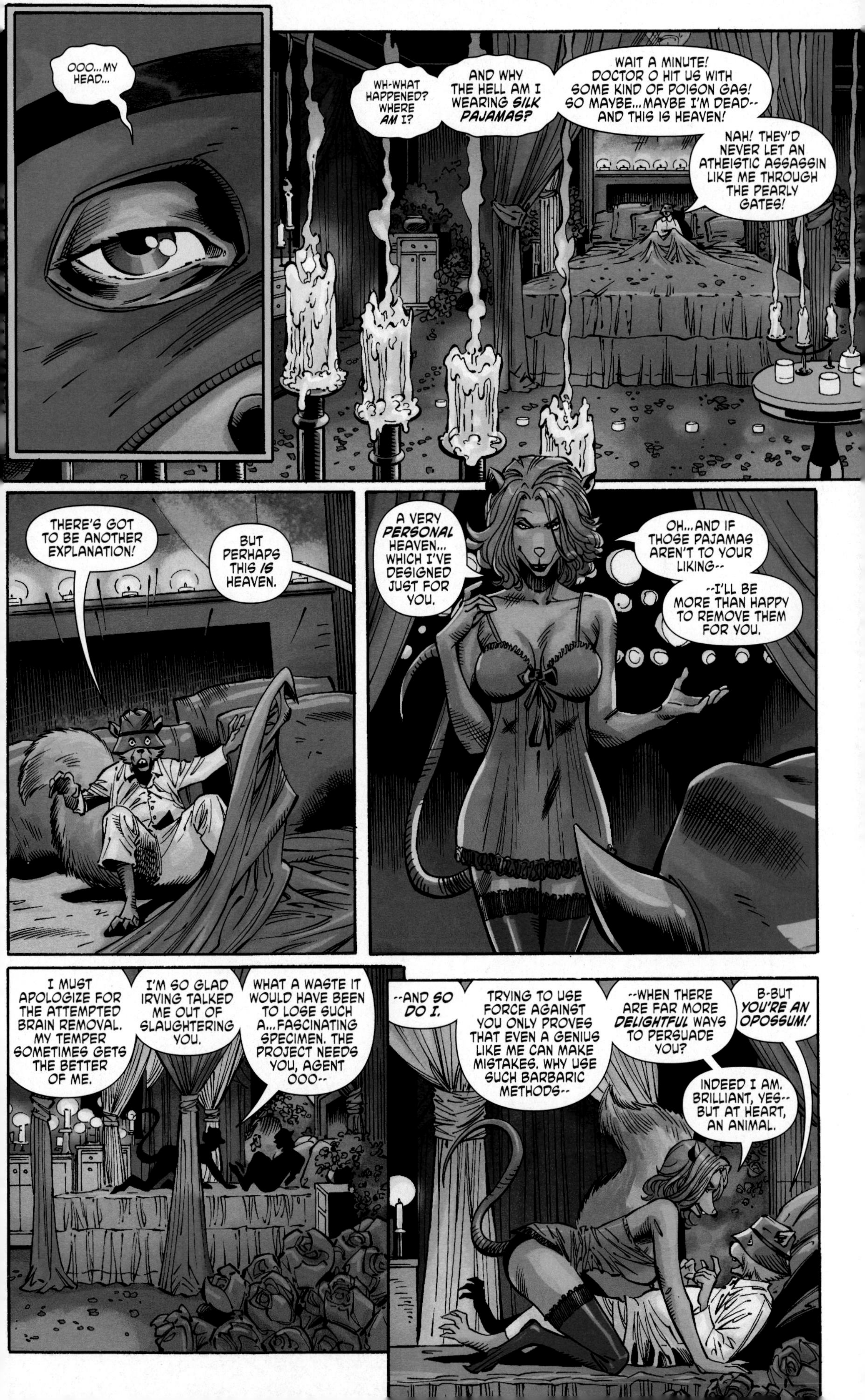

OOO...MY HEAD...
WH-WHAT HAPPENED? WHERE AM I?
AND WHY THE HELL AM I WEARING SILK PAJAMAS?
WAIT A MINUTE! DOCTOR O HIT US WITH SOME KIND OF POISON GAS! SO MAYBE...MAYBE I'M DEAD-- AND THIS IS HEAVEN!
NAH! THEY'D NEVER LET AN ATHEISTIC ASSASSIN LIKE ME THROUGH THE PEARLY GATES!
THERE'S GOT TO BE ANOTHER EXPLANATION!
BUT PERHAPS THIS IS HEAVEN.
A VERY PERSONAL HEAVEN... WHICH I'VE DESIGNED JUST FOR YOU.
OH...AND IF THOSE PAJAMAS AREN'T TO YOUR LIKING--
--I'LL BE MORE THAN HAPPY TO REMOVE THEM FOR YOU.
I MUST APOLOGIZE FOR THE ATTEMPTED BRAIN REMOVAL. MY TEMPER SOMETIMES GETS THE BETTER OF ME.
I'M SO GLAD IRVING TALKED ME OUT OF SLAUGHTERING YOU.
WHAT A WASTE IT WOULD HAVE BEEN TO LOSE SUCH A...FASCINATING SPECIMEN. THE PROJECT NEEDS YOU, AGENT OOO--
--AND SO DO I.
TRYING TO USE FORCE AGAINST YOU ONLY PROVES THAT EVEN A GENIUS LIKE ME CAN MAKE MISTAKES. WHY USE SUCH BARBARIC METHODS--
--WHEN THERE ARE FAR MORE DELIGHTFUL WAYS TO PERSUADE YOU?
B-BUT YOU'RE AN OPOSSUM!
INDEED I AM. BRILLIANT, YES-- BUT AT HEART, AN ANIMAL.

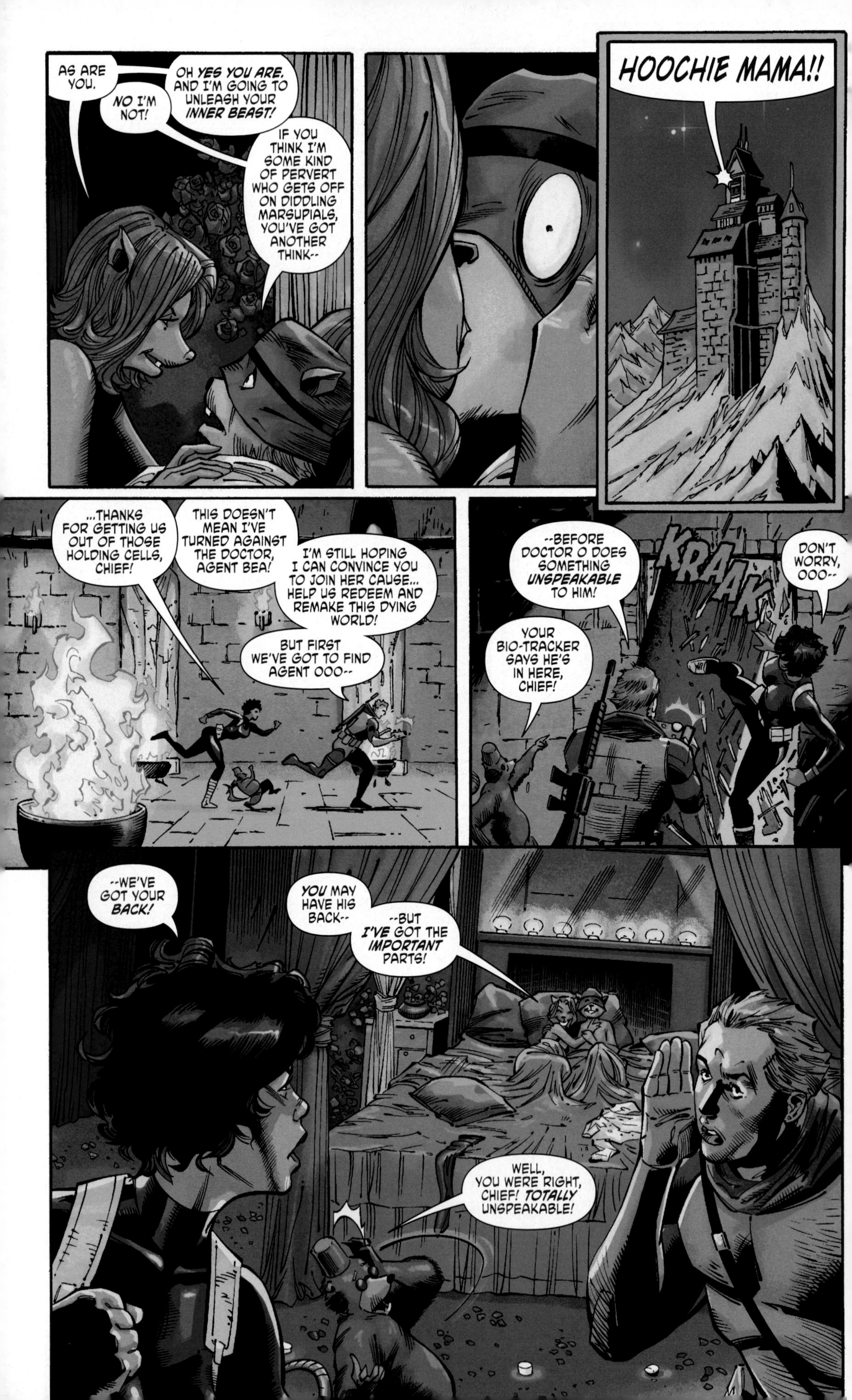

AS ARE YOU.
OH YES YOU ARE. AND I'M GOING TO UNLEASH YOUR INNER BEAST!
NO I'M NOT!
IF YOU THINK I'M SOME KIND OF PERVERT WHO GETS OFF ON DIDDLING MARSUPIALS, YOU'VE GOT ANOTHER THINK--
HOOCHIE MAMA!!
...THANKS FOR GETTING US OUT OF THOSE HOLDING CELLS, CHIEF!
THIS DOESN'T MEAN I'VE TURNED AGAINST THE DOCTOR, AGENT BEA!
I'M STILL HOPING I CAN CONVINCE YOU TO JOIN HER CAUSE... HELP US REDEEM AND REMAKE THIS DYING WORLD!
BUT FIRST WE'VE GOT TO FIND AGENT OOO--
KRAAK
DON'T WORRY, OOO--
--BEFORE DOCTOR O DOES SOMETHING UNSPEAKABLE TO HIM!
YOUR BIO-TRACKER SAYS HE'S IN HERE, CHIEF!
--WE'VE GOT YOUR BACK!
YOU MAY HAVE HIS BACK--
--BUT I'VE GOT THE IMPORTANT PARTS!
WELL, YOU WERE RIGHT, CHIEF! TOTALLY UNSPEAKABLE!

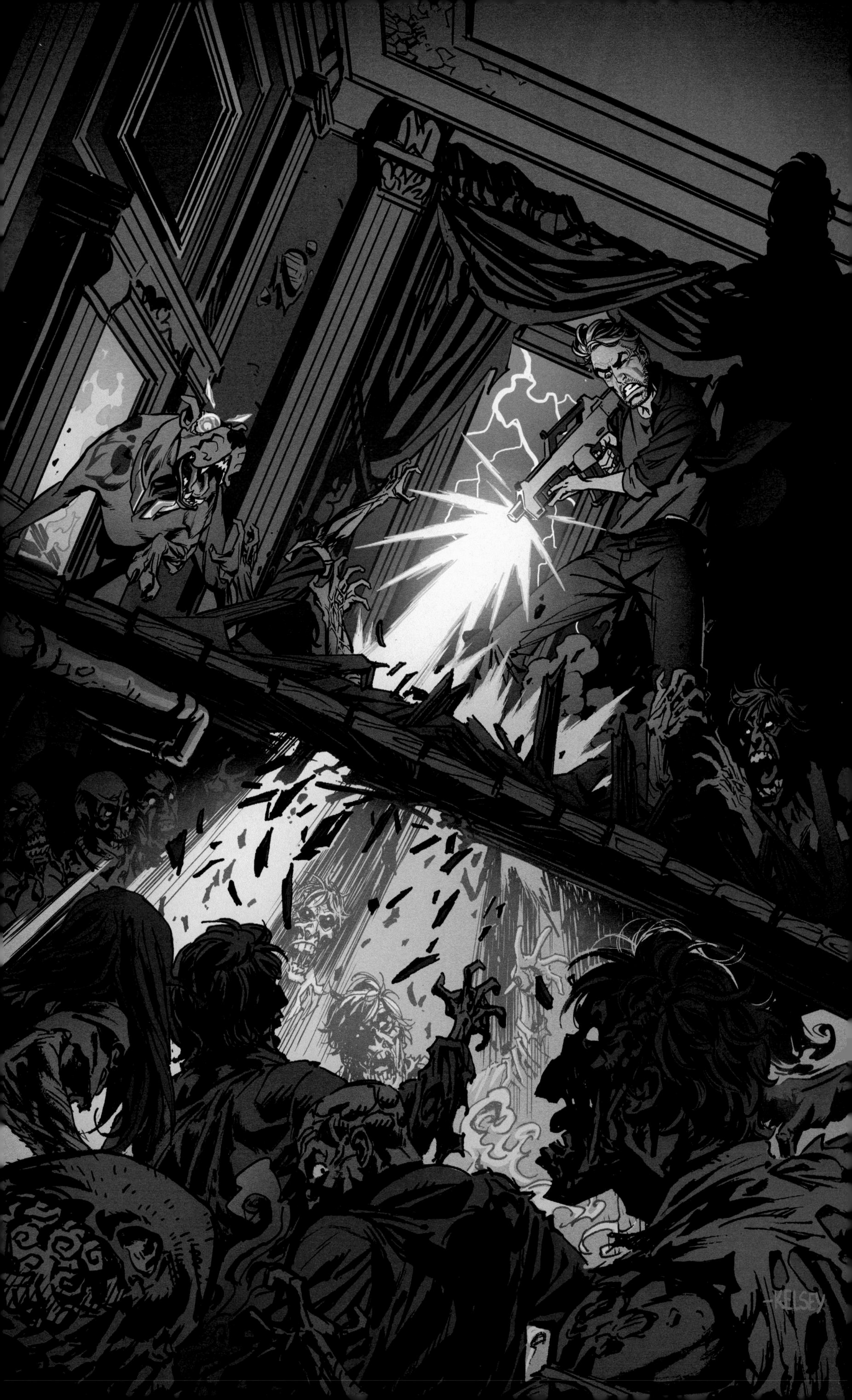
-KELSEY

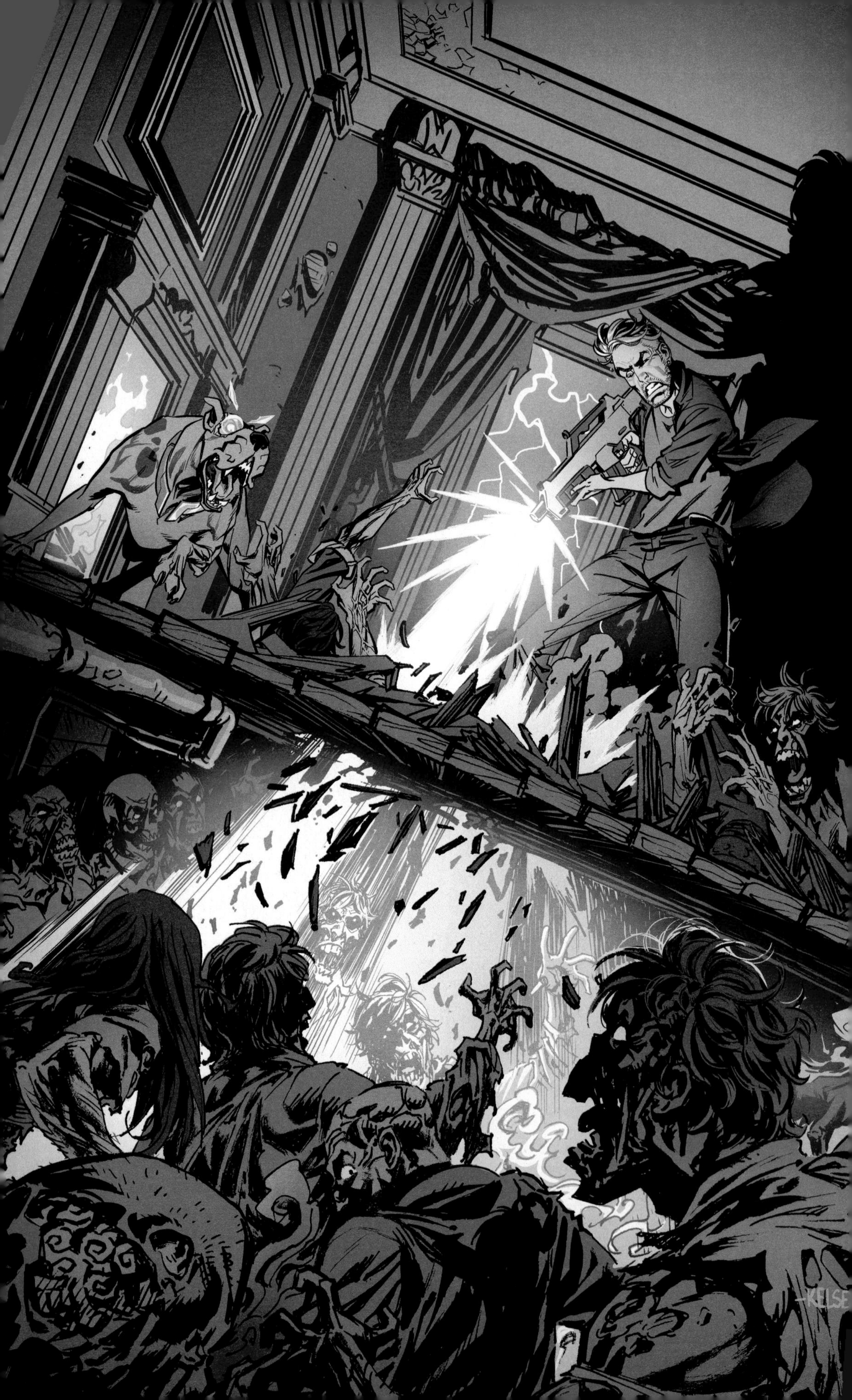
KELSE

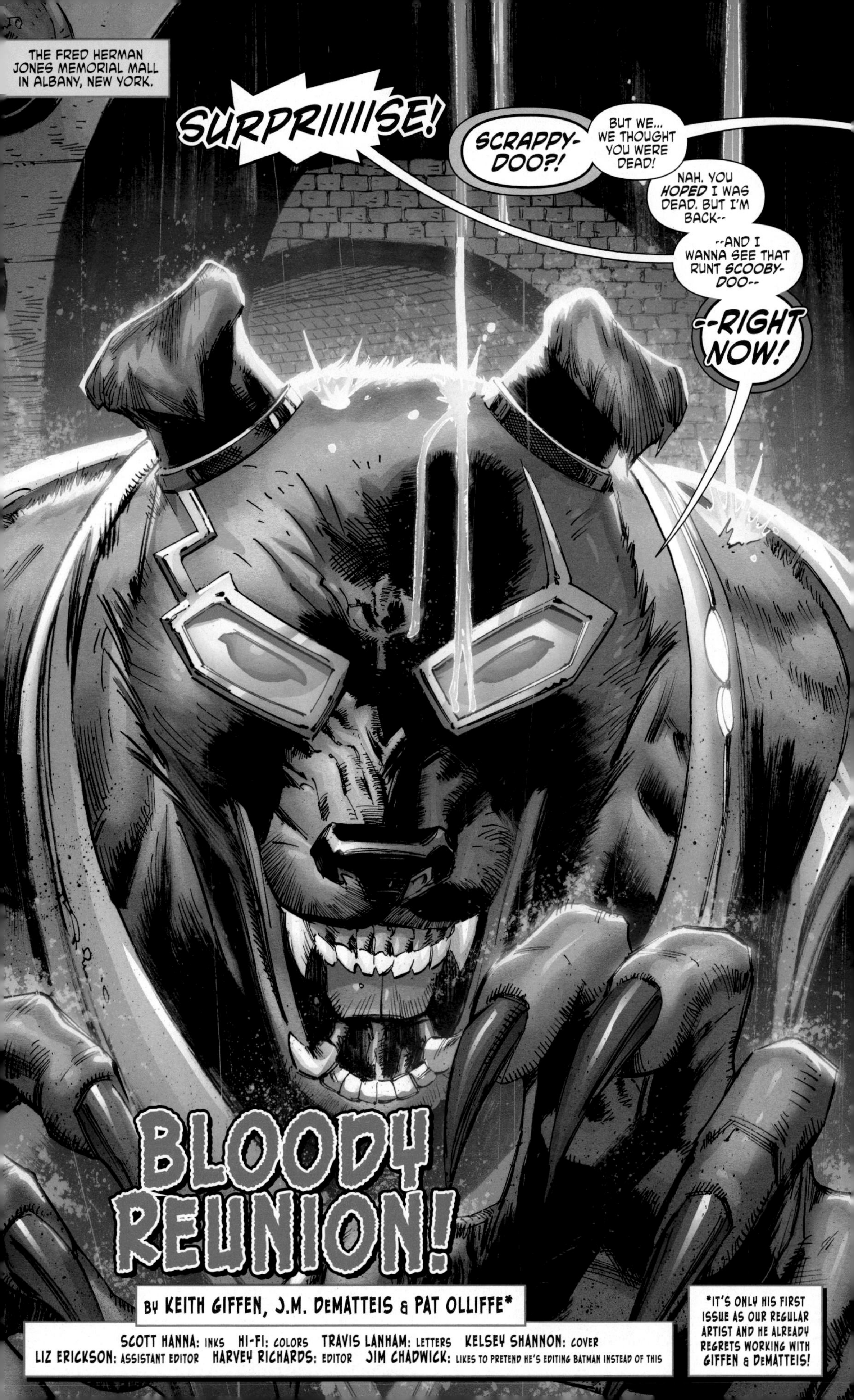
THE FRED HERMAN JONES MEMORIAL MALL IN ALBANY, NEW YORK.
SURPRIIIIISE!
SCRAPPY-DOO?!
BUT WE... WE THOUGHT YOU WERE DEAD!
NAH. YOU HOPED I WAS DEAD. BUT I'M BACK--
--AND I WANNA SEE THAT RUNT SCOOBY-DOO--
--RIGHT NOW!
BLOODY REUNION!
BY KEITH GIFFEN, J.M. DEMATTEIS & PAT OLLIFFE*
SCOTT HANNA: INKS HI-FI: COLORS TRAVIS LANHAM: LETTERS KELSEY SHANNON: COVER
LIZ ERICKSON: ASSISTANT EDITOR HARVEY RICHARDS: EDITOR JIM CHADWICK: LIKES TO PRETEND HE'S EDITING BATMAN INSTEAD OF THIS
*IT'S ONLY HIS FIRST ISSUE AS OUR REGULAR ARTIST AND HE ALREADY REGRETS WORKING WITH GIFFEN & DEMATTEIS!

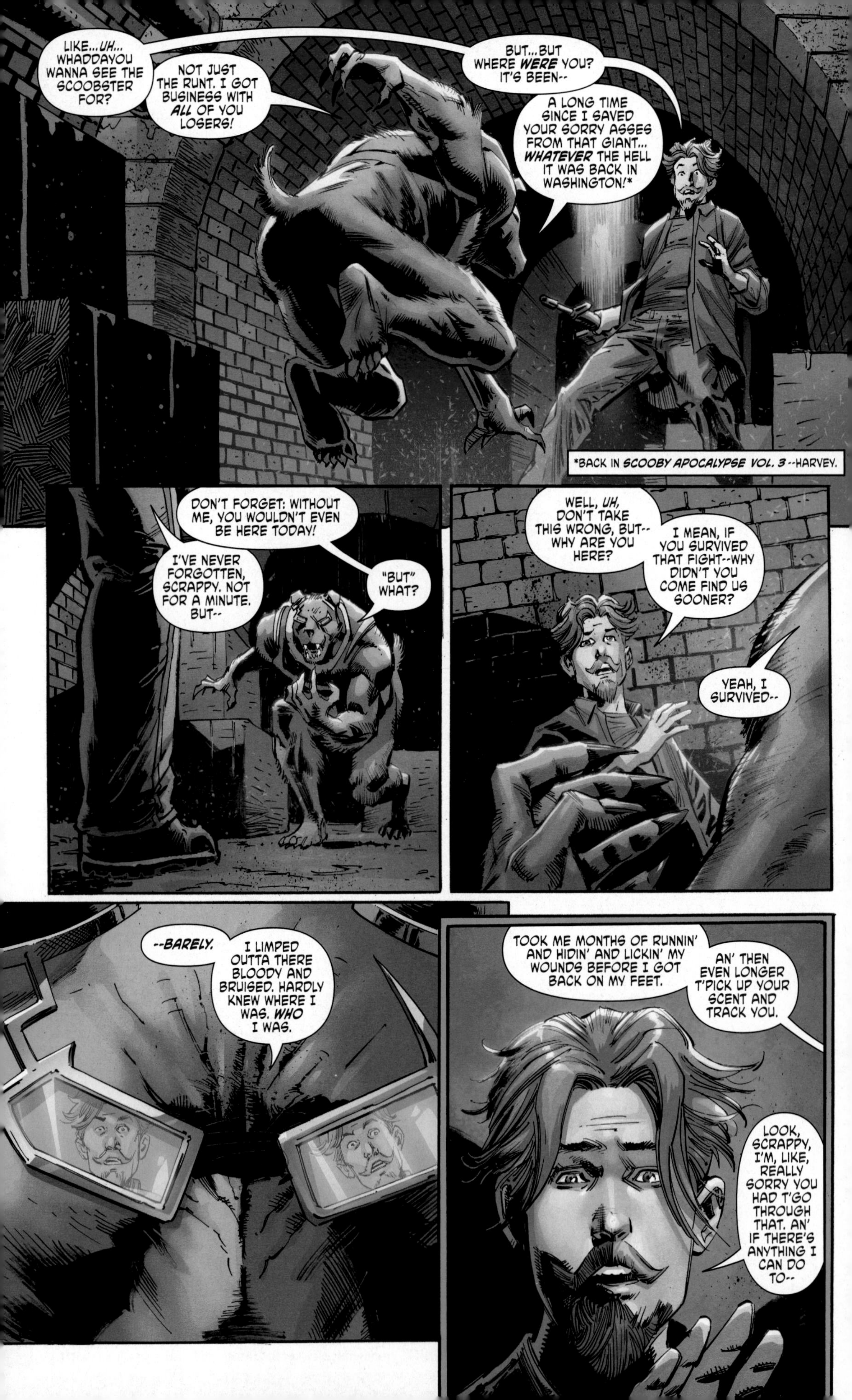
LIKE...UH... WHADDAYOU WANNA SEE THE SCOOBSTER FOR?
NOT JUST THE RUNT. I GOT BUSINESS WITH ALL OF YOU LOSERS!
BUT...BUT WHERE WERE YOU? IT'S BEEN--
A LONG TIME SINCE I SAVED YOUR SORRY ASSES FROM THAT GIANT... WHATEVER THE HELL IT WAS BACK IN WASHINGTON!*
*BACK IN SCOOBY APOCALYPSE VOL. 3 --HARVEY.
DON'T FORGET: WITHOUT ME, YOU WOULDN'T EVEN BE HERE TODAY!
I'VE NEVER FORGOTTEN, SCRAPPY. NOT FOR A MINUTE. BUT--
"BUT" WHAT?
WELL, UH, DON'T TAKE THIS WRONG, BUT-- WHY ARE YOU HERE?
I MEAN, IF YOU SURVIVED THAT FIGHT--WHY DIDN'T YOU COME FIND US SOONER?
YEAH, I SURVIVED--
--BARELY.
I LIMPED OUTTA THERE BLOODY AND BRUISED. HARDLY KNEW WHERE I WAS. WHO I WAS.
TOOK ME MONTHS OF RUNNIN' AND HIDIN' AND LICKIN' MY WOUNDS BEFORE I GOT BACK ON MY FEET.
AN' THEN EVEN LONGER T'PICK UP YOUR SCENT AND TRACK YOU.
LOOK, SCRAPPY, I'M, LIKE, REALLY SORRY YOU HAD T'GO THROUGH THAT. AN' IF THERE'S ANYTHING I CAN DO TO--

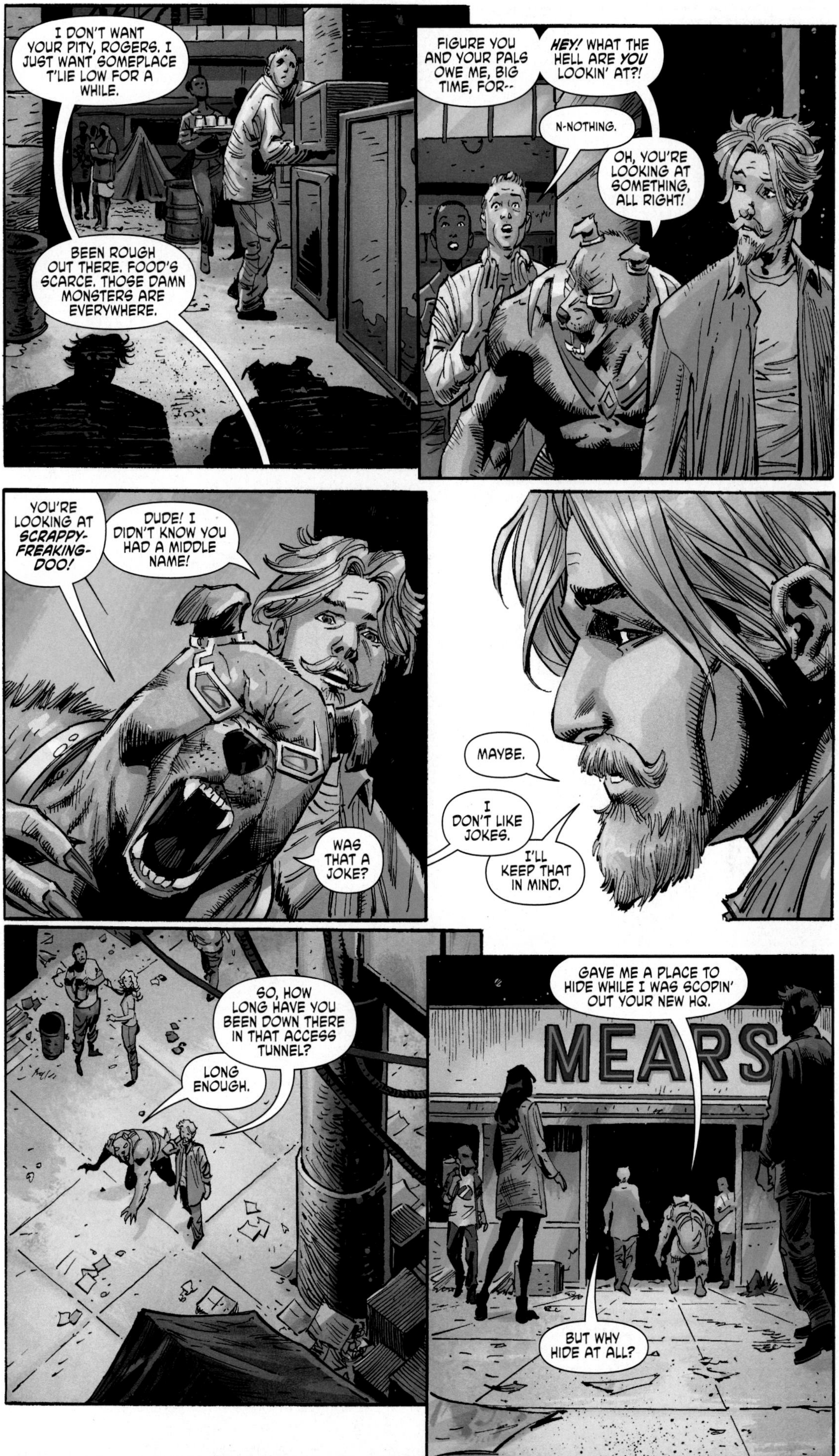
I DON'T WANT YOUR PITY, ROGERS. I JUST WANT SOMEPLACE T'LIE LOW FOR A WHILE.
BEEN ROUGH OUT THERE. FOOD'S SCARCE. THOSE DAMN MONSTERS ARE EVERYWHERE.
FIGURE YOU AND YOUR PALS OWE ME, BIG TIME, FOR--
HEY! WHAT THE HELL ARE YOU LOOKIN' AT?!
N-NOTHING.
OH, YOU'RE LOOKING AT SOMETHING, ALL RIGHT!
YOU'RE LOOKING AT SCRAPPY-FREAKING-DOO!
DUDE! I DIDN'T KNOW YOU HAD A MIDDLE NAME!
MAYBE.
WAS THAT A JOKE?
I DON'T LIKE JOKES.
I'LL KEEP THAT IN MIND.
SO, HOW LONG HAVE YOU BEEN DOWN THERE IN THAT ACCESS TUNNEL?
LONG ENOUGH.
GAVE ME A PLACE TO HIDE WHILE I WAS SCOPIN' OUT YOUR NEW HQ.
MEARS
BUT WHY HIDE AT ALL?

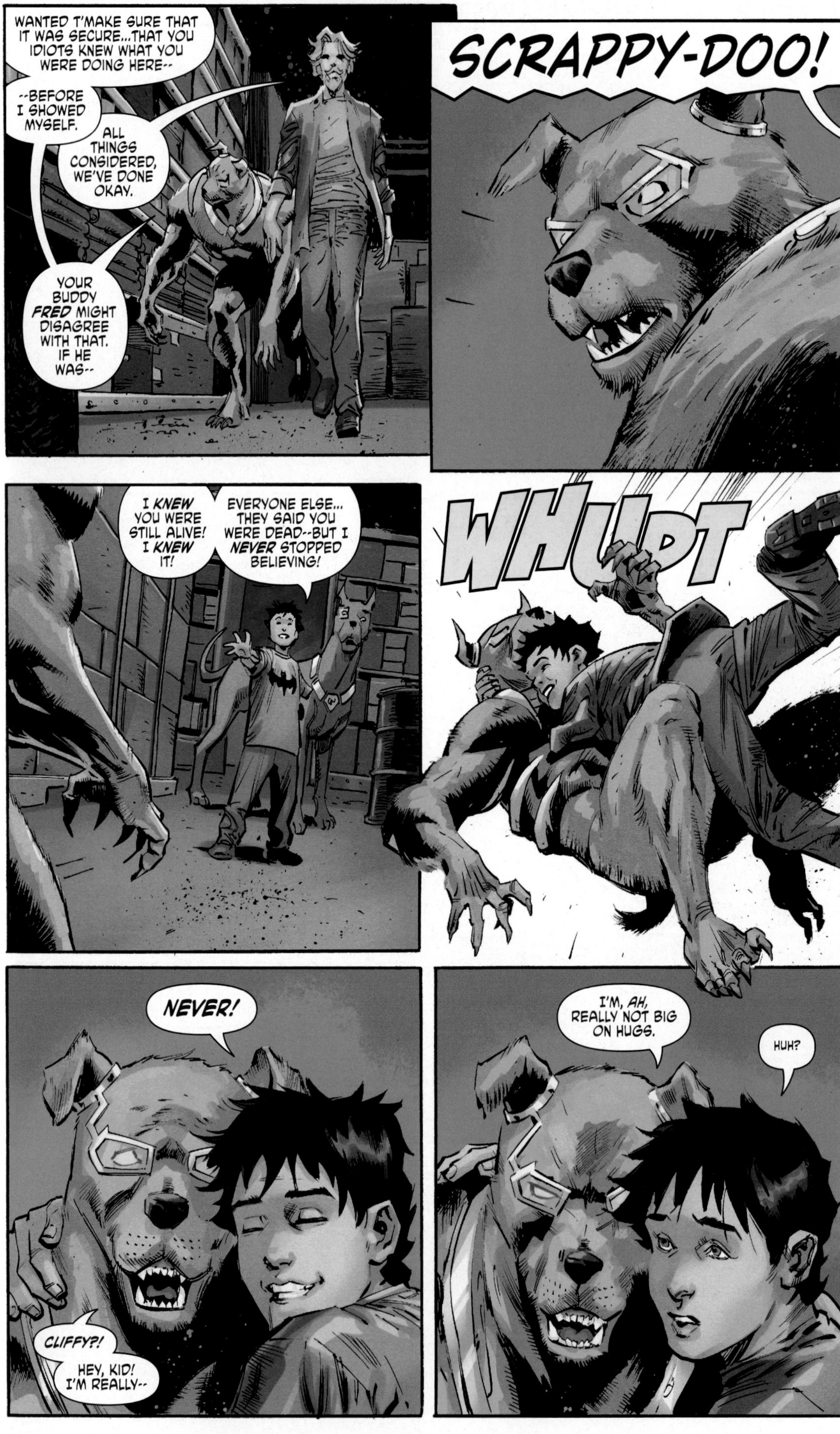
WANTED T'MAKE SURE THAT IT WAS SECURE...THAT YOU IDIOTS KNEW WHAT YOU WERE DOING HERE--
--BEFORE I SHOWED MYSELF.
ALL THINGS CONSIDERED, WE'VE DONE OKAY.
YOUR BUDDY FRED MIGHT DISAGREE WITH THAT. IF HE WAS--
SCRAPPY-DOO!
I KNEW YOU WERE STILL ALIVE! I KNEW IT!
EVERYONE ELSE... THEY SAID YOU WERE DEAD--BUT I NEVER STOPPED BELIEVING!
WHUDT
NEVER!
CLIFFY?!
HEY, KID! I'M REALLY--
I'M, AH, REALLY NOT BIG ON HUGS.
HUH?

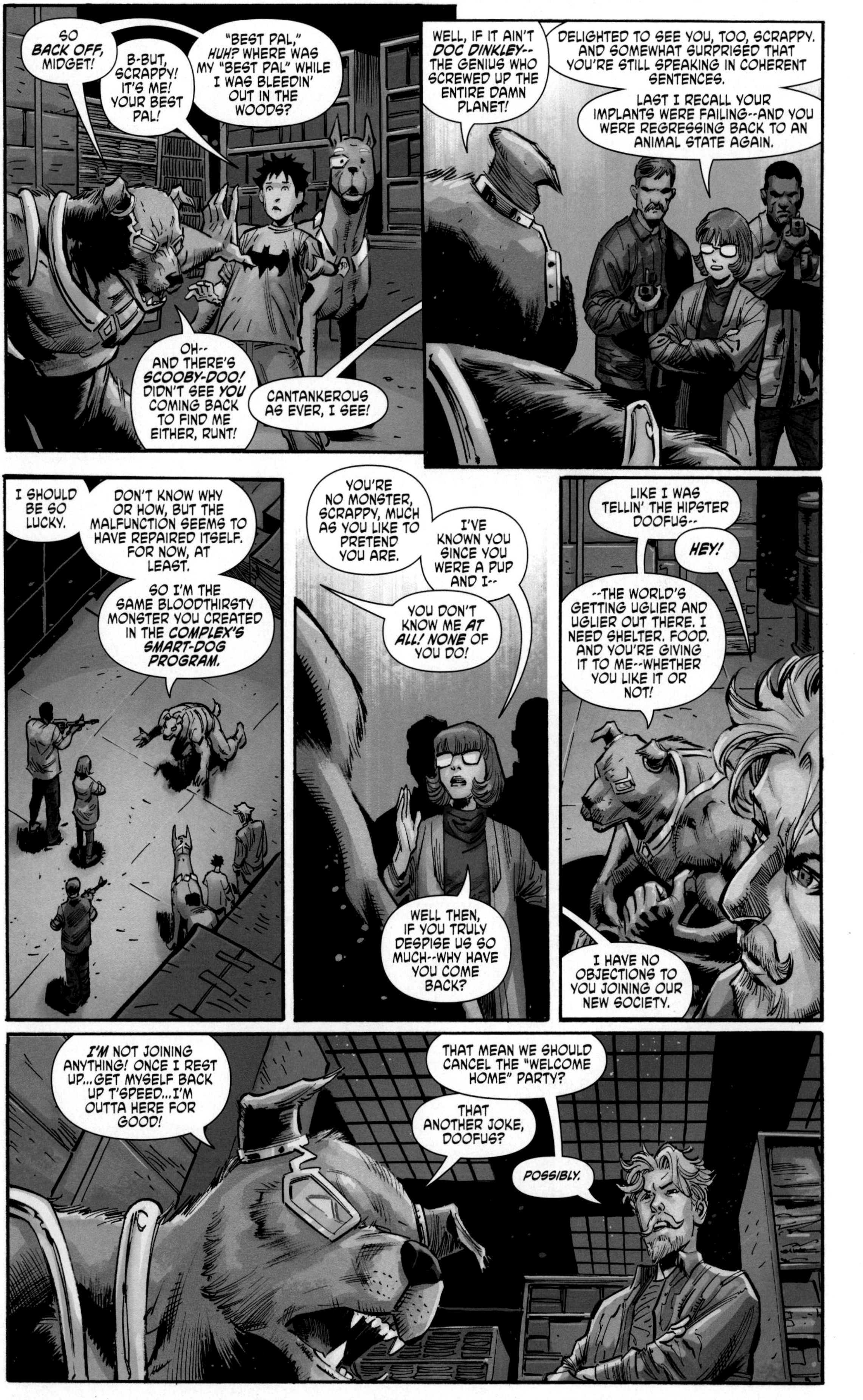
SO BACK OFF, MIDGET!
B-BUT, SCRAPPY! IT'S ME! YOUR BEST PAL!
"BEST PAL," HUH? WHERE WAS MY "BEST PAL" WHILE I WAS BLEEDIN' OUT IN THE WOODS?
OH-- AND THERE'S SCOOBY-DOO! DIDN'T SEE YOU COMING BACK TO FIND ME EITHER, RUNT!
CANTANKEROUS AS EVER, I SEE!
WELL, IF IT AIN'T DOC DINKLEY-- THE GENIUS WHO SCREWED UP THE ENTIRE DAMN PLANET!
DELIGHTED TO SEE YOU, TOO, SCRAPPY. AND SOMEWHAT SURPRISED THAT YOU'RE STILL SPEAKING IN COHERENT SENTENCES.
LAST I RECALL YOUR IMPLANTS WERE FAILING--AND YOU WERE REGRESSING BACK TO AN ANIMAL STATE AGAIN.
I SHOULD BE SO LUCKY.
DON'T KNOW WHY OR HOW, BUT THE MALFUNCTION SEEMS TO HAVE REPAIRED ITSELF. FOR NOW, AT LEAST.
SO I'M THE SAME BLOODTHIRSTY MONSTER YOU CREATED IN THE COMPLEX'S SMART-DOG PROGRAM.
YOU'RE NO MONSTER, SCRAPPY, MUCH AS YOU LIKE TO PRETEND YOU ARE.
I'VE KNOWN YOU SINCE YOU WERE A PUP AND I--
YOU DON'T KNOW ME AT ALL! NONE OF YOU DO!
WELL THEN, IF YOU TRULY DESPISE US SO MUCH--WHY HAVE YOU COME BACK?
LIKE I WAS TELLIN' THE HIPSTER DOOFUS--
HEY!
--THE WORLD'S GETTING UGLIER AND UGLIER OUT THERE. I NEED SHELTER. FOOD. AND YOU'RE GIVING IT TO ME--WHETHER YOU LIKE IT OR NOT!
I HAVE NO OBJECTIONS TO YOU JOINING OUR NEW SOCIETY.
I'M NOT JOINING ANYTHING! ONCE I REST UP...GET MYSELF BACK UP T'SPEED...I'M OUTTA HERE FOR GOOD!
THAT MEAN WE SHOULD CANCEL THE "WELCOME HOME" PARTY?
THAT ANOTHER JOKE, DOOFUS?
POSSIBLY.

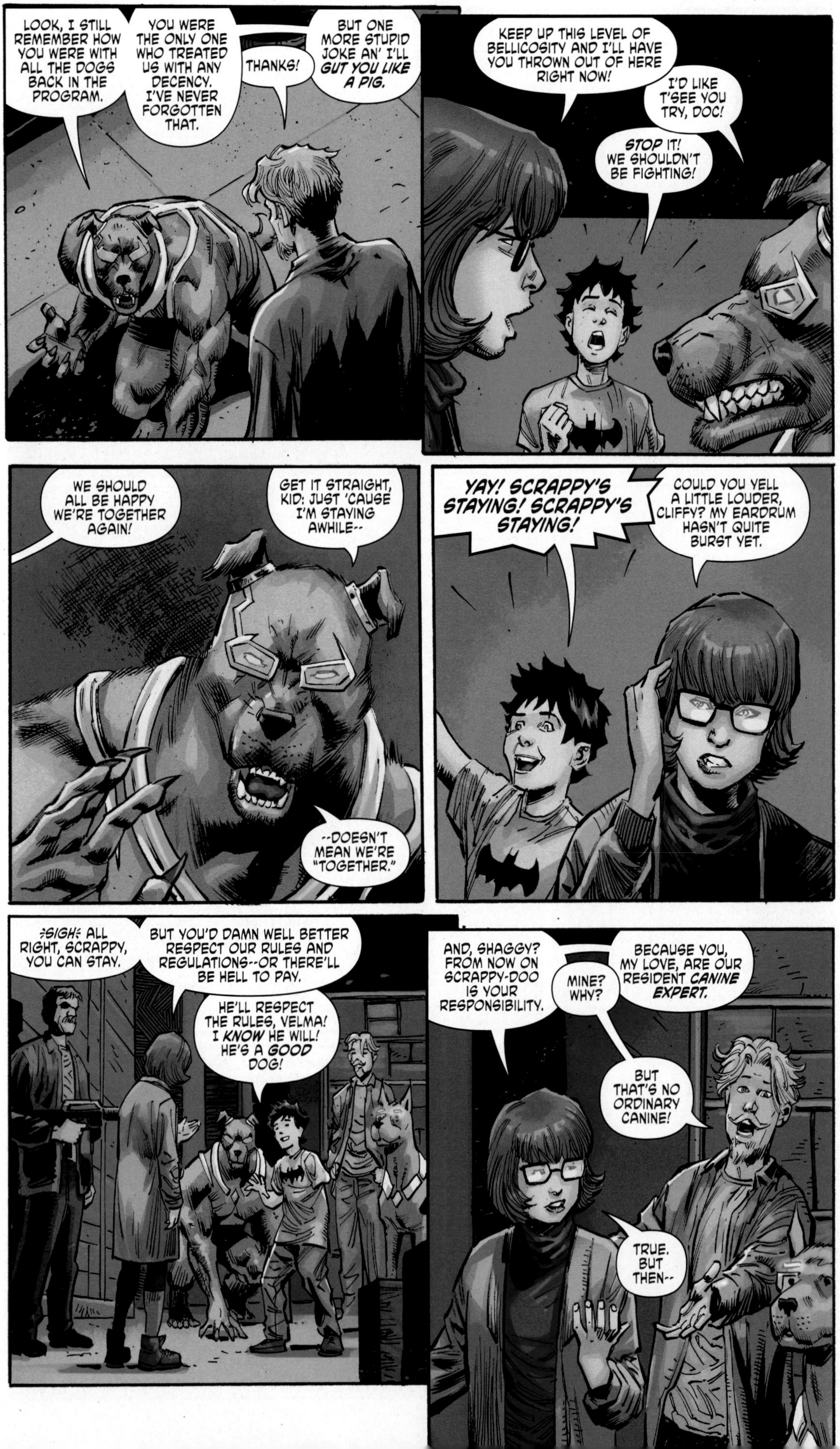

LOOK, I STILL REMEMBER HOW YOU WERE WITH ALL THE DOGS BACK IN THE PROGRAM.
YOU WERE THE ONLY ONE WHO TREATED US WITH ANY DECENCY. I'VE NEVER FORGOTTEN THAT.
THANKS!
BUT ONE MORE STUPID JOKE AN' I'LL *GUT YOU LIKE A PIG.*
KEEP UP THIS LEVEL OF BELLICOSITY AND I'LL HAVE YOU THROWN OUT OF HERE RIGHT NOW!
I'D LIKE T'SEE YOU TRY, DOC!
STOP IT! WE SHOULDN'T BE FIGHTING!
WE SHOULD ALL BE HAPPY WE'RE TOGETHER AGAIN!
GET IT STRAIGHT, KID: JUST 'CAUSE I'M STAYING AWHILE--
--DOESN'T MEAN WE'RE "TOGETHER."
YAY! SCRAPPY'S STAYING! SCRAPPY'S STAYING!
COULD YOU YELL A LITTLE LOUDER, CLIFFY? MY EARDRUM HASN'T QUITE BURST YET.
SIGH ALL RIGHT, SCRAPPY, YOU CAN STAY.
BUT YOU'D DAMN WELL BETTER RESPECT OUR RULES AND REGULATIONS--OR THERE'LL BE HELL TO PAY.
HE'LL RESPECT THE RULES, VELMA! I *KNOW* HE WILL! HE'S A *GOOD* DOG!
AND, SHAGGY? FROM NOW ON SCRAPPY-DOO IS YOUR RESPONSIBILITY.
MINE? WHY?
BECAUSE YOU, MY LOVE, ARE OUR RESIDENT *CANINE EXPERT.*
BUT THAT'S NO ORDINARY CANINE!
TRUE. BUT THEN--

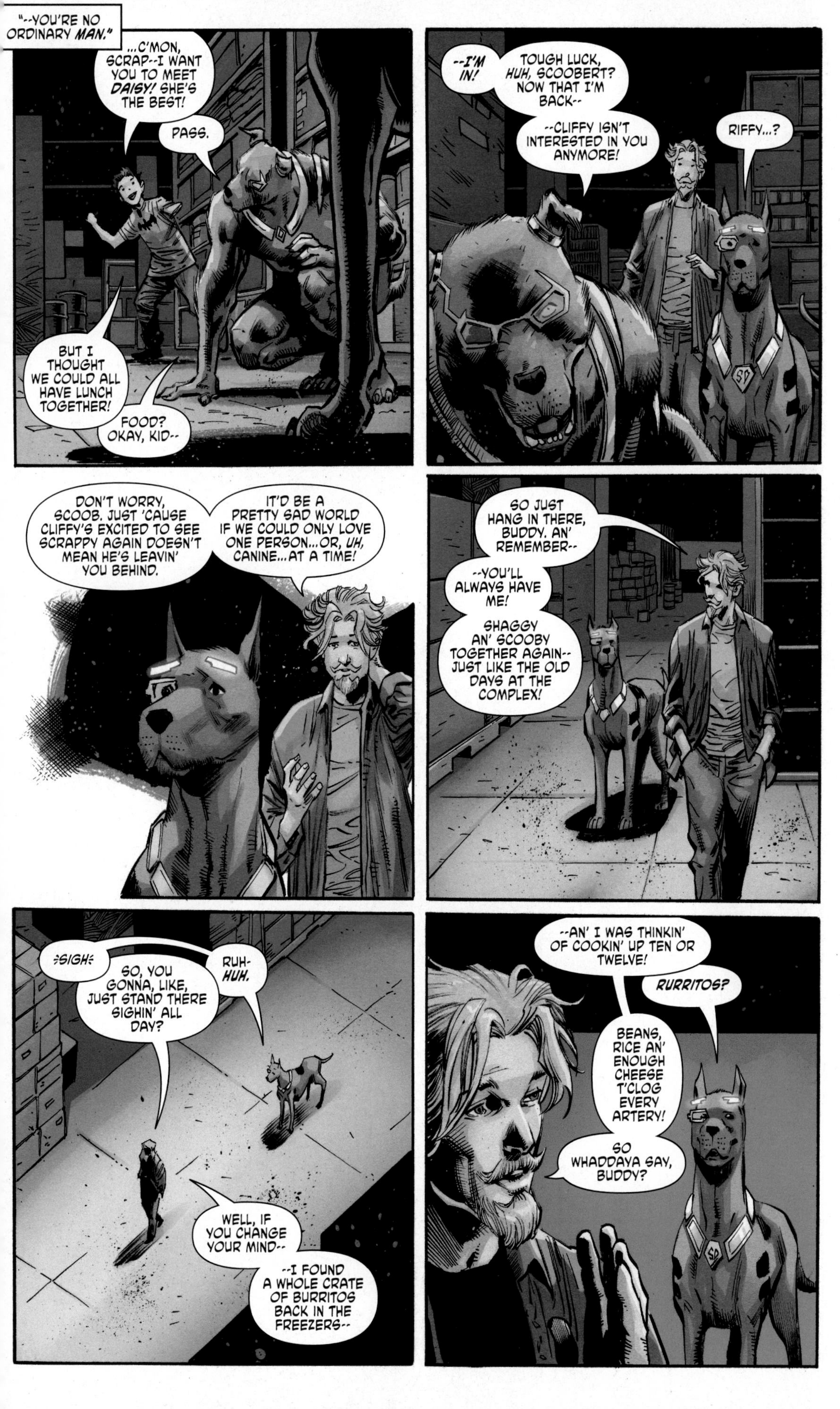
"--YOU'RE NO ORDINARY MAN."
...C'MON, SCRAP--I WANT YOU TO MEET DAISY! SHE'S THE BEST!
PASS.
BUT I THOUGHT WE COULD ALL HAVE LUNCH TOGETHER!
FOOD? OKAY, KID--
--I'M IN!
TOUGH LUCK, HUH, SCOOBERT? NOW THAT I'M BACK--
--CLIFFY ISN'T INTERESTED IN YOU ANYMORE!
RIFFY...?
DON'T WORRY, SCOOB. JUST 'CAUSE CLIFFY'S EXCITED TO SEE SCRAPPY AGAIN DOESN'T MEAN HE'S LEAVIN' YOU BEHIND.
IT'D BE A PRETTY SAD WORLD IF WE COULD ONLY LOVE ONE PERSON...OR, UH, CANINE...AT A TIME!
SO JUST HANG IN THERE, BUDDY. AN' REMEMBER--
--YOU'LL ALWAYS HAVE ME!
SHAGGY AN' SCOOBY TOGETHER AGAIN--JUST LIKE THE OLD DAYS AT THE COMPLEX!
SIGH
SO, YOU GONNA, LIKE, JUST STAND THERE SIGHIN' ALL DAY?
RUH-HUH.
WELL, IF YOU CHANGE YOUR MIND--
--I FOUND A WHOLE CRATE OF BURRITOS BACK IN THE FREEZERS--
--AN' I WAS THINKIN' OF COOKIN' UP TEN OR TWELVE!
RURRITOS?
BEANS, RICE AN' ENOUGH CHEESE T'CLOG EVERY ARTERY!
SO WHADDAYA SAY, BUDDY?

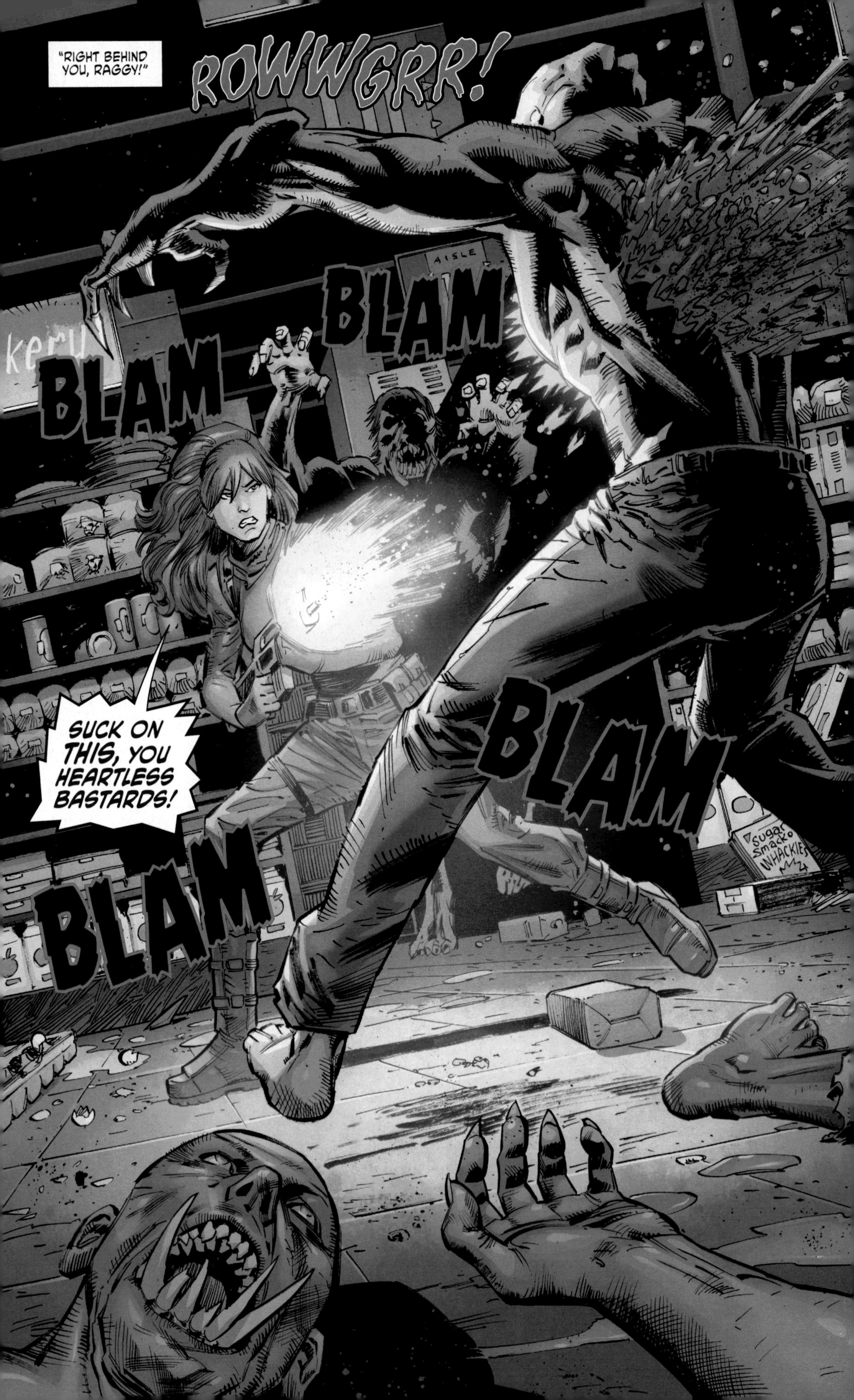
"RIGHT BEHIND YOU, RAGGY!"
ROWWGRR!
BLAM
BLAM
SUCK ON THIS, YOU HEARTLESS BASTARDS!
BLAM
BLAM
AISLE
Sugar Smacko WHACKIES

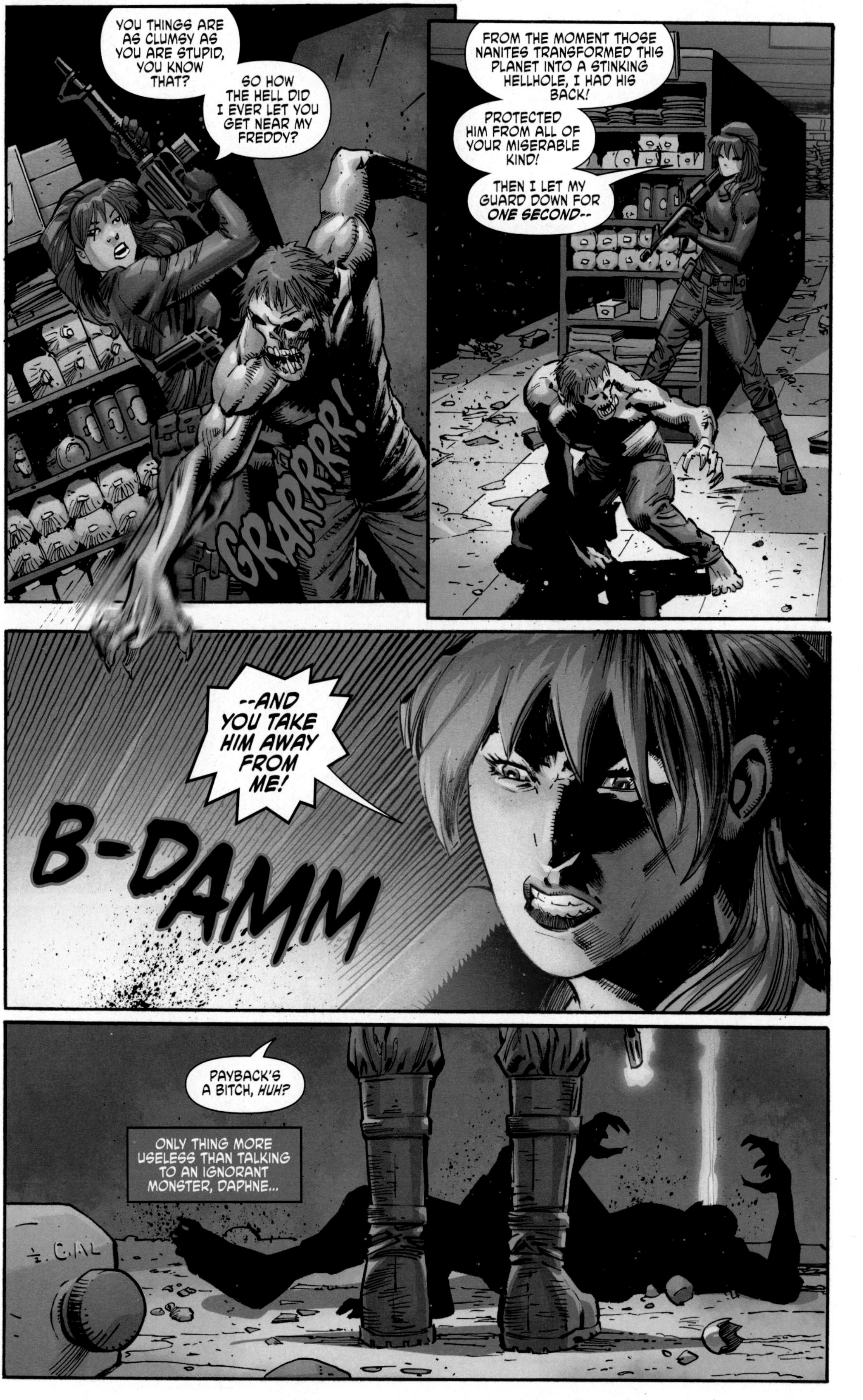
YOU THINGS ARE AS CLUMSY AS YOU ARE STUPID, YOU KNOW THAT?
SO HOW THE HELL DID I EVER LET YOU GET NEAR MY FREDDY?
GRARRRR!
FROM THE MOMENT THOSE NANITES TRANSFORMED THIS PLANET INTO A STINKING HELLHOLE, I HAD HIS BACK!
PROTECTED HIM FROM ALL OF YOUR MISERABLE KIND!
THEN I LET MY GUARD DOWN FOR *ONE SECOND*--
--AND YOU TAKE HIM AWAY FROM ME!
B-DAMM
PAYBACK'S A BITCH, *HUH?*
ONLY THING MORE USELESS THAN TALKING TO AN IGNORANT MONSTER, DAPHNE...
½ GAL

...IS TALKING TO A *DEAD* IGNORANT MONSTER.

BUT I GUESS ANYTHING'S BETTER THAN BEING STUCK IN MY OWN HEAD...

...TORTURED BY GUILT.

VELMA KEEPS TELLING ME THERE WAS NOTHING I COULD HAVE DONE.

THAT GIVEN THE SAVAGE WORLD WE'RE LIVING IN, IT'S AMAZING THAT *MORE* OF US HAVEN'T DIED.

AND SHAGGY--THE KINDHEARTED IDIOT--KEEPS SAYING THAT THE ONLY THING THAT WILL DISSOLVE MY GUILT IS SELF-FORGIVENESS.

BUT WHAT IF I DON'T *WANT* TO FORGIVE MYSELF? WHAT IF I DON'T *DESERVE* FORGIVENESS?

WELL, I COULD ALWAYS PUT THIS GUN IN MY MOUTH AND END IT ALL.

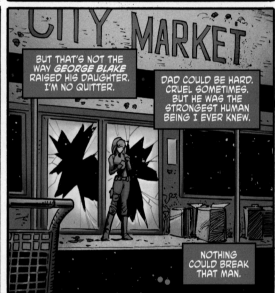

BUT THAT'S NOT THE WAY *GEORGE BLAKE* RAISED HIS DAUGHTER. I'M NO QUITTER.

DAD COULD BE HARD. CRUEL SOMETIMES. BUT HE WAS THE STRONGEST HUMAN BEING I EVER KNEW.

NOTHING COULD BREAK THAT MAN.

AND NOTHING'S GONNA BREAK *ME* EITHER.

DAD TAUGHT ME THAT AS LONG AS WE HAVE A FOCUS IN LIFE, A PURPOSE, WE WON'T JUST SURVIVE...

...WE'LL TRIUMPH.

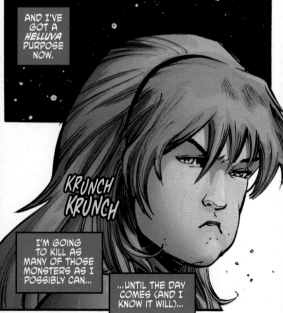

AND I'VE GOT A *HELLUVA* PURPOSE NOW.

KRUNCH KRUNCH

I'M GOING TO KILL AS MANY OF THOSE MONSTERS AS I POSSIBLY CAN...

...UNTIL THE DAY COMES (AND I KNOW IT WILL)...

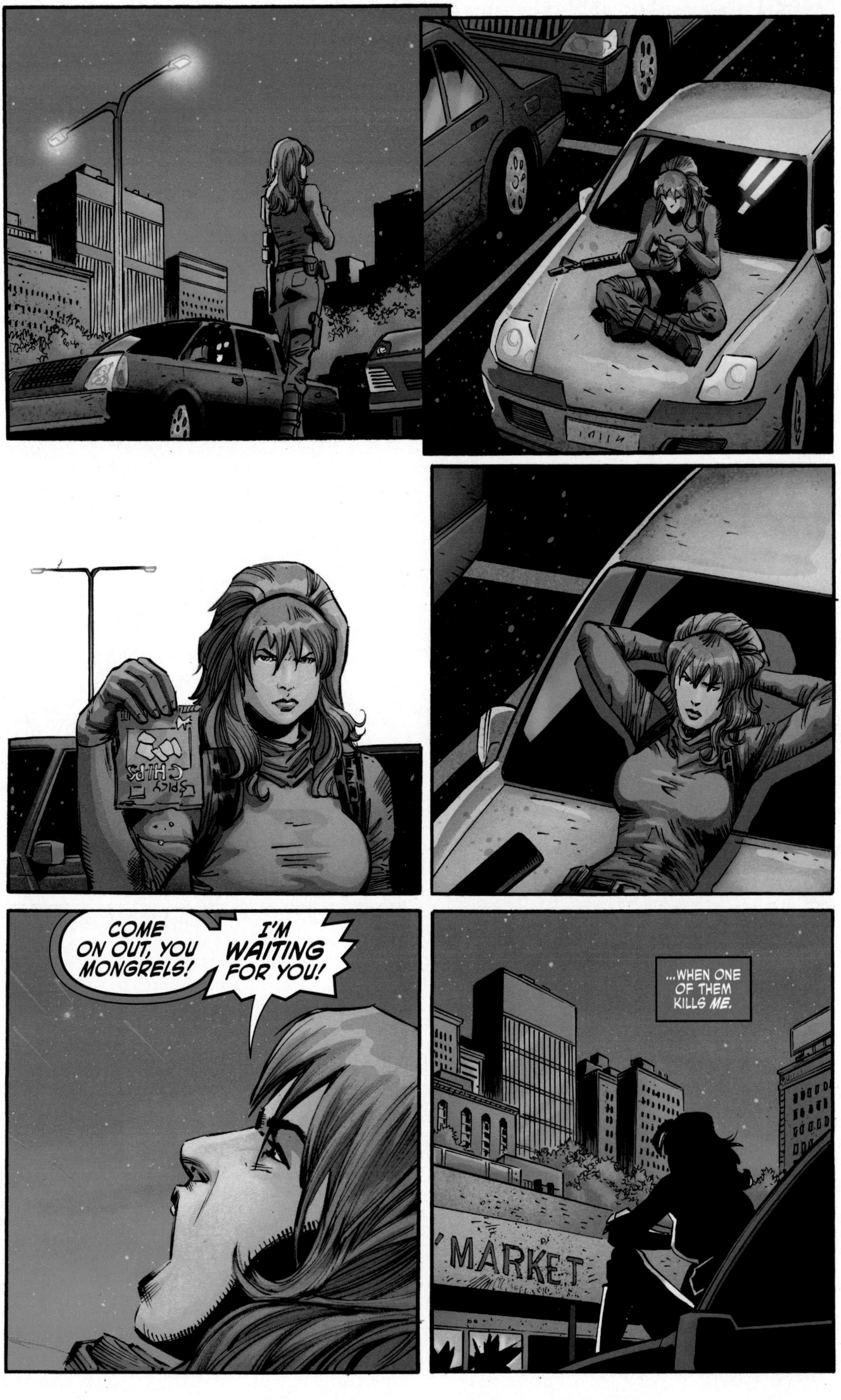
SPICY CHIPS
COME ON OUT, YOU MONGRELS!
I'M WAITING FOR YOU!
...WHEN ONE OF THEM KILLS ME.
MARKET

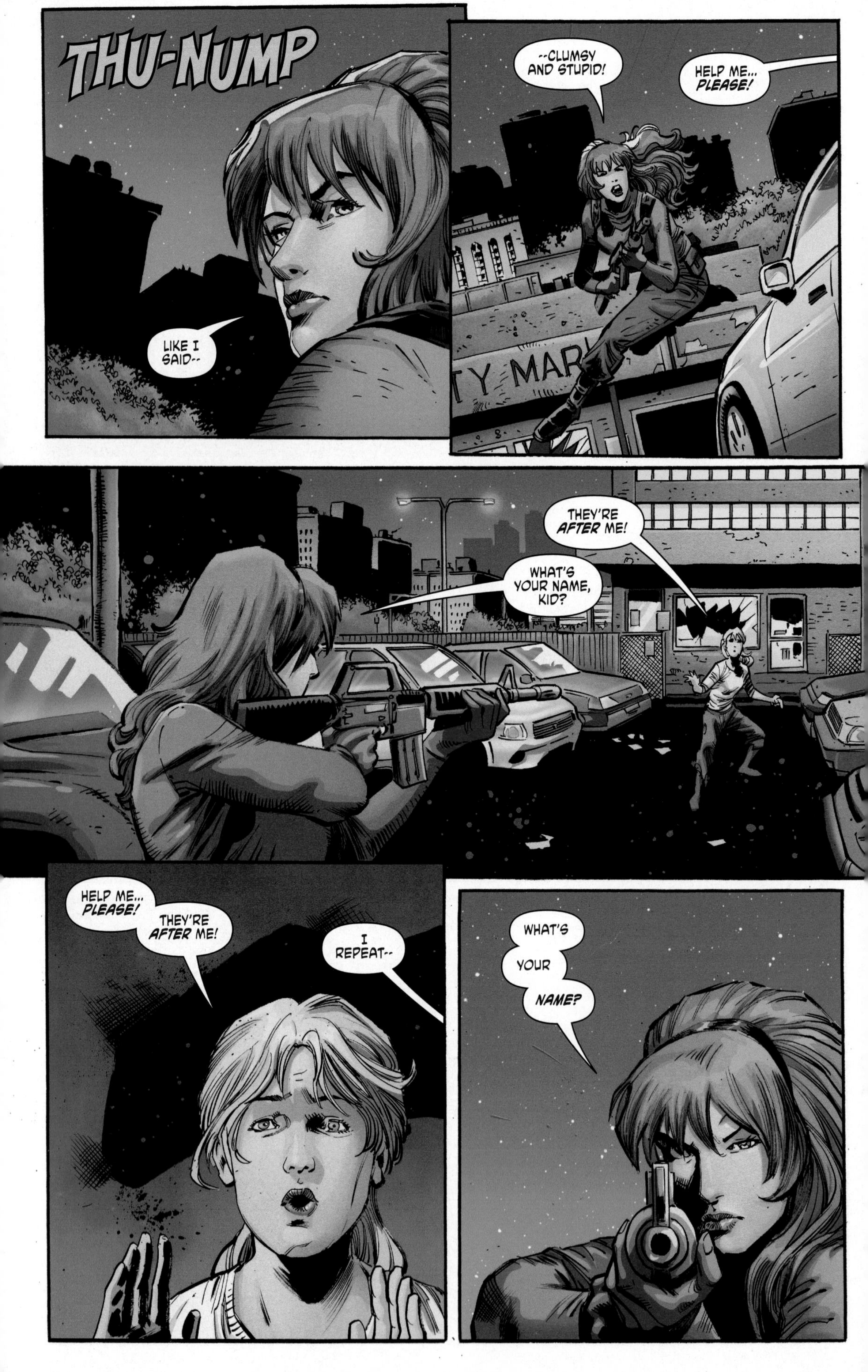
THU-NUMP
LIKE I SAID--
--CLUMSY AND STUPID!
HELP ME... PLEASE!
TY MAR
THEY'RE AFTER ME!
WHAT'S YOUR NAME, KID?
HELP ME... PLEASE!
THEY'RE AFTER ME!
I REPEAT--
WHAT'S
YOUR
NAME?

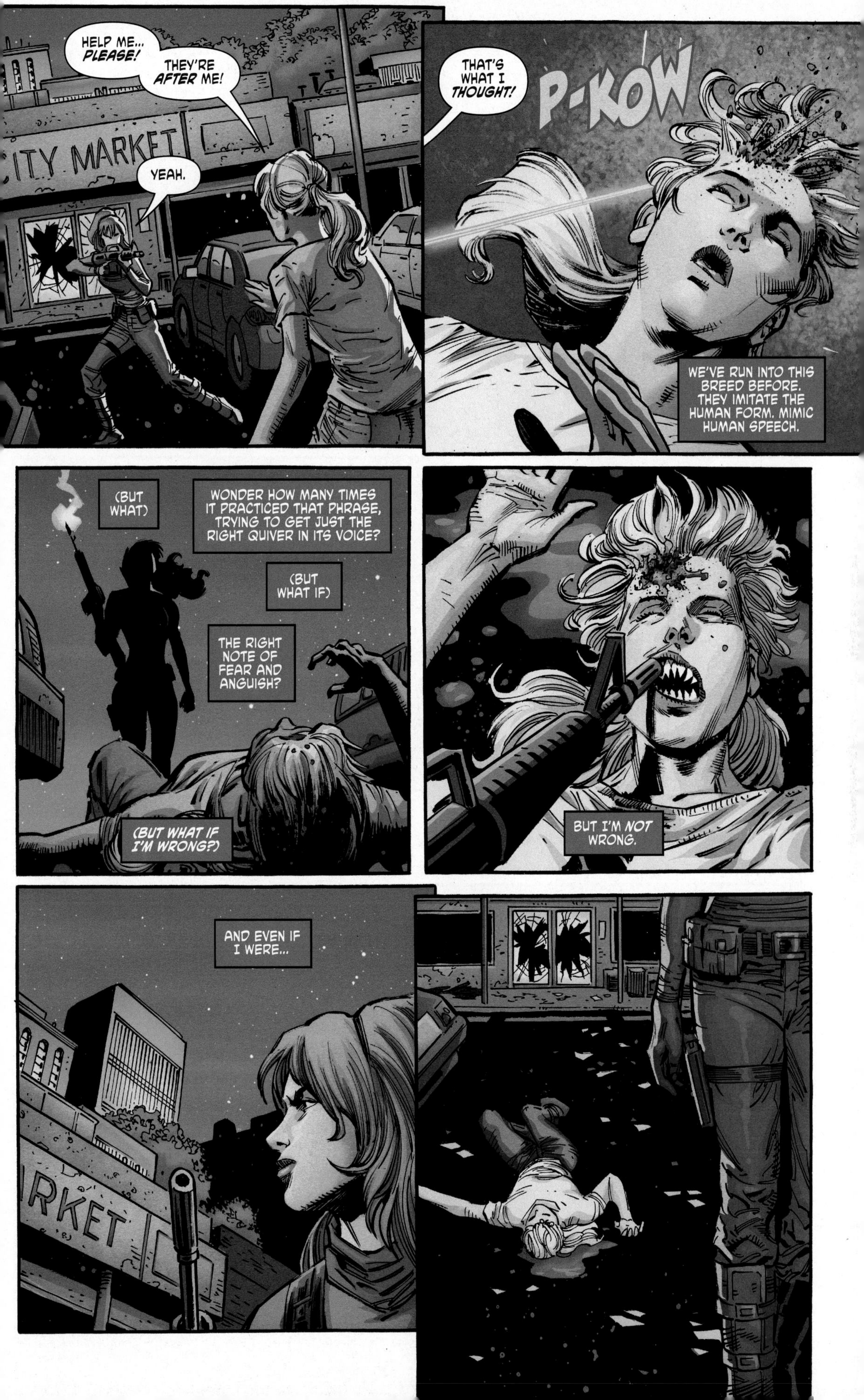
HELP ME... PLEASE!
THEY'RE AFTER ME!
YEAH.
ITY MARKET
THAT'S WHAT I THOUGHT!
P-KOW
WE'VE RUN INTO THIS BREED BEFORE. THEY IMITATE THE HUMAN FORM. MIMIC HUMAN SPEECH.
(BUT WHAT)
WONDER HOW MANY TIMES IT PRACTICED THAT PHRASE, TRYING TO GET JUST THE RIGHT QUIVER IN ITS VOICE?
(BUT WHAT IF)
THE RIGHT NOTE OF FEAR AND ANGUISH?
(BUT WHAT IF I'M WRONG?)
BUT I'M NOT WRONG.
AND EVEN IF I WERE...
RKET

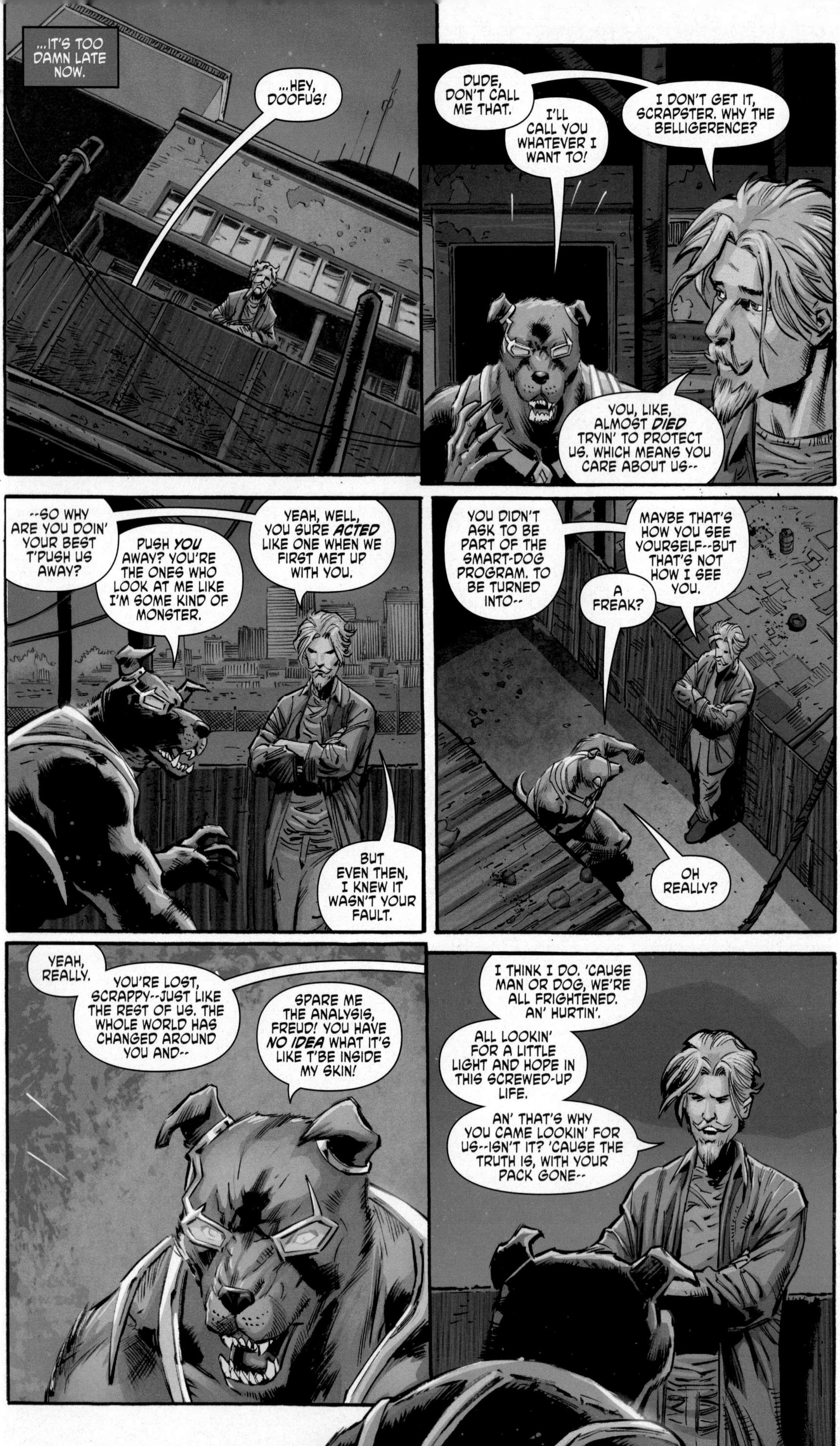
...IT'S TOO DAMN LATE NOW.
...HEY, DOOFUS!
DUDE, DON'T CALL ME THAT.
I'LL CALL YOU WHATEVER I WANT TO!
I DON'T GET IT, SCRAPSTER. WHY THE BELLIGERENCE?
YOU, LIKE, ALMOST DIED TRYIN' TO PROTECT US. WHICH MEANS YOU CARE ABOUT US--
--SO WHY ARE YOU DOIN' YOUR BEST T'PUSH US AWAY?
PUSH YOU AWAY? YOU'RE THE ONES WHO LOOK AT ME LIKE I'M SOME KIND OF MONSTER.
YEAH, WELL, YOU SURE ACTED LIKE ONE WHEN WE FIRST MET UP WITH YOU.
BUT EVEN THEN, I KNEW IT WASN'T YOUR FAULT.
YOU DIDN'T ASK TO BE PART OF THE SMART-DOG PROGRAM. TO BE TURNED INTO--
A FREAK?
MAYBE THAT'S HOW YOU SEE YOURSELF--BUT THAT'S NOT HOW I SEE YOU.
OH REALLY?
YEAH, REALLY.
YOU'RE LOST, SCRAPPY--JUST LIKE THE REST OF US. THE WHOLE WORLD HAS CHANGED AROUND YOU AND--
SPARE ME THE ANALYSIS, FREUD! YOU HAVE NO IDEA WHAT IT'S LIKE T'BE INSIDE MY SKIN!
I THINK I DO. 'CAUSE MAN OR DOG, WE'RE ALL FRIGHTENED. AN' HURTIN'.
ALL LOOKIN' FOR A LITTLE LIGHT AND HOPE IN THIS SCREWED-UP LIFE.
AN' THAT'S WHY YOU CAME LOOKIN' FOR US--ISN'T IT? 'CAUSE THE TRUTH IS, WITH YOUR PACK GONE--

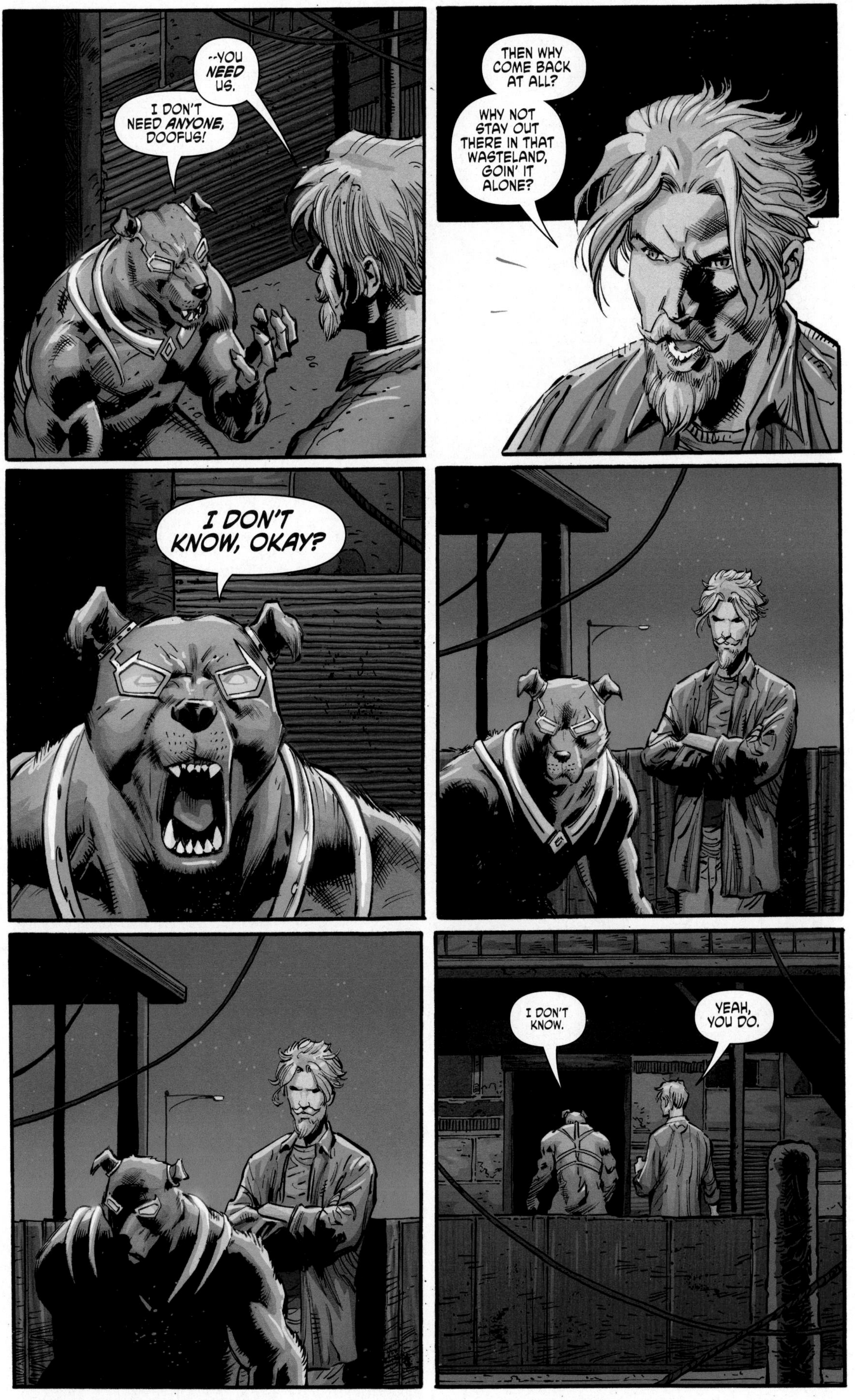
--YOU *NEED* US.
I DON'T NEED *ANYONE*, DOOFUS!
THEN WHY COME BACK AT ALL?
WHY NOT STAY OUT THERE IN THAT WASTELAND, GOIN' IT ALONE?
I DON'T KNOW, OKAY?
I DON'T KNOW.
YEAH, YOU DO.

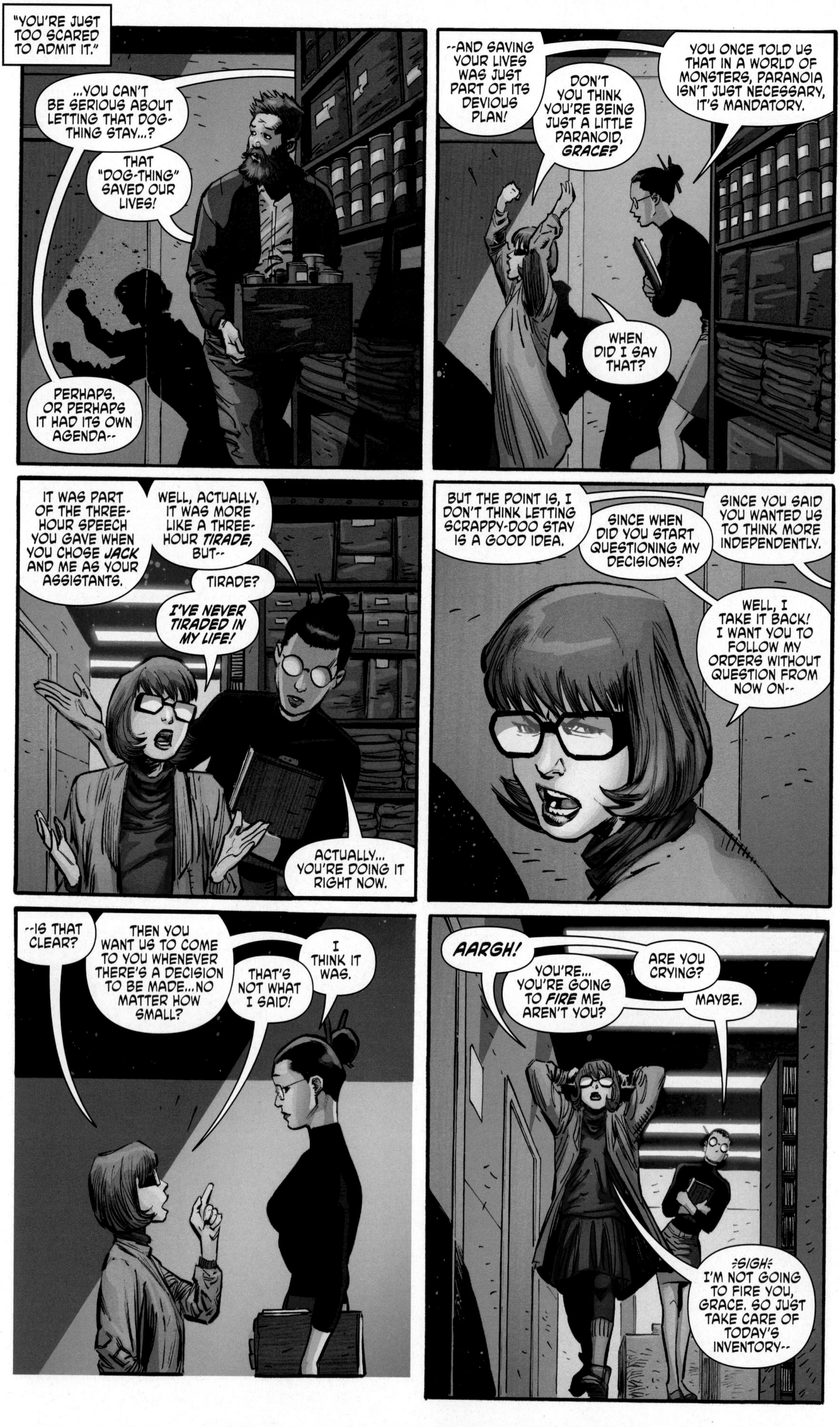
"YOU'RE JUST TOO SCARED TO ADMIT IT."
...YOU CAN'T BE SERIOUS ABOUT LETTING THAT DOG-THING STAY...?
THAT "DOG-THING" SAVED OUR LIVES!
PERHAPS. OR PERHAPS IT HAD ITS OWN AGENDA--
--AND SAVING YOUR LIVES WAS JUST PART OF ITS DEVIOUS PLAN!
DON'T YOU THINK YOU'RE BEING JUST A LITTLE PARANOID, GRACE?
YOU ONCE TOLD US THAT IN A WORLD OF MONSTERS, PARANOIA ISN'T JUST NECESSARY, IT'S MANDATORY.
WHEN DID I SAY THAT?
IT WAS PART OF THE THREE-HOUR SPEECH YOU GAVE WHEN YOU CHOSE JACK AND ME AS YOUR ASSISTANTS.
WELL, ACTUALLY, IT WAS MORE LIKE A THREE-HOUR TIRADE, BUT--
TIRADE?
I'VE NEVER TIRADED IN MY LIFE!
ACTUALLY... YOU'RE DOING IT RIGHT NOW.
BUT THE POINT IS, I DON'T THINK LETTING SCRAPPY-DOO STAY IS A GOOD IDEA.
SINCE WHEN DID YOU START QUESTIONING MY DECISIONS?
SINCE YOU SAID YOU WANTED US TO THINK MORE INDEPENDENTLY.
WELL, I TAKE IT BACK! I WANT YOU TO FOLLOW MY ORDERS WITHOUT QUESTION FROM NOW ON--
--IS THAT CLEAR?
THEN YOU WANT US TO COME TO YOU WHENEVER THERE'S A DECISION TO BE MADE...NO MATTER HOW SMALL?
THAT'S NOT WHAT I SAID!
I THINK IT WAS.
AARGH!
YOU'RE... YOU'RE GOING TO FIRE ME, AREN'T YOU?
ARE YOU CRYING?
MAYBE.
SIGH
I'M NOT GOING TO FIRE YOU, GRACE. SO JUST TAKE CARE OF TODAY'S INVENTORY--

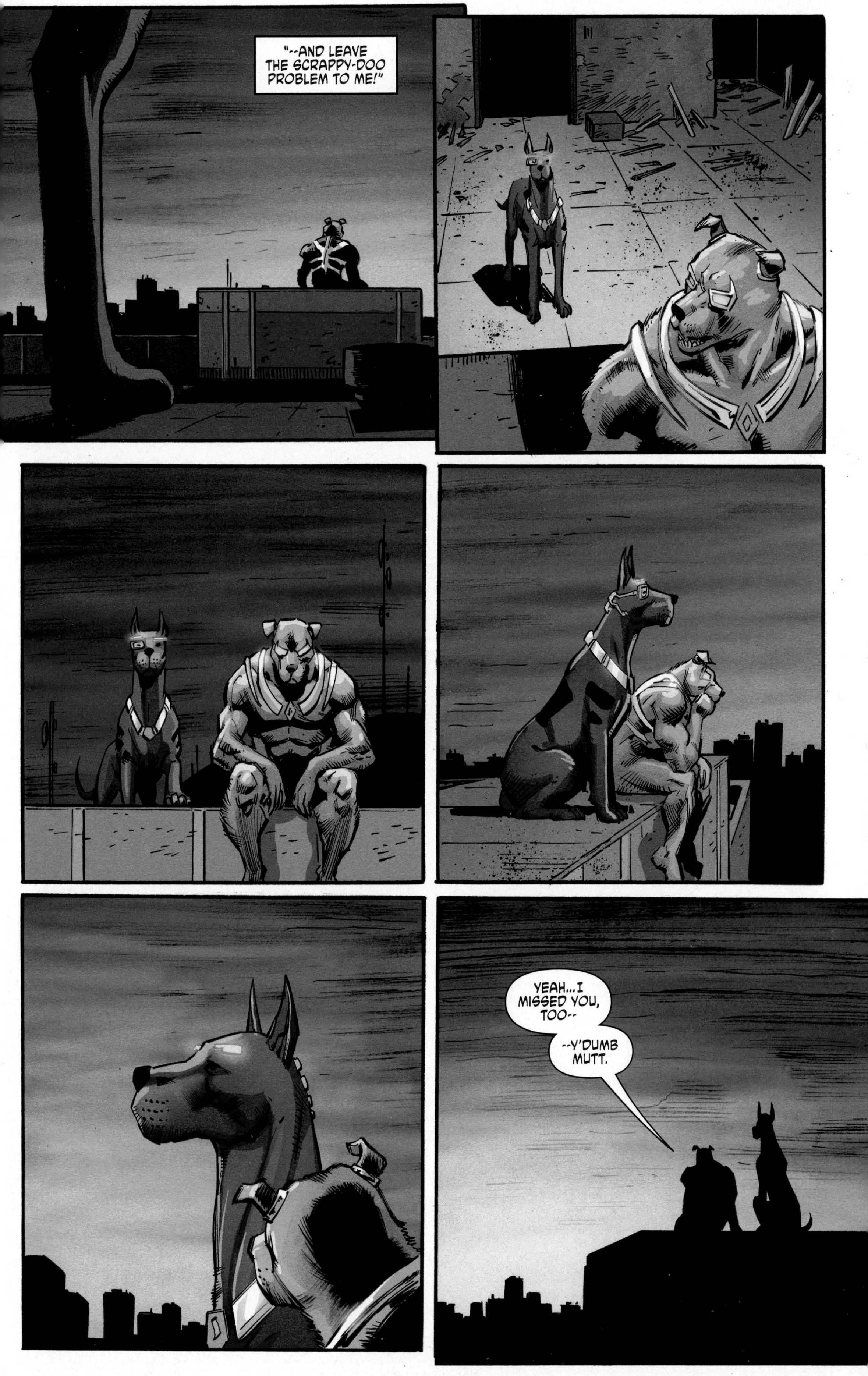
"--AND LEAVE THE SCRAPPY-DOO PROBLEM TO ME!"
YEAH...I MISSED YOU, TOO--
--Y'DUMB MUTT.

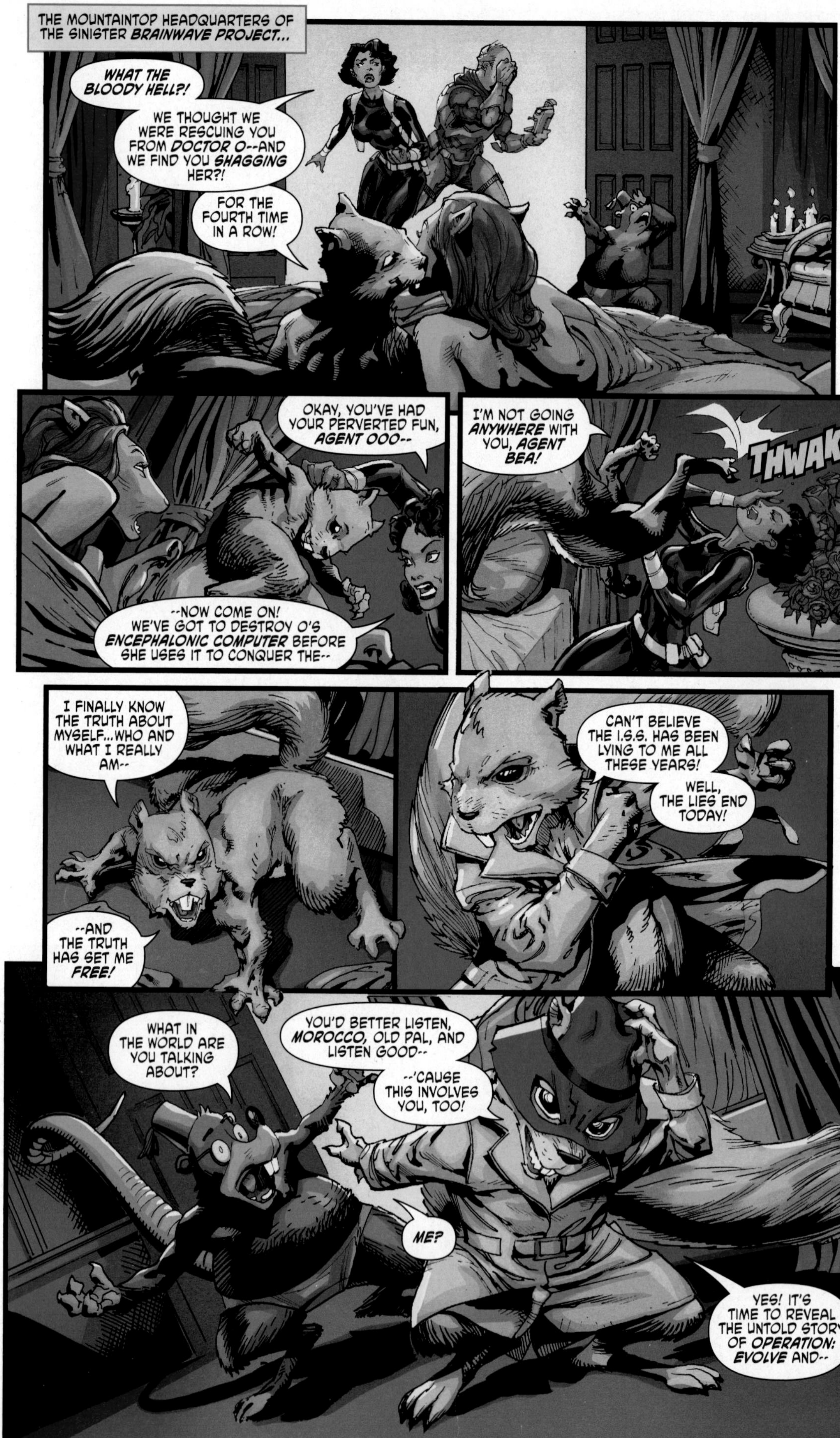
THE MOUNTAINTOP HEADQUARTERS OF THE SINISTER BRAINWAVE PROJECT...
WHAT THE BLOODY HELL?!
WE THOUGHT WE WERE RESCUING YOU FROM DOCTOR O--AND WE FIND YOU SHAGGING HER?!
FOR THE FOURTH TIME IN A ROW!
OKAY, YOU'VE HAD YOUR PERVERTED FUN, AGENT OOO--
--NOW COME ON! WE'VE GOT TO DESTROY O'S ENCEPHALONIC COMPUTER BEFORE SHE USES IT TO CONQUER THE--
I'M NOT GOING ANYWHERE WITH YOU, AGENT BEA!
THWAK
I FINALLY KNOW THE TRUTH ABOUT MYSELF...WHO AND WHAT I REALLY AM--
--AND THE TRUTH HAS SET ME FREE!
CAN'T BELIEVE THE I.S.S. HAS BEEN LYING TO ME ALL THESE YEARS!
WELL, THE LIES END TODAY!
WHAT IN THE WORLD ARE YOU TALKING ABOUT?
YOU'D BETTER LISTEN, MOROCCO, OLD PAL, AND LISTEN GOOD--
--'CAUSE THIS INVOLVES YOU, TOO!
ME?
YES! IT'S TIME TO REVEAL THE UNTOLD STORY OF OPERATION: EVOLVE AND--

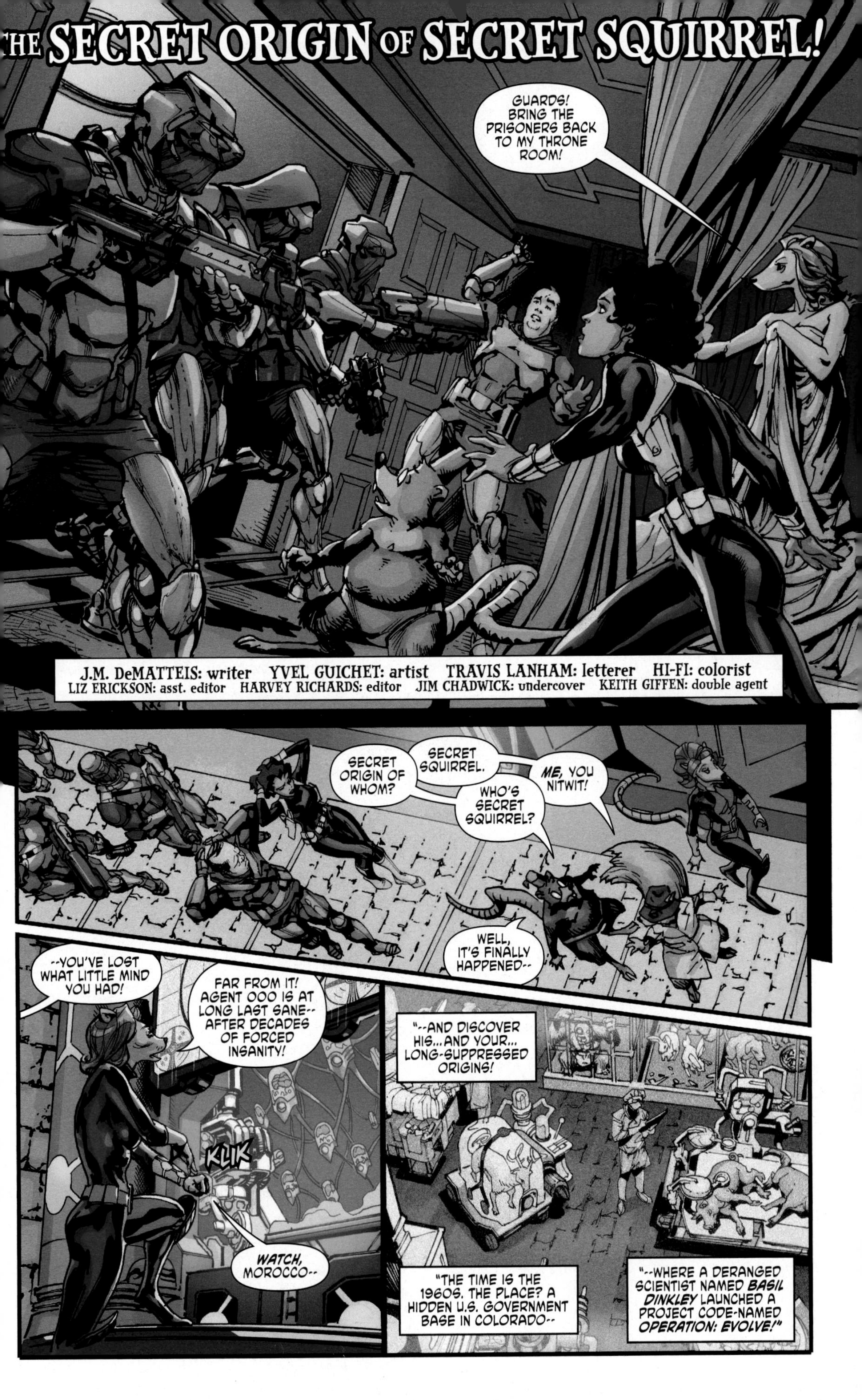
THE SECRET ORIGIN OF SECRET SQUIRREL!
GUARDS! BRING THE PRISONERS BACK TO MY THRONE ROOM!
J.M. DeMATTEIS: writer YVEL GUICHET: artist TRAVIS LANHAM: letterer HI-FI: colorist
LIZ ERICKSON: asst. editor HARVEY RICHARDS: editor JIM CHADWICK: undercover KEITH GIFFEN: double agent
SECRET ORIGIN OF WHOM?
SECRET SQUIRREL.
WHO'S SECRET SQUIRREL?
ME, YOU NITWIT!
WELL, IT'S FINALLY HAPPENED--
--YOU'VE LOST WHAT LITTLE MIND YOU HAD!
FAR FROM IT! AGENT OOO IS AT LONG LAST SANE-- AFTER DECADES OF FORCED INSANITY!
KLIK
WATCH, MOROCCO--
"--AND DISCOVER HIS...AND YOUR... LONG-SUPPRESSED ORIGINS!
"THE TIME IS THE 1960S. THE PLACE? A HIDDEN U.S. GOVERNMENT BASE IN COLORADO--
"--WHERE A DERANGED SCIENTIST NAMED BASIL DINKLEY LAUNCHED A PROJECT CODE-NAMED OPERATION: EVOLVE!"

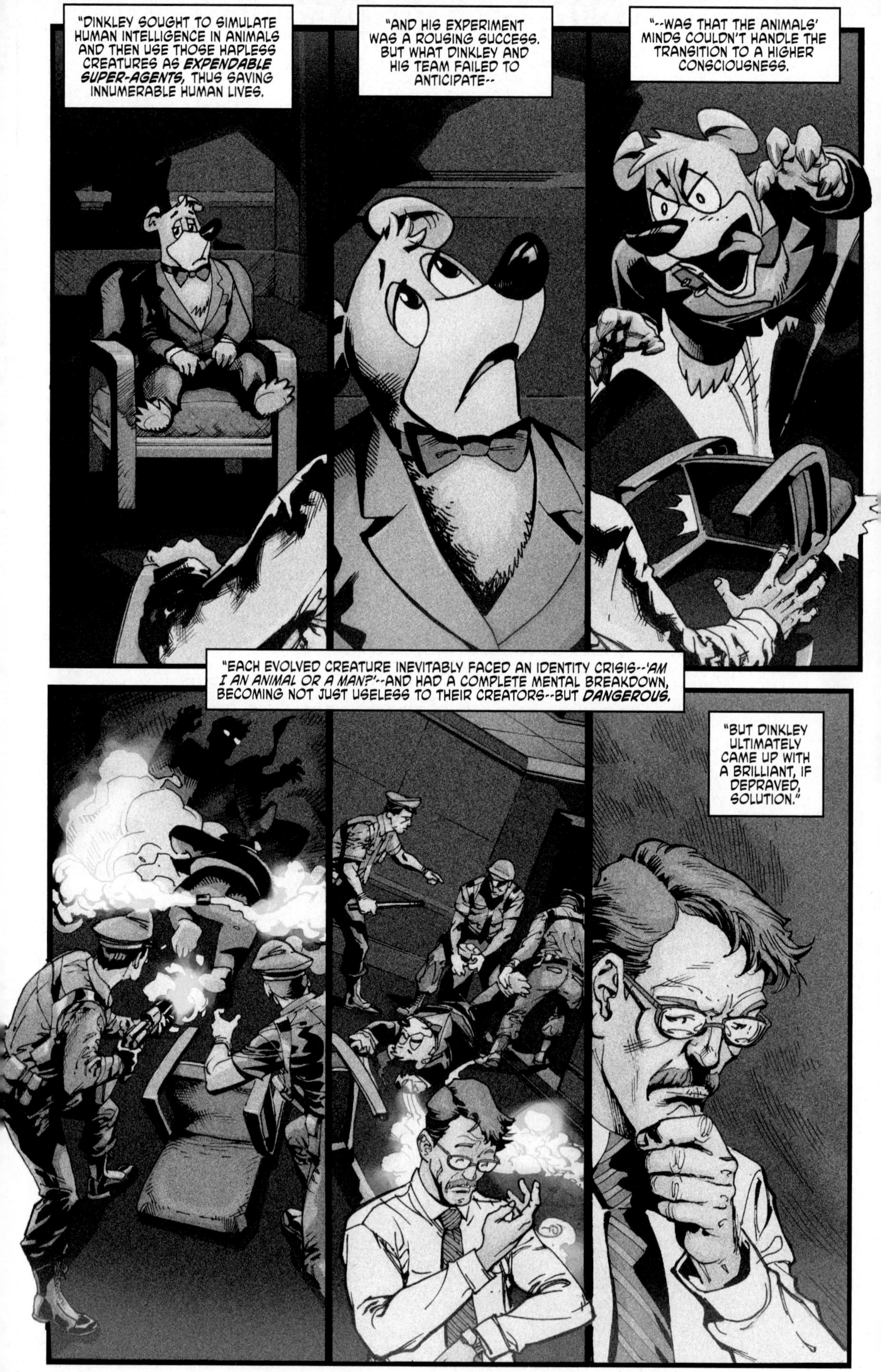
"DINKLEY SOUGHT TO SIMULATE HUMAN INTELLIGENCE IN ANIMALS AND THEN USE THOSE HAPLESS CREATURES AS EXPENDABLE SUPER-AGENTS, THUS SAVING INNUMERABLE HUMAN LIVES.
"AND HIS EXPERIMENT WAS A ROUSING SUCCESS. BUT WHAT DINKLEY AND HIS TEAM FAILED TO ANTICIPATE--
"--WAS THAT THE ANIMALS' MINDS COULDN'T HANDLE THE TRANSITION TO A HIGHER CONSCIOUSNESS.
"EACH EVOLVED CREATURE INEVITABLY FACED AN IDENTITY CRISIS--'AM I AN ANIMAL OR A MAN?'--AND HAD A COMPLETE MENTAL BREAKDOWN, BECOMING NOT JUST USELESS TO THEIR CREATORS--BUT DANGEROUS.
"BUT DINKLEY ULTIMATELY CAME UP WITH A BRILLIANT, IF DEPRAVED, SOLUTION."

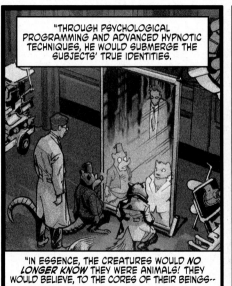

"THROUGH PSYCHOLOGICAL PROGRAMMING AND ADVANCED HYPNOTIC TECHNIQUES, HE WOULD SUBMERGE THE SUBJECTS' TRUE IDENTITIES.

"IN ESSENCE, THE CREATURES WOULD *NO LONGER KNOW* THEY WERE ANIMALS! THEY WOULD BELIEVE, TO THE CORES OF THEIR BEINGS--

ARTIST'S RENDITION

"--THAT *THEY WERE HUMAN.*

"ALTHOUGH OPERATION: EVOLVE WAS EVENTUALLY SHUT DOWN BY THE I.S.S.--

"--DINKLEY MANAGED TO CREATE THREE SUCCESSFUL 'HUMAN' SUPER-AGENTS--

--SECRET SQUIRREL, MOROCCO MOLE-- AND *ME!*

BUT MY INTELLIGENCE WAS SO FORMIDABLE THAT I SOON BROKE THROUGH THE HYPNOTIC BLOCKS--

--MAINTAINING BOTH MY EVOLVED MIND *AND* MY TRUE ANIMAL NATURE... AND ESCAPING MY CAPTORS!

Y'SEE, BUDDY--

--WE WERE JUST A COUPLE OF DUPES!

DOUBLE-Q AND HIS CRONIES HAVE BEEN USING US FOR YEARS!

AND *YOU* KNEW ALL ALONG, DIDN'T YOU, *HONEY?*

PRETENDED T'CARE ABOUT ME WHEN I WAS NOTHING BUT AN *EXPERIMENT* TO YOU!

WELL, YOU'RE GONNA *PAY* FOR THAT, BABE--

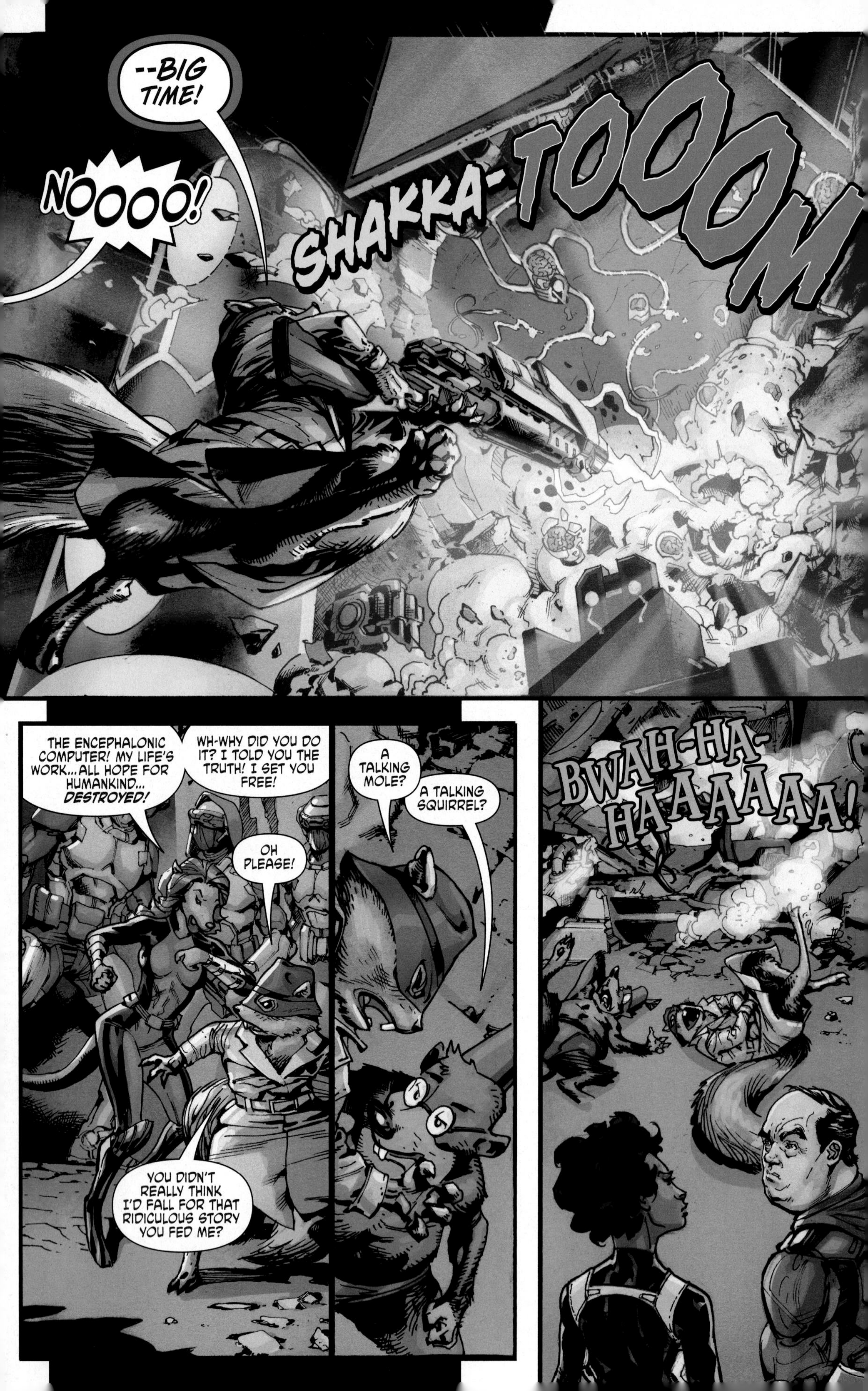
--BIG TIME!
NOOOO!
SHAKKA-TOOOOM
THE ENCEPHALONIC COMPUTER! MY LIFE'S WORK...ALL HOPE FOR HUMANKIND... DESTROYED!
WH-WHY DID YOU DO IT? I TOLD YOU THE TRUTH! I SET YOU FREE!
OH PLEASE!
YOU DIDN'T REALLY THINK I'D FALL FOR THAT RIDICULOUS STORY YOU FED ME?
A TALKING MOLE?
A TALKING SQUIRREL?
BWAH-HA-HA-AAAAAA!

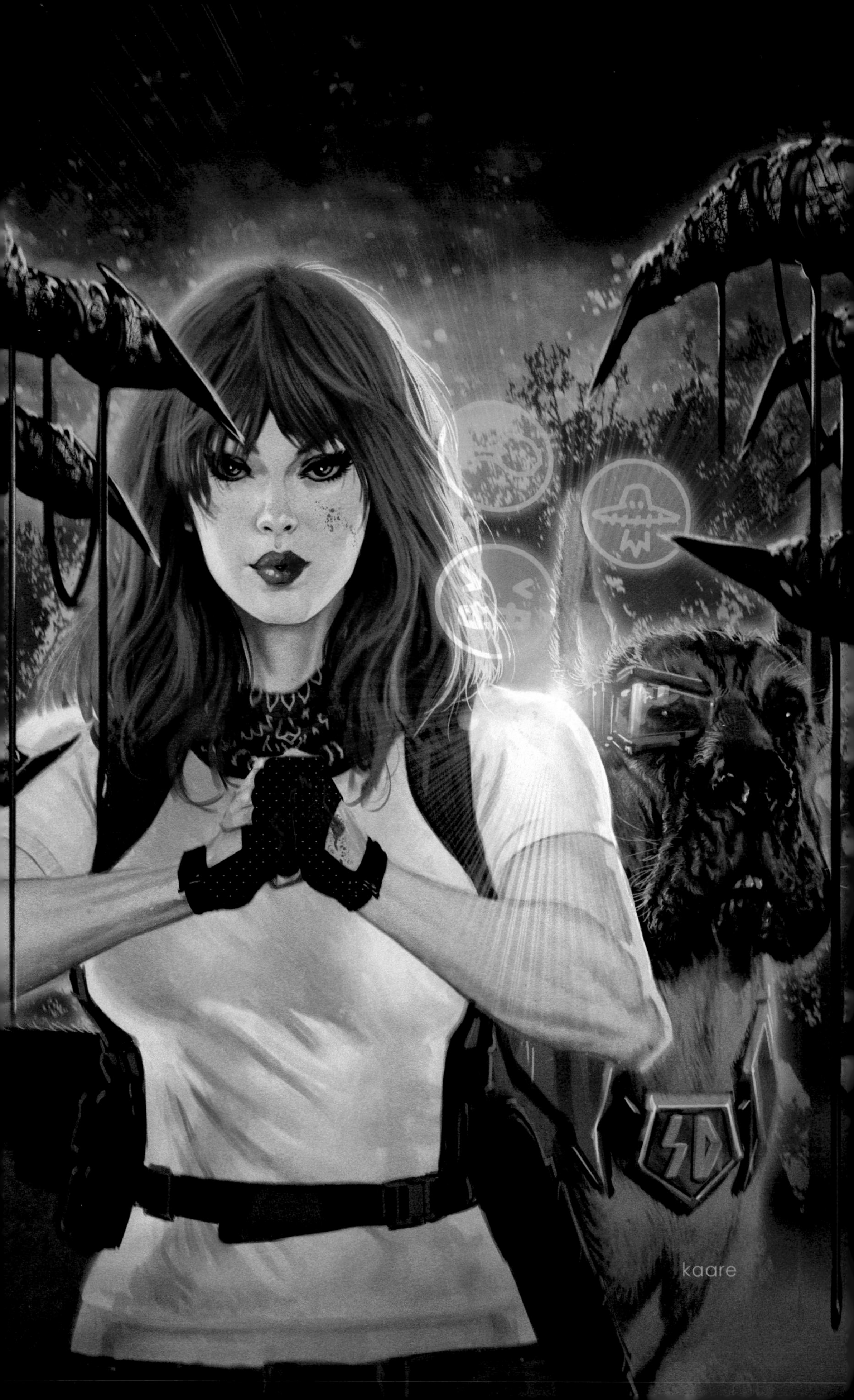
kaare

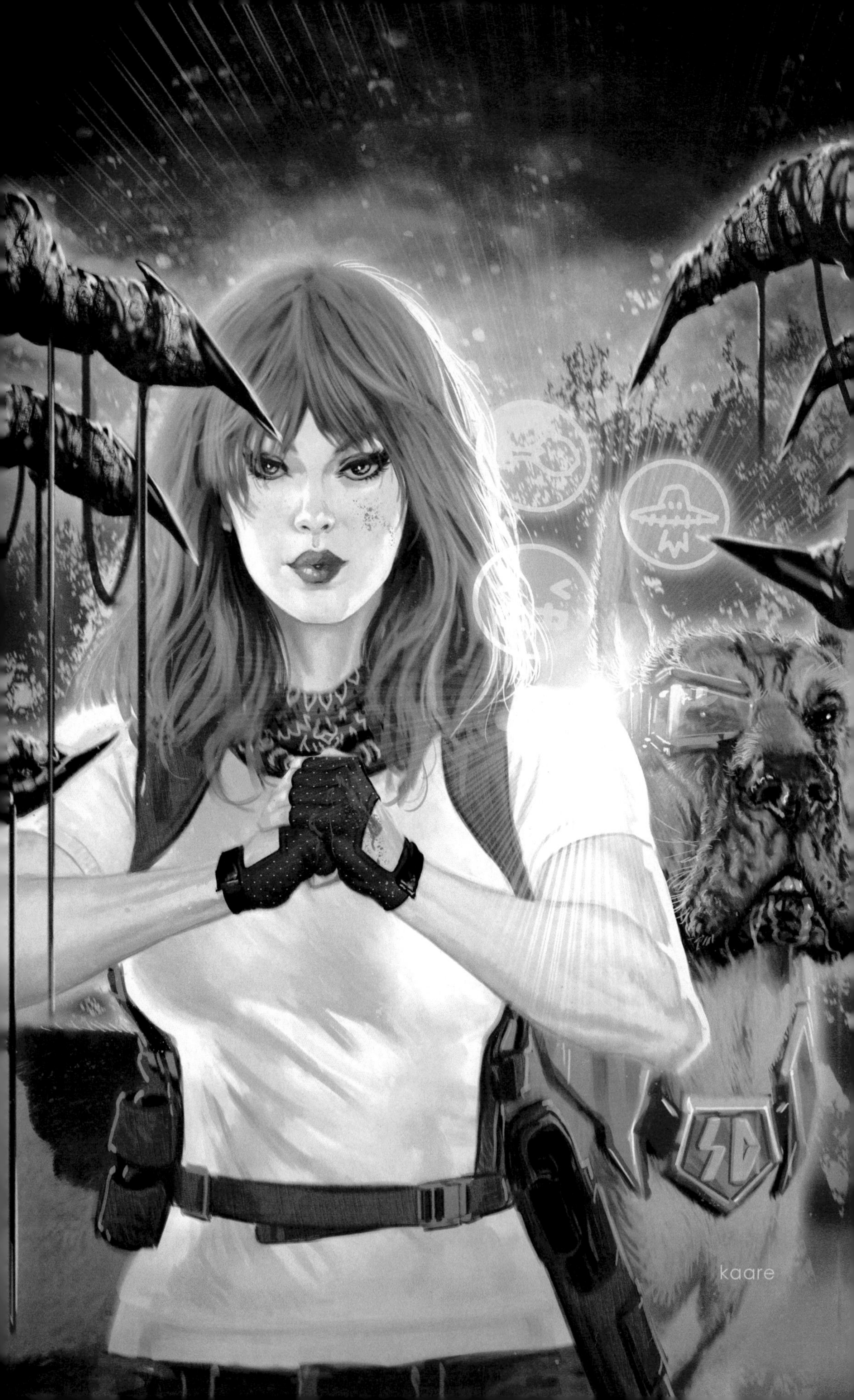
kaare

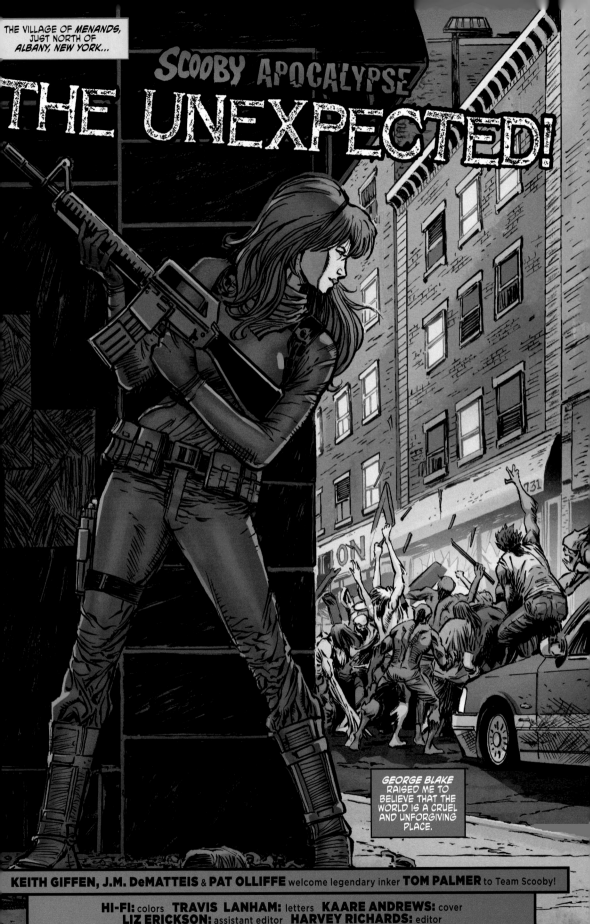

THE VILLAGE OF *MENANDS,* JUST NORTH OF *ALBANY, NEW YORK...*

SCOOBY APOCALYPSE

THE UNEXPECTED!

731

GEORGE BLAKE RAISED ME TO BELIEVE THAT THE WORLD IS A *CRUEL* AND *UNFORGIVING* PLACE.

KEITH GIFFEN, J.M. DeMATTEIS & PAT OLLIFFE welcome legendary inker **TOM PALMER** to Team Scooby!

HI-FI: colors **TRAVIS LANHAM:** letters **KAARE ANDREWS:** cover
LIZ ERICKSON: assistant editor **HARVEY RICHARDS:** editor
JIM CHADWICK: is wondering how long it will take for **GIFFEN & DeMATTEIS** to drive **PALMER** away

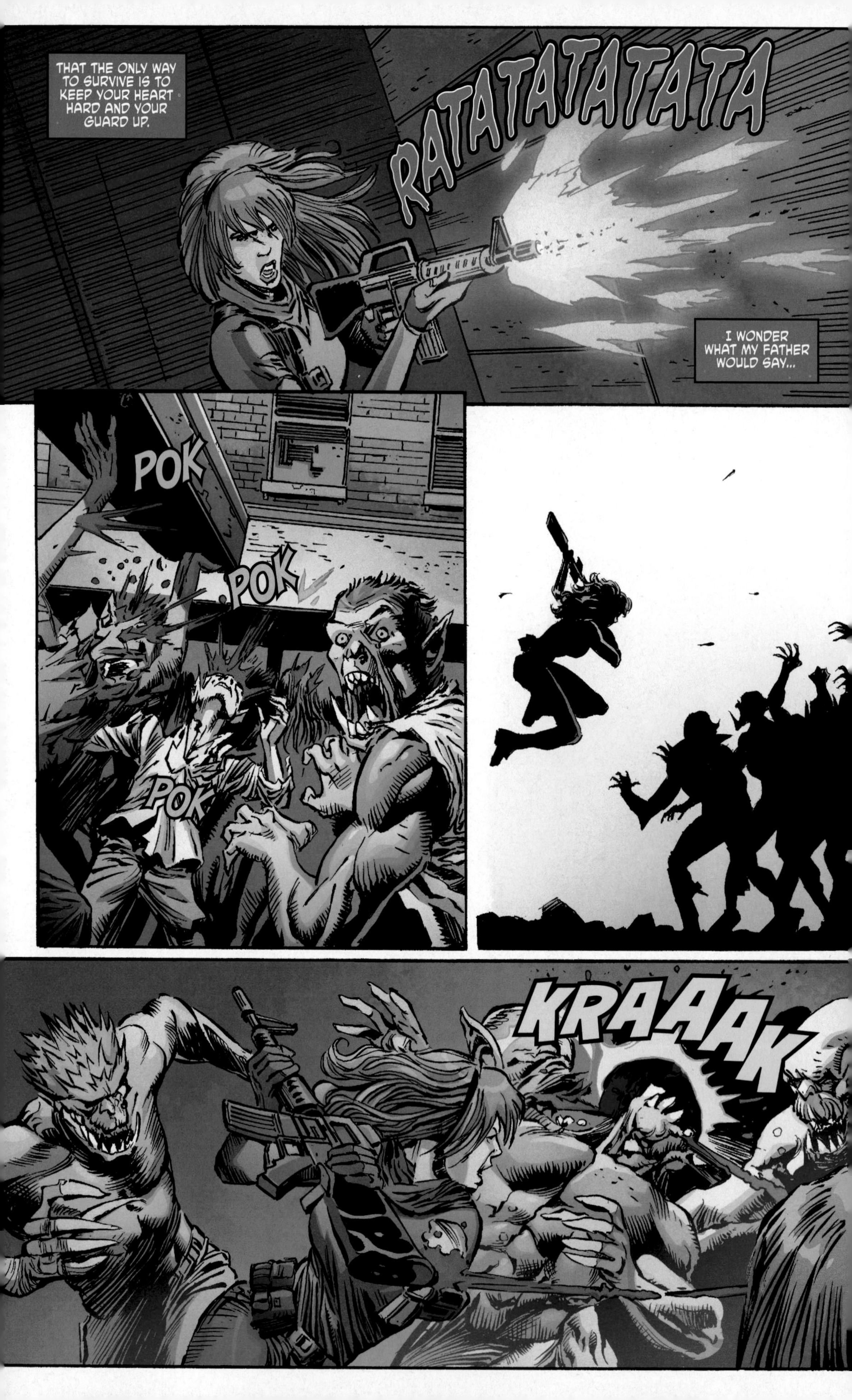

THAT THE ONLY WAY TO SURVIVE IS TO KEEP YOUR HEART HARD AND YOUR GUARD UP.
RATATATATATATA
I WONDER WHAT MY FATHER WOULD SAY...
POK
POK
POK
KRAAAK

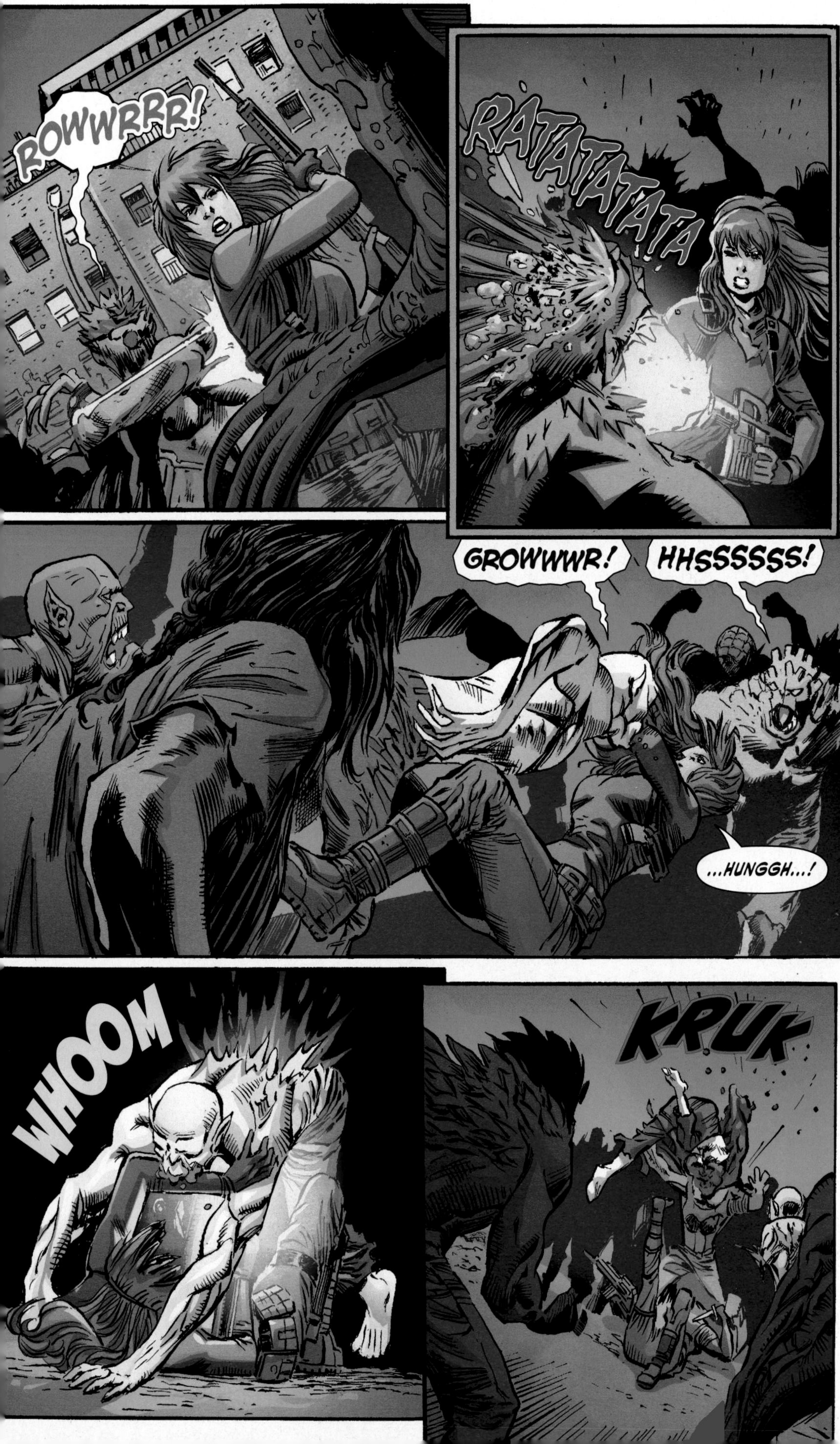
ROWWRRR!
RATATATATATA
GROWWWR!
HHSSSSSS!
...HUNGGH...!
WHOOM
KRUK

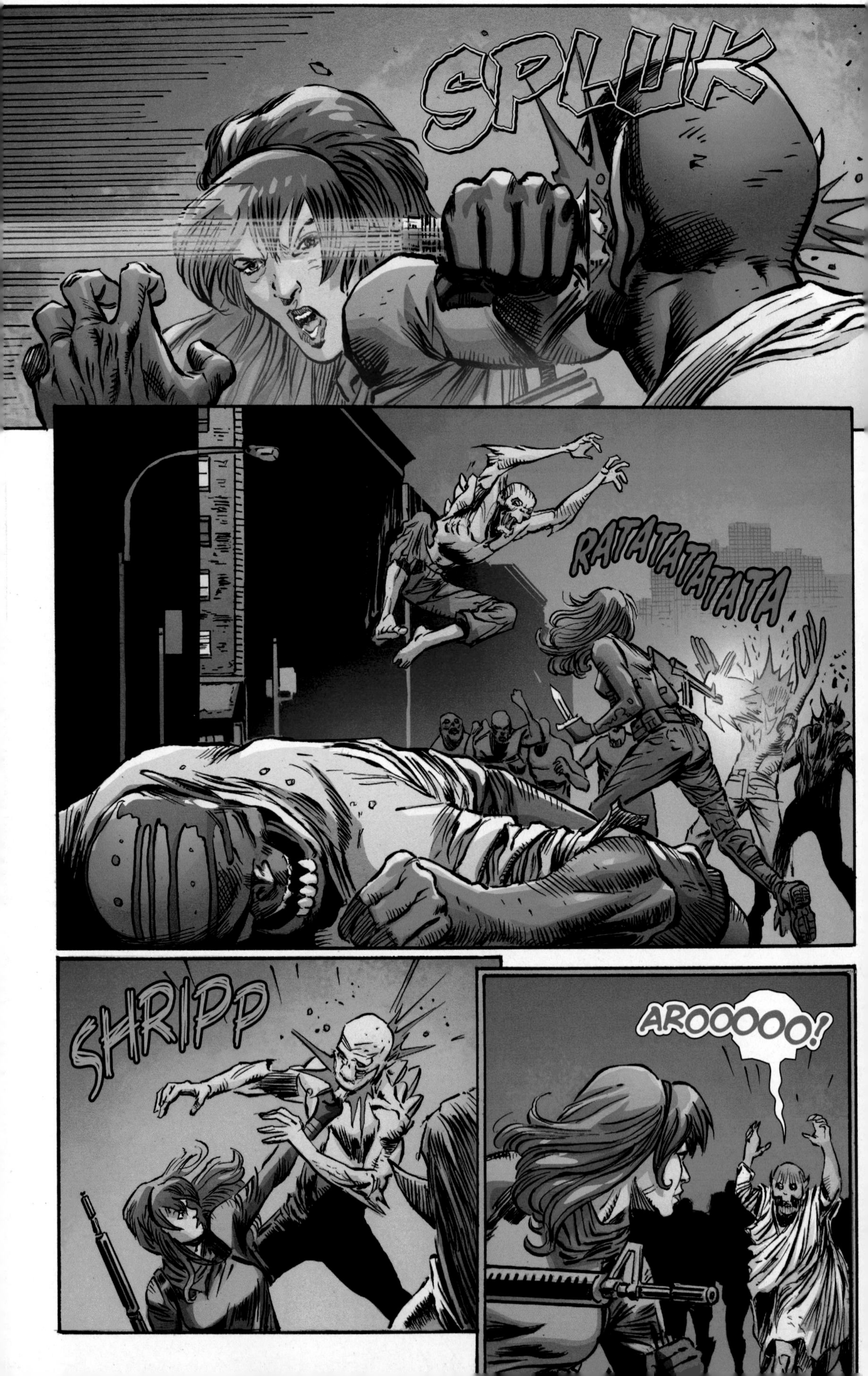
SPLUK
RATATATATATATA
SHRIPP
AROOOOOO!

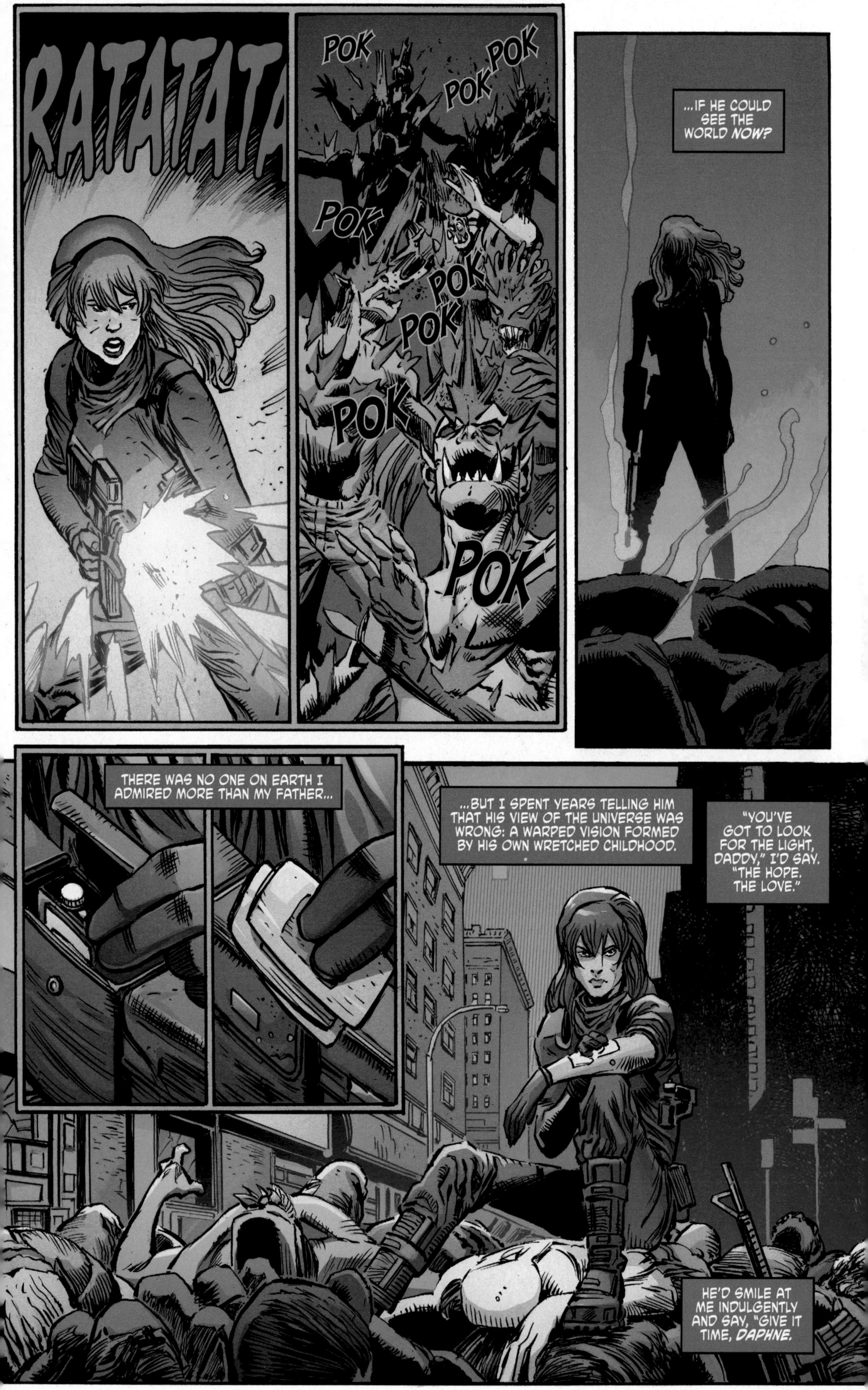
RATATATA
POK
POK
POK
POK
POK
POK
POK
POK
POK
...IF HE COULD SEE THE WORLD *NOW?*
THERE WAS NO ONE ON EARTH I ADMIRED MORE THAN MY FATHER...
...BUT I SPENT YEARS TELLING HIM THAT HIS VIEW OF THE UNIVERSE WAS WRONG: A WARPED VISION FORMED BY HIS OWN WRETCHED CHILDHOOD.
"YOU'VE GOT TO LOOK FOR THE LIGHT, DADDY," I'D SAY. "THE HOPE. THE LOVE."
HE'D SMILE AT ME INDULGENTLY AND SAY, "GIVE IT TIME, *DAPHNE.*

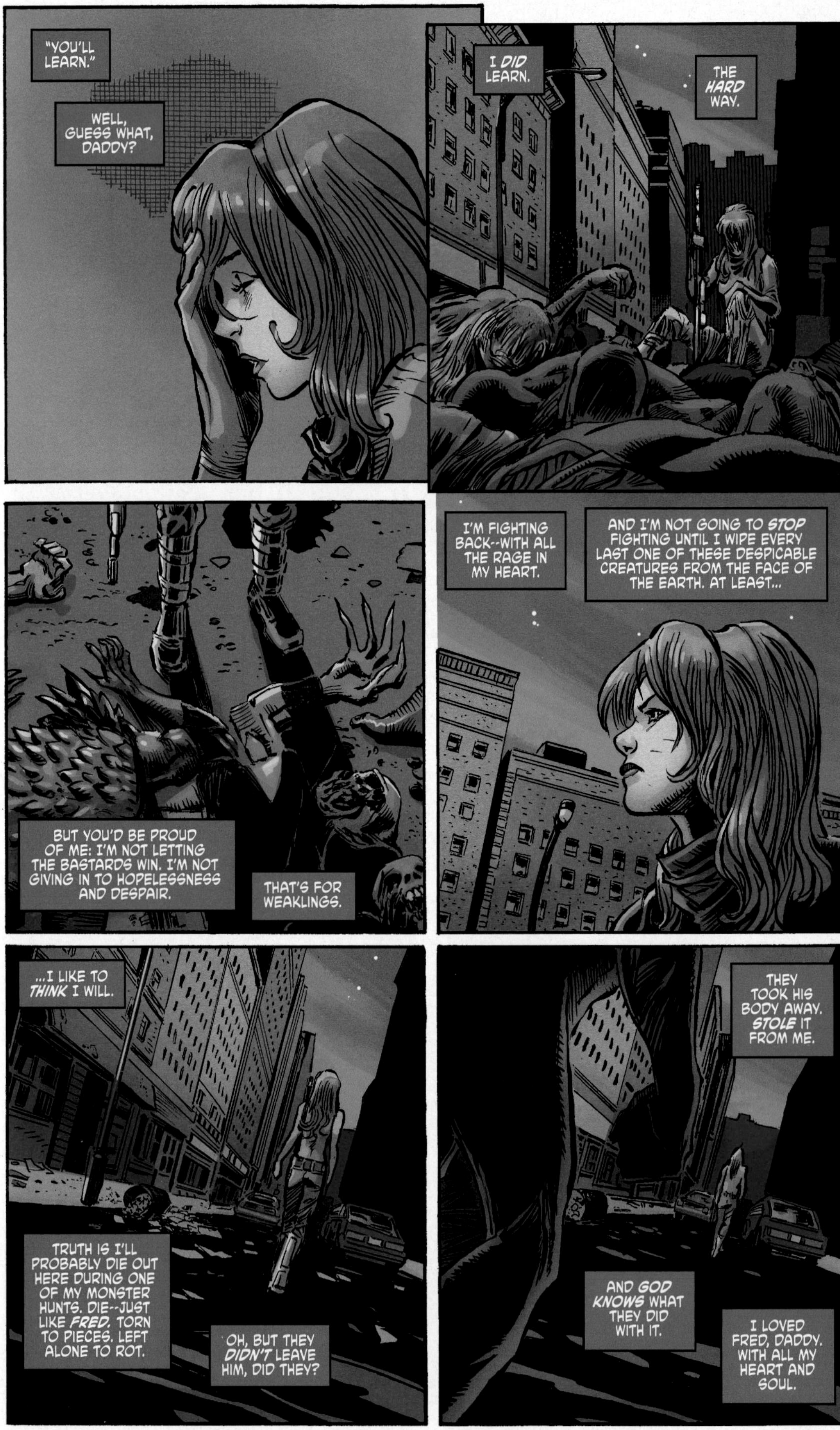
"YOU'LL LEARN."
WELL, GUESS WHAT, DADDY?
I *DID* LEARN.
THE *HARD* WAY.
BUT YOU'D BE PROUD OF ME: I'M NOT LETTING THE BASTARDS WIN. I'M NOT GIVING IN TO HOPELESSNESS AND DESPAIR.
THAT'S FOR WEAKLINGS.
I'M FIGHTING BACK--WITH ALL THE RAGE IN MY HEART.
AND I'M NOT GOING TO *STOP* FIGHTING UNTIL I WIPE EVERY LAST ONE OF THESE DESPICABLE CREATURES FROM THE FACE OF THE EARTH. AT LEAST...
...I LIKE TO *THINK* I WILL.
TRUTH IS I'LL PROBABLY DIE OUT HERE DURING ONE OF MY MONSTER HUNTS. DIE--JUST LIKE *FRED*. TORN TO PIECES. LEFT ALONE TO ROT.
OH, BUT THEY *DIDN'T* LEAVE HIM, DID THEY?
THEY TOOK HIS BODY AWAY. *STOLE* IT FROM ME.
AND *GOD KNOWS* WHAT THEY DID WITH IT.
I LOVED FRED, DADDY. WITH ALL MY HEART AND SOUL.

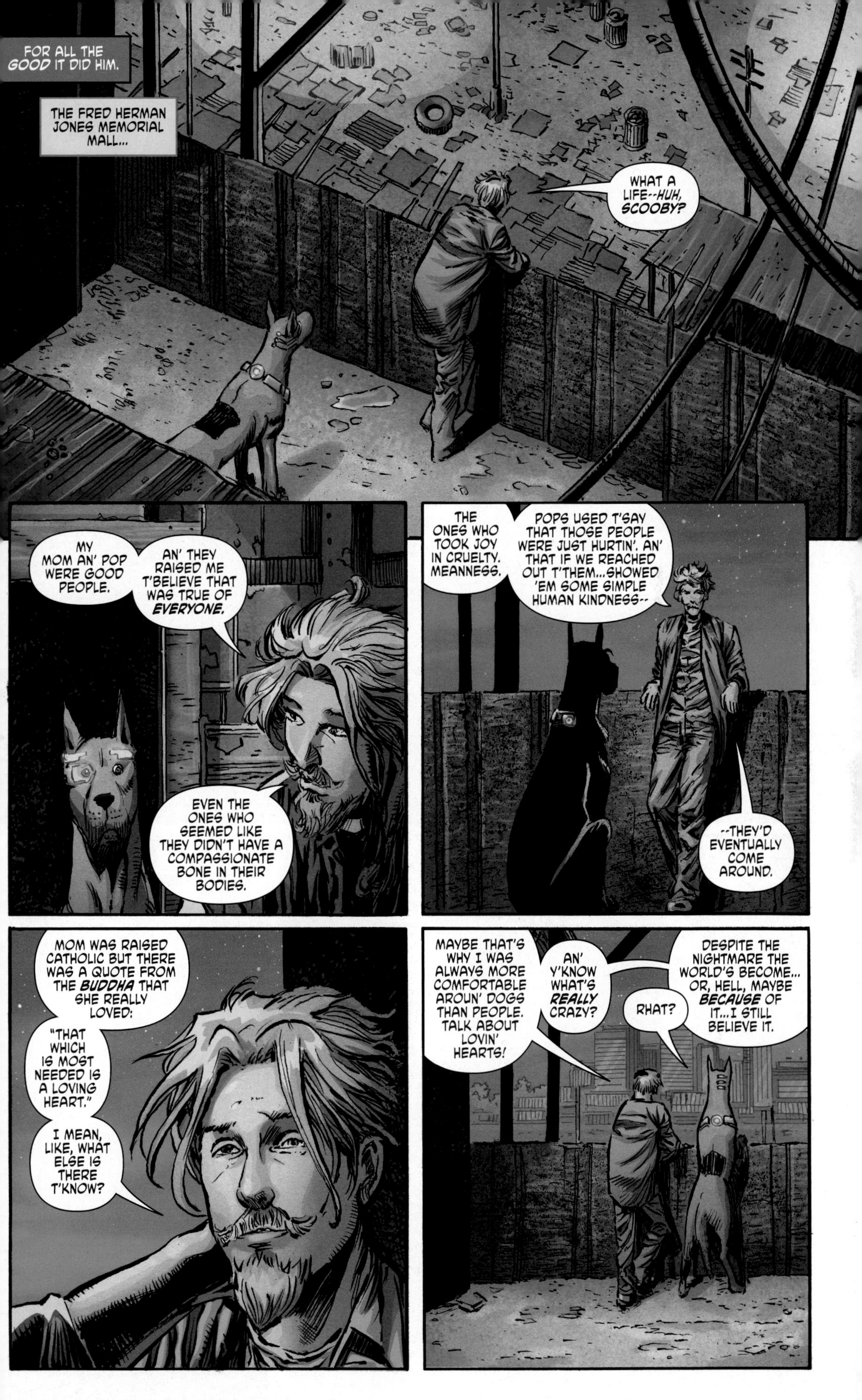

FOR ALL THE GOOD IT DID HIM.
THE FRED HERMAN JONES MEMORIAL MALL...
WHAT A LIFE--HUH, SCOOBY?
MY MOM AN' POP WERE GOOD PEOPLE.
AN' THEY RAISED ME T'BELIEVE THAT WAS TRUE OF EVERYONE.
EVEN THE ONES WHO SEEMED LIKE THEY DIDN'T HAVE A COMPASSIONATE BONE IN THEIR BODIES.
THE ONES WHO TOOK JOY IN CRUELTY. MEANNESS.
POPS USED T'SAY THAT THOSE PEOPLE WERE JUST HURTIN'. AN' THAT IF WE REACHED OUT T'THEM...SHOWED 'EM SOME SIMPLE HUMAN KINDNESS--
--THEY'D EVENTUALLY COME AROUND.
MOM WAS RAISED CATHOLIC BUT THERE WAS A QUOTE FROM THE BUDDHA THAT SHE REALLY LOVED:
"THAT WHICH IS MOST NEEDED IS A LOVING HEART."
I MEAN, LIKE, WHAT ELSE IS THERE T'KNOW?
MAYBE THAT'S WHY I WAS ALWAYS MORE COMFORTABLE AROUN' DOGS THAN PEOPLE. TALK ABOUT LOVIN' HEARTS!
AN' Y'KNOW WHAT'S REALLY CRAZY?
RHAT?
DESPITE THE NIGHTMARE THE WORLD'S BECOME... OR, HELL, MAYBE BECAUSE OF IT...I STILL BELIEVE IT.

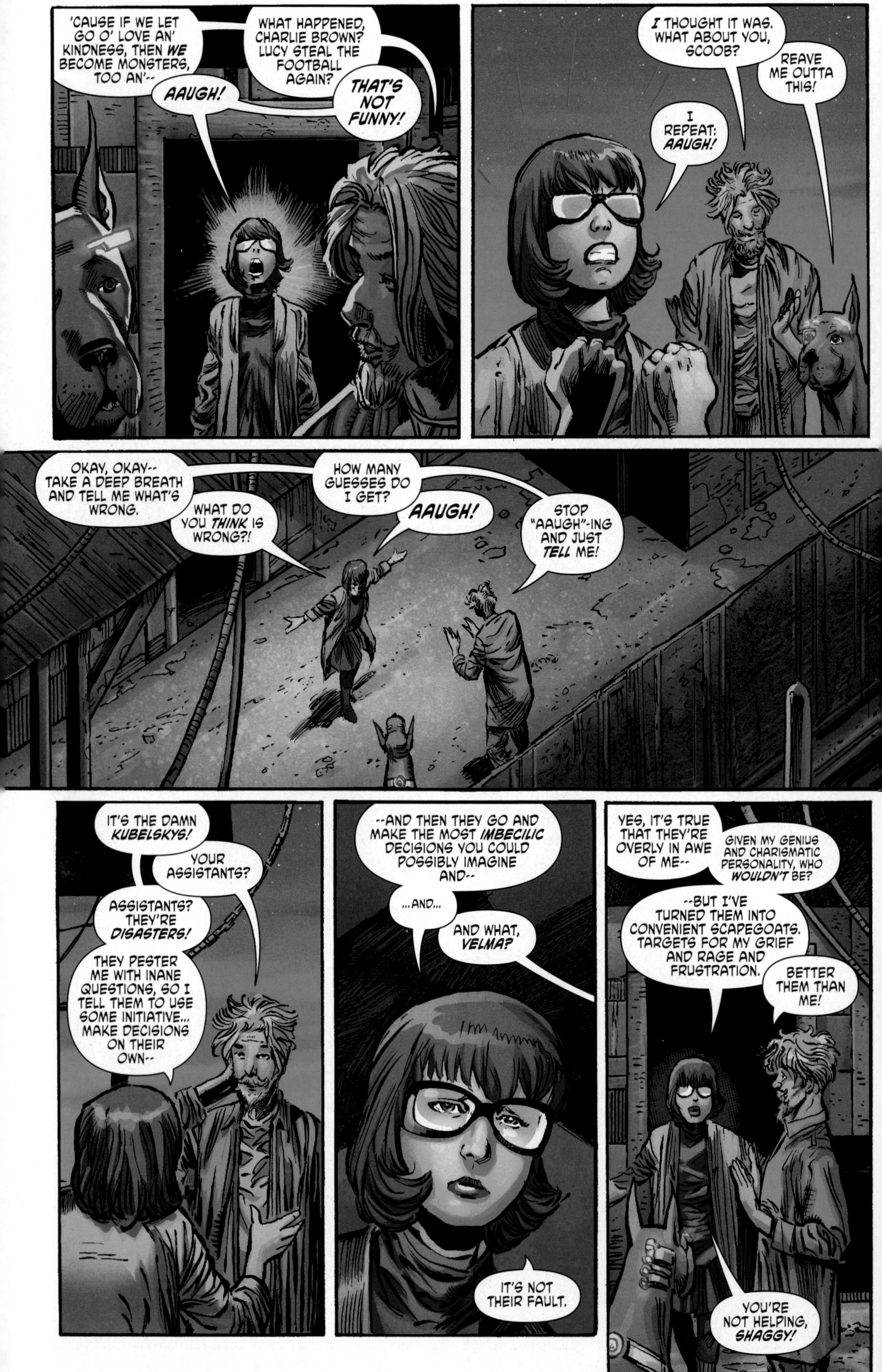
'CAUSE IF WE LET GO O' LOVE AN' KINDNESS, THEN WE BECOME MONSTERS, TOO AN'--
AAUGH!
WHAT HAPPENED, CHARLIE BROWN? LUCY STEAL THE FOOTBALL AGAIN?
THAT'S NOT FUNNY!
I THOUGHT IT WAS. WHAT ABOUT YOU, SCOOB?
REAVE ME OUTTA THIS!
I REPEAT: AAUGH!
OKAY, OKAY-- TAKE A DEEP BREATH AND TELL ME WHAT'S WRONG.
WHAT DO YOU THINK IS WRONG?!
HOW MANY GUESSES DO I GET?
AAUGH!
STOP "AAUGH"-ING AND JUST TELL ME!
IT'S THE DAMN KUBELSKYS!
YOUR ASSISTANTS?
ASSISTANTS? THEY'RE DISASTERS!
THEY PESTER ME WITH INANE QUESTIONS, SO I TELL THEM TO USE SOME INITIATIVE... MAKE DECISIONS ON THEIR OWN--
--AND THEN THEY GO AND MAKE THE MOST IMBECILIC DECISIONS YOU COULD POSSIBLY IMAGINE AND--
...AND...
AND WHAT, VELMA?
IT'S NOT THEIR FAULT.
YES, IT'S TRUE THAT THEY'RE OVERLY IN AWE OF ME--
GIVEN MY GENIUS AND CHARISMATIC PERSONALITY, WHO WOULDN'T BE?
--BUT I'VE TURNED THEM INTO CONVENIENT SCAPEGOATS. TARGETS FOR MY GRIEF AND RAGE AND FRUSTRATION.
BETTER THEM THAN ME!
YOU'RE NOT HELPING, SHAGGY!

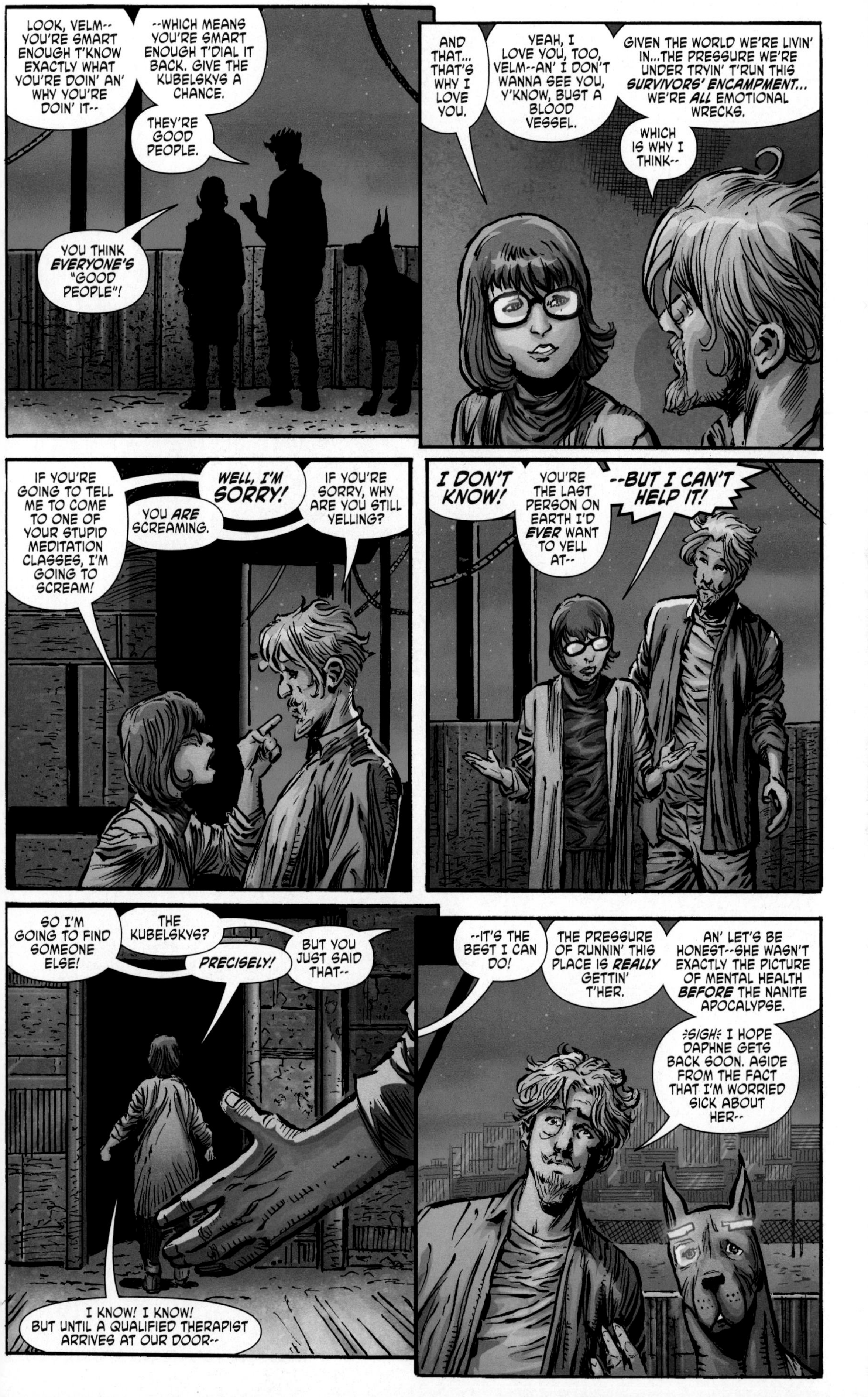
LOOK, VELM-- YOU'RE SMART ENOUGH T'KNOW EXACTLY WHAT YOU'RE DOIN' AN' WHY YOU'RE DOIN' IT--
--WHICH MEANS YOU'RE SMART ENOUGH T'DIAL IT BACK. GIVE THE KUBELSKYS A CHANCE.
THEY'RE GOOD PEOPLE.
YOU THINK EVERYONE'S "GOOD PEOPLE"!
AND THAT... THAT'S WHY I LOVE YOU.
YEAH, I LOVE YOU, TOO, VELM--AN' I DON'T WANNA SEE YOU, Y'KNOW, BUST A BLOOD VESSEL.
GIVEN THE WORLD WE'RE LIVIN' IN...THE PRESSURE WE'RE UNDER TRYIN' T'RUN THIS SURVIVORS' ENCAMPMENT... WE'RE ALL EMOTIONAL WRECKS.
WHICH IS WHY I THINK--
IF YOU'RE GOING TO TELL ME TO COME TO ONE OF YOUR STUPID MEDITATION CLASSES, I'M GOING TO SCREAM!
YOU ARE SCREAMING.
WELL, I'M SORRY!
IF YOU'RE SORRY, WHY ARE YOU STILL YELLING?
I DON'T KNOW!
YOU'RE THE LAST PERSON ON EARTH I'D EVER WANT TO YELL AT--
--BUT I CAN'T HELP IT!
SO I'M GOING TO FIND SOMEONE ELSE!
THE KUBELSKYS?
PRECISELY!
BUT YOU JUST SAID THAT--
I KNOW! I KNOW! BUT UNTIL A QUALIFIED THERAPIST ARRIVES AT OUR DOOR--
--IT'S THE BEST I CAN DO!
THE PRESSURE OF RUNNIN' THIS PLACE IS REALLY GETTIN' T'HER.
AN' LET'S BE HONEST--SHE WASN'T EXACTLY THE PICTURE OF MENTAL HEALTH BEFORE THE NANITE APOCALYPSE.
SIGH I HOPE DAPHNE GETS BACK SOON. ASIDE FROM THE FACT THAT I'M WORRIED SICK ABOUT HER--

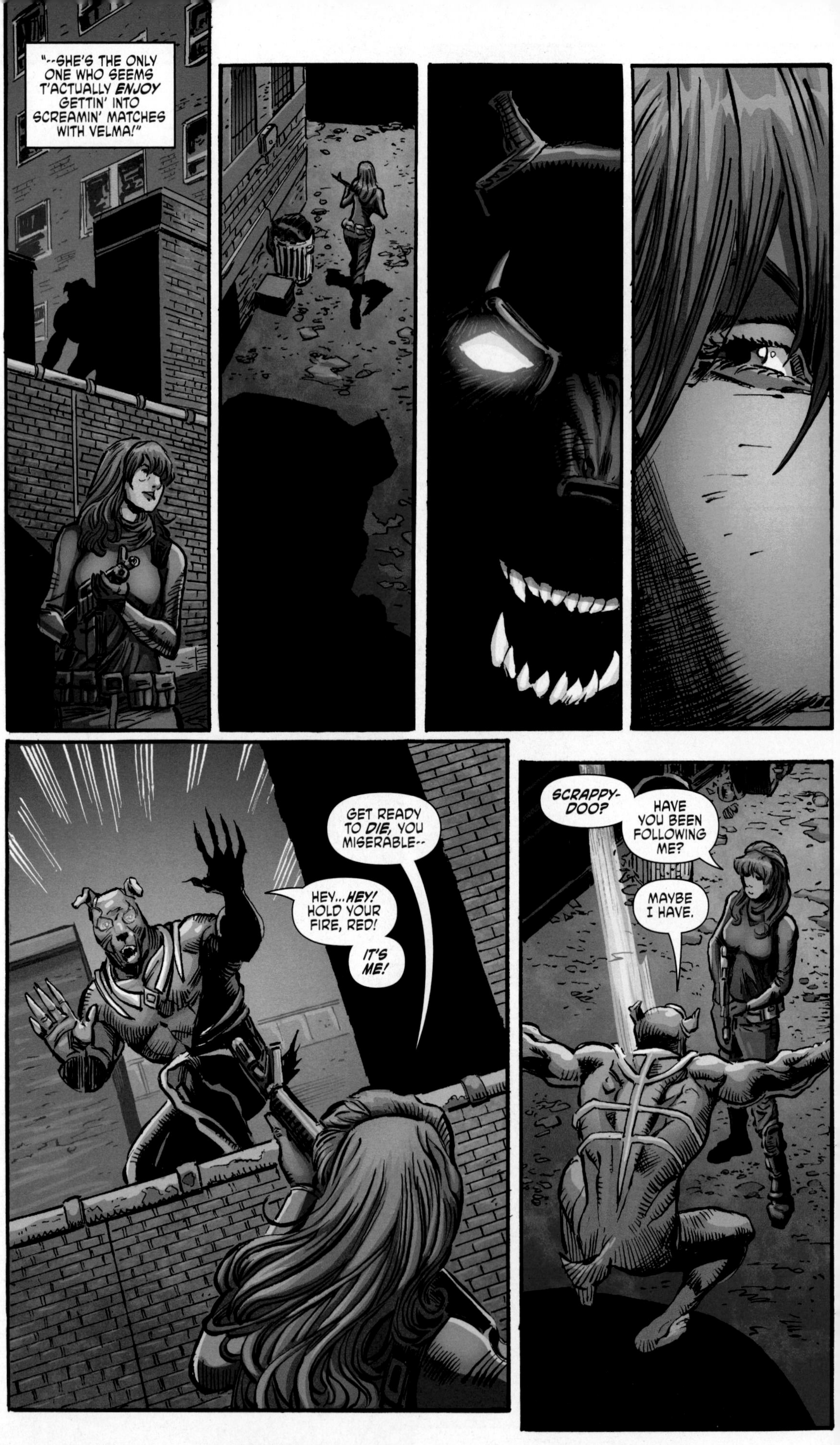
"--SHE'S THE ONLY ONE WHO SEEMS T'ACTUALLY *ENJOY* GETTIN' INTO SCREAMIN' MATCHES WITH VELMA!"
GET READY TO *DIE*, YOU MISERABLE--
HEY... *HEY!* HOLD YOUR FIRE, RED!
IT'S ME!
SCRAPPY-DOO?
HAVE YOU BEEN FOLLOWING ME?
MAYBE I HAVE.

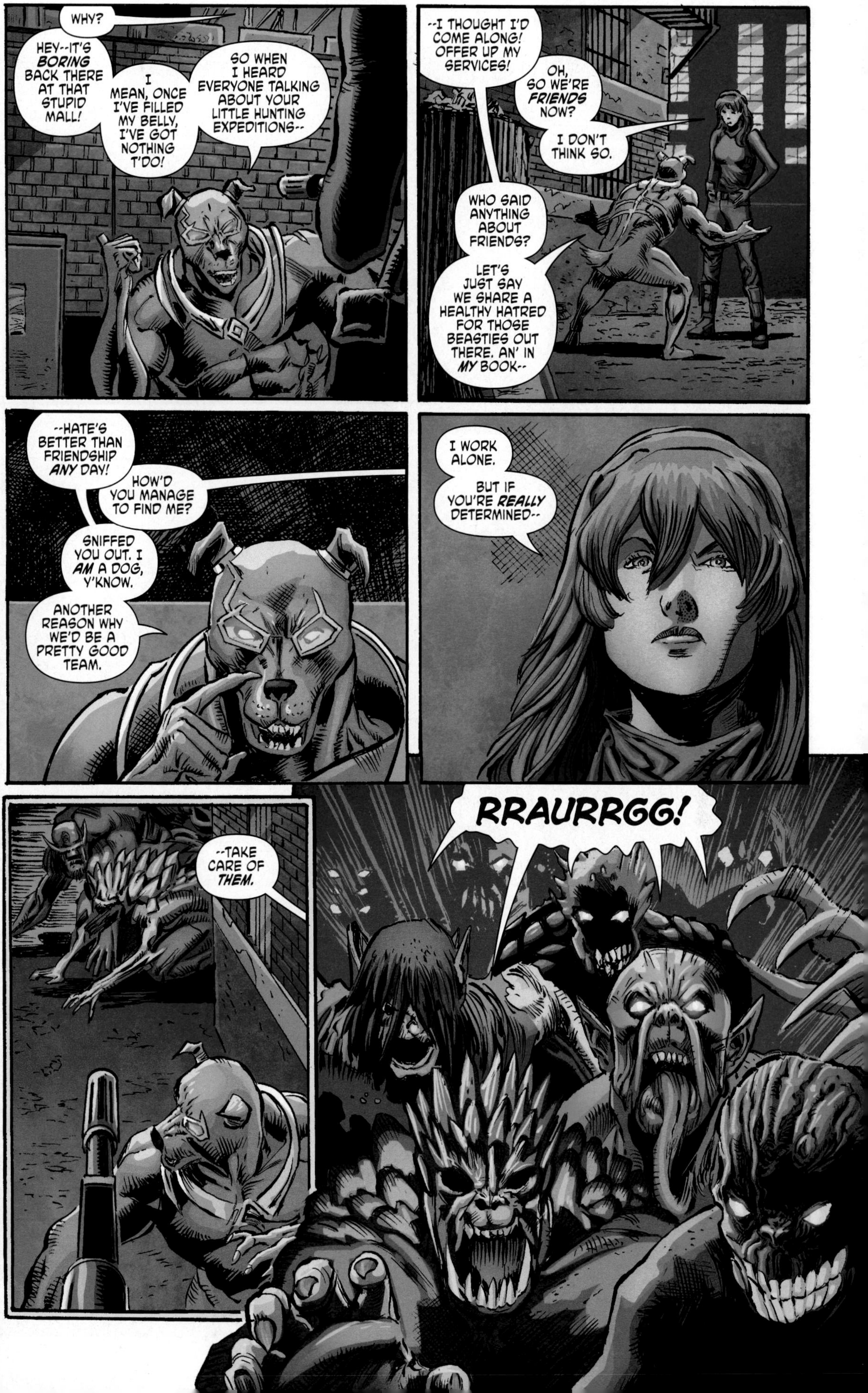
WHY?
HEY--IT'S *BORING* BACK THERE AT THAT STUPID MALL!
I MEAN, ONCE I'VE FILLED MY BELLY, I'VE GOT NOTHING T'DO!
SO WHEN I HEARD EVERYONE TALKING ABOUT YOUR LITTLE HUNTING EXPEDITIONS--
--I THOUGHT I'D COME ALONG! OFFER UP MY SERVICES!
OH, SO WE'RE *FRIENDS* NOW?
I DON'T THINK SO.
WHO SAID ANYTHING ABOUT FRIENDS?
LET'S JUST SAY WE SHARE A HEALTHY HATRED FOR THOSE BEASTIES OUT THERE. AN' IN *MY* BOOK--
--HATE'S BETTER THAN FRIENDSHIP *ANY* DAY!
HOW'D YOU MANAGE TO FIND ME?
SNIFFED YOU OUT. I *AM* A DOG, Y'KNOW.
ANOTHER REASON WHY WE'D BE A PRETTY GOOD TEAM.
I WORK ALONE.
BUT IF YOU'RE *REALLY* DETERMINED--
--TAKE CARE OF *THEM.*
RRAURRGG!

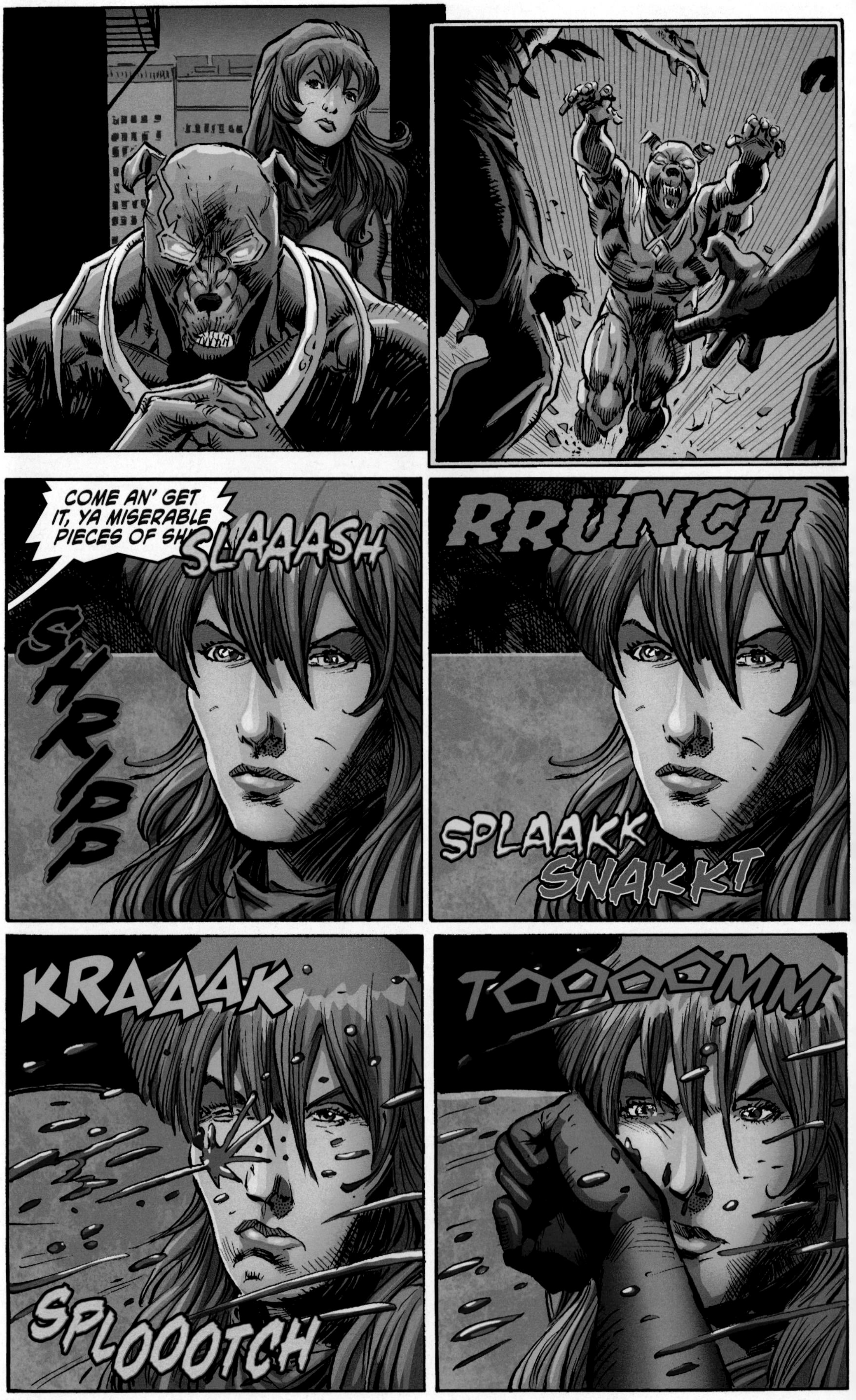

COME AN' GET IT, YA MISERABLE PIECES OF SH--
SLAAASH
SHRIPP
RRUNCH
SPLAAKK
SNAKKT
KRAAAK
SPLOOOTCH
TOOOOMM

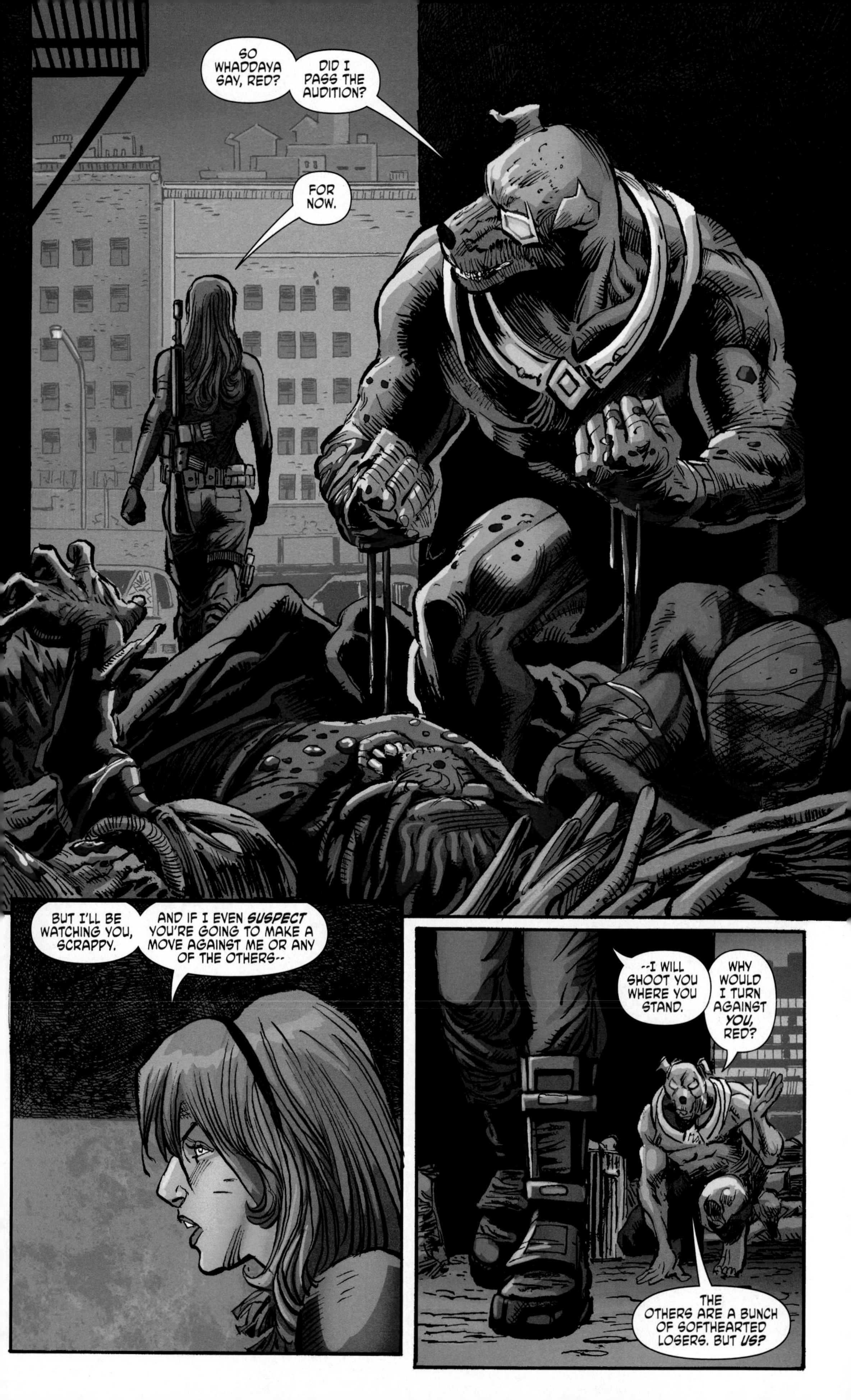
SO WHADDAYA SAY, RED?
DID I PASS THE AUDITION?
FOR NOW.
BUT I'LL BE WATCHING YOU, SCRAPPY.
AND IF I EVEN SUSPECT YOU'RE GOING TO MAKE A MOVE AGAINST ME OR ANY OF THE OTHERS--
--I WILL SHOOT YOU WHERE YOU STAND.
WHY WOULD I TURN AGAINST YOU, RED?
THE OTHERS ARE A BUNCH OF SOFTHEARTED LOSERS. BUT US?

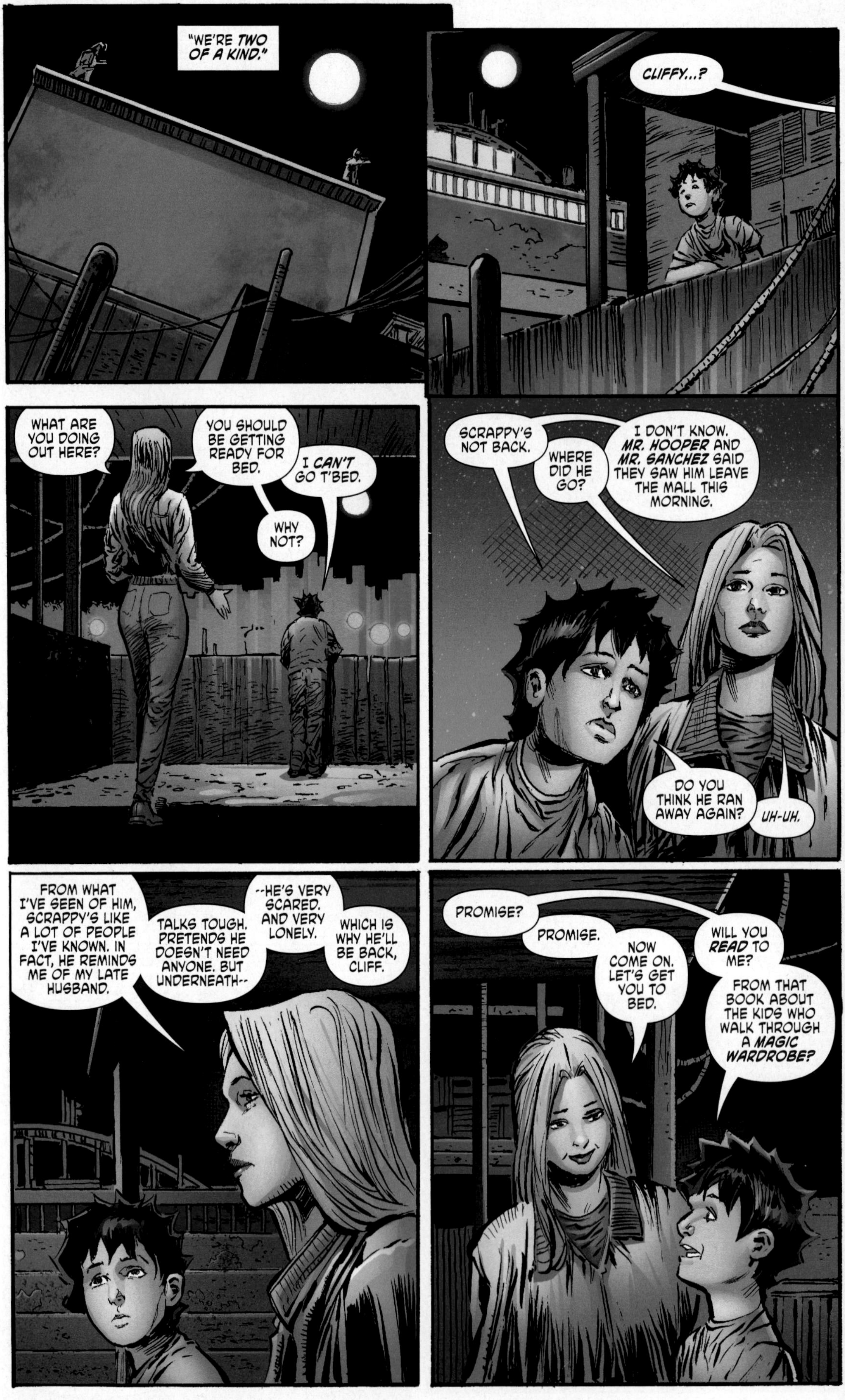
"WE'RE *TWO OF A KIND.*"
CLIFFY...?
WHAT ARE YOU DOING OUT HERE?
YOU SHOULD BE GETTING READY FOR BED.
I *CAN'T* GO T'BED.
WHY NOT?
SCRAPPY'S NOT BACK.
WHERE DID HE GO?
I DON'T KNOW. *MR. HOOPER* AND *MR. SANCHEZ* SAID THEY SAW HIM LEAVE THE MALL THIS MORNING.
DO YOU THINK HE RAN AWAY AGAIN?
UH-UH.
FROM WHAT I'VE SEEN OF HIM, SCRAPPY'S LIKE A LOT OF PEOPLE I'VE KNOWN. IN FACT, HE REMINDS ME OF MY LATE HUSBAND.
TALKS TOUGH. PRETENDS HE DOESN'T NEED ANYONE. BUT UNDERNEATH--
--HE'S VERY SCARED. AND VERY LONELY.
WHICH IS WHY HE'LL BE BACK, CLIFF.
PROMISE?
PROMISE.
NOW COME ON. LET'S GET YOU TO BED.
WILL YOU *READ* TO ME?
FROM THAT BOOK ABOUT THE KIDS WHO WALK THROUGH A *MAGIC WARDROBE?*

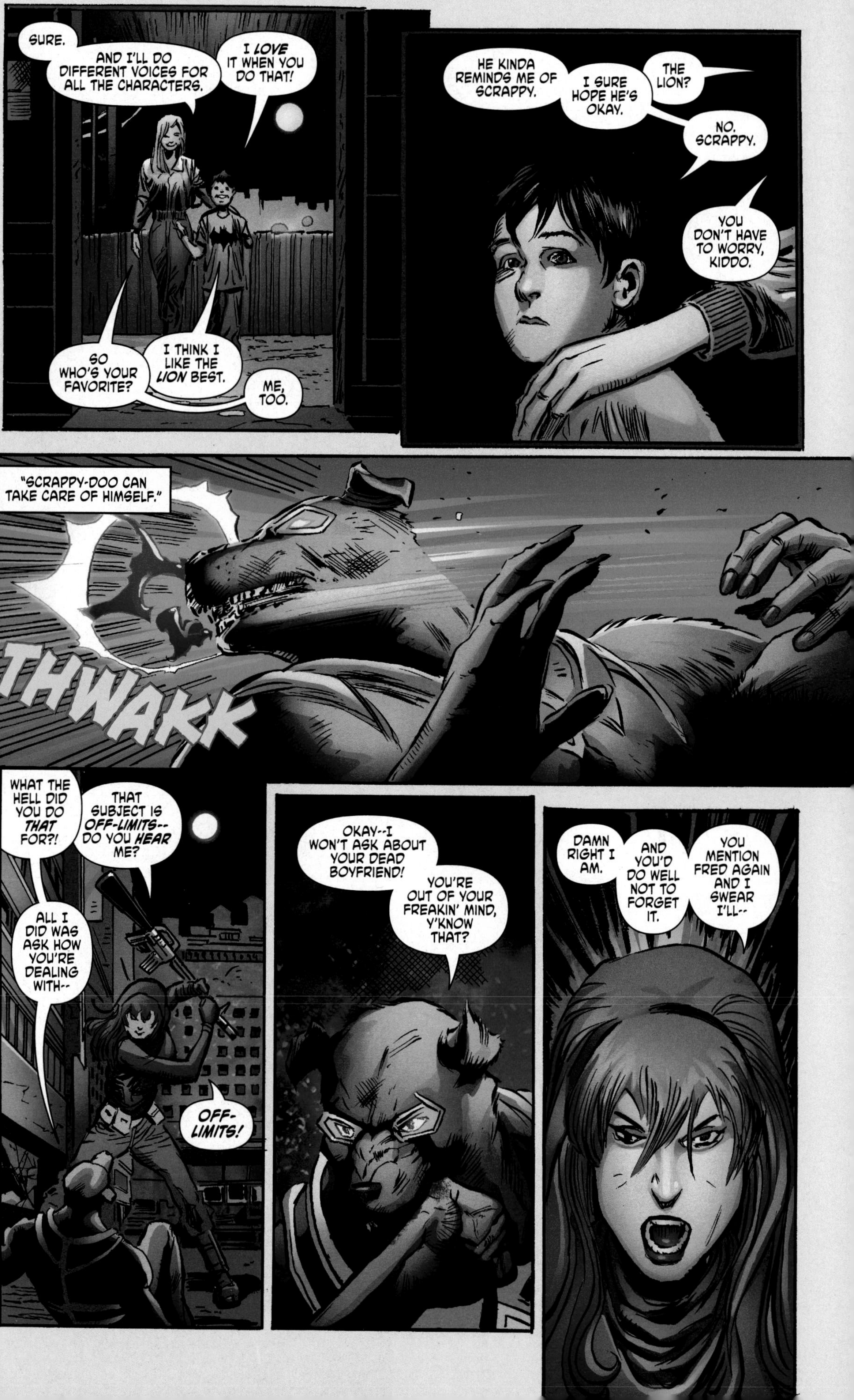
SURE.
AND I'LL DO DIFFERENT VOICES FOR ALL THE CHARACTERS.
I *LOVE* IT WHEN YOU DO THAT!
SO WHO'S YOUR FAVORITE?
I THINK I LIKE THE *LION* BEST.
ME, TOO.
HE KINDA REMINDS ME OF SCRAPPY.
I SURE HOPE HE'S OKAY.
THE LION?
NO. SCRAPPY.
YOU DON'T HAVE TO WORRY, KIDDO.
"SCRAPPY-DOO CAN TAKE CARE OF HIMSELF."
THWAKK
WHAT THE HELL DID YOU DO *THAT* FOR?!
THAT SUBJECT IS *OFF-LIMITS*-- DO YOU *HEAR* ME?
ALL I DID WAS ASK HOW YOU'RE DEALING WITH--
OFF-LIMITS!
OKAY--I WON'T ASK ABOUT YOUR DEAD BOYFRIEND!
YOU'RE OUT OF YOUR FREAKIN' MIND, Y'KNOW THAT?
DAMN RIGHT I AM.
AND YOU'D DO WELL NOT TO FORGET IT.
YOU MENTION FRED AGAIN AND I SWEAR I'LL--

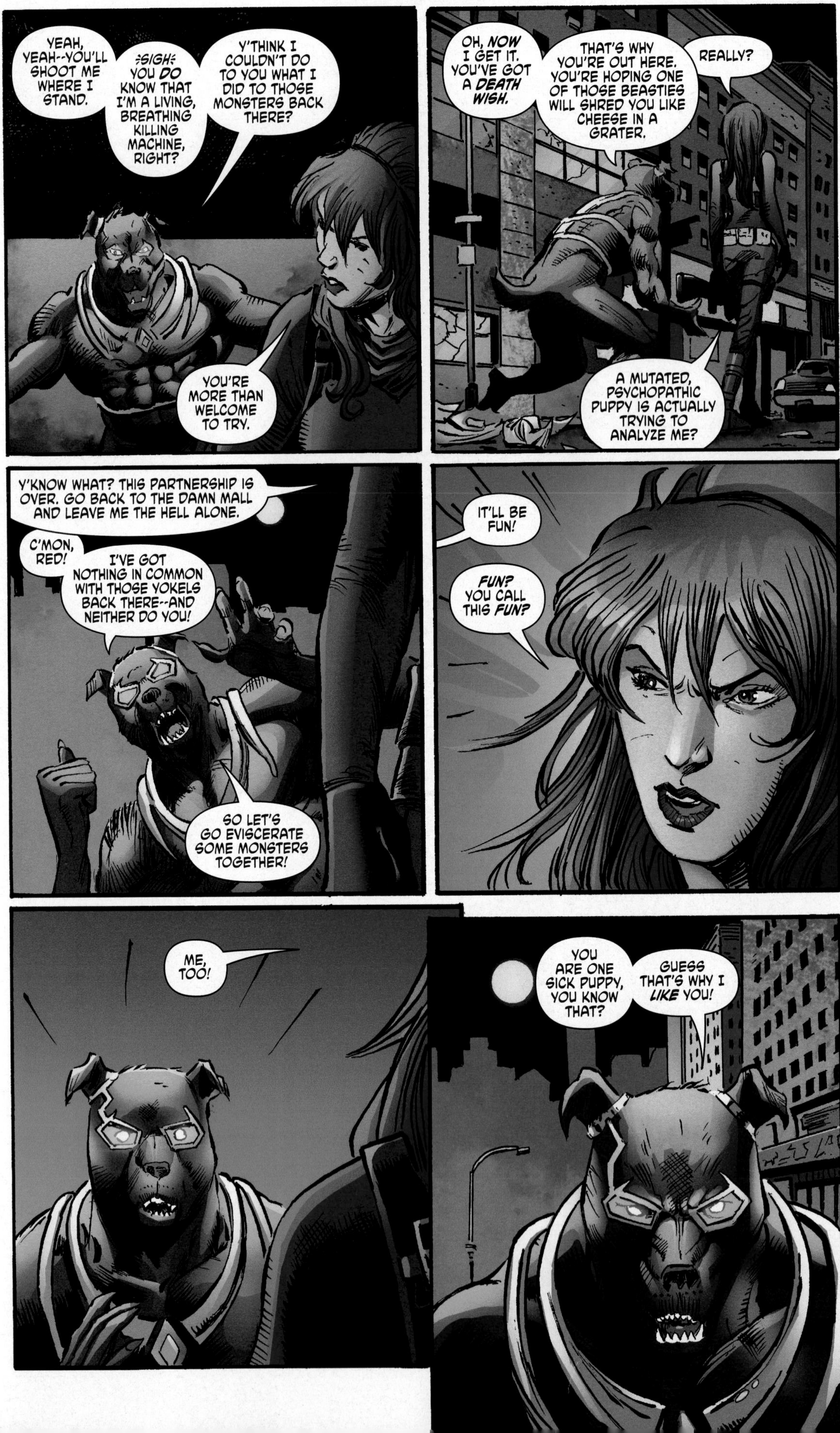
YEAH, YEAH--YOU'LL SHOOT ME WHERE I STAND.
SIGH YOU DO KNOW THAT I'M A LIVING, BREATHING KILLING MACHINE, RIGHT?
Y'THINK I COULDN'T DO TO YOU WHAT I DID TO THOSE MONSTERS BACK THERE?
YOU'RE MORE THAN WELCOME TO TRY.
OH, NOW I GET IT. YOU'VE GOT A DEATH WISH.
THAT'S WHY YOU'RE OUT HERE. YOU'RE HOPING ONE OF THOSE BEASTIES WILL SHRED YOU LIKE CHEESE IN A GRATER.
REALLY?
A MUTATED, PSYCHOPATHIC PUPPY IS ACTUALLY TRYING TO ANALYZE ME?
Y'KNOW WHAT? THIS PARTNERSHIP IS OVER. GO BACK TO THE DAMN MALL AND LEAVE ME THE HELL ALONE.
C'MON, RED!
I'VE GOT NOTHING IN COMMON WITH THOSE YOKELS BACK THERE--AND NEITHER DO YOU!
SO LET'S GO EVISCERATE SOME MONSTERS TOGETHER!
IT'LL BE FUN!
FUN? YOU CALL THIS FUN?
ME, TOO!
YOU ARE ONE SICK PUPPY, YOU KNOW THAT?
GUESS THAT'S WHY I LIKE YOU!

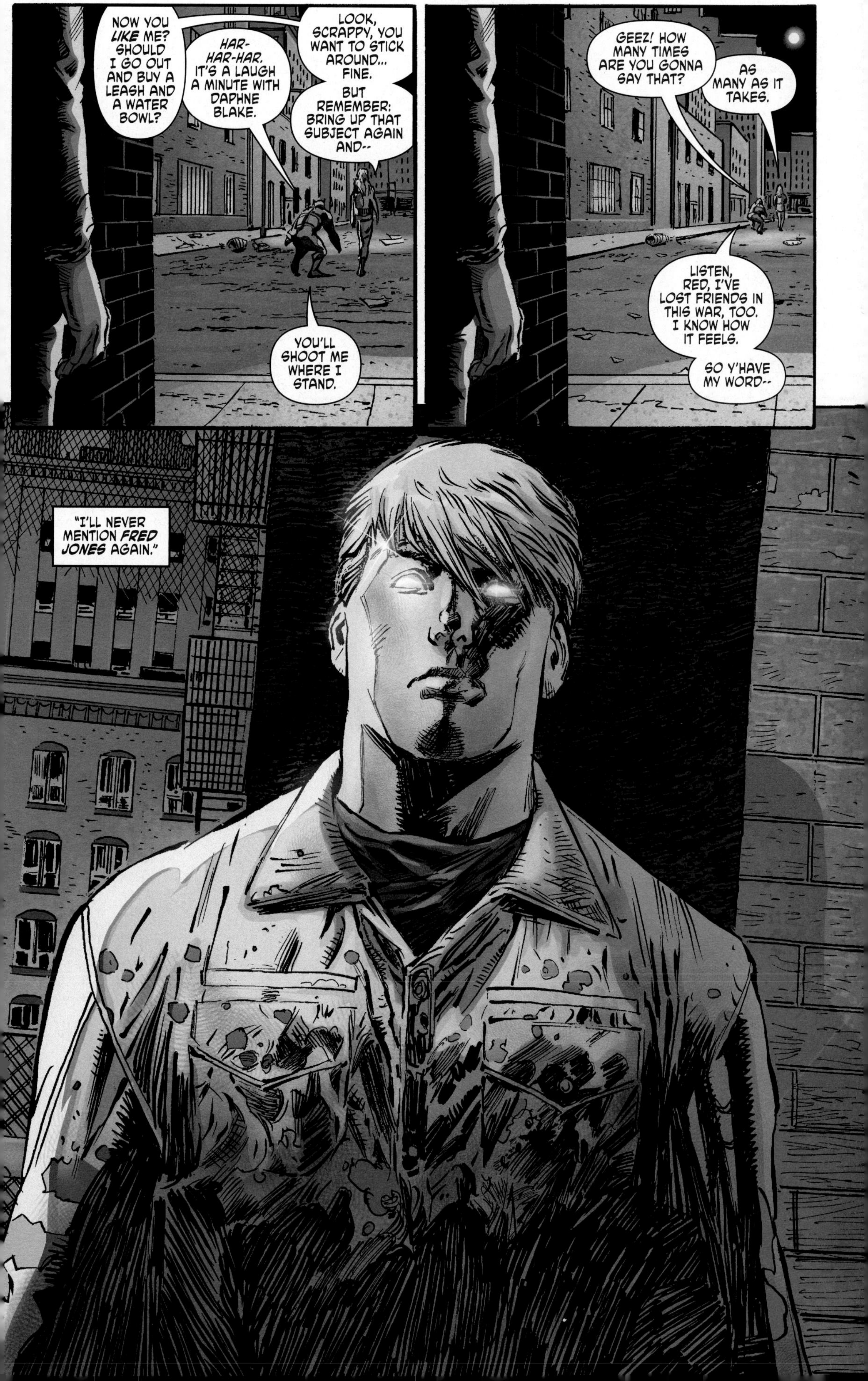

NOW YOU *LIKE* ME? SHOULD I GO OUT AND BUY A LEASH AND A WATER BOWL?
HAR-HAR-HAR. IT'S A LAUGH A MINUTE WITH DAPHNE BLAKE.
LOOK, SCRAPPY, YOU WANT TO STICK AROUND... FINE.
BUT REMEMBER: BRING UP THAT SUBJECT AGAIN AND--
YOU'LL SHOOT ME WHERE I STAND.
GEEZ! HOW MANY TIMES ARE YOU GONNA SAY THAT?
AS MANY AS IT TAKES.
LISTEN, RED, I'VE LOST FRIENDS IN THIS WAR, TOO. I KNOW HOW IT FEELS.
SO Y'HAVE MY WORD--
"I'LL NEVER MENTION *FRED JONES* AGAIN."

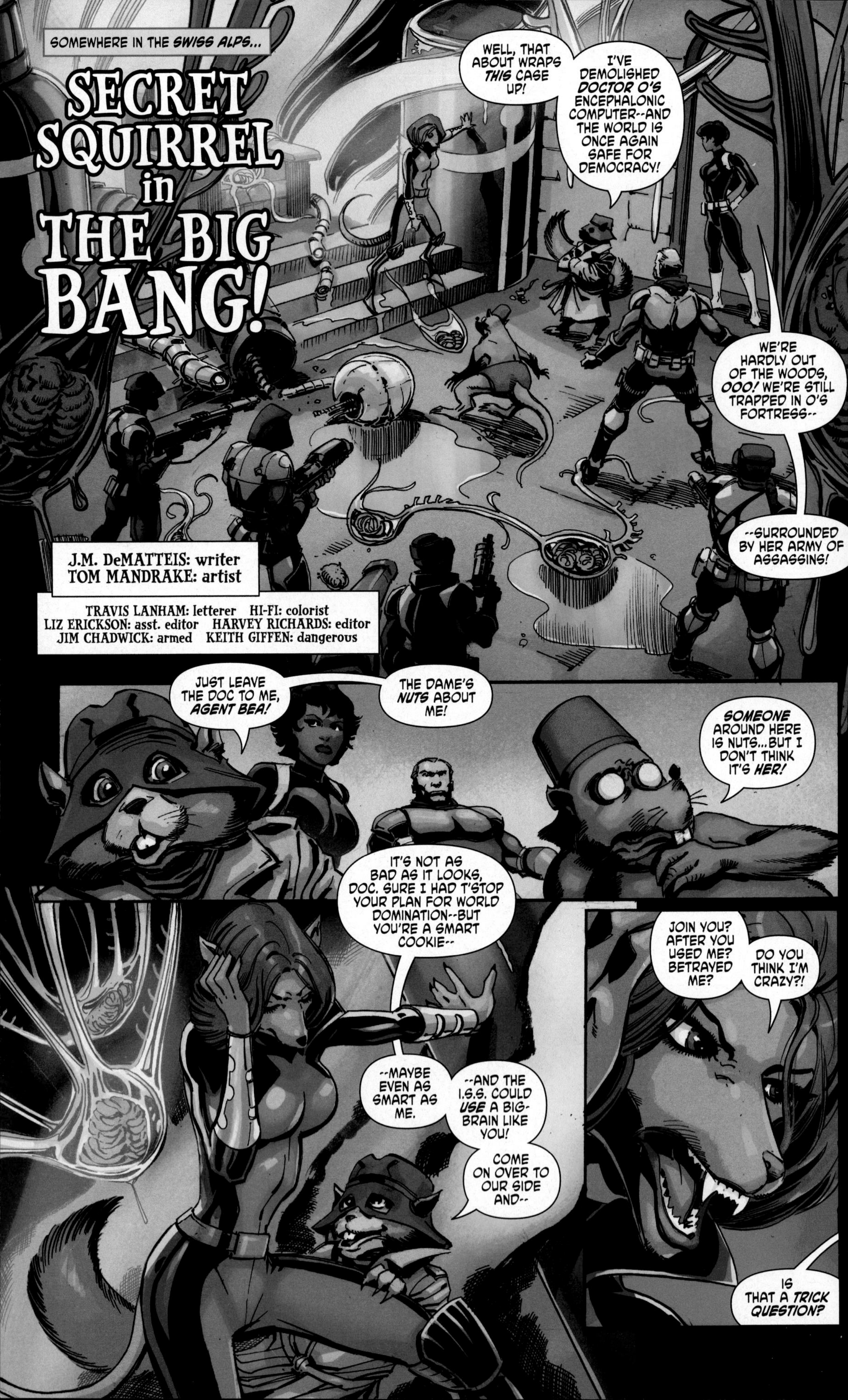
SOMEWHERE IN THE SWISS ALPS...
SECRET SQUIRREL in THE BIG BANG!
WELL, THAT ABOUT WRAPS THIS CASE UP!
I'VE DEMOLISHED DOCTOR O'S ENCEPHALONIC COMPUTER--AND THE WORLD IS ONCE AGAIN SAFE FOR DEMOCRACY!
WE'RE HARDLY OUT OF THE WOODS, OOO! WE'RE STILL TRAPPED IN O'S FORTRESS--
--SURROUNDED BY HER ARMY OF ASSASSINS!
J.M. DeMATTEIS: writer
TOM MANDRAKE: artist
TRAVIS LANHAM: letterer HI-FI: colorist
LIZ ERICKSON: asst. editor HARVEY RICHARDS: editor
JIM CHADWICK: armed KEITH GIFFEN: dangerous
JUST LEAVE THE DOC TO ME, AGENT BEA!
THE DAME'S NUTS ABOUT ME!
SOMEONE AROUND HERE IS NUTS...BUT I DON'T THINK IT'S HER!
IT'S NOT AS BAD AS IT LOOKS, DOC. SURE I HAD T'STOP YOUR PLAN FOR WORLD DOMINATION--BUT YOU'RE A SMART COOKIE--
--MAYBE EVEN AS SMART AS ME.
--AND THE I.S.S. COULD USE A BIG-BRAIN LIKE YOU!
COME ON OVER TO OUR SIDE AND--
JOIN YOU? AFTER YOU USED ME? BETRAYED ME?
DO YOU THINK I'M CRAZY?!
IS THAT A TRICK QUESTION?

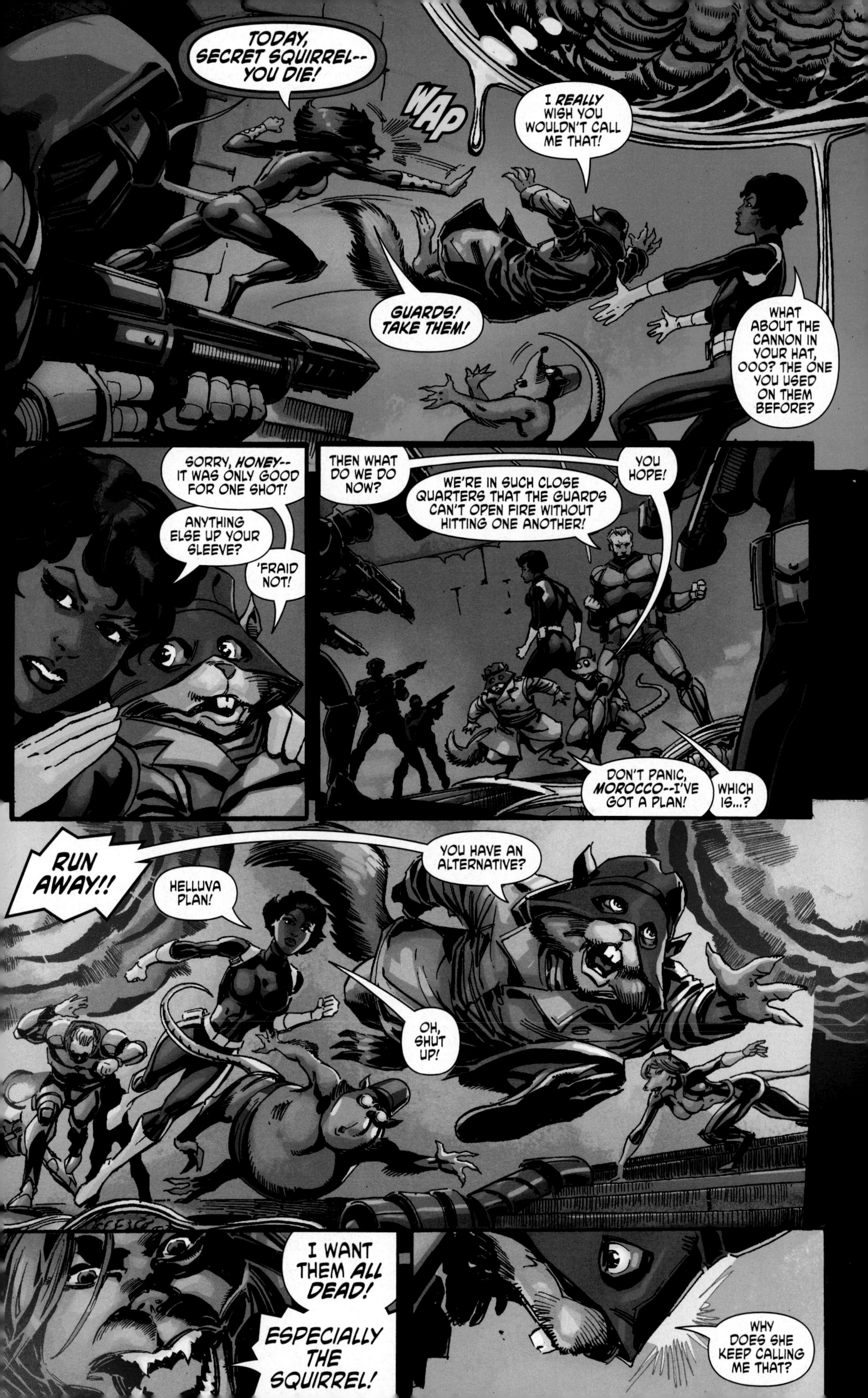
TODAY, SECRET SQUIRREL-- YOU DIE!
WAP
I REALLY WISH YOU WOULDN'T CALL ME THAT!
GUARDS! TAKE THEM!
WHAT ABOUT THE CANNON IN YOUR HAT, OOO? THE ONE YOU USED ON THEM BEFORE?
SORRY, HONEY-- IT WAS ONLY GOOD FOR ONE SHOT!
ANYTHING ELSE UP YOUR SLEEVE?
'FRAID NOT!
THEN WHAT DO WE DO NOW?
WE'RE IN SUCH CLOSE QUARTERS THAT THE GUARDS CAN'T OPEN FIRE WITHOUT HITTING ONE ANOTHER!
YOU HOPE!
DON'T PANIC, MOROCCO--I'VE GOT A PLAN!
WHICH IS...?
RUN AWAY!!
YOU HAVE AN ALTERNATIVE?
HELLUVA PLAN!
OH, SHUT UP!
I WANT THEM ALL DEAD!
ESPECIALLY THE SQUIRREL!
WHY DOES SHE KEEP CALLING ME THAT?

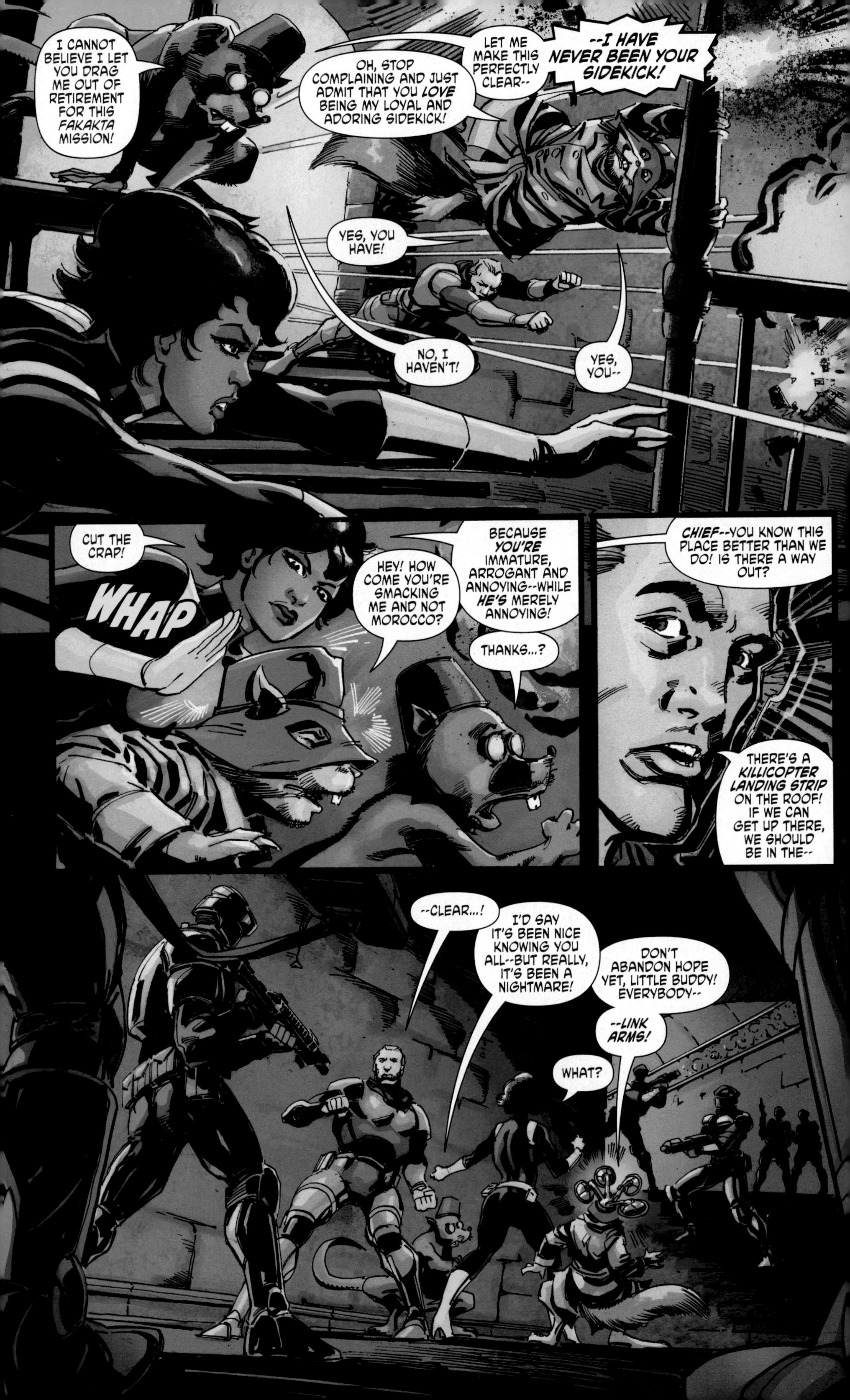
I CANNOT BELIEVE I LET YOU DRAG ME OUT OF RETIREMENT FOR THIS FAKAKTA MISSION!
OH, STOP COMPLAINING AND JUST ADMIT THAT YOU LOVE BEING MY LOYAL AND ADORING SIDEKICK!
LET ME MAKE THIS PERFECTLY CLEAR--
--I HAVE NEVER BEEN YOUR SIDEKICK!
YES, YOU HAVE!
NO, I HAVEN'T!
YES, YOU--
CUT THE CRAP!
WHAP
HEY! HOW COME YOU'RE SMACKING ME AND NOT MOROCCO?
BECAUSE YOU'RE IMMATURE, ARROGANT AND ANNOYING--WHILE HE'S MERELY ANNOYING!
THANKS...?
CHIEF--YOU KNOW THIS PLACE BETTER THAN WE DO! IS THERE A WAY OUT?
THERE'S A KILLICOPTER LANDING STRIP ON THE ROOF! IF WE CAN GET UP THERE, WE SHOULD BE IN THE--
--CLEAR...!
I'D SAY IT'S BEEN NICE KNOWING YOU ALL--BUT REALLY, IT'S BEEN A NIGHTMARE!
DON'T ABANDON HOPE YET, LITTLE BUDDY! EVERYBODY--
--LINK ARMS!
WHAT?

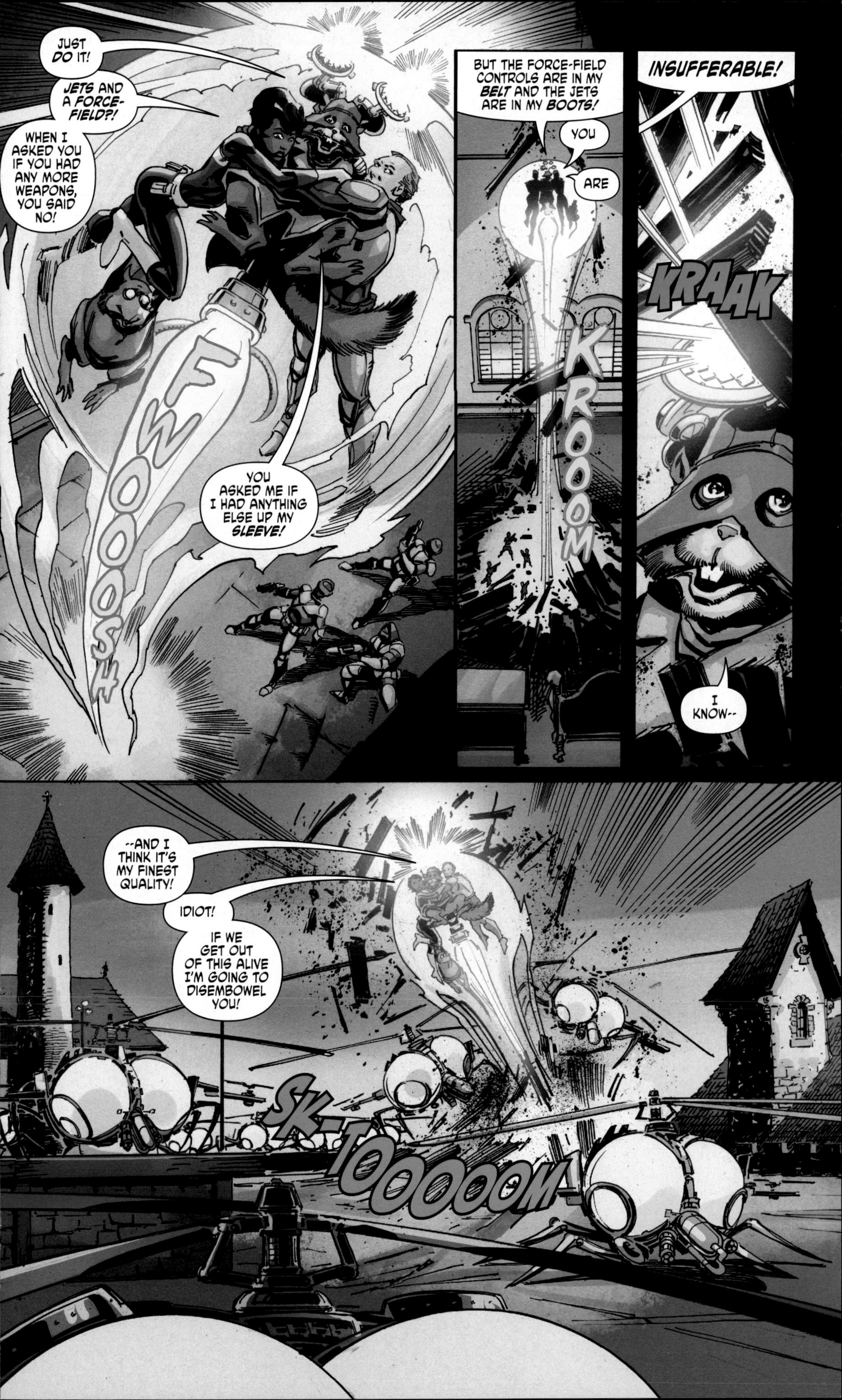
JUST DO IT!
JETS AND A FORCE-FIELD?!
WHEN I ASKED YOU IF YOU HAD ANY MORE WEAPONS, YOU SAID NO!
YOU ASKED ME IF I HAD ANYTHING ELSE UP MY SLEEVE!
FWOOOOOSH
BUT THE FORCE-FIELD CONTROLS ARE IN MY BELT AND THE JETS ARE IN MY BOOTS!
YOU
ARE
KROOOOM
INSUFFERABLE!
KRAAAK
I KNOW--
--AND I THINK IT'S MY FINEST QUALITY!
IDIOT!
IF WE GET OUT OF THIS ALIVE I'M GOING TO DISEMBOWEL YOU!
SK-TOOOOOOM

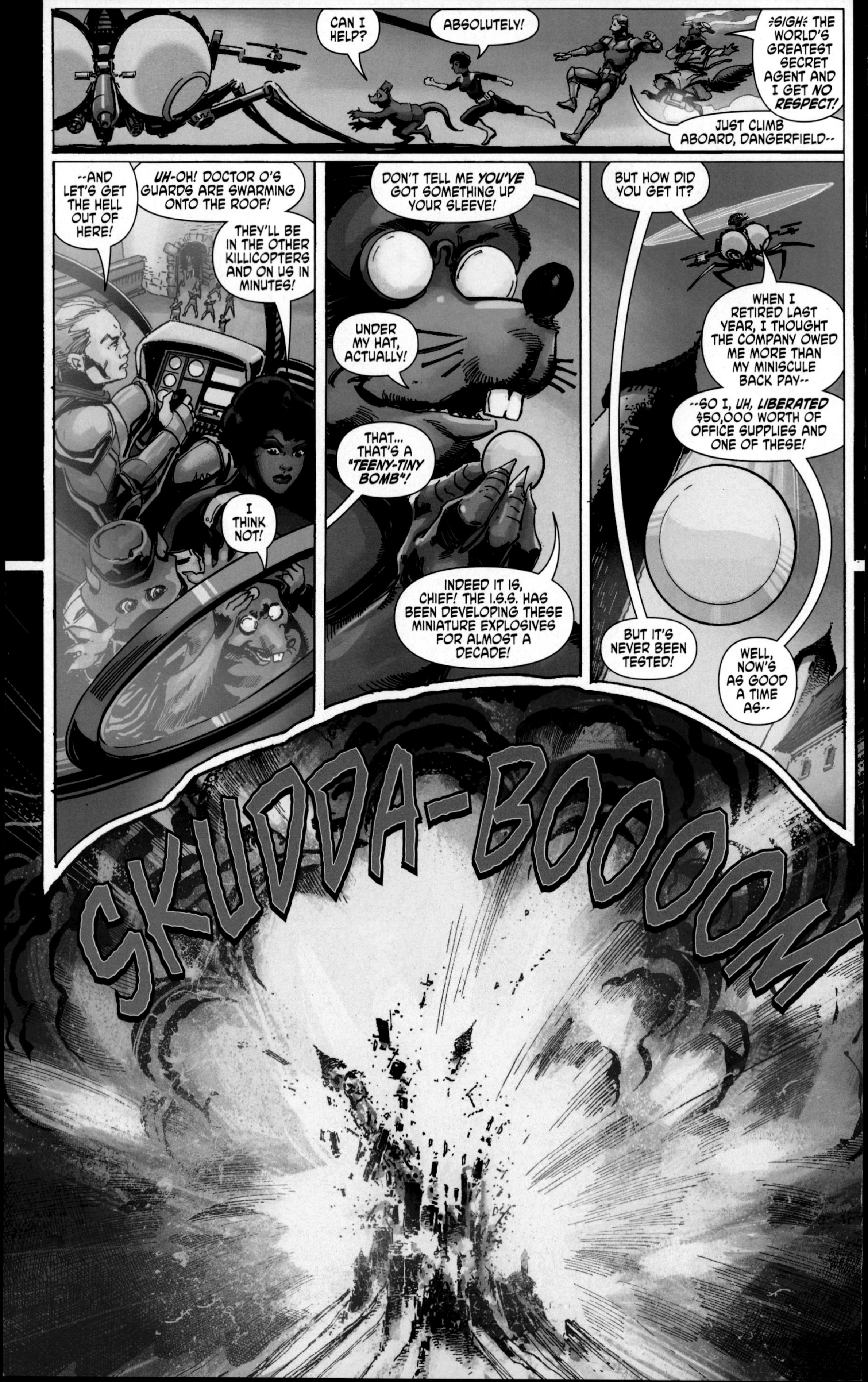
CAN I HELP?
ABSOLUTELY!
SIGH THE WORLD'S GREATEST SECRET AGENT AND I GET NO RESPECT!
JUST CLIMB ABOARD, DANGERFIELD--
--AND LET'S GET THE HELL OUT OF HERE!
UH-OH! DOCTOR O'S GUARDS ARE SWARMING ONTO THE ROOF!
THEY'LL BE IN THE OTHER KILLICOPTERS AND ON US IN MINUTES!
I THINK NOT!
DON'T TELL ME YOU'VE GOT SOMETHING UP YOUR SLEEVE!
UNDER MY HAT, ACTUALLY!
THAT... THAT'S A "TEENY-TINY BOMB"!
INDEED IT IS, CHIEF! THE I.S.S. HAS BEEN DEVELOPING THESE MINIATURE EXPLOSIVES FOR ALMOST A DECADE!
BUT HOW DID YOU GET IT?
WHEN I RETIRED LAST YEAR, I THOUGHT THE COMPANY OWED ME MORE THAN MY MINISCULE BACK PAY--
--SO I, UH, LIBERATED $50,000 WORTH OF OFFICE SUPPLIES AND ONE OF THESE!
BUT IT'S NEVER BEEN TESTED!
WELL, NOW'S AS GOOD A TIME AS--
SKUDDA-BOOOOOM

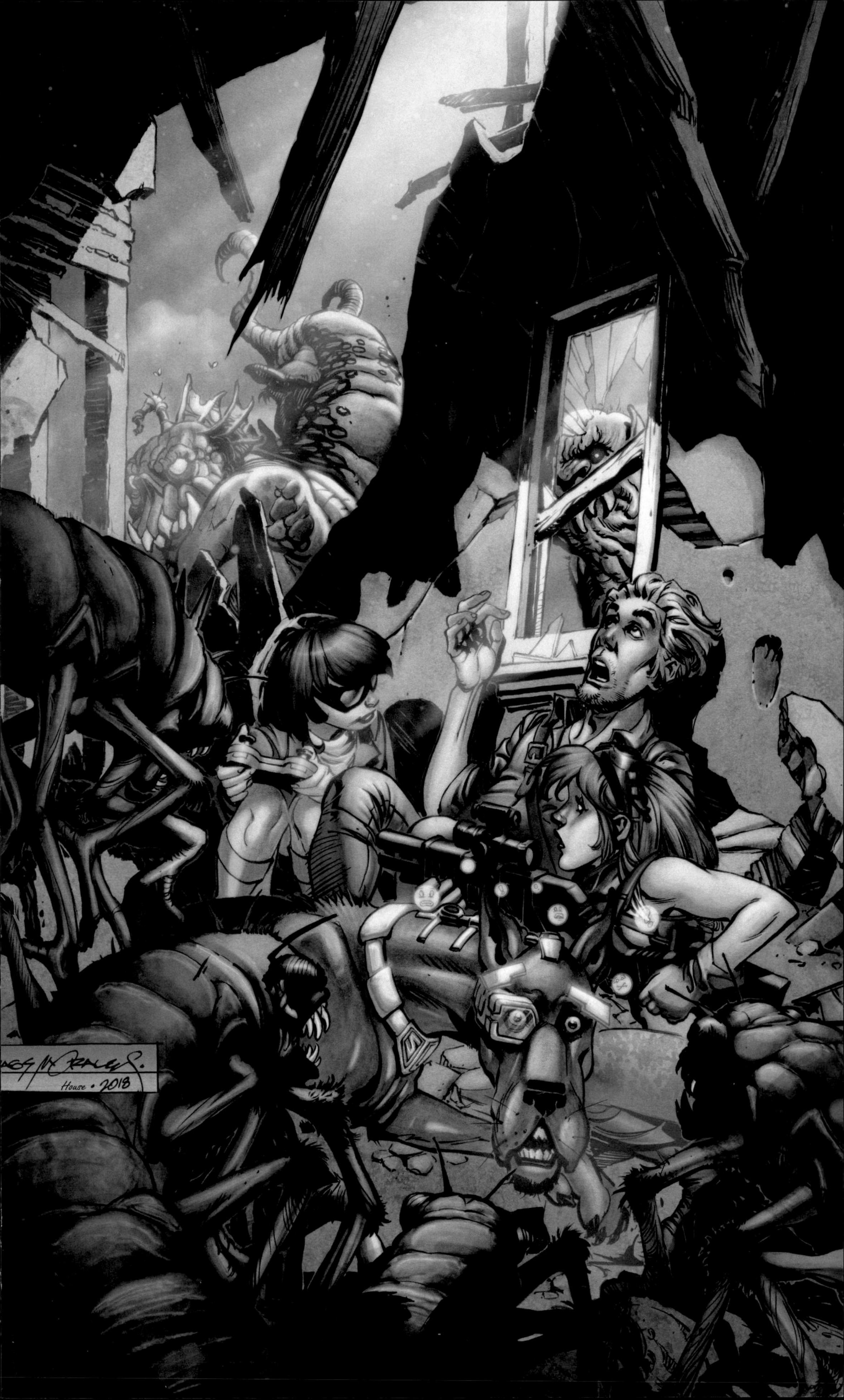
House • 2018

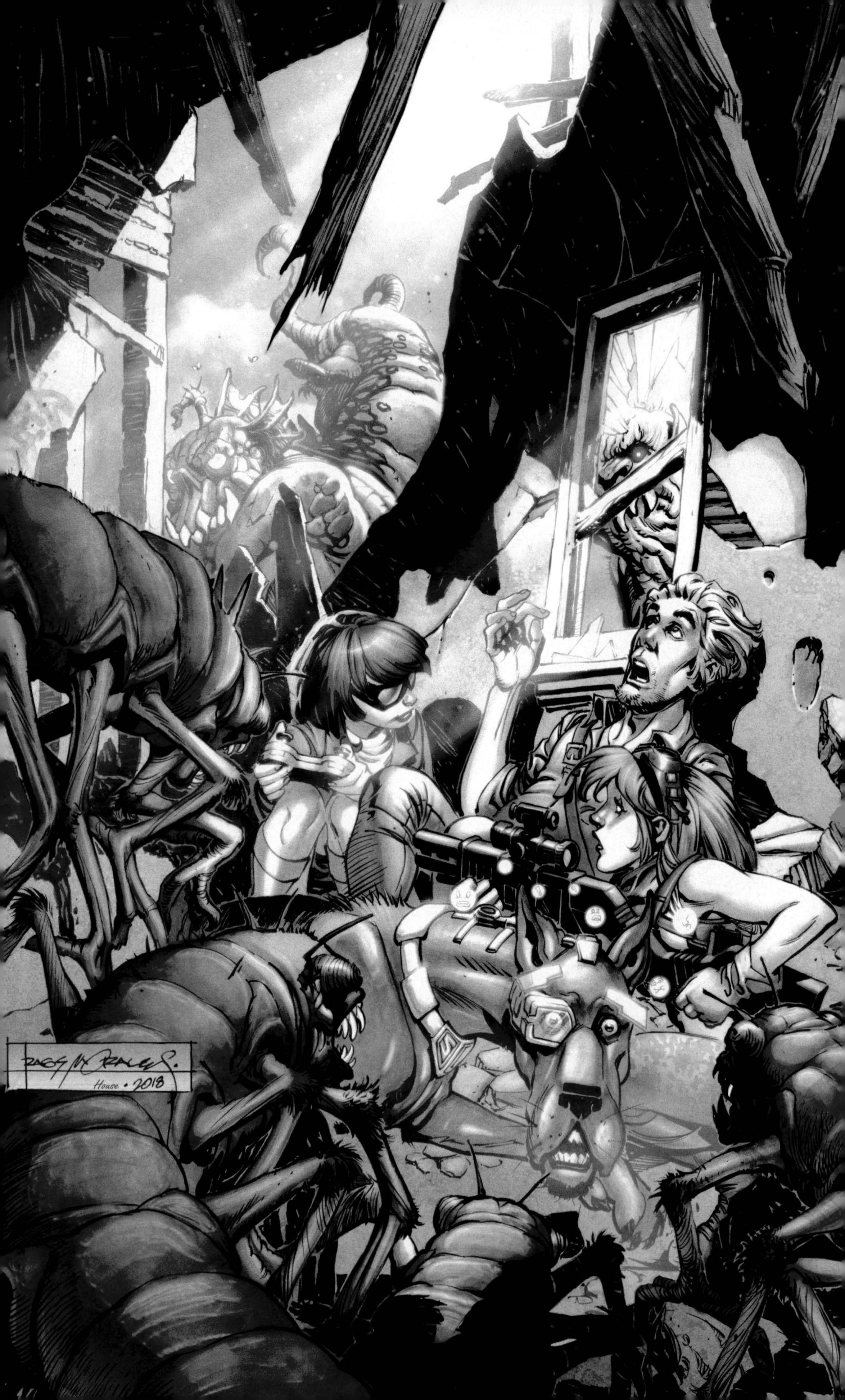
House • 2018

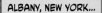

ALBANY, NEW YORK...

SIX MONTHS AGO...

SCOOBY APOCALYPSE

Fred(ish)!

KEITH GIFFEN & J.M. DeMATTEIS: writers   PAT OLLIFFE & TOM PALMER: artists

HI-FI: colors   TRAVIS LANHAM: letters   RAGS MORALES with ANDREW DALHOUSE: cover
LIZ ERICKSON: assistant editor   HARVEY RICHARDS: editor   JIM CHADWICK: nerves of steel

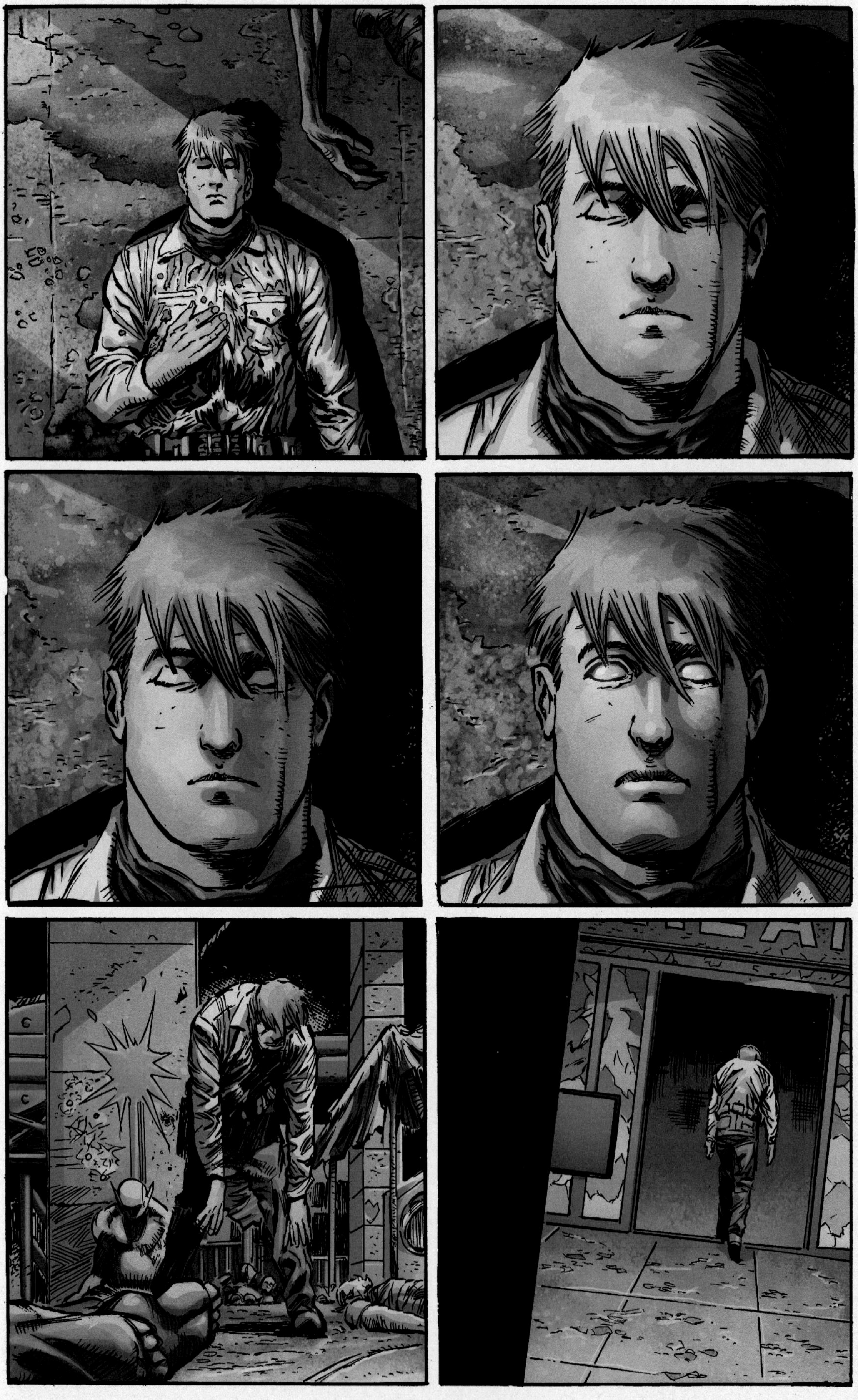

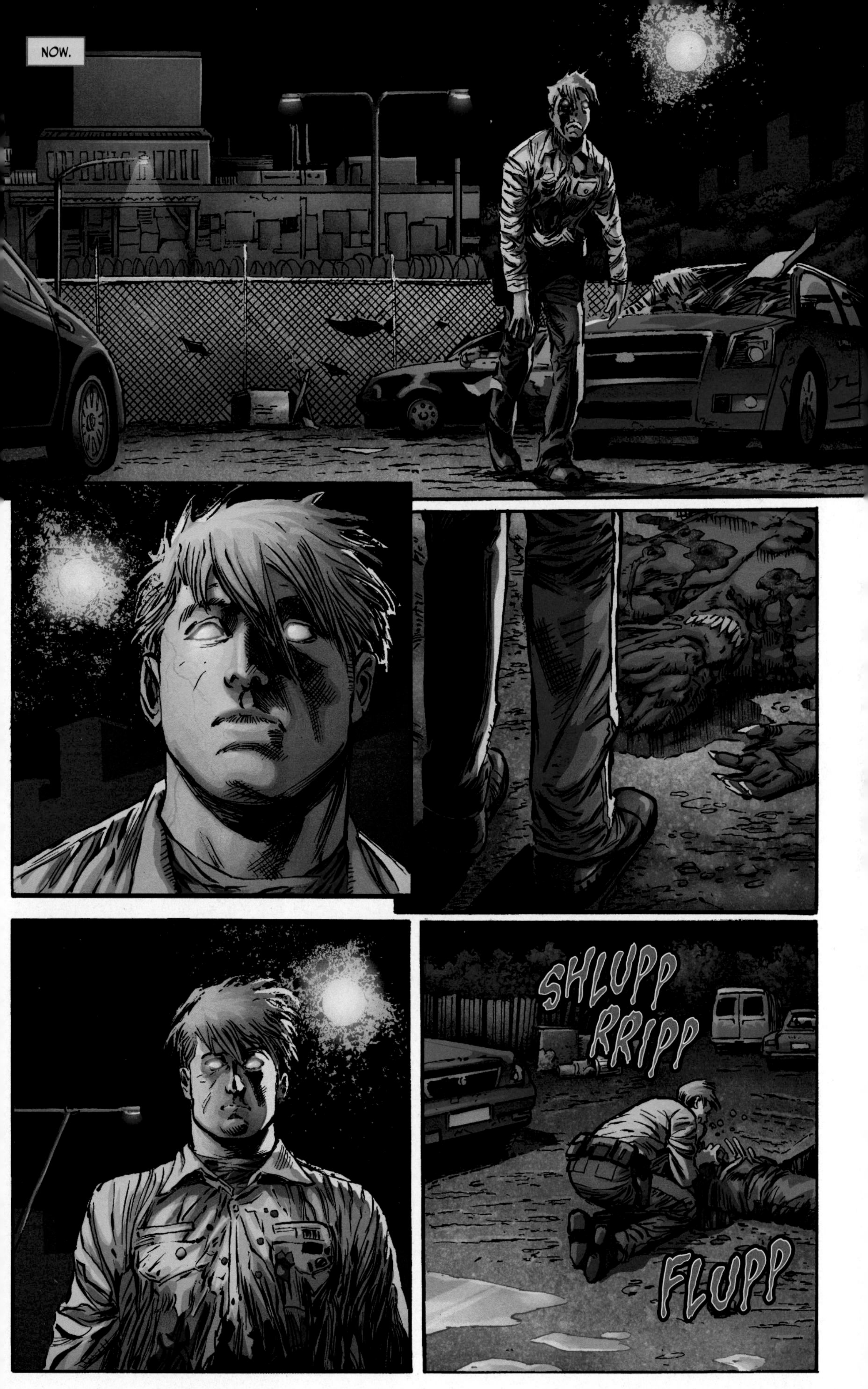
NOW.
SHLUPP
RRIPP
FLUPP

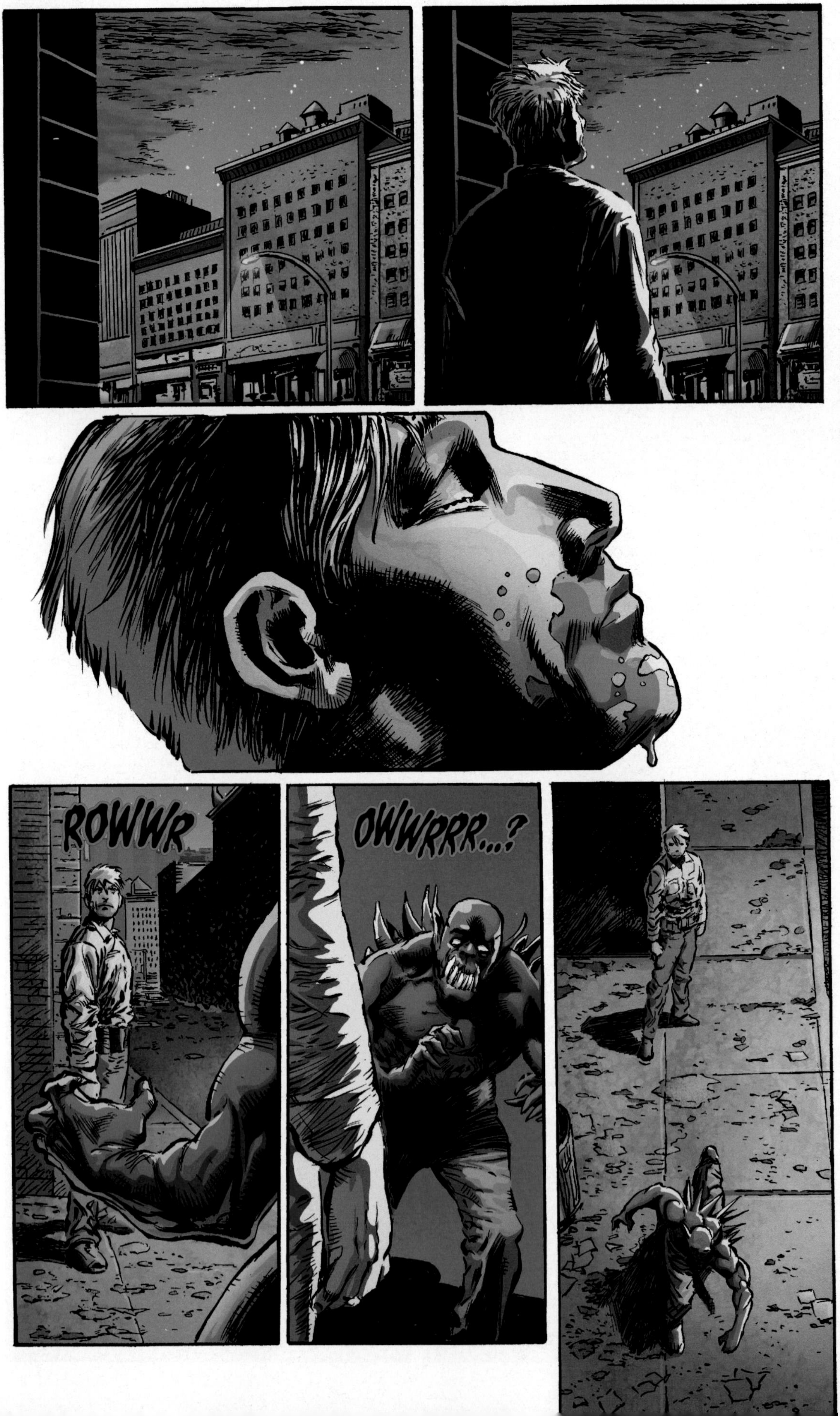
ROWWR
OWWRRR...?

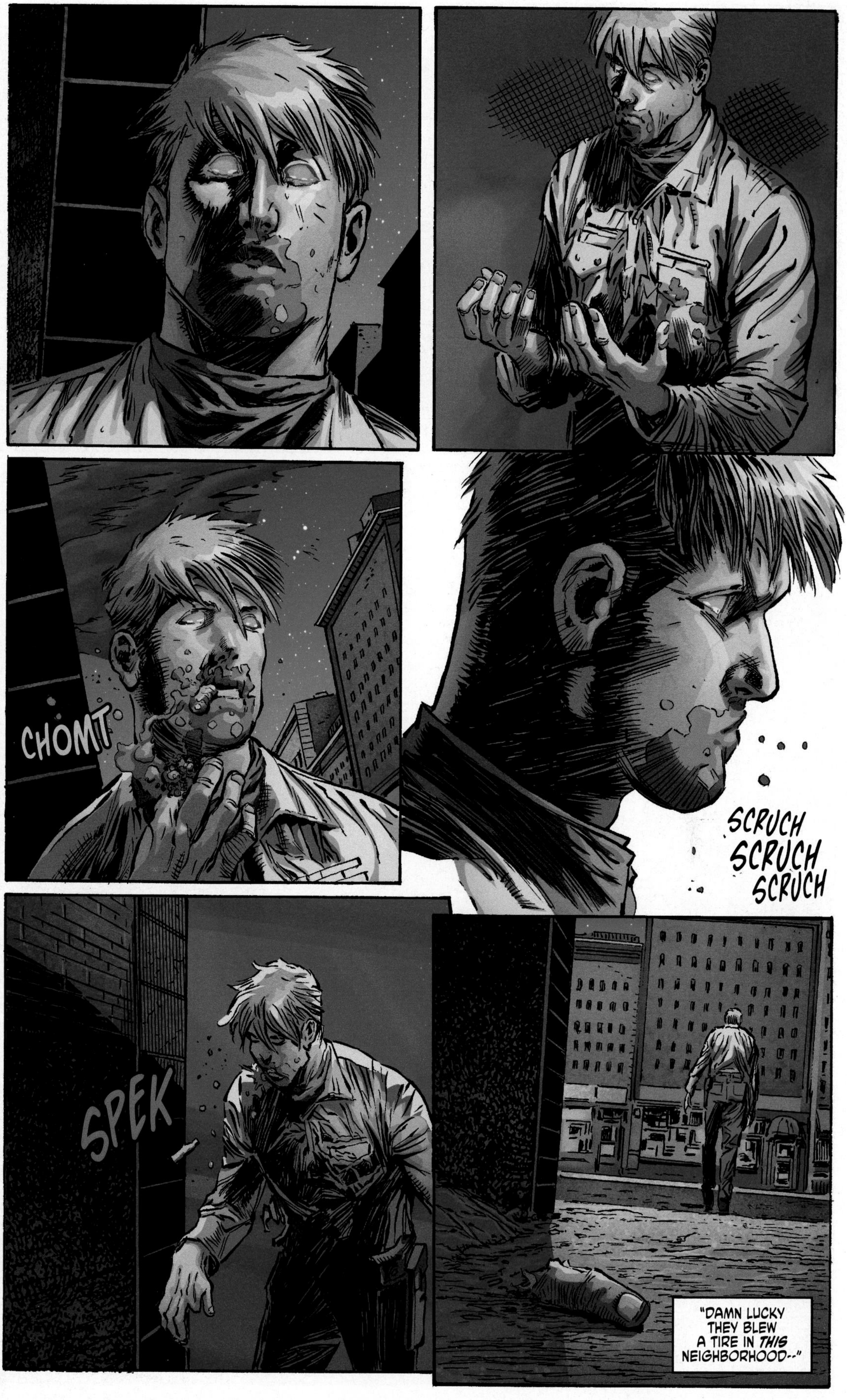
CHOMT
SCRUCH
SCRUCH
SCRUCH
SPEK
"DAMN LUCKY THEY BLEW A TIRE IN *THIS* NEIGHBORHOOD--"

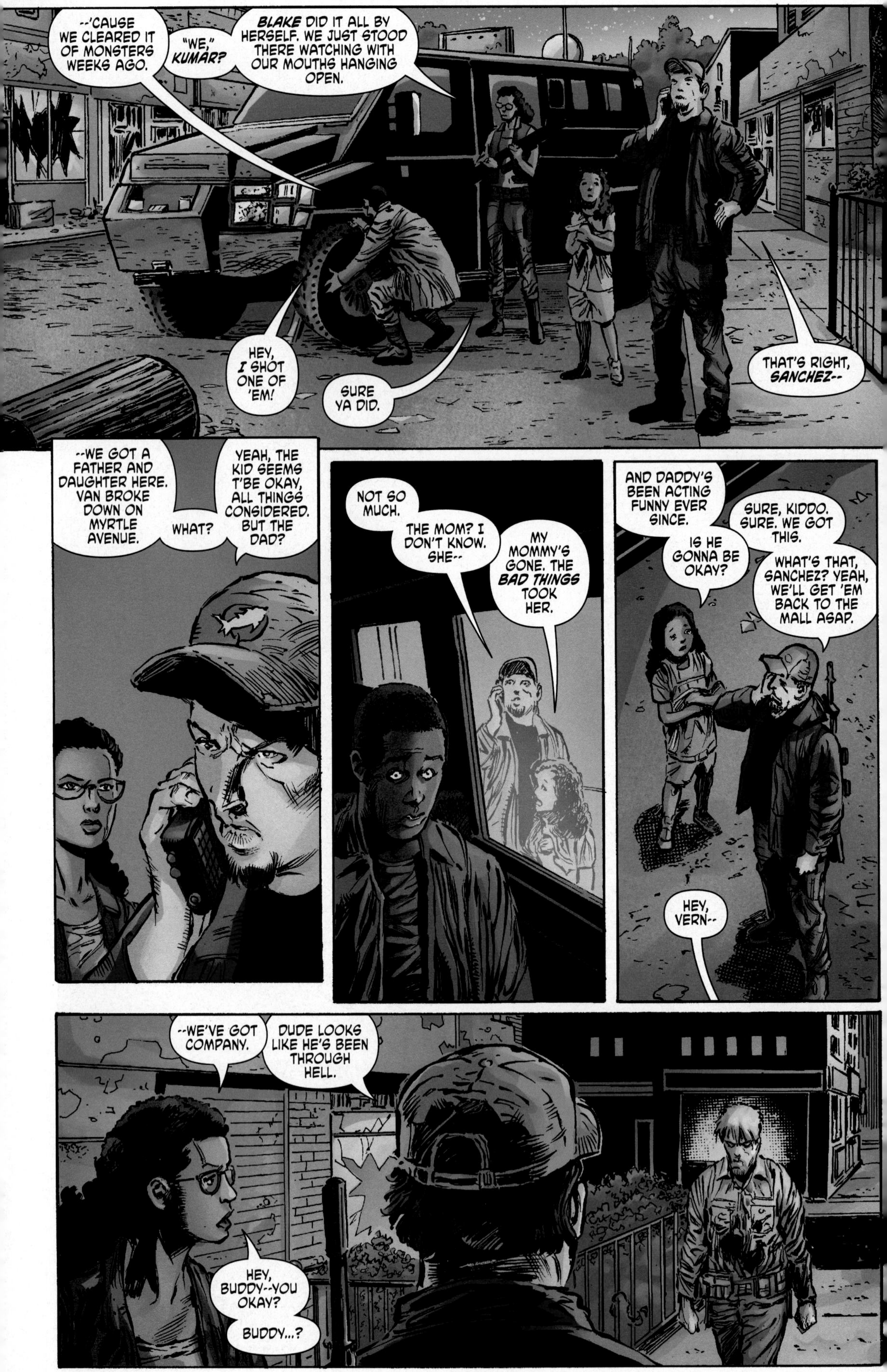
--'CAUSE WE CLEARED IT OF MONSTERS WEEKS AGO.
"WE," KUMAR?
BLAKE DID IT ALL BY HERSELF. WE JUST STOOD THERE WATCHING WITH OUR MOUTHS HANGING OPEN.
HEY, I SHOT ONE OF 'EM!
SURE YA DID.
THAT'S RIGHT, SANCHEZ--
--WE GOT A FATHER AND DAUGHTER HERE. VAN BROKE DOWN ON MYRTLE AVENUE.
WHAT?
YEAH, THE KID SEEMS T'BE OKAY, ALL THINGS CONSIDERED. BUT THE DAD?
NOT SO MUCH.
THE MOM? I DON'T KNOW. SHE--
MY MOMMY'S GONE. THE BAD THINGS TOOK HER.
AND DADDY'S BEEN ACTING FUNNY EVER SINCE.
IS HE GONNA BE OKAY?
SURE, KIDDO. SURE. WE GOT THIS.
WHAT'S THAT, SANCHEZ? YEAH, WE'LL GET 'EM BACK TO THE MALL ASAP.
HEY, VERN--
--WE'VE GOT COMPANY.
DUDE LOOKS LIKE HE'S BEEN THROUGH HELL.
HEY, BUDDY--YOU OKAY?
BUDDY...?

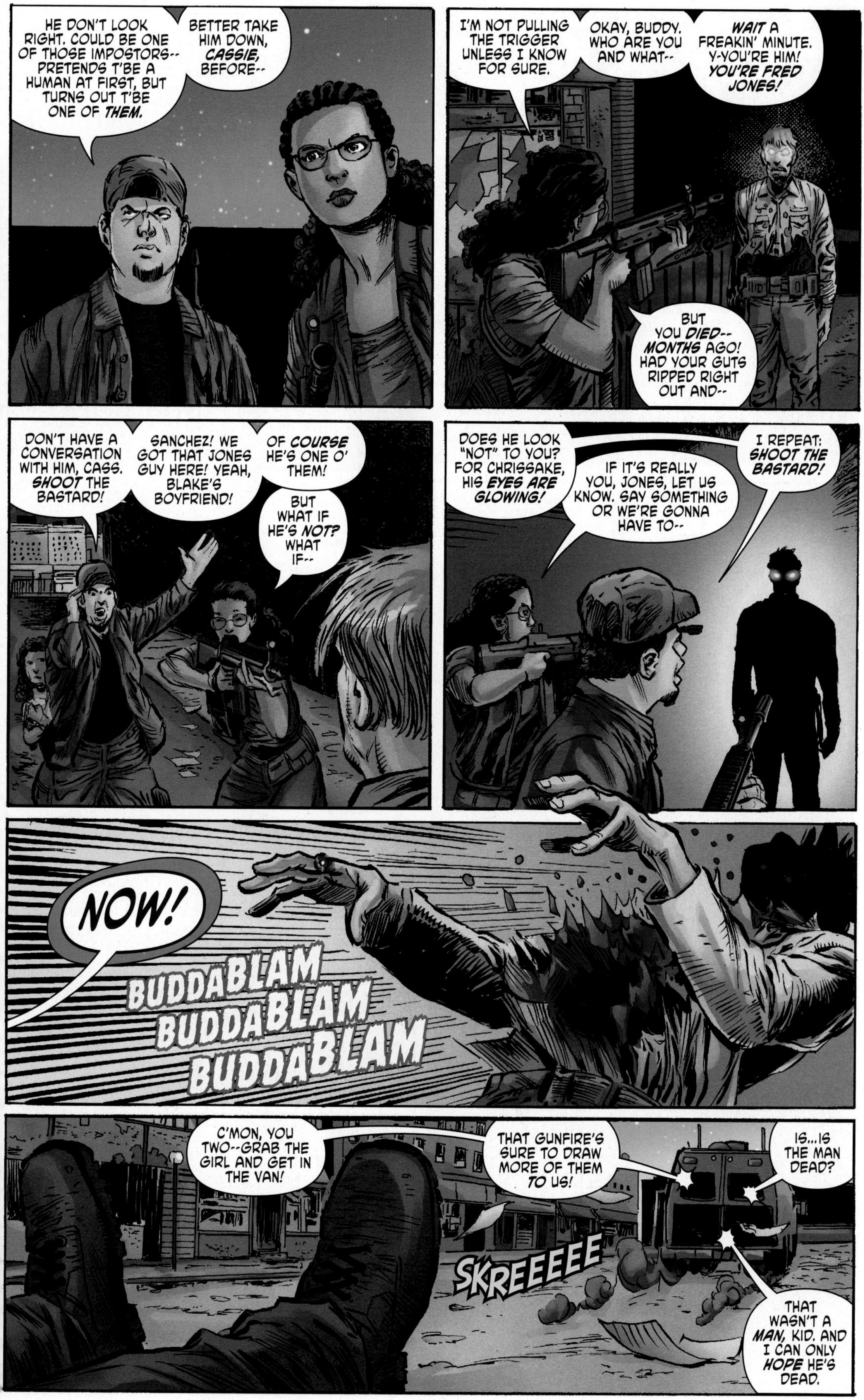
HE DON'T LOOK RIGHT. COULD BE ONE OF THOSE IMPOSTORS--PRETENDS T'BE A HUMAN AT FIRST, BUT TURNS OUT T'BE ONE OF *THEM.*
BETTER TAKE HIM DOWN, *CASSIE,* BEFORE--
I'M NOT PULLING THE TRIGGER UNLESS I KNOW FOR SURE.
OKAY, BUDDY. WHO ARE YOU AND WHAT--
WAIT A FREAKIN' MINUTE. Y-YOU'RE HIM! *YOU'RE FRED JONES!*
BUT YOU *DIED--MONTHS* AGO! HAD YOUR GUTS RIPPED RIGHT OUT AND--
DON'T HAVE A CONVERSATION WITH HIM, CASS. *SHOOT* THE BASTARD!
SANCHEZ! WE GOT THAT JONES GUY HERE! YEAH, BLAKE'S BOYFRIEND!
OF *COURSE* HE'S ONE O' THEM!
BUT WHAT IF HE'S *NOT?* WHAT IF--
DOES HE LOOK "NOT" TO YOU? FOR CHRISSAKE, HIS *EYES ARE GLOWING!*
IF IT'S REALLY YOU, JONES, LET US KNOW. SAY SOMETHING OR WE'RE GONNA HAVE TO--
I REPEAT: *SHOOT THE BASTARD!*
NOW!
BUDDABLAM BUDDABLAM BUDDABLAM
C'MON, YOU TWO--GRAB THE GIRL AND GET IN THE VAN!
THAT GUNFIRE'S SURE TO DRAW MORE OF THEM *TO* US!
IS...IS THE MAN DEAD?
SKREEEEE
THAT WASN'T A *MAN,* KID. AND I CAN ONLY *HOPE* HE'S DEAD.

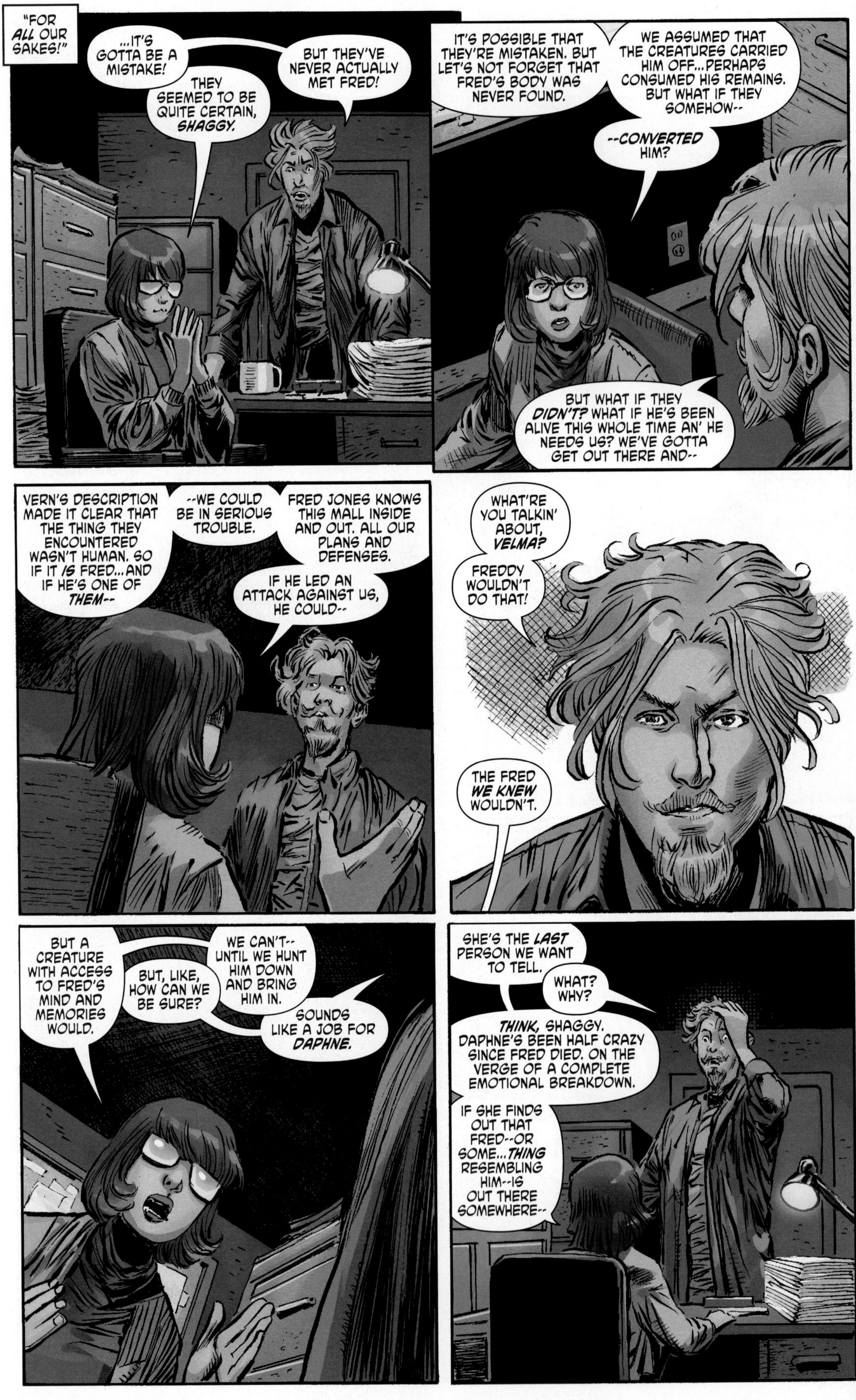
"FOR *ALL* OUR SAKES!"
...IT'S GOTTA BE A MISTAKE!
BUT THEY'VE NEVER ACTUALLY MET FRED!
THEY SEEMED TO BE QUITE CERTAIN, *SHAGGY.*
IT'S POSSIBLE THAT THEY'RE MISTAKEN. BUT LET'S NOT FORGET THAT FRED'S BODY WAS NEVER FOUND.
WE ASSUMED THAT THE CREATURES CARRIED HIM OFF...PERHAPS CONSUMED HIS REMAINS. BUT WHAT IF THEY SOMEHOW--
--CONVERTED HIM?
BUT WHAT IF THEY *DIDN'T?* WHAT IF HE'S BEEN ALIVE THIS WHOLE TIME AN' HE NEEDS US? WE'VE GOTTA GET OUT THERE AND--
VERN'S DESCRIPTION MADE IT CLEAR THAT THE THING THEY ENCOUNTERED WASN'T HUMAN. SO IF IT *IS* FRED...AND IF HE'S ONE OF *THEM--*
--WE COULD BE IN SERIOUS TROUBLE.
FRED JONES KNOWS THIS MALL INSIDE AND OUT. ALL OUR PLANS AND DEFENSES.
IF HE LED AN ATTACK AGAINST US, HE COULD--
WHAT'RE YOU TALKIN' ABOUT, *VELMA?*
FREDDY WOULDN'T DO THAT!
THE FRED *WE KNEW* WOULDN'T.
BUT A CREATURE WITH ACCESS TO FRED'S MIND AND MEMORIES WOULD.
BUT, LIKE, HOW CAN WE BE SURE?
WE CAN'T-- UNTIL WE HUNT HIM DOWN AND BRING HIM IN.
SOUNDS LIKE A JOB FOR *DAPHNE.*
SHE'S THE *LAST* PERSON WE WANT TO TELL.
WHAT? WHY?
THINK, SHAGGY. DAPHNE'S BEEN HALF CRAZY SINCE FRED DIED. ON THE VERGE OF A COMPLETE EMOTIONAL BREAKDOWN.
IF SHE FINDS OUT THAT FRED--OR SOME...*THING* RESEMBLING HIM--IS OUT THERE SOMEWHERE--

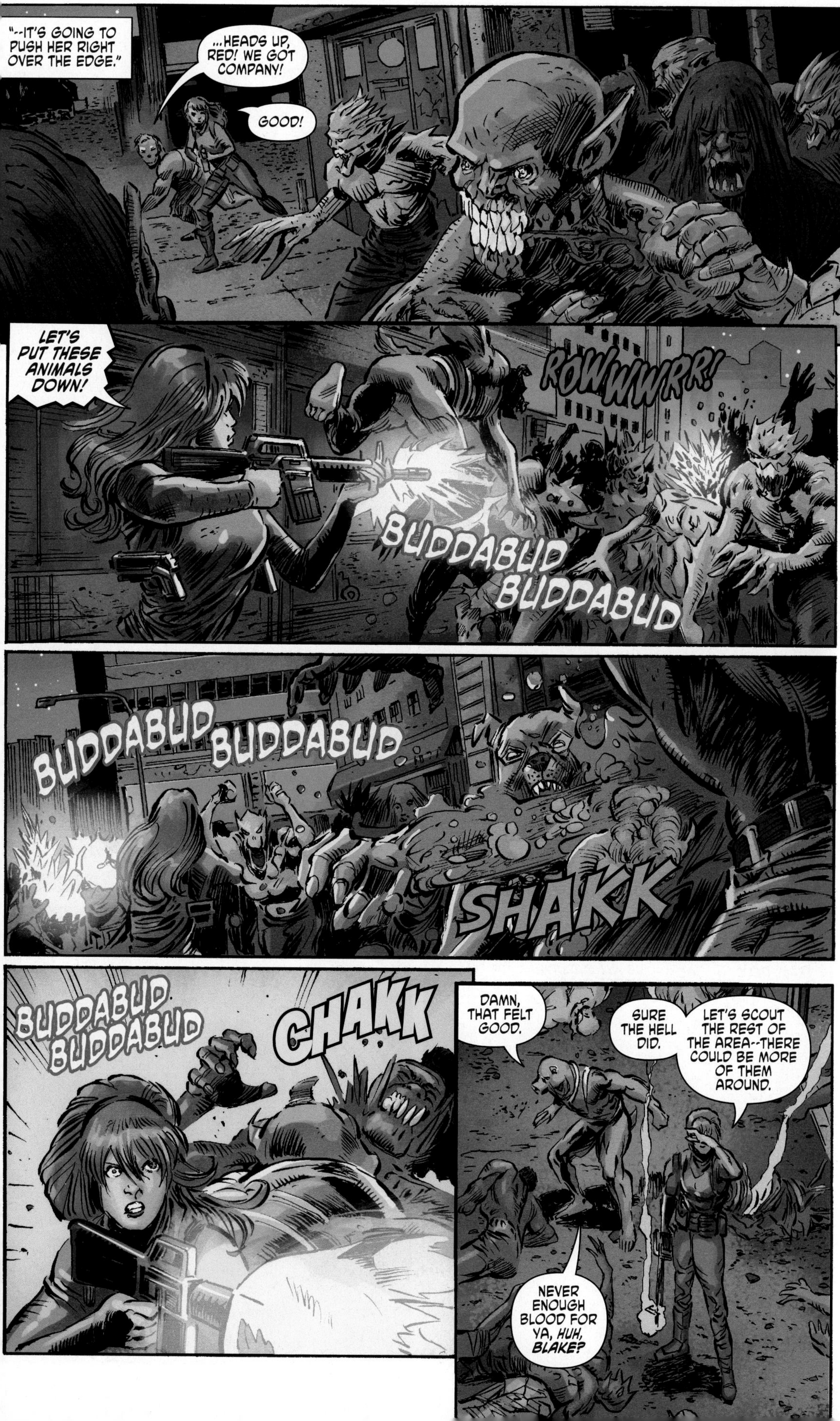
"--IT'S GOING TO PUSH HER RIGHT OVER THE EDGE."
...HEADS UP, RED! WE GOT COMPANY!
GOOD!
LET'S PUT THESE ANIMALS DOWN!
ROWWWRR!
BUDDABUD BUDDABUD
BUDDABUD BUDDABUD
SHAKK
BUDDABUD BUDDABUD
CHAKK
DAMN, THAT FELT GOOD.
SURE THE HELL DID.
LET'S SCOUT THE REST OF THE AREA--THERE COULD BE MORE OF THEM AROUND.
NEVER ENOUGH BLOOD FOR YA, HUH, BLAKE?

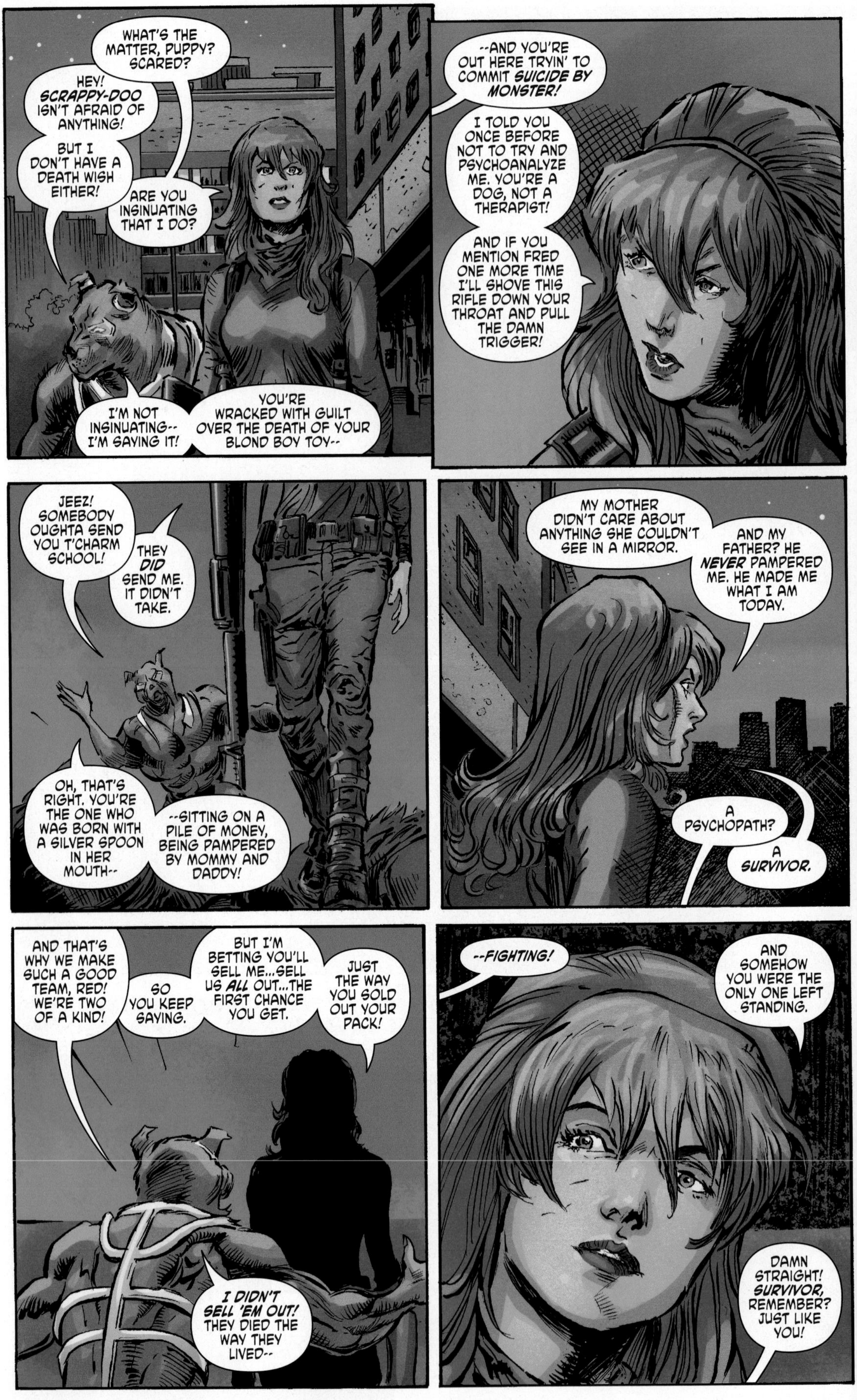
WHAT'S THE MATTER, PUPPY? SCARED?
HEY! SCRAPPY-DOO ISN'T AFRAID OF ANYTHING!
BUT I DON'T HAVE A DEATH WISH EITHER!
ARE YOU INSINUATING THAT I DO?
I'M NOT INSINUATING-- I'M SAYING IT!
YOU'RE WRACKED WITH GUILT OVER THE DEATH OF YOUR BLOND BOY TOY--
--AND YOU'RE OUT HERE TRYIN' TO COMMIT SUICIDE BY MONSTER!
I TOLD YOU ONCE BEFORE NOT TO TRY AND PSYCHOANALYZE ME. YOU'RE A DOG, NOT A THERAPIST!
AND IF YOU MENTION FRED ONE MORE TIME I'LL SHOVE THIS RIFLE DOWN YOUR THROAT AND PULL THE DAMN TRIGGER!
JEEZ! SOMEBODY OUGHTA SEND YOU T'CHARM SCHOOL!
THEY DID SEND ME. IT DIDN'T TAKE.
OH, THAT'S RIGHT. YOU'RE THE ONE WHO WAS BORN WITH A SILVER SPOON IN HER MOUTH--
--SITTING ON A PILE OF MONEY, BEING PAMPERED BY MOMMY AND DADDY!
MY MOTHER DIDN'T CARE ABOUT ANYTHING SHE COULDN'T SEE IN A MIRROR.
AND MY FATHER? HE NEVER PAMPERED ME. HE MADE ME WHAT I AM TODAY.
A PSYCHOPATH?
A SURVIVOR.
AND THAT'S WHY WE MAKE SUCH A GOOD TEAM, RED! WE'RE TWO OF A KIND!
SO YOU KEEP SAYING.
BUT I'M BETTING YOU'LL SELL ME...SELL US ALL OUT...THE FIRST CHANCE YOU GET.
JUST THE WAY YOU SOLD OUT YOUR PACK!
I DIDN'T SELL 'EM OUT! THEY DIED THE WAY THEY LIVED--
--FIGHTING!
AND SOMEHOW YOU WERE THE ONLY ONE LEFT STANDING.
DAMN STRAIGHT! SURVIVOR, REMEMBER? JUST LIKE YOU!

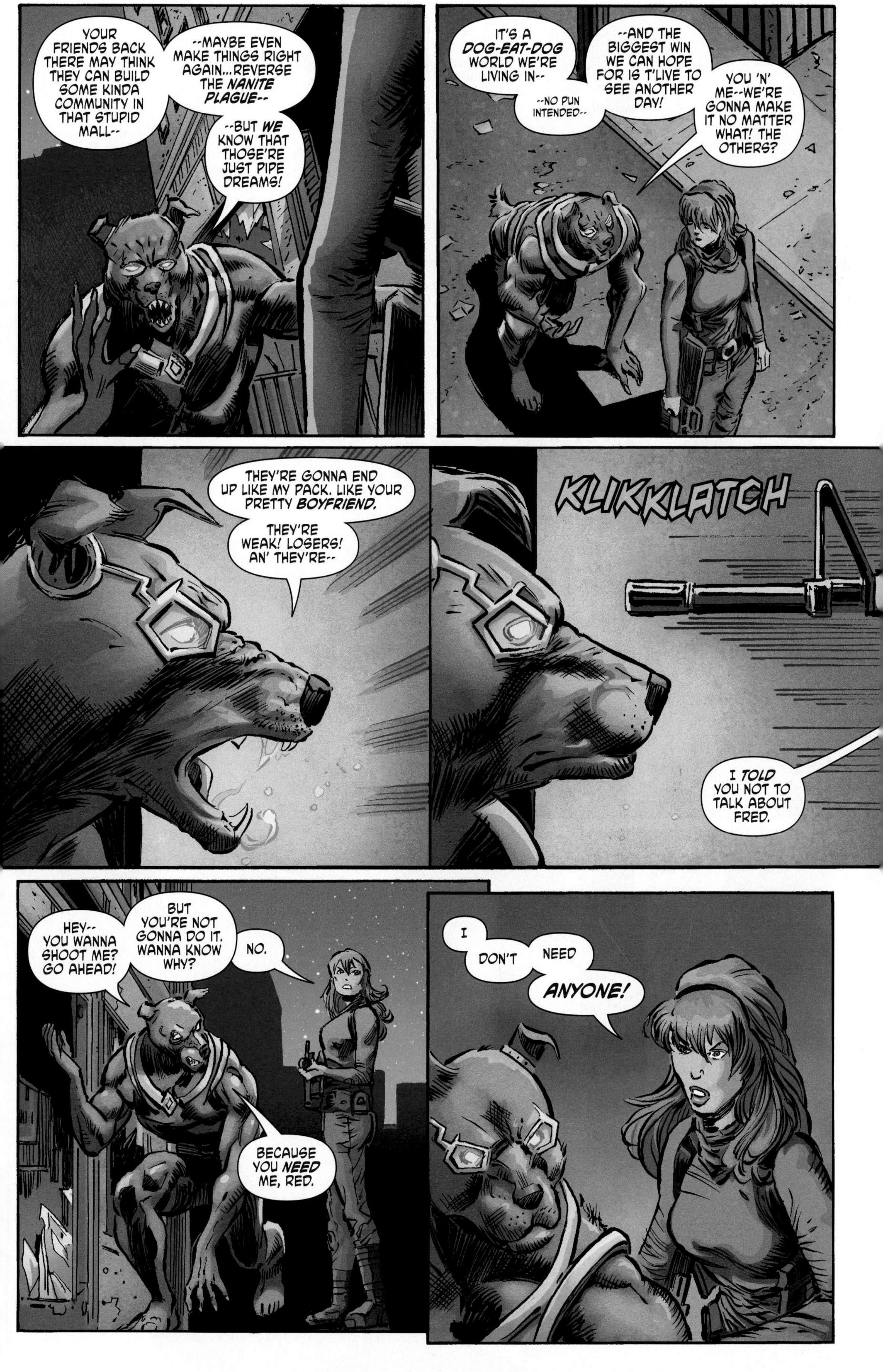
YOUR FRIENDS BACK THERE MAY THINK THEY CAN BUILD SOME KINDA COMMUNITY IN THAT STUPID MALL--
--MAYBE EVEN MAKE THINGS RIGHT AGAIN...REVERSE THE NANITE PLAGUE--
--BUT WE KNOW THAT THOSE'RE JUST PIPE DREAMS!
IT'S A DOG-EAT-DOG WORLD WE'RE LIVING IN--
--NO PUN INTENDED--
--AND THE BIGGEST WIN WE CAN HOPE FOR IS T'LIVE TO SEE ANOTHER DAY!
YOU 'N' ME--WE'RE GONNA MAKE IT NO MATTER WHAT! THE OTHERS?
THEY'RE GONNA END UP LIKE MY PACK. LIKE YOUR PRETTY BOYFRIEND.
THEY'RE WEAK! LOSERS! AN' THEY'RE--
KLIKKLATCH
I TOLD YOU NOT TO TALK ABOUT FRED.
HEY-- YOU WANNA SHOOT ME? GO AHEAD!
BUT YOU'RE NOT GONNA DO IT. WANNA KNOW WHY?
NO.
BECAUSE YOU NEED ME, RED.
I
DON'T
NEED
ANYONE!

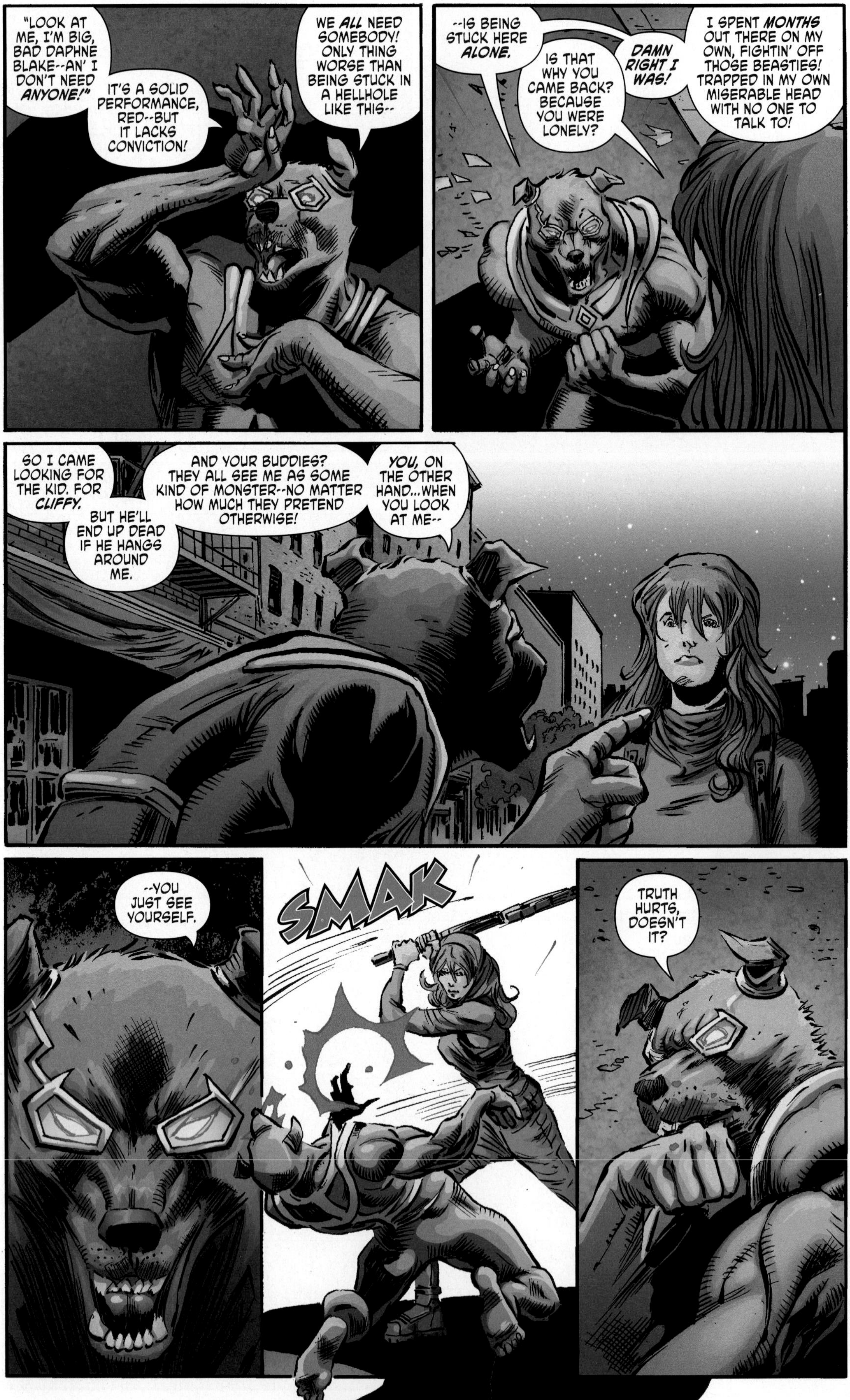
"LOOK AT ME, I'M BIG, BAD DAPHNE BLAKE--AN' I DON'T NEED ANYONE!"
IT'S A SOLID PERFORMANCE, RED--BUT IT LACKS CONVICTION!
WE ALL NEED SOMEBODY! ONLY THING WORSE THAN BEING STUCK IN A HELLHOLE LIKE THIS--
--IS BEING STUCK HERE ALONE.
IS THAT WHY YOU CAME BACK? BECAUSE YOU WERE LONELY?
DAMN RIGHT I WAS!
I SPENT MONTHS OUT THERE ON MY OWN, FIGHTIN' OFF THOSE BEASTIES! TRAPPED IN MY OWN MISERABLE HEAD WITH NO ONE TO TALK TO!
SO I CAME LOOKING FOR THE KID. FOR CLIFFY.
BUT HE'LL END UP DEAD IF HE HANGS AROUND ME.
AND YOUR BUDDIES? THEY ALL SEE ME AS SOME KIND OF MONSTER--NO MATTER HOW MUCH THEY PRETEND OTHERWISE!
YOU, ON THE OTHER HAND...WHEN YOU LOOK AT ME--
--YOU JUST SEE YOURSELF.
SMAK
TRUTH HURTS, DOESN'T IT?

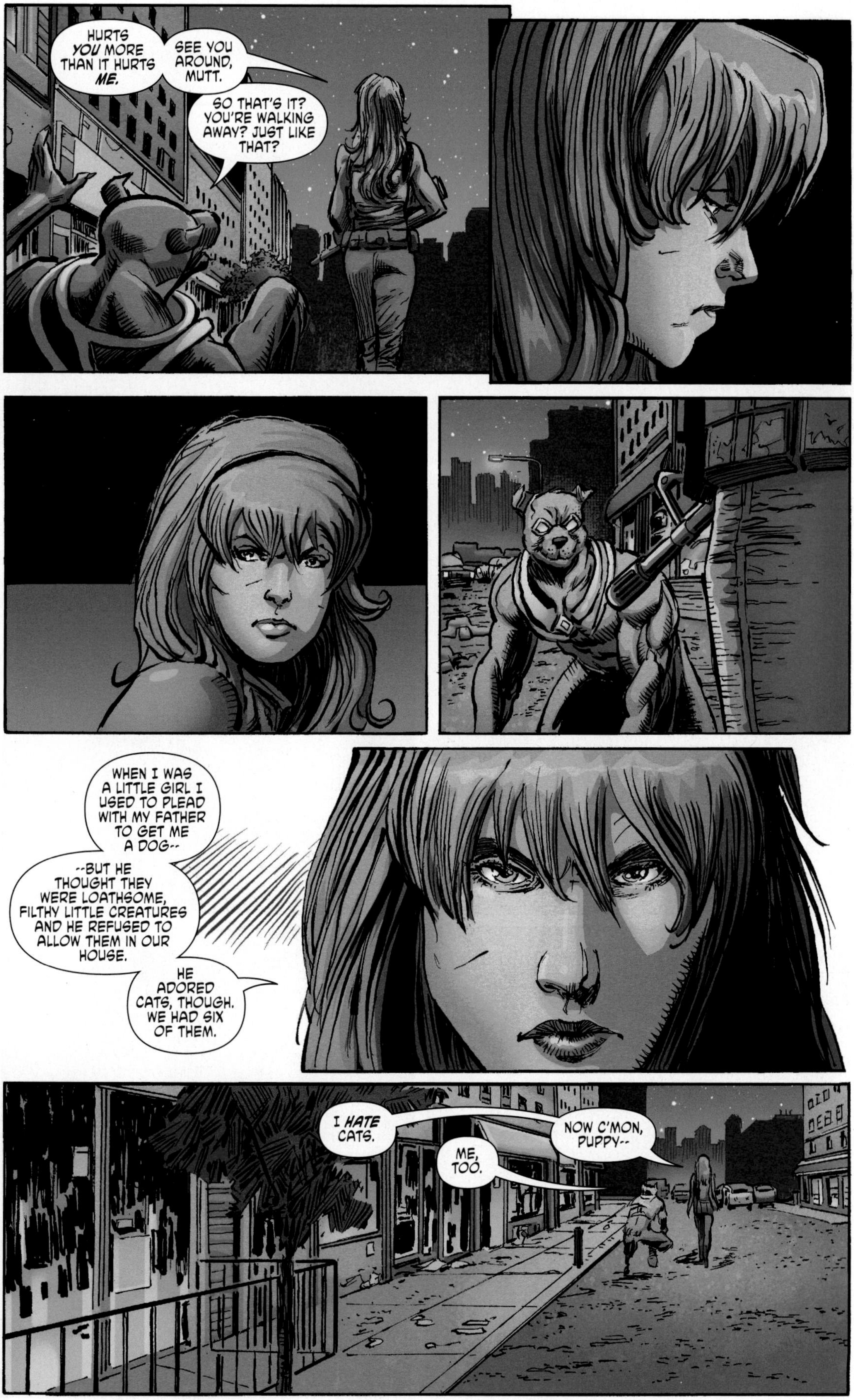
HURTS *YOU* MORE THAN IT HURTS *ME.*
SEE YOU AROUND, MUTT.
SO THAT'S IT? YOU'RE WALKING AWAY? JUST LIKE THAT?
WHEN I WAS A LITTLE GIRL I USED TO PLEAD WITH MY FATHER TO GET ME A DOG--
--BUT HE THOUGHT THEY WERE LOATHSOME, FILTHY LITTLE CREATURES AND HE REFUSED TO ALLOW THEM IN OUR HOUSE.
HE ADORED CATS, THOUGH. WE HAD SIX OF THEM.
I *HATE* CATS.
ME, TOO.
NOW C'MON, PUPPY--

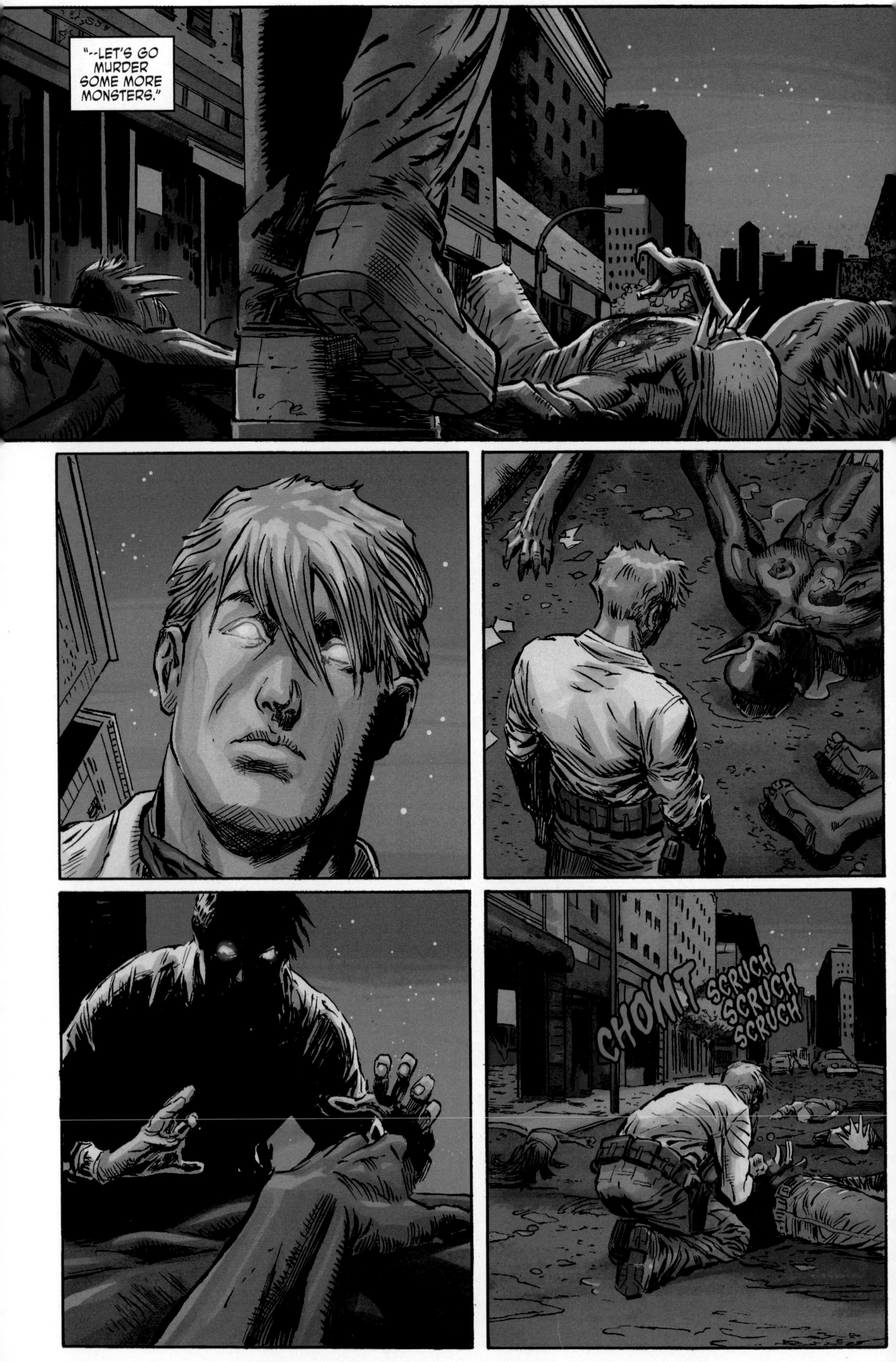
"--LET'S GO MURDER SOME MORE MONSTERS."
CHOMT
SCRUCH SCRUCH SCRUCH

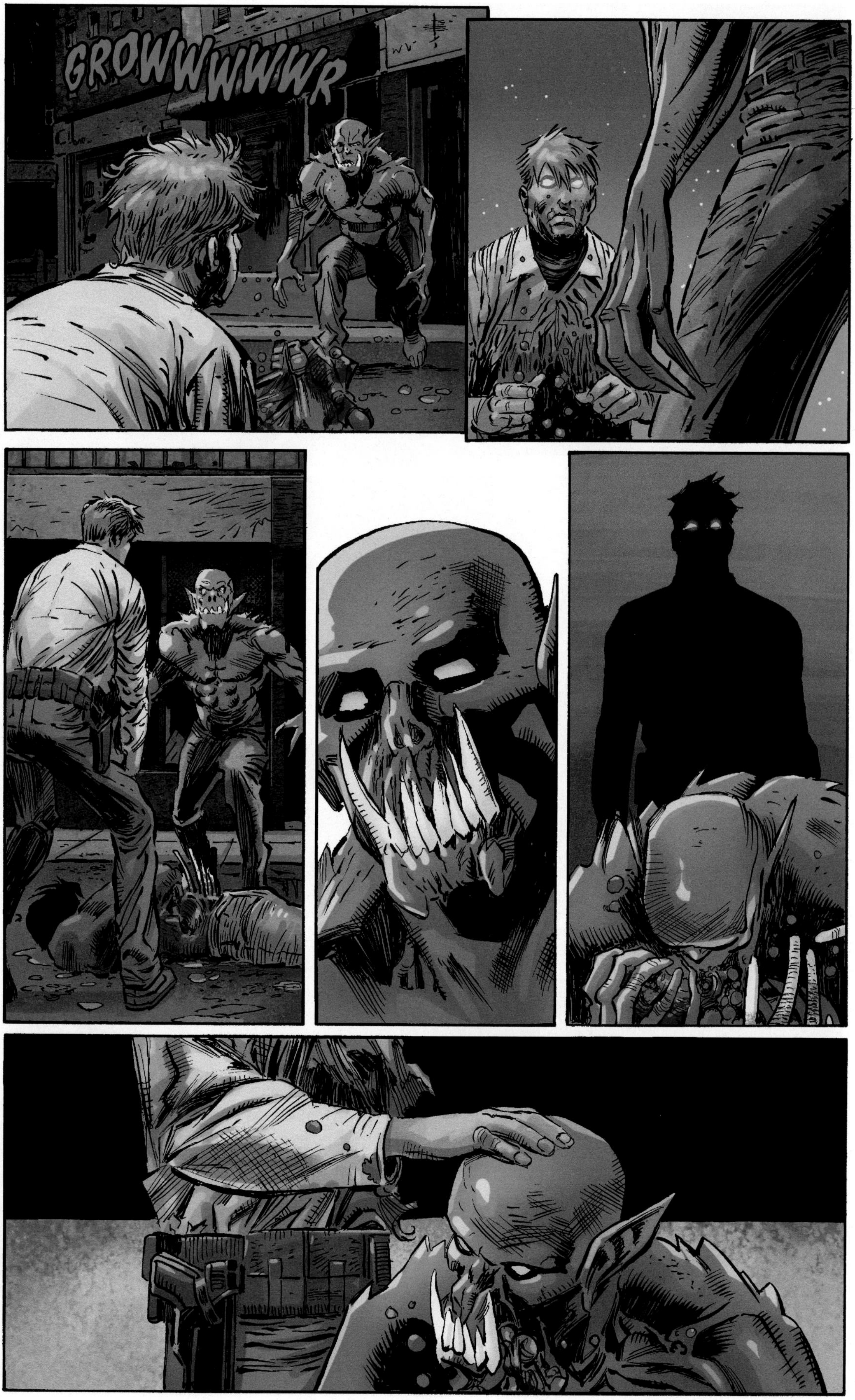
GROWWWWWWR

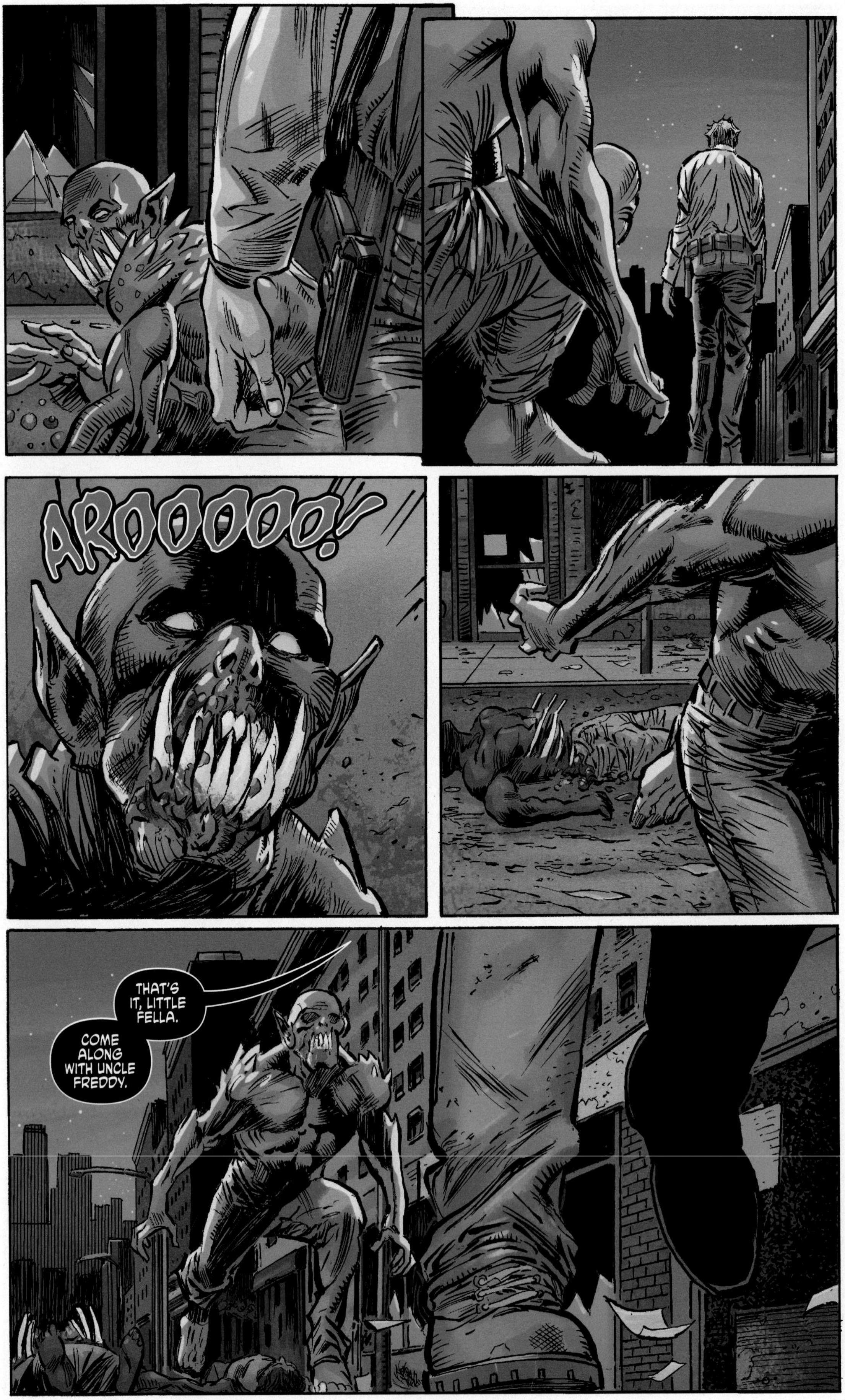
AROOOOO!
THAT'S IT, LITTLE FELLA.
COME ALONG WITH UNCLE FREDDY.

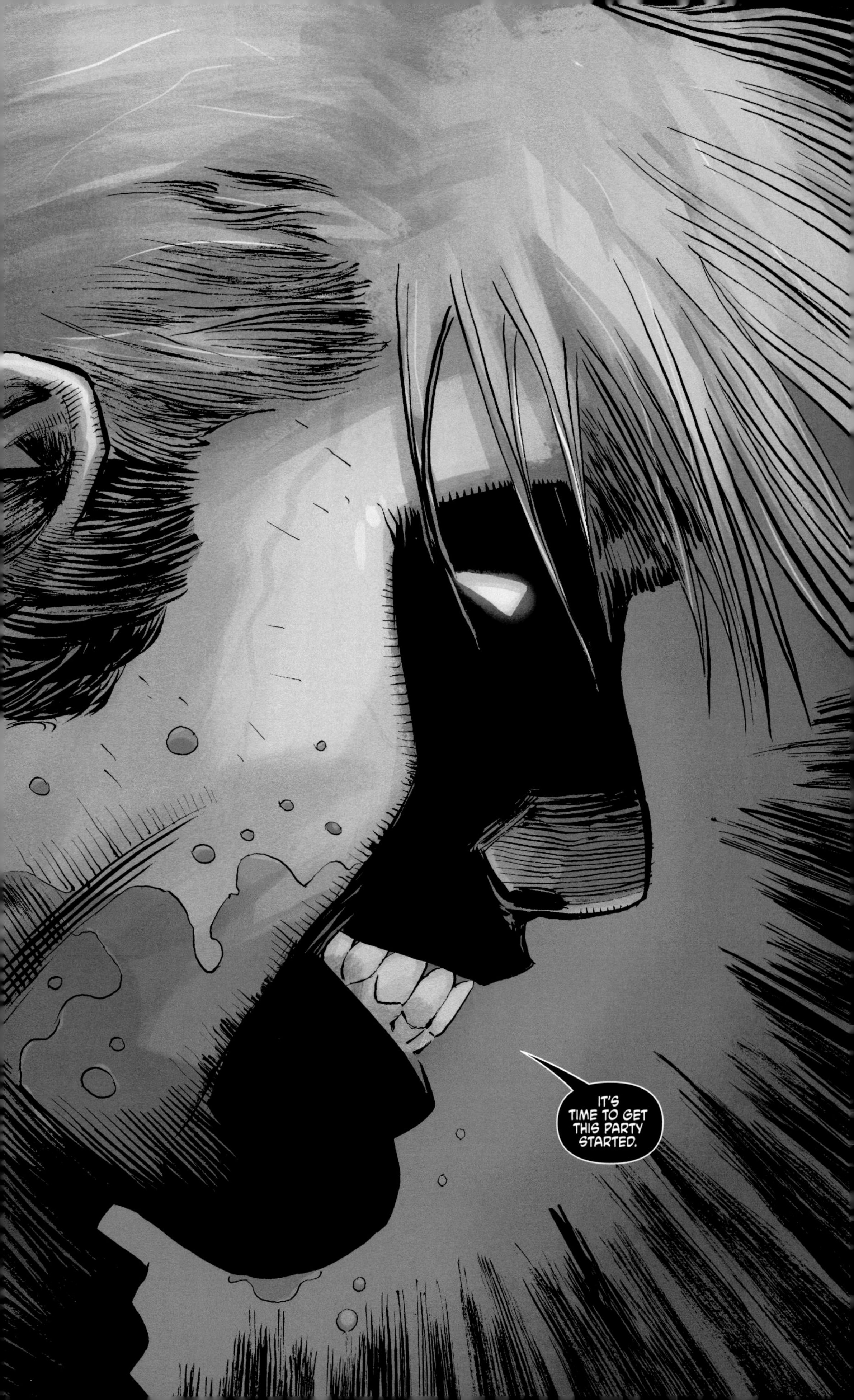
IT'S TIME TO GET THIS PARTY STARTED.

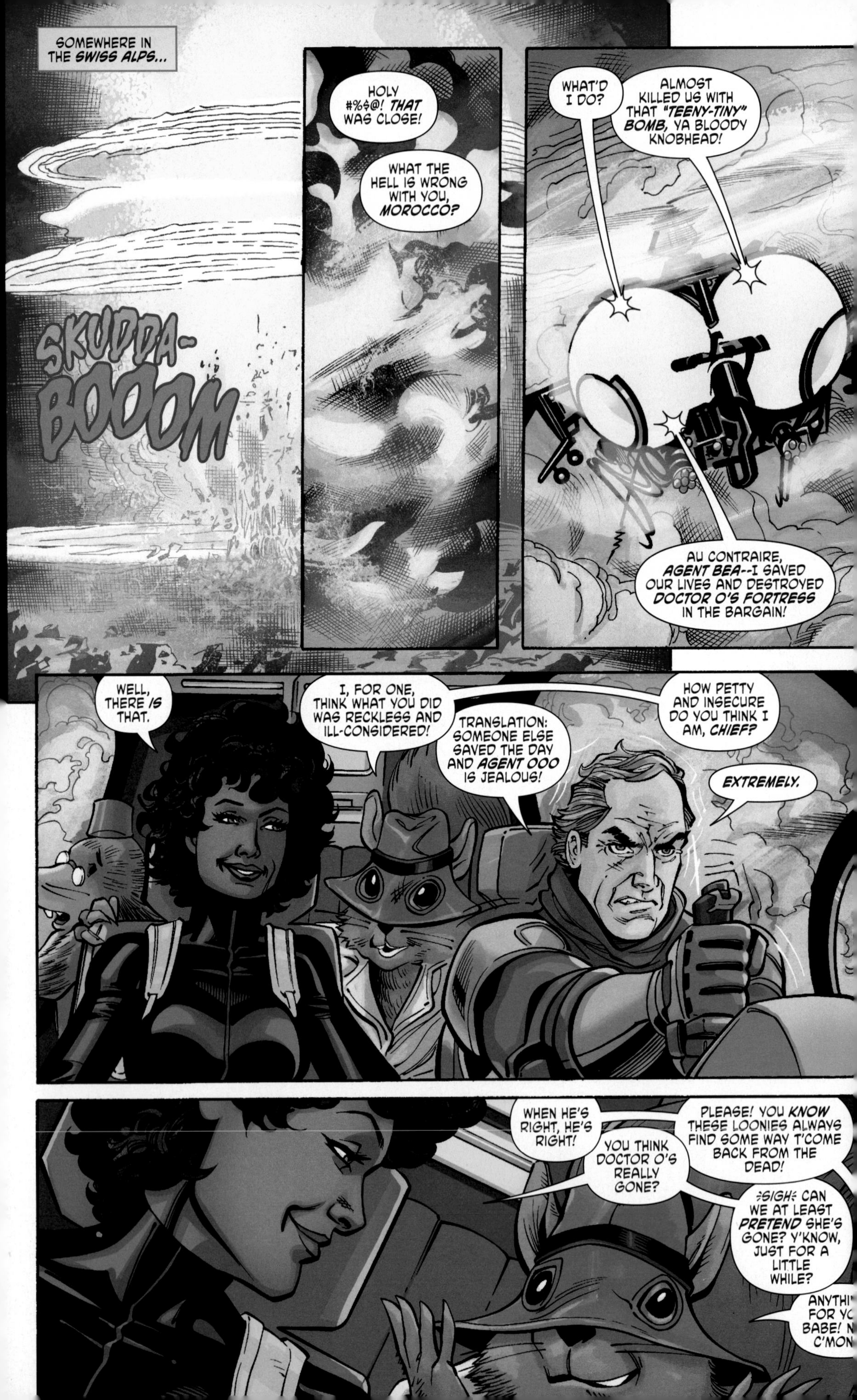
SOMEWHERE IN THE SWISS ALPS...
SKUDDA-BOOOM
HOLY #%$@! THAT WAS CLOSE!
WHAT THE HELL IS WRONG WITH YOU, MOROCCO?
WHAT'D I DO?
ALMOST KILLED US WITH THAT "TEENY-TINY" BOMB, YA BLOODY KNOBHEAD!
AU CONTRAIRE, AGENT BEA--I SAVED OUR LIVES AND DESTROYED DOCTOR O'S FORTRESS IN THE BARGAIN!
WELL, THERE IS THAT.
I, FOR ONE, THINK WHAT YOU DID WAS RECKLESS AND ILL-CONSIDERED!
TRANSLATION: SOMEONE ELSE SAVED THE DAY AND AGENT OOO IS JEALOUS!
HOW PETTY AND INSECURE DO YOU THINK I AM, CHIEF?
EXTREMELY.
WHEN HE'S RIGHT, HE'S RIGHT!
YOU THINK DOCTOR O'S REALLY GONE?
PLEASE! YOU KNOW THESE LOONIES ALWAYS FIND SOME WAY T'COME BACK FROM THE DEAD!
=SIGH= CAN WE AT LEAST PRETEND SHE'S GONE? Y'KNOW, JUST FOR A LITTLE WHILE?

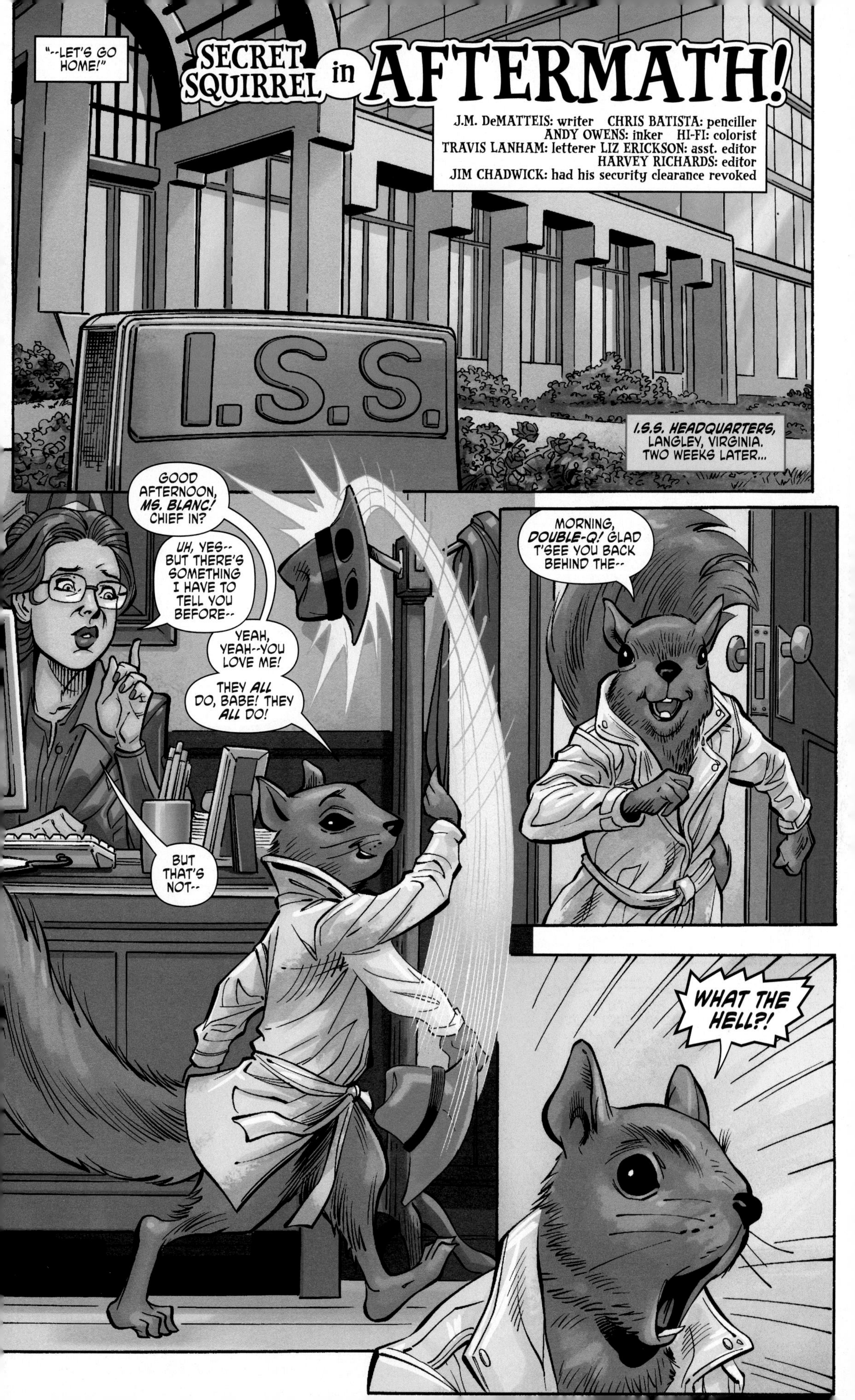
"--LET'S GO HOME!"
SECRET SQUIRREL in AFTERMATH!
J.M. DeMATTEIS: writer CHRIS BATISTA: penciller
ANDY OWENS: inker HI-FI: colorist
TRAVIS LANHAM: letterer LIZ ERICKSON: asst. editor
HARVEY RICHARDS: editor
JIM CHADWICK: had his security clearance revoked
I.S.S.
I.S.S. HEADQUARTERS, LANGLEY, VIRGINIA. TWO WEEKS LATER...
GOOD AFTERNOON, MS. BLANC! CHIEF IN?
UH, YES--BUT THERE'S SOMETHING I HAVE TO TELL YOU BEFORE--
YEAH, YEAH--YOU LOVE ME!
THEY ALL DO, BABE! THEY ALL DO!
BUT THAT'S NOT--
MORNING, DOUBLE-Q! GLAD T'SEE YOU BACK BEHIND THE--
WHAT THE HELL?!

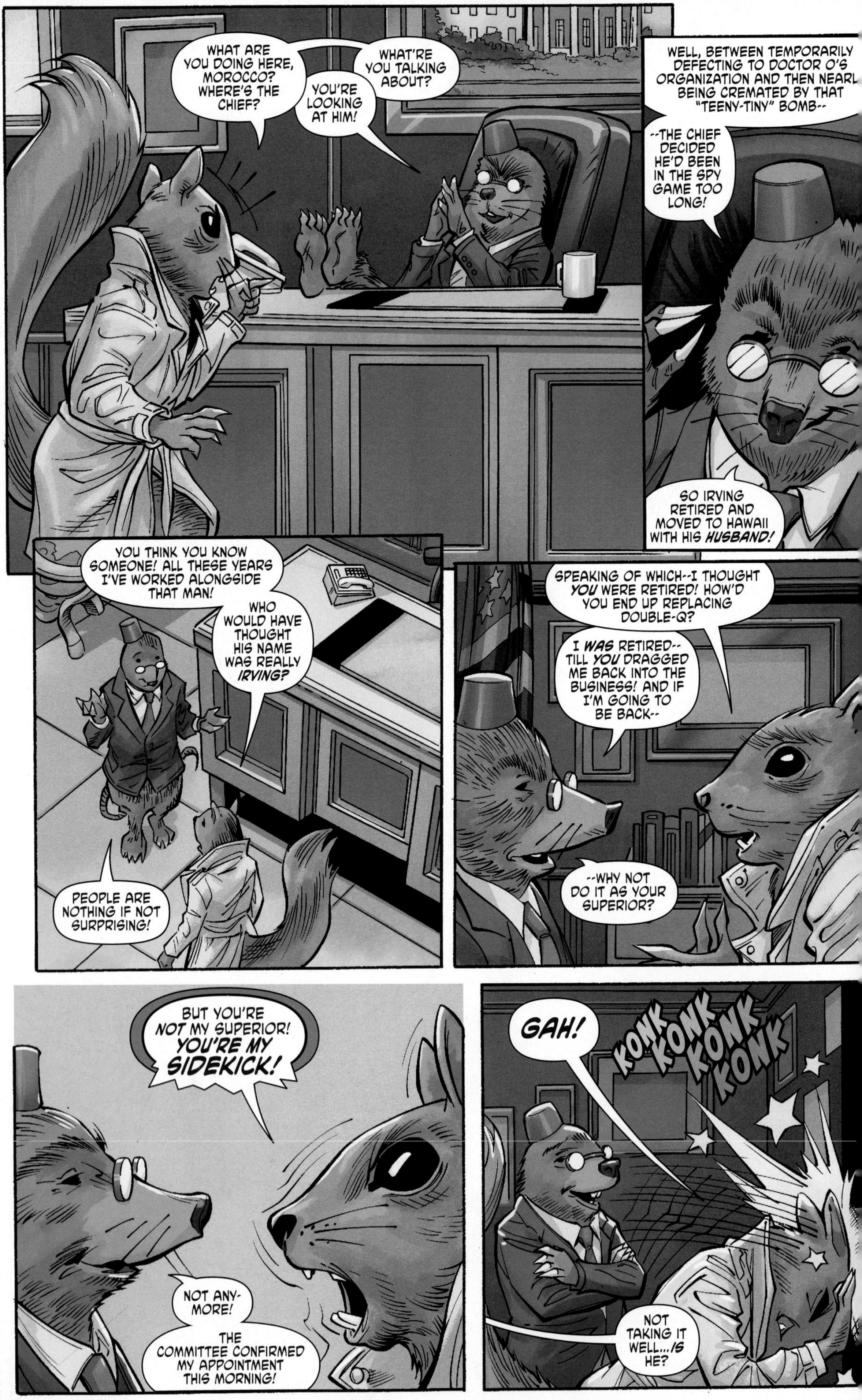
WHAT ARE YOU DOING HERE, MOROCCO? WHERE'S THE CHIEF?
WHAT'RE YOU TALKING ABOUT?
YOU'RE LOOKING AT HIM!
WELL, BETWEEN TEMPORARILY DEFECTING TO DOCTOR O'S ORGANIZATION AND THEN NEARL BEING CREMATED BY THAT "TEENY-TINY" BOMB--
--THE CHIEF DECIDED HE'D BEEN IN THE SPY GAME TOO LONG!
SO IRVING RETIRED AND MOVED TO HAWAII WITH HIS HUSBAND!
YOU THINK YOU KNOW SOMEONE! ALL THESE YEARS I'VE WORKED ALONGSIDE THAT MAN!
WHO WOULD HAVE THOUGHT HIS NAME WAS REALLY IRVING?
PEOPLE ARE NOTHING IF NOT SURPRISING!
SPEAKING OF WHICH--I THOUGHT YOU WERE RETIRED! HOW'D YOU END UP REPLACING DOUBLE-Q?
I WAS RETIRED-- TILL YOU DRAGGED ME BACK INTO THE BUSINESS! AND IF I'M GOING TO BE BACK--
--WHY NOT DO IT AS YOUR SUPERIOR?
BUT YOU'RE NOT MY SUPERIOR! YOU'RE MY SIDEKICK!
NOT ANY-MORE!
THE COMMITTEE CONFIRMED MY APPOINTMENT THIS MORNING!
GAH!
KONK KONK KONK KONK
NOT TAKING IT WELL...IS HE?

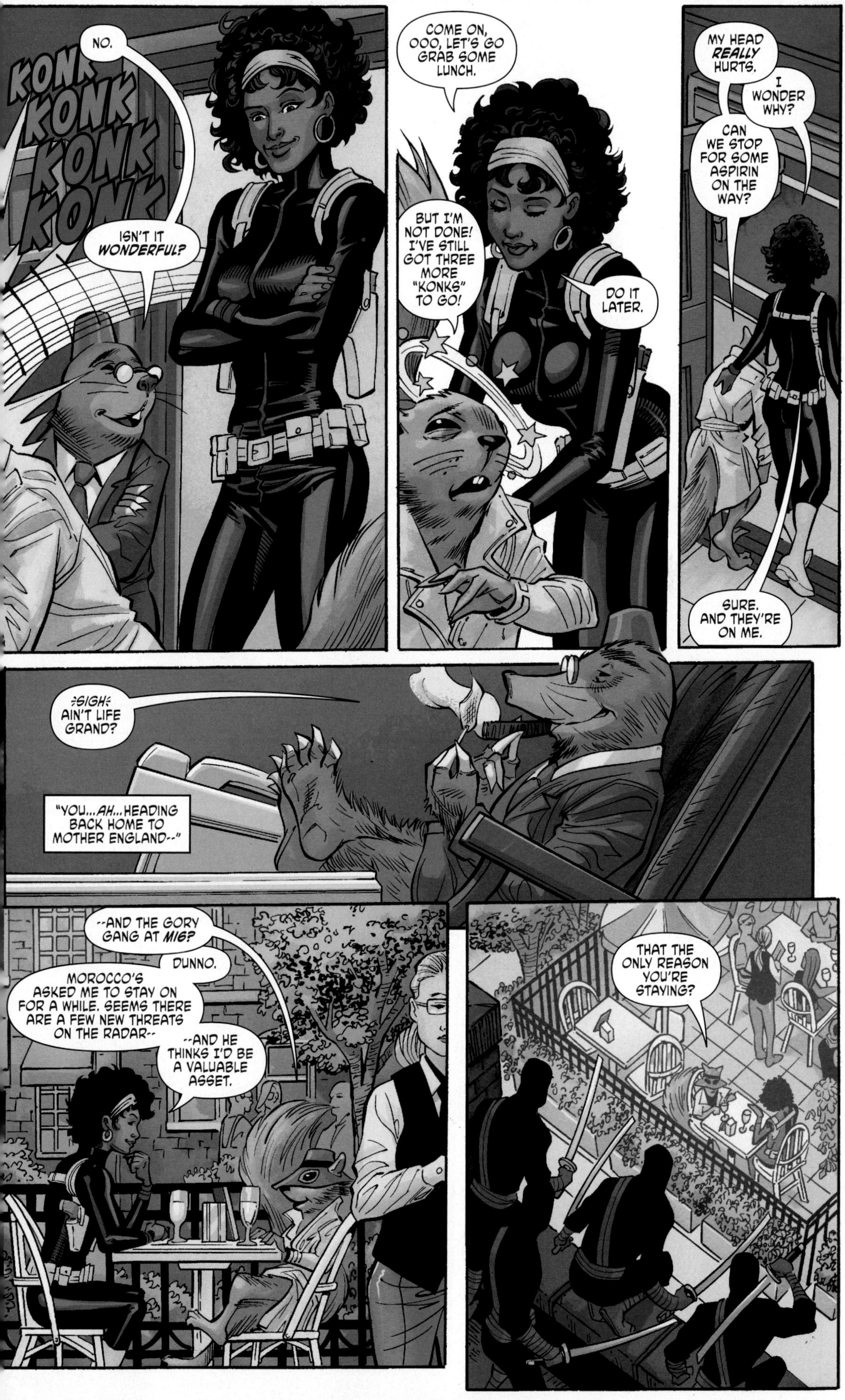
KONK KONK KONK KONK KONK
NO.
ISN'T IT *WONDERFUL?*
COME ON, OOO, LET'S GO GRAB SOME LUNCH.
BUT I'M NOT DONE! I'VE STILL GOT THREE MORE "KONKS" TO GO!
DO IT LATER.
MY HEAD *REALLY* HURTS.
I WONDER WHY?
CAN WE STOP FOR SOME ASPIRIN ON THE WAY?
SURE. AND THEY'RE ON ME.
SIGH AIN'T LIFE GRAND?
"YOU...*AH*...HEADING BACK HOME TO MOTHER ENGLAND--"
--AND THE GORY GANG AT *MI6?*
DUNNO.
MOROCCO'S ASKED ME TO STAY ON FOR A WHILE. SEEMS THERE ARE A FEW NEW THREATS ON THE RADAR--
--AND HE THINKS I'D BE A VALUABLE ASSET.
THAT THE ONLY REASON YOU'RE STAYING?

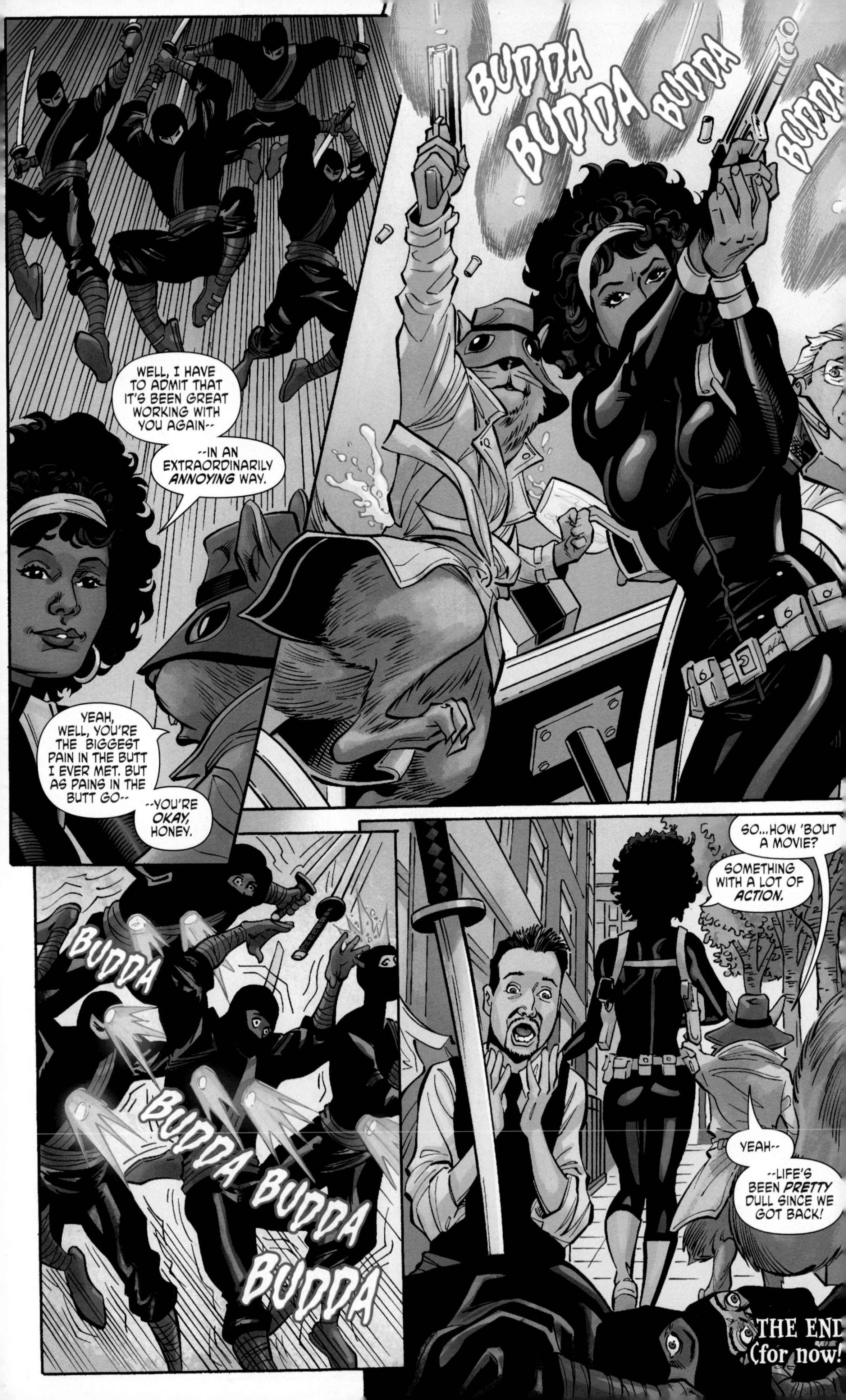

BUDDA BUDDA BUDDA BUDDA
WELL, I HAVE TO ADMIT THAT IT'S BEEN GREAT WORKING WITH YOU AGAIN--
--IN AN EXTRAORDINARILY *ANNOYING* WAY.
YEAH, WELL, YOU'RE THE BIGGEST PAIN IN THE BUTT I EVER MET. BUT AS PAINS IN THE BUTT GO--
--YOU'RE *OKAY,* HONEY.
BUDDA
BUDDA BUDDA BUDDA
SO...HOW 'BOUT A MOVIE?
SOMETHING WITH A LOT OF *ACTION.*
YEAH--
--LIFE'S BEEN *PRETTY* DULL SINCE WE GOT BACK!
THE END (for now!

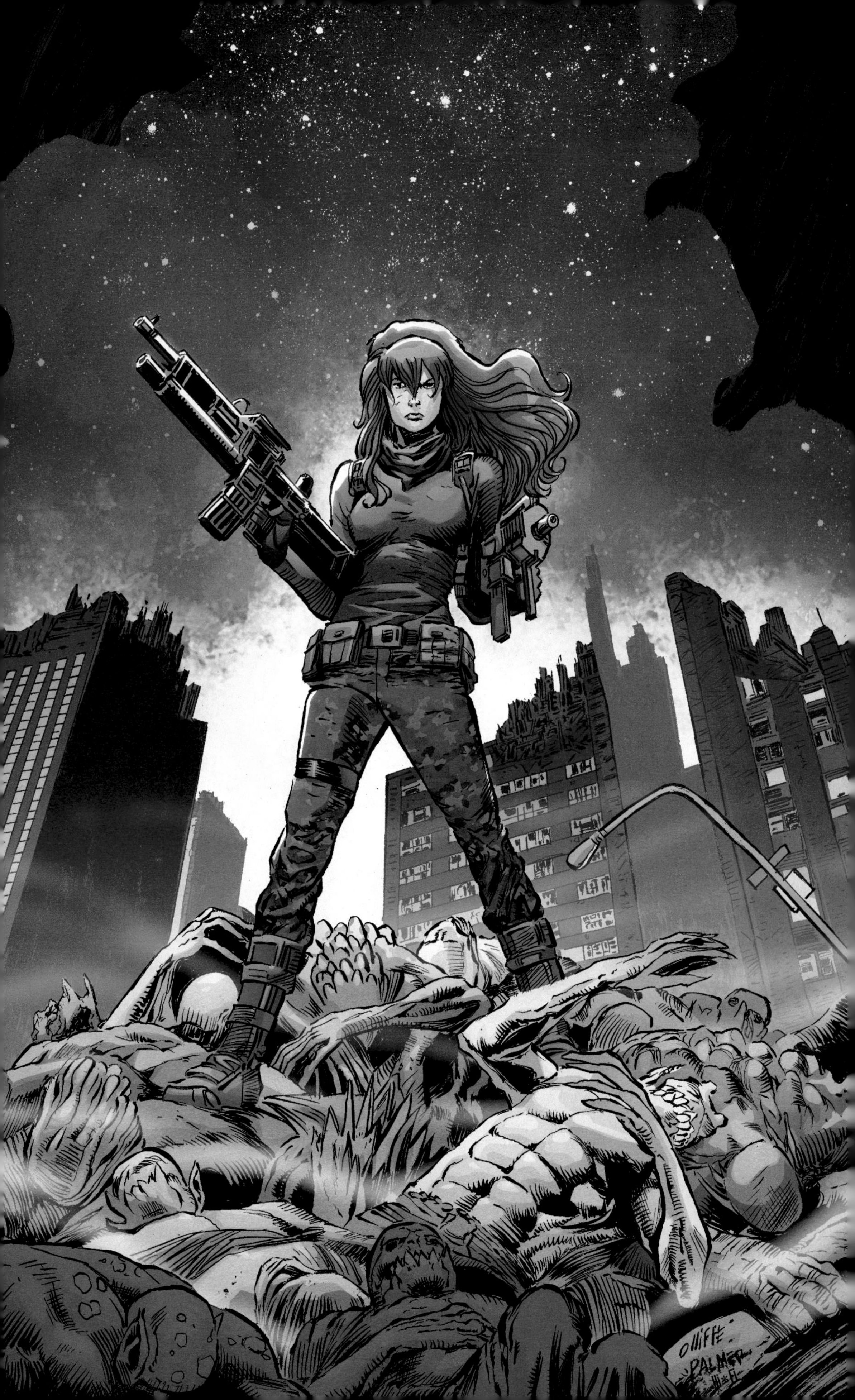
OLIFF
PALMER

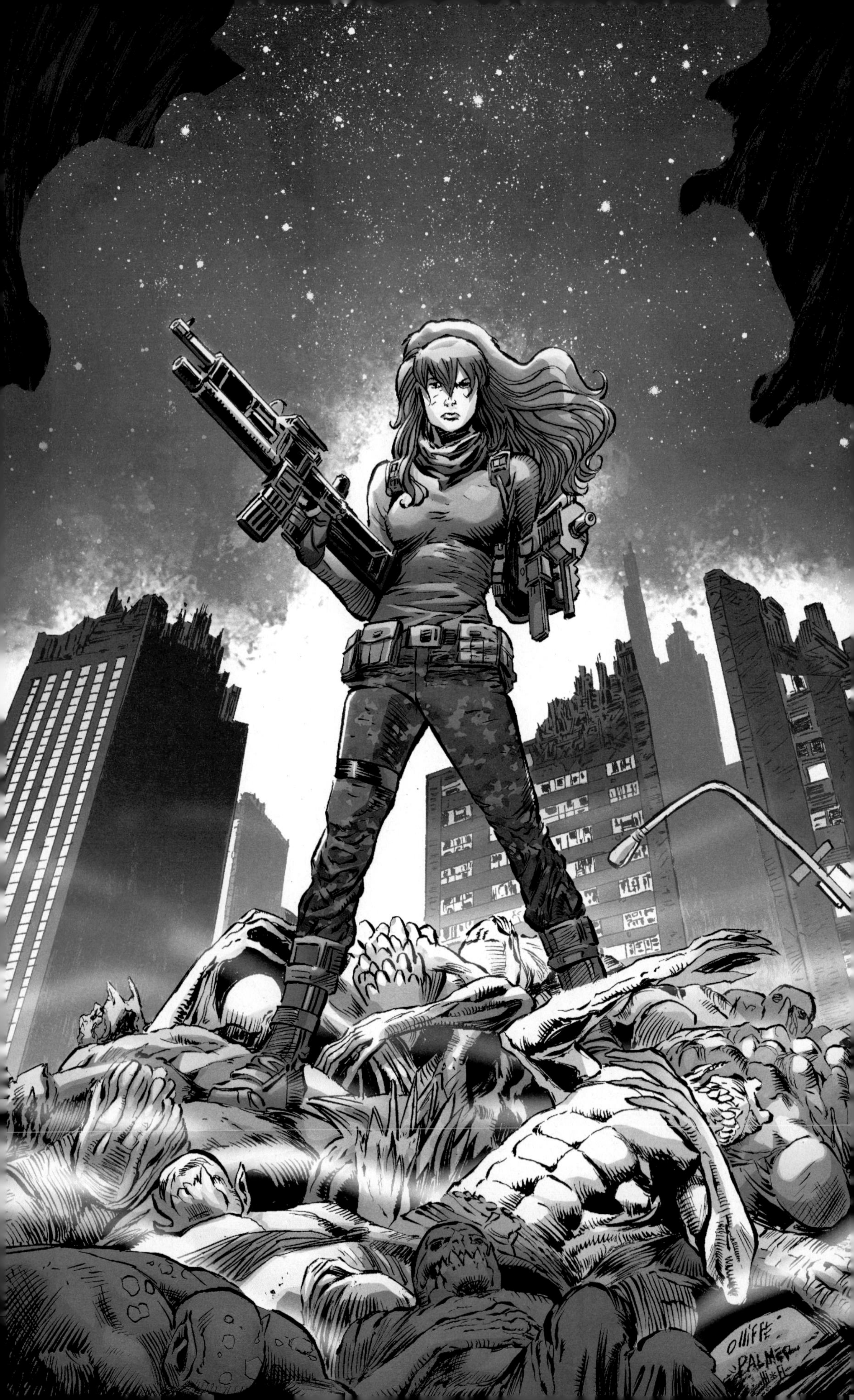
OLLIFFE
PALMER

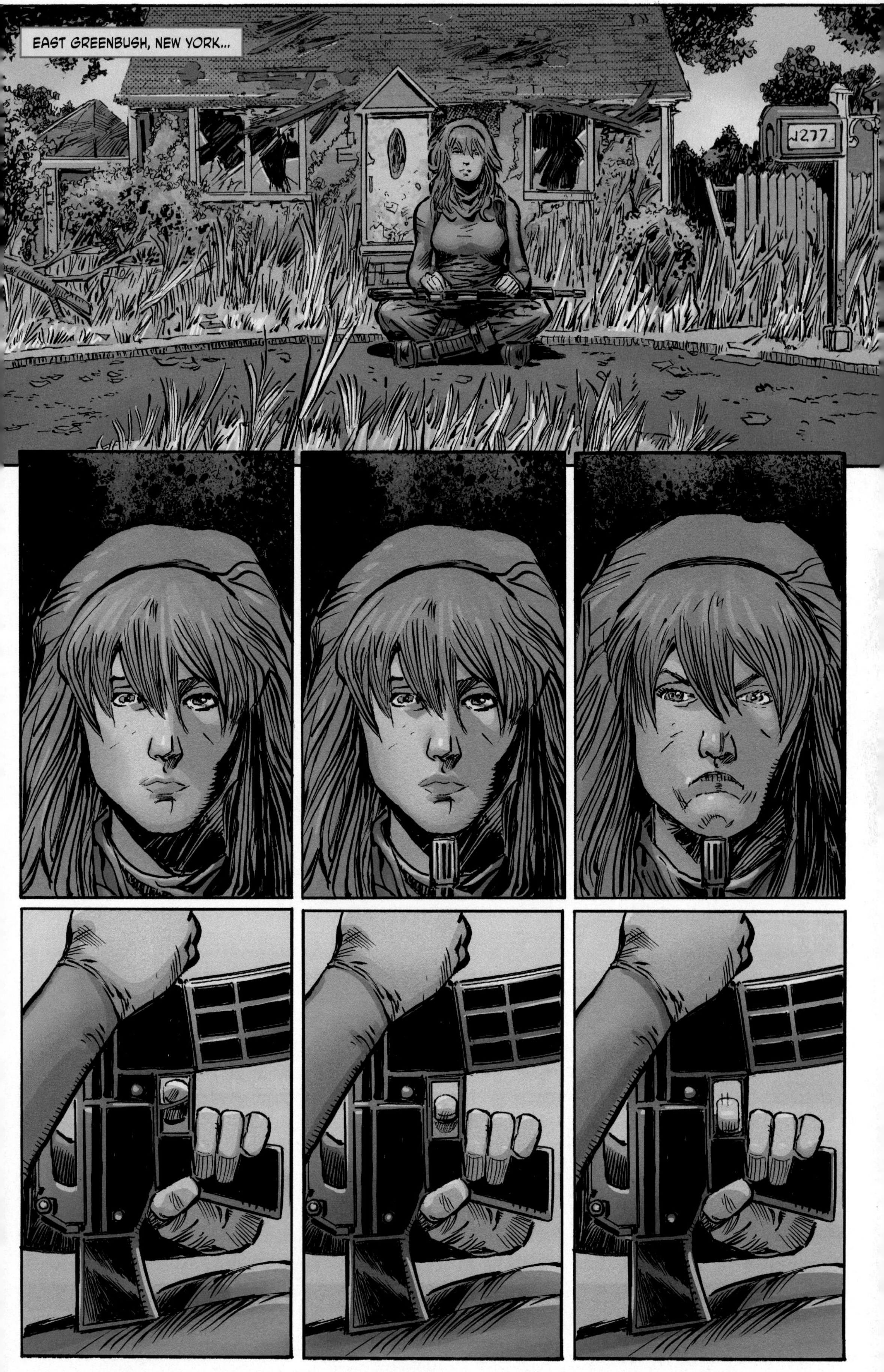
EAST GREENBUSH, NEW YORK...
1277

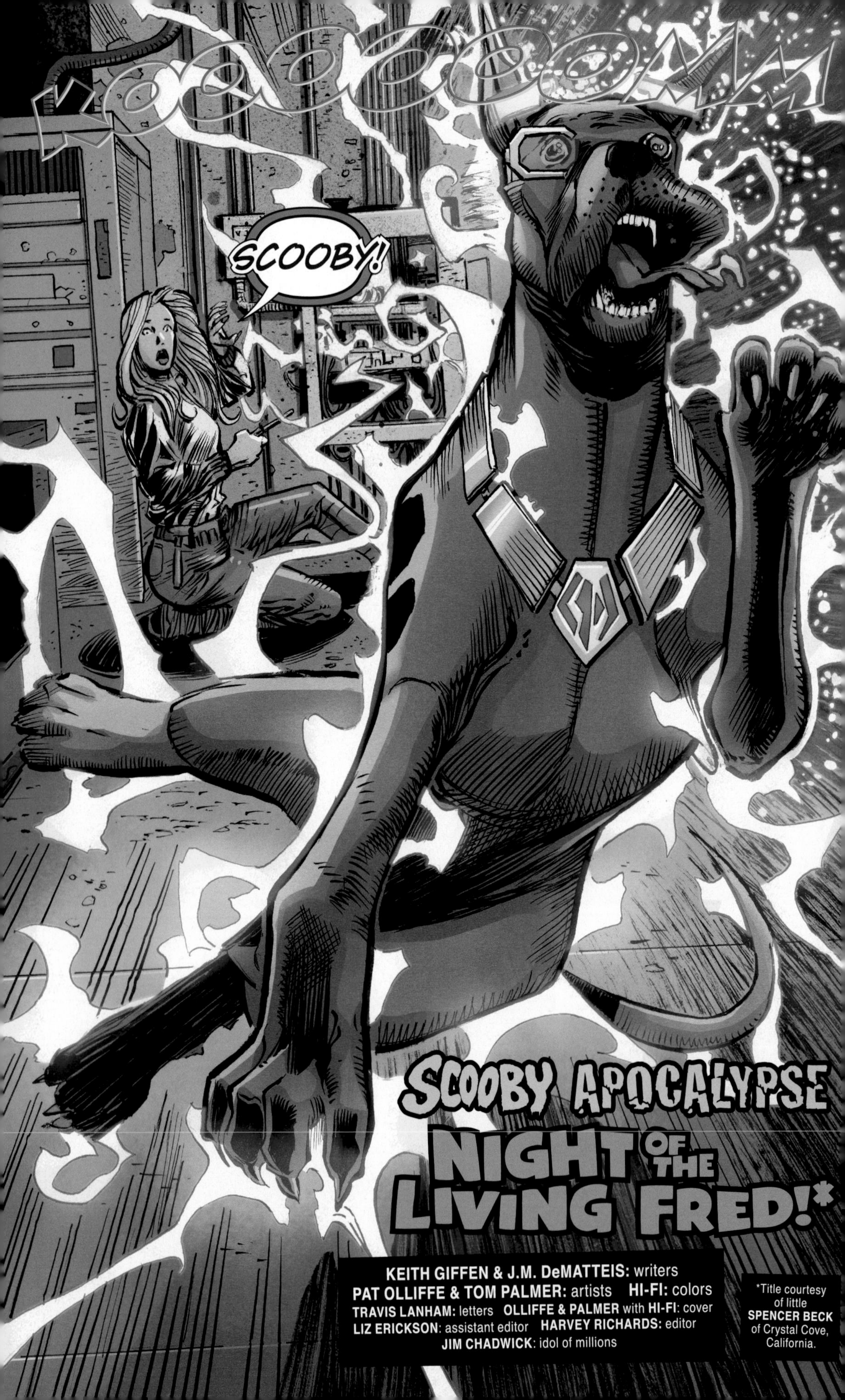

SCOOBY!
SCOOBY APOCALYPSE
NIGHT OF THE LIVING FRED!*
KEITH GIFFEN & J.M. DeMATTEIS: writers
PAT OLLIFFE & TOM PALMER: artists HI-FI: colors
TRAVIS LANHAM: letters OLLIFFE & PALMER with HI-FI: cover
LIZ ERICKSON: assistant editor HARVEY RICHARDS: editor
JIM CHADWICK: idol of millions
*Title courtesy of little SPENCER BECK of Crystal Cove, California.

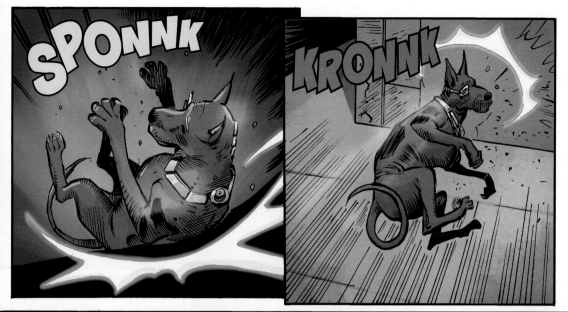

WHAT THE HELL DID YOU DO, DAISY?

"DO"? *NOTHING!*

I WAS IN THE MIDDLE OF SOME ELECTRICAL REPAIRS! SCOOBY CAME ALONG... INADVERTENTLY TOUCHED SOME LIVE WIRES AND--

AND YOU *KILLED* HIM!

DAPHNE BLAKE--

--WHY DO YOU ALWAYS INSIST ON SEEING THE ABSOLUTE WORST IN EVERY SITUATION?

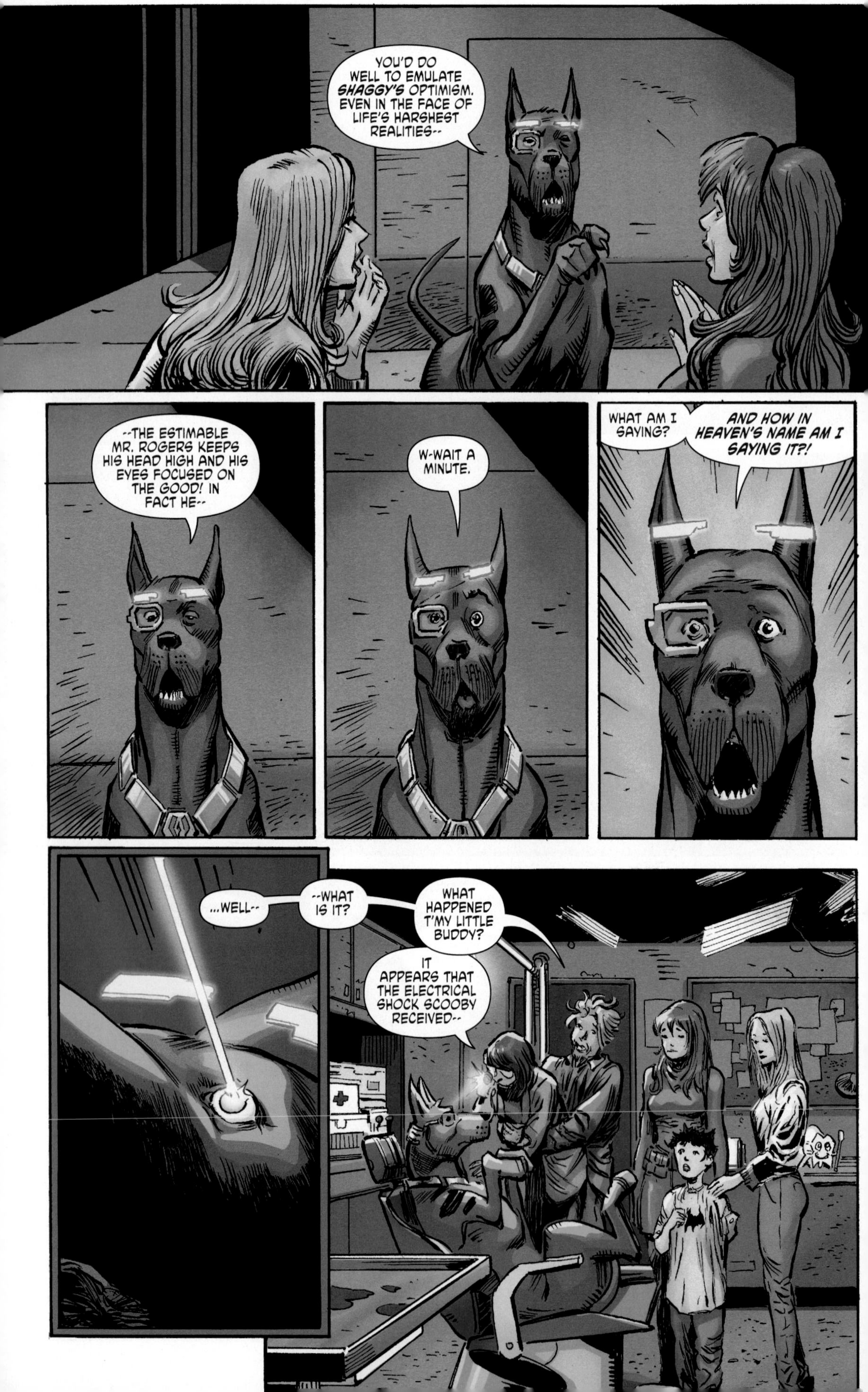
YOU'D DO WELL TO EMULATE SHAGGY'S OPTIMISM. EVEN IN THE FACE OF LIFE'S HARSHEST REALITIES--
--THE ESTIMABLE MR. ROGERS KEEPS HIS HEAD HIGH AND HIS EYES FOCUSED ON THE GOOD! IN FACT HE--
W-WAIT A MINUTE.
WHAT AM I SAYING?
AND HOW IN HEAVEN'S NAME AM I SAYING IT?!
...WELL--
--WHAT IS IT?
WHAT HAPPENED T'MY LITTLE BUDDY?
IT APPEARS THAT THE ELECTRICAL SHOCK SCOOBY RECEIVED--

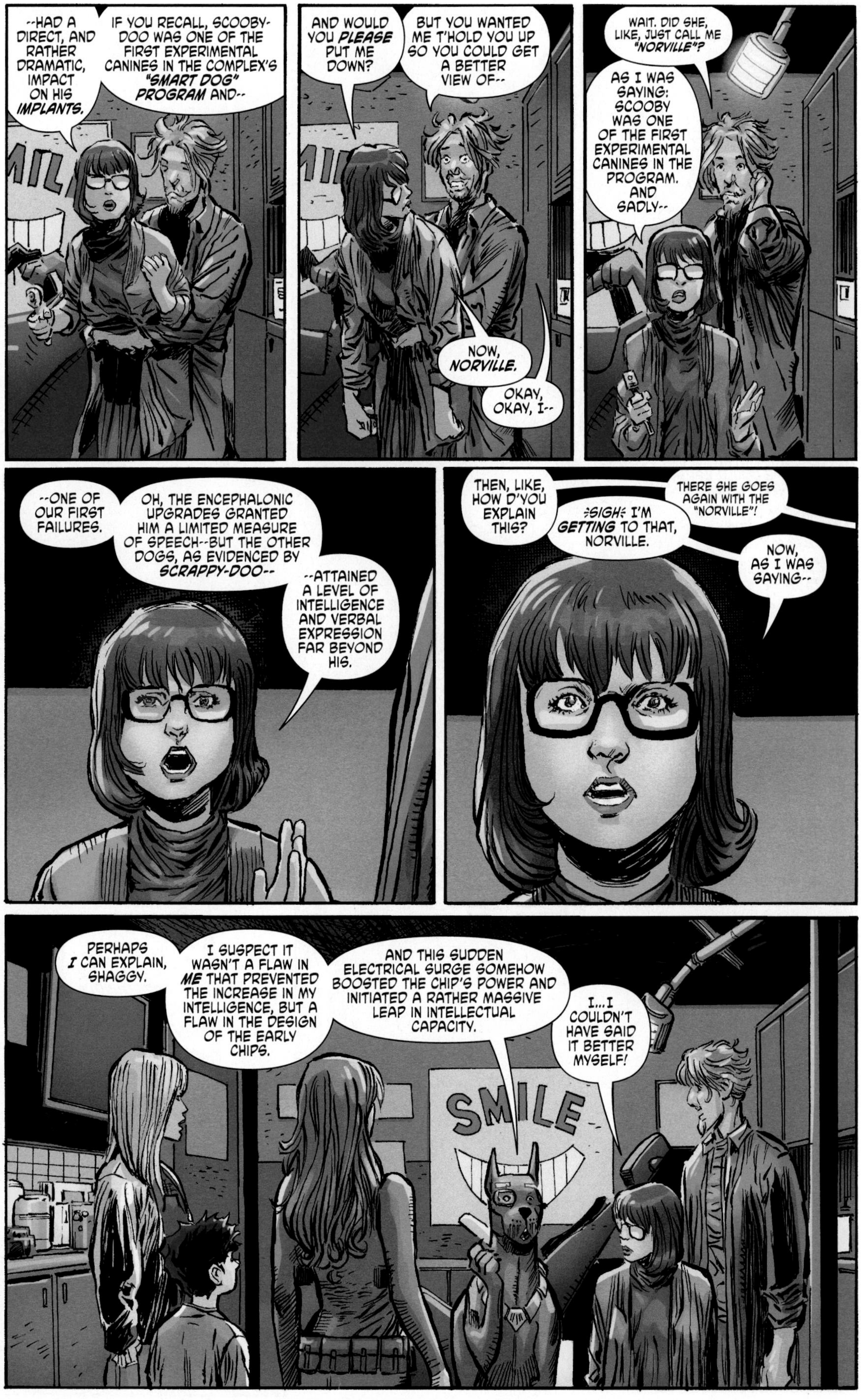
--HAD A DIRECT, AND RATHER DRAMATIC, IMPACT ON HIS IMPLANTS.
IF YOU RECALL, SCOOBY-DOO WAS ONE OF THE FIRST EXPERIMENTAL CANINES IN THE COMPLEX'S "SMART DOG" PROGRAM AND--
SMIL
AND WOULD YOU PLEASE PUT ME DOWN?
BUT YOU WANTED ME T'HOLD YOU UP SO YOU COULD GET A BETTER VIEW OF--
NOW, NORVILLE.
OKAY, OKAY, I--
WAIT. DID SHE, LIKE, JUST CALL ME "NORVILLE"?
AS I WAS SAYING: SCOOBY WAS ONE OF THE FIRST EXPERIMENTAL CANINES IN THE PROGRAM. AND SADLY--
--ONE OF OUR FIRST FAILURES.
OH, THE ENCEPHALONIC UPGRADES GRANTED HIM A LIMITED MEASURE OF SPEECH--BUT THE OTHER DOGS, AS EVIDENCED BY SCRAPPY-DOO--
--ATTAINED A LEVEL OF INTELLIGENCE AND VERBAL EXPRESSION FAR BEYOND HIS.
THEN, LIKE, HOW D'YOU EXPLAIN THIS?
THERE SHE GOES AGAIN WITH THE "NORVILLE"!
SIGH I'M GETTING TO THAT, NORVILLE.
NOW, AS I WAS SAYING--
PERHAPS I CAN EXPLAIN, SHAGGY.
I SUSPECT IT WASN'T A FLAW IN ME THAT PREVENTED THE INCREASE IN MY INTELLIGENCE, BUT A FLAW IN THE DESIGN OF THE EARLY CHIPS.
AND THIS SUDDEN ELECTRICAL SURGE SOMEHOW BOOSTED THE CHIP'S POWER AND INITIATED A RATHER MASSIVE LEAP IN INTELLECTUAL CAPACITY.
I...I COULDN'T HAVE SAID IT BETTER MYSELF!
SMILE

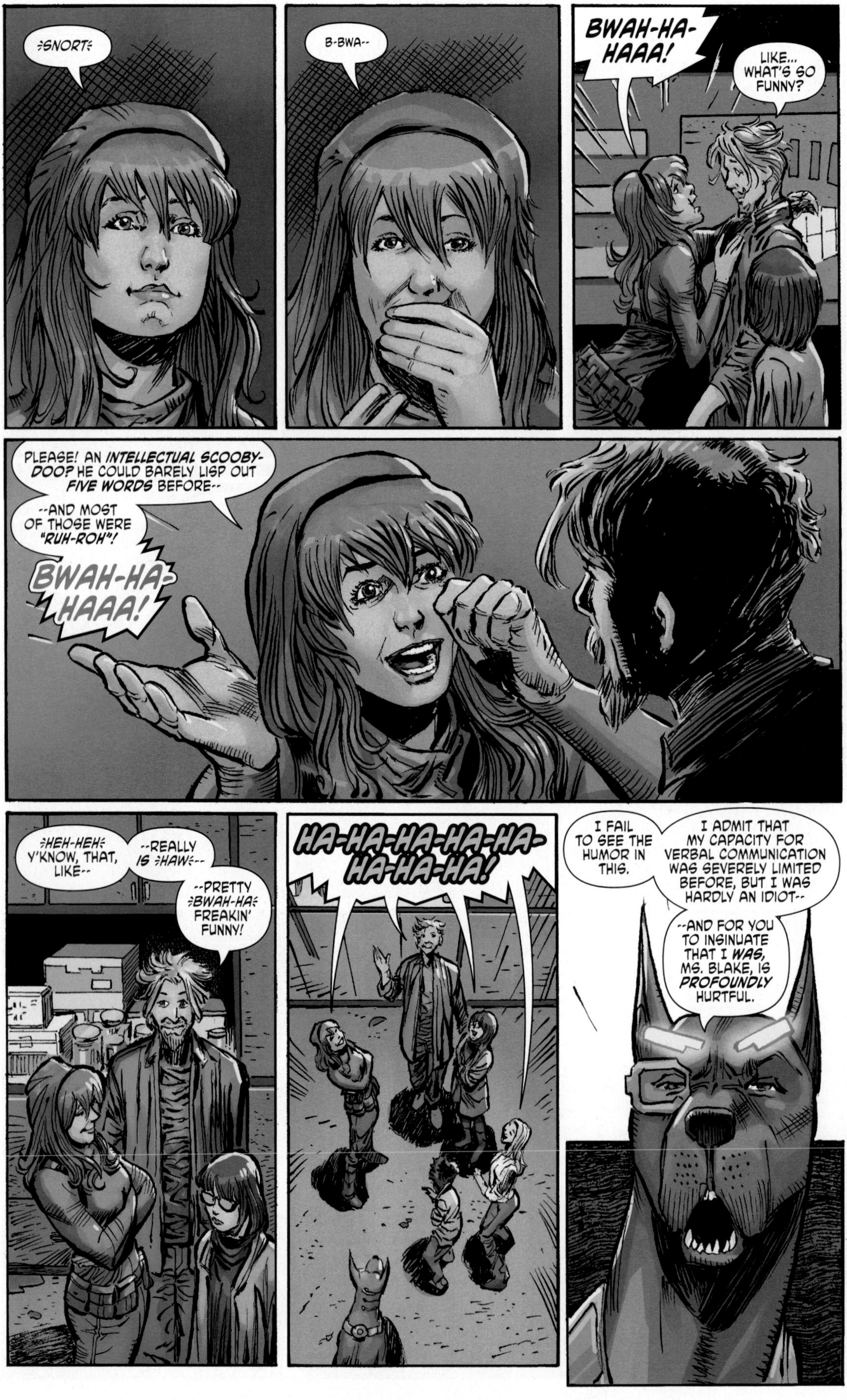

SNORT
B-BWA--
BWAH-HA-HAAA!
LIKE... WHAT'S SO FUNNY?
PLEASE! AN INTELLECTUAL SCOOBY-DOO? HE COULD BARELY LISP OUT FIVE WORDS BEFORE--
--AND MOST OF THOSE WERE "RUH-ROH"!
BWAH-HA-HAAA!
HEH-HEH Y'KNOW, THAT, LIKE--
--REALLY IS HAW--
--PRETTY BWAH-HA FREAKIN' FUNNY!
HA-HA-HA-HA-HA-HA-HA-HA!
I FAIL TO SEE THE HUMOR IN THIS.
I ADMIT THAT MY CAPACITY FOR VERBAL COMMUNICATION WAS SEVERELY LIMITED BEFORE, BUT I WAS HARDLY AN IDIOT--
--AND FOR YOU TO INSINUATE THAT I WAS, MS. BLAKE, IS PROFOUNDLY HURTFUL.

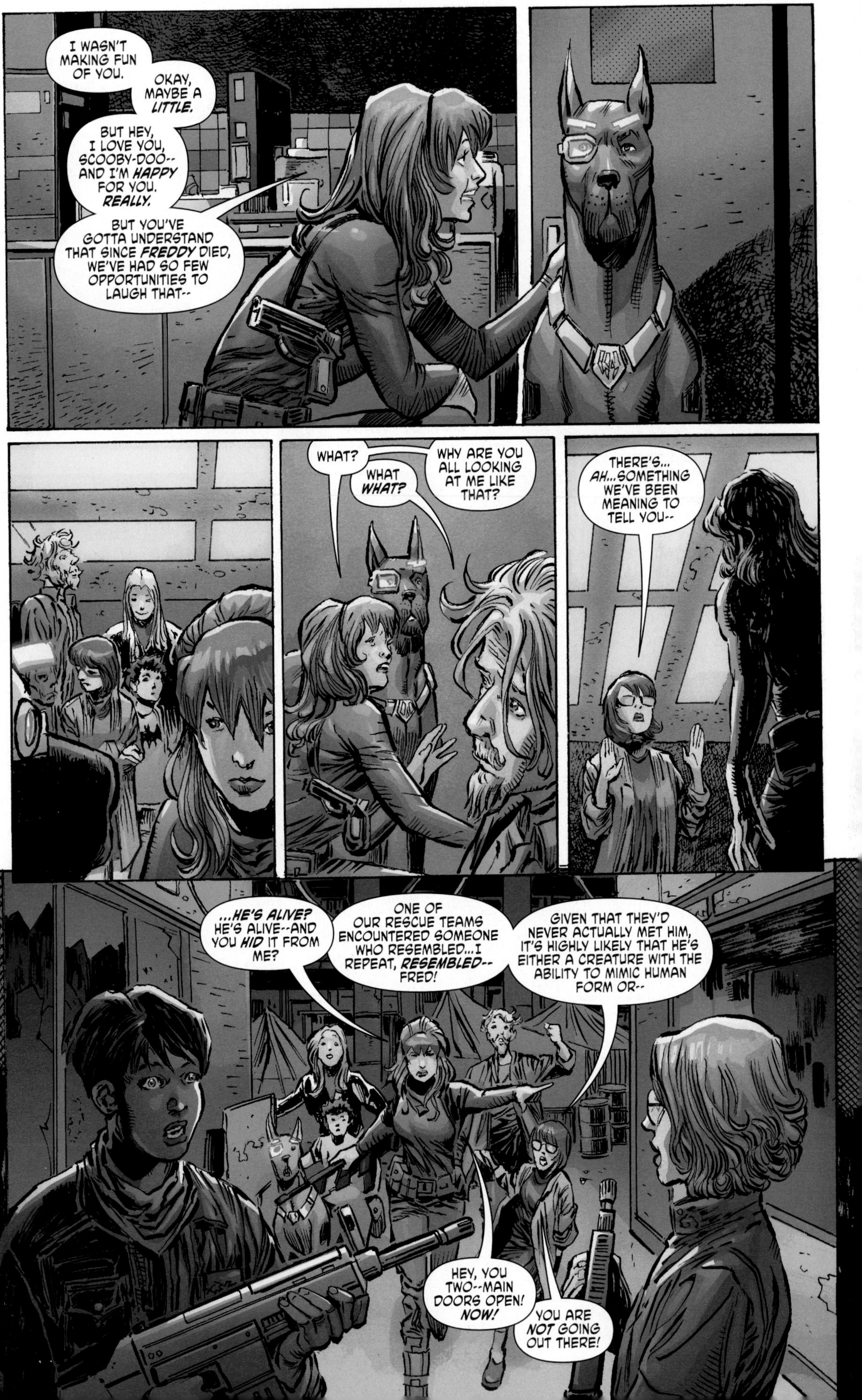
I WASN'T MAKING FUN OF YOU.
OKAY, MAYBE A *LITTLE.*
BUT HEY, I LOVE YOU, SCOOBY-DOO-- AND I'M *HAPPY* FOR YOU. *REALLY.*
BUT YOU'VE GOTTA UNDERSTAND THAT SINCE *FREDDY* DIED, WE'VE HAD SO FEW OPPORTUNITIES TO LAUGH THAT--
WHAT?
WHAT *WHAT?*
WHY ARE YOU ALL LOOKING AT ME LIKE THAT?
THERE'S... *AH*...SOMETHING WE'VE BEEN MEANING TO TELL YOU--
...HE'S ALIVE? HE'S ALIVE--AND YOU *HID* IT FROM ME?
ONE OF OUR RESCUE TEAMS ENCOUNTERED SOMEONE WHO RESEMBLED...I REPEAT, *RESEMBLED*--FRED!
GIVEN THAT THEY'D NEVER ACTUALLY MET HIM, IT'S HIGHLY LIKELY THAT HE'S EITHER A CREATURE WITH THE ABILITY TO MIMIC HUMAN FORM OR--
HEY, YOU TWO--MAIN DOORS OPEN! *NOW!*
YOU ARE *NOT* GOING OUT THERE!

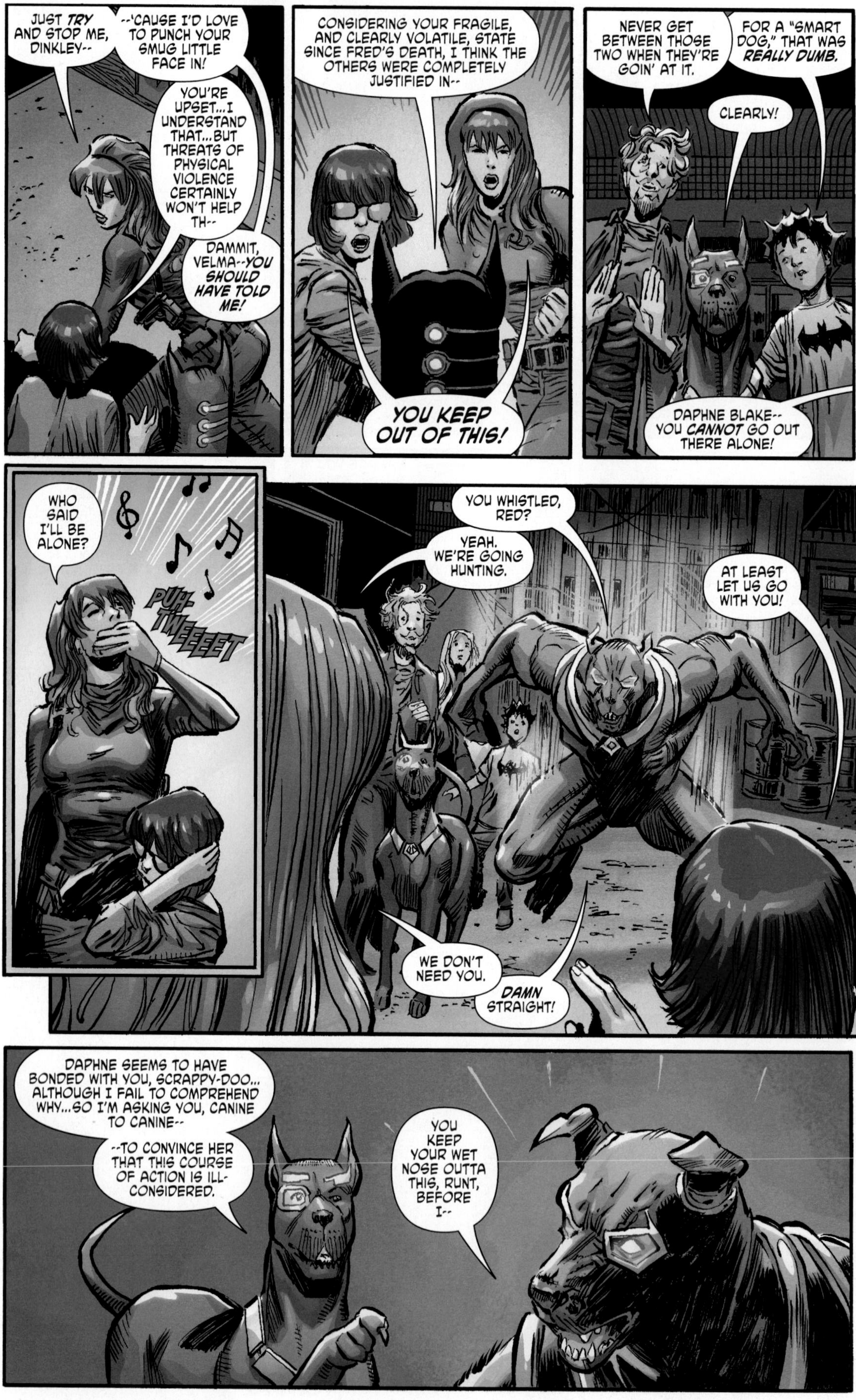

JUST TRY AND STOP ME, DINKLEY--
--'CAUSE I'D LOVE TO PUNCH YOUR SMUG LITTLE FACE IN!
YOU'RE UPSET...I UNDERSTAND THAT...BUT THREATS OF PHYSICAL VIOLENCE CERTAINLY WON'T HELP TH--
DAMMIT, VELMA--YOU SHOULD HAVE TOLD ME!
CONSIDERING YOUR FRAGILE, AND CLEARLY VOLATILE, STATE SINCE FRED'S DEATH, I THINK THE OTHERS WERE COMPLETELY JUSTIFIED IN--
YOU KEEP OUT OF THIS!
NEVER GET BETWEEN THOSE TWO WHEN THEY'RE GOIN' AT IT.
FOR A "SMART DOG," THAT WAS REALLY DUMB.
CLEARLY!
DAPHNE BLAKE-- YOU CANNOT GO OUT THERE ALONE!
WHO SAID I'LL BE ALONE?
PUH-TWEEEET
YOU WHISTLED, RED?
YEAH. WE'RE GOING HUNTING.
AT LEAST LET US GO WITH YOU!
WE DON'T NEED YOU.
DAMN STRAIGHT!
DAPHNE SEEMS TO HAVE BONDED WITH YOU, SCRAPPY-DOO... ALTHOUGH I FAIL TO COMPREHEND WHY...SO I'M ASKING YOU, CANINE TO CANINE--
--TO CONVINCE HER THAT THIS COURSE OF ACTION IS ILL-CONSIDERED.
YOU KEEP YOUR WET NOSE OUTTA THIS, RUNT, BEFORE I--

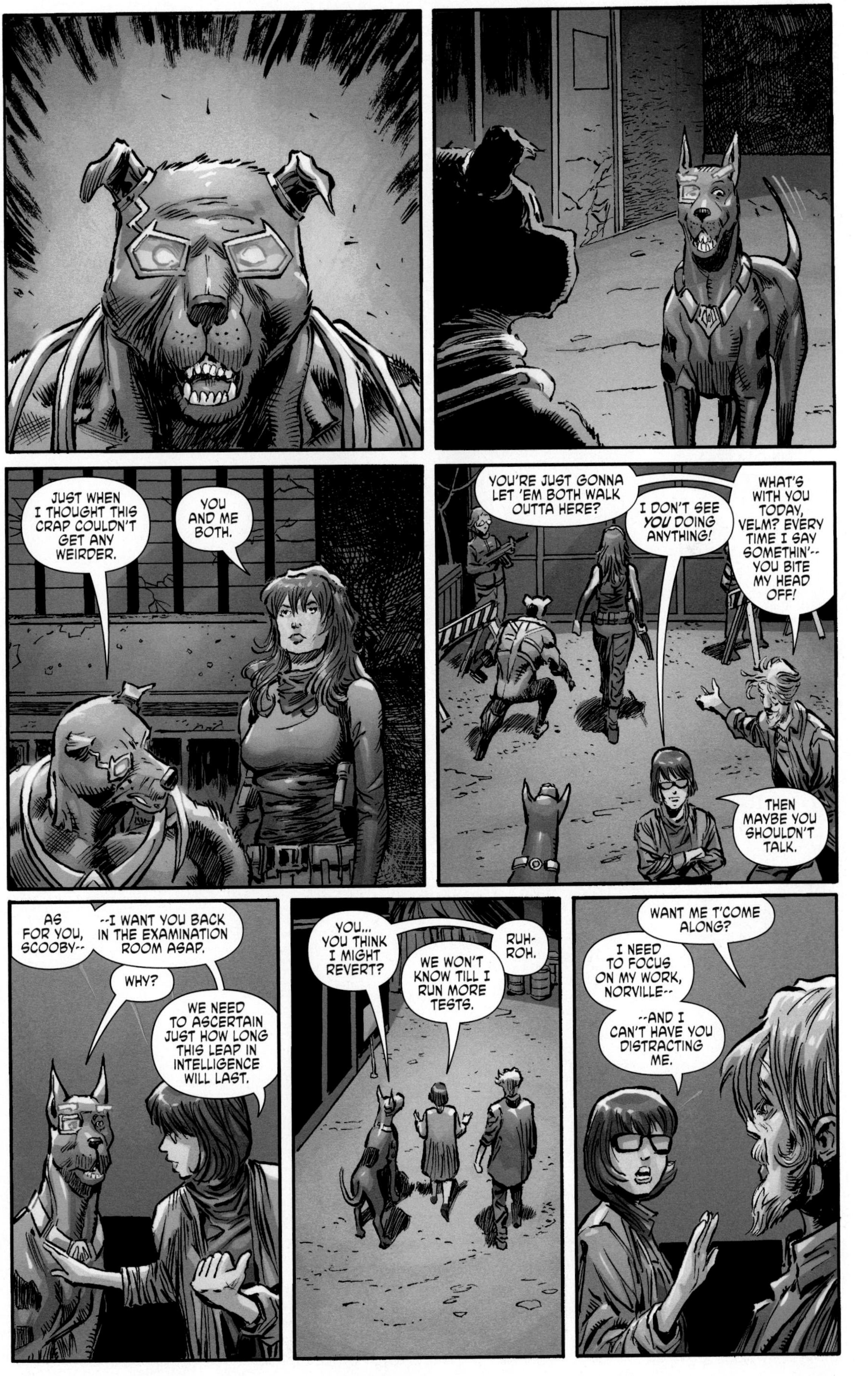
JUST WHEN I THOUGHT THIS CRAP COULDN'T GET ANY WEIRDER.
YOU AND ME BOTH.
YOU'RE JUST GONNA LET 'EM BOTH WALK OUTTA HERE?
I DON'T SEE *YOU* DOING ANYTHING!
WHAT'S WITH YOU TODAY, VELM? EVERY TIME I SAY SOMETHIN'-- YOU BITE MY HEAD OFF!
THEN MAYBE YOU SHOULDN'T TALK.
AS FOR YOU, SCOOBY--
--I WANT YOU BACK IN THE EXAMINATION ROOM ASAP.
WHY?
WE NEED TO ASCERTAIN JUST HOW LONG THIS LEAP IN INTELLIGENCE WILL LAST.
YOU... YOU THINK I MIGHT REVERT?
RUH-ROH.
WE WON'T KNOW TILL I RUN MORE TESTS.
WANT ME T'COME ALONG?
I NEED TO FOCUS ON MY WORK, NORVILLE--
--AND I CAN'T HAVE YOU DISTRACTING ME.

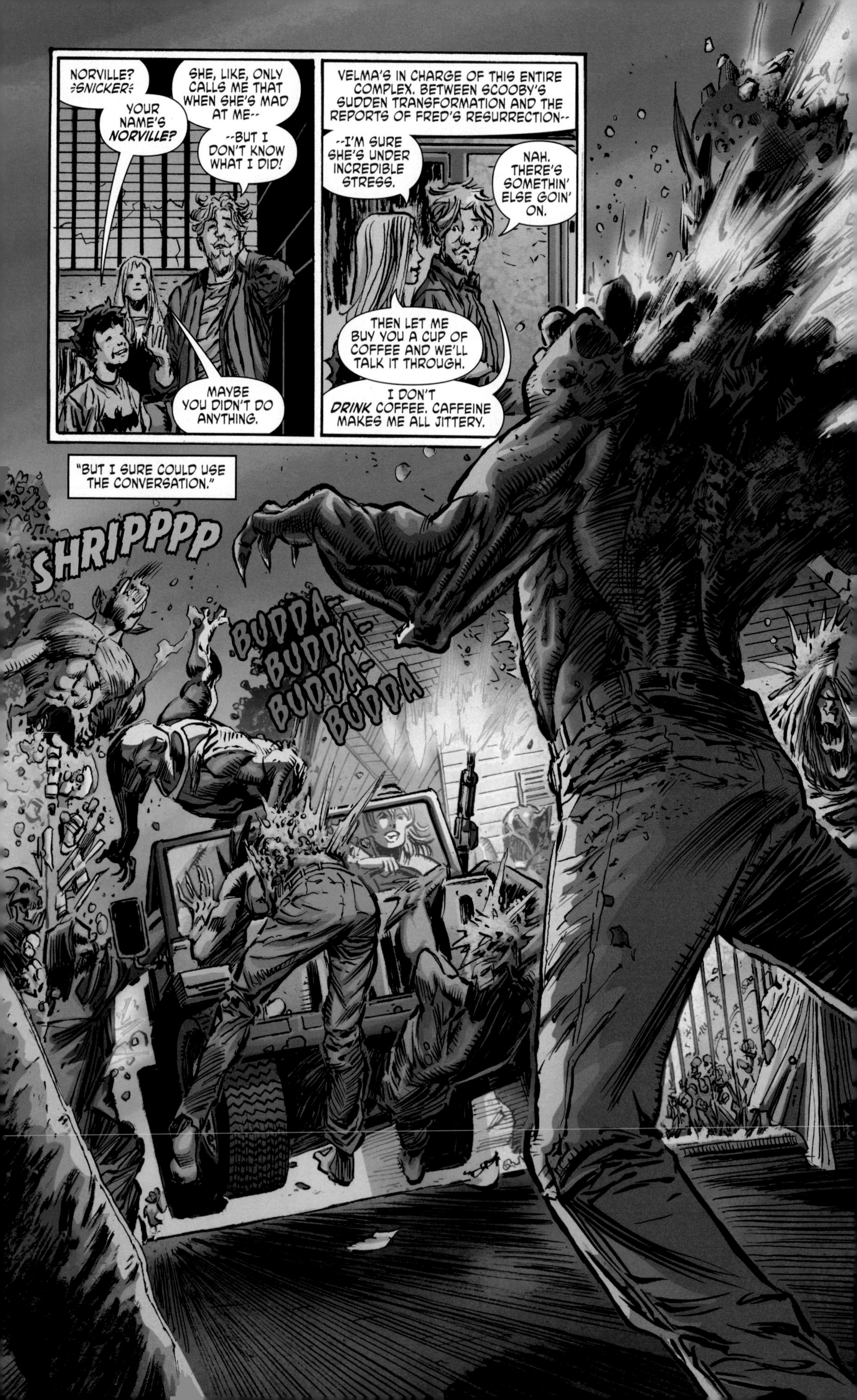
NORVILLE? ≈SNICKER≈
YOUR NAME'S NORVILLE?
SHE, LIKE, ONLY CALLS ME THAT WHEN SHE'S MAD AT ME--
--BUT I DON'T KNOW WHAT I DID!
MAYBE YOU DIDN'T DO ANYTHING.
VELMA'S IN CHARGE OF THIS ENTIRE COMPLEX. BETWEEN SCOOBY'S SUDDEN TRANSFORMATION AND THE REPORTS OF FRED'S RESURRECTION--
--I'M SURE SHE'S UNDER INCREDIBLE STRESS.
NAH. THERE'S SOMETHIN' ELSE GOIN' ON.
THEN LET ME BUY YOU A CUP OF COFFEE AND WE'LL TALK IT THROUGH.
I DON'T DRINK COFFEE. CAFFEINE MAKES ME ALL JITTERY.
"BUT I SURE COULD USE THE CONVERSATION."
SHRIPPPP
BUDDA-BUDDA-BUDDA-BUDDA

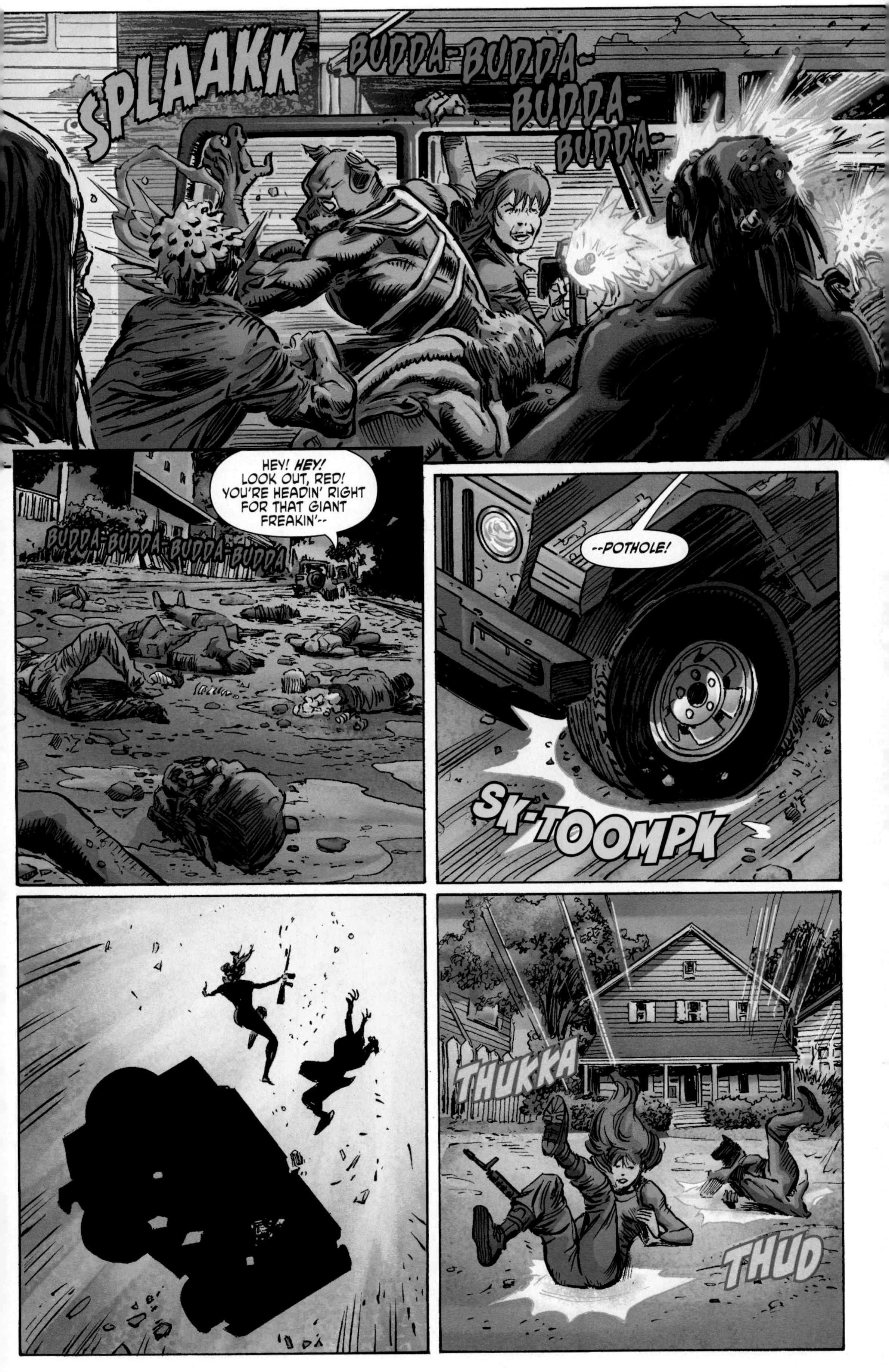
SPLAAKK
BUDDA-BUDDA-BUDDA-BUDDA-
BUDDA-BUDDA-BUDDA-BUDDA
HEY! HEY! LOOK OUT, RED! YOU'RE HEADIN' RIGHT FOR THAT GIANT FREAKIN'--
--POTHOLE!
SK-TOOMPK
THUKKA
THUD

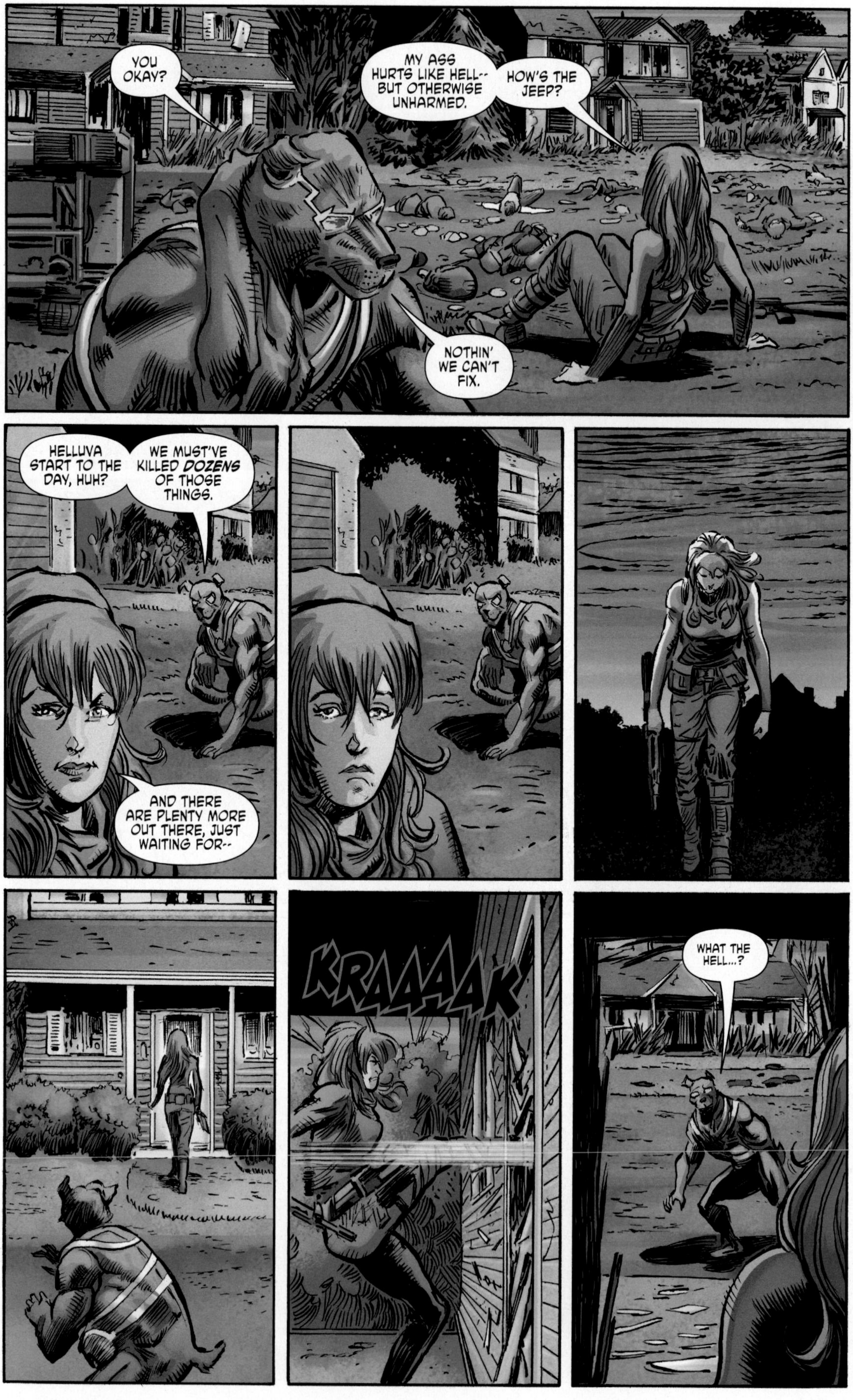
YOU OKAY?
MY ASS HURTS LIKE HELL-- BUT OTHERWISE UNHARMED.
HOW'S THE JEEP?
NOTHIN' WE CAN'T FIX.
HELLUVA START TO THE DAY, HUH?
WE MUST'VE KILLED DOZENS OF THOSE THINGS.
AND THERE ARE PLENTY MORE OUT THERE, JUST WAITING FOR--
KRAAAK
WHAT THE HELL...?

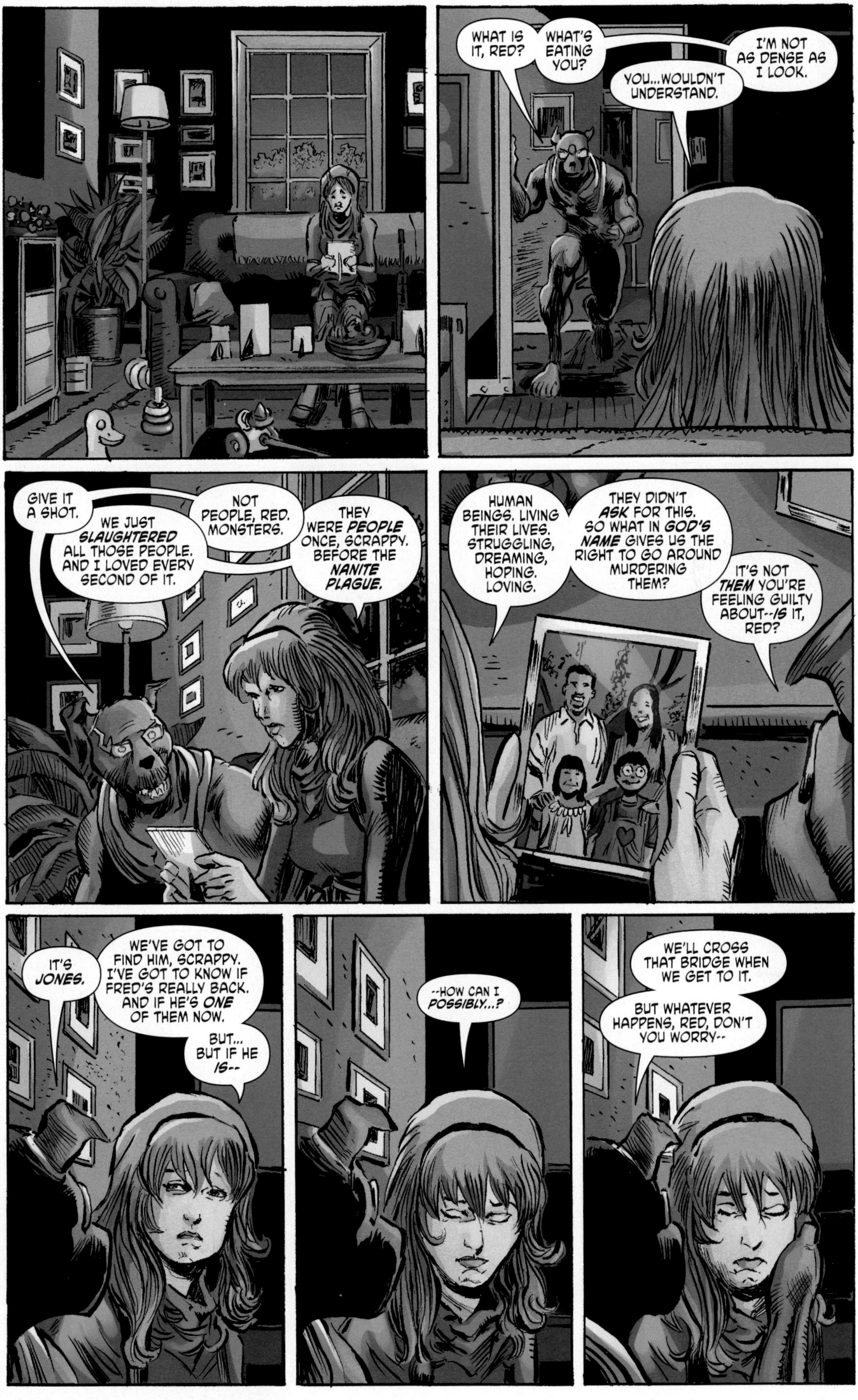
WHAT IS IT, RED?
WHAT'S EATING YOU?
I'M NOT AS DENSE AS I LOOK.
YOU...WOULDN'T UNDERSTAND.
GIVE IT A SHOT.
WE JUST SLAUGHTERED ALL THOSE PEOPLE. AND I LOVED EVERY SECOND OF IT.
NOT PEOPLE, RED. MONSTERS.
THEY WERE PEOPLE ONCE, SCRAPPY. BEFORE THE NANITE PLAGUE.
HUMAN BEINGS. LIVING THEIR LIVES. STRUGGLING, DREAMING, HOPING. LOVING.
THEY DIDN'T ASK FOR THIS. SO WHAT IN GOD'S NAME GIVES US THE RIGHT TO GO AROUND MURDERING THEM?
IT'S NOT THEM YOU'RE FEELING GUILTY ABOUT--IS IT, RED?
IT'S JONES.
WE'VE GOT TO FIND HIM, SCRAPPY. I'VE GOT TO KNOW IF FRED'S REALLY BACK. AND IF HE'S ONE OF THEM NOW.
BUT... BUT IF HE IS--
--HOW CAN I POSSIBLY...?
WE'LL CROSS THAT BRIDGE WHEN WE GET TO IT.
BUT WHATEVER HAPPENS, RED, DON'T YOU WORRY--

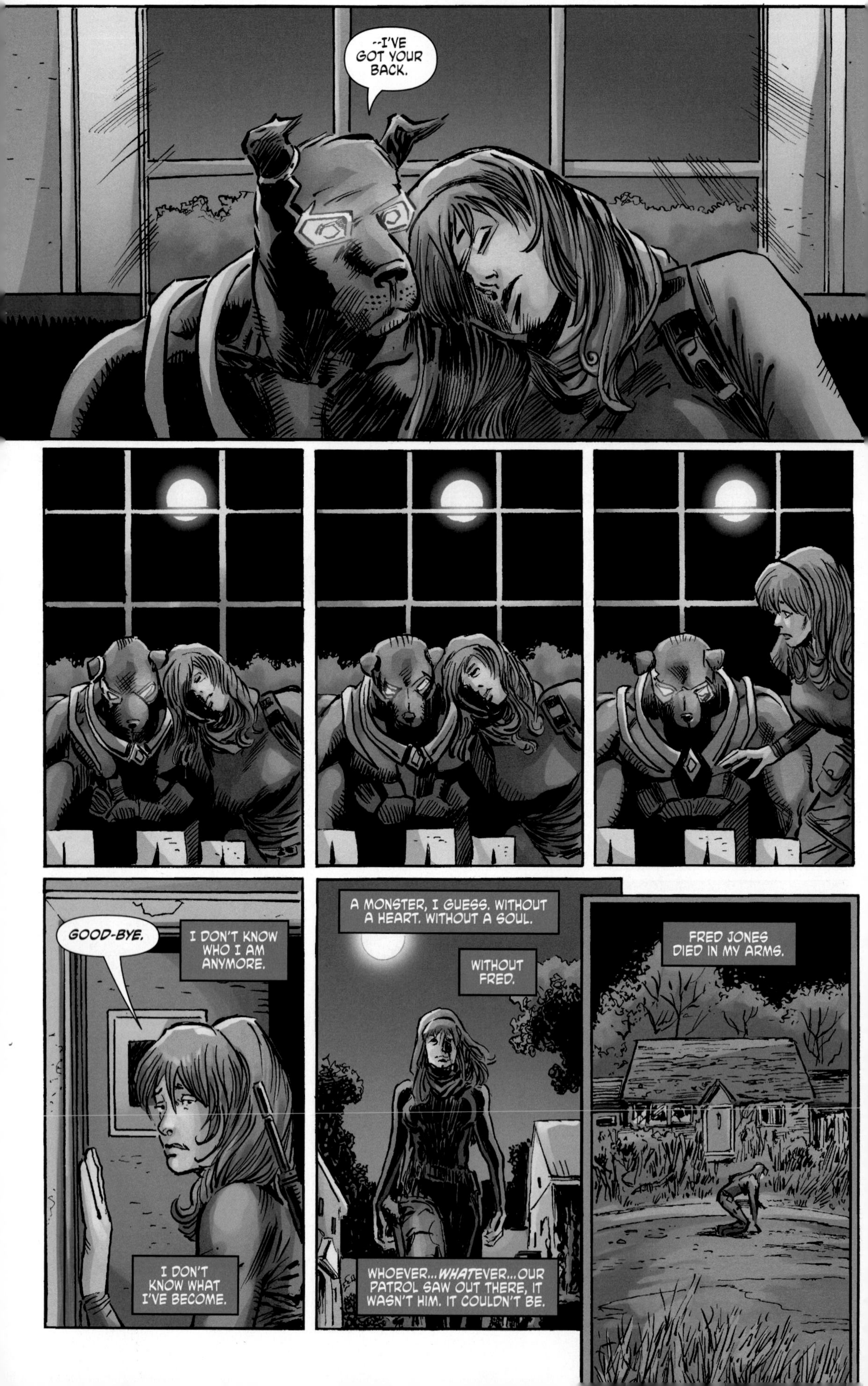
--I'VE GOT YOUR BACK.
GOOD-BYE.
I DON'T KNOW WHO I AM ANYMORE.
I DON'T KNOW WHAT I'VE BECOME.
A MONSTER, I GUESS. WITHOUT A HEART. WITHOUT A SOUL.
WITHOUT FRED.
WHOEVER...WHATEVER...OUR PATROL SAW OUT THERE, IT WASN'T HIM. IT COULDN'T BE.
FRED JONES DIED IN MY ARMS.

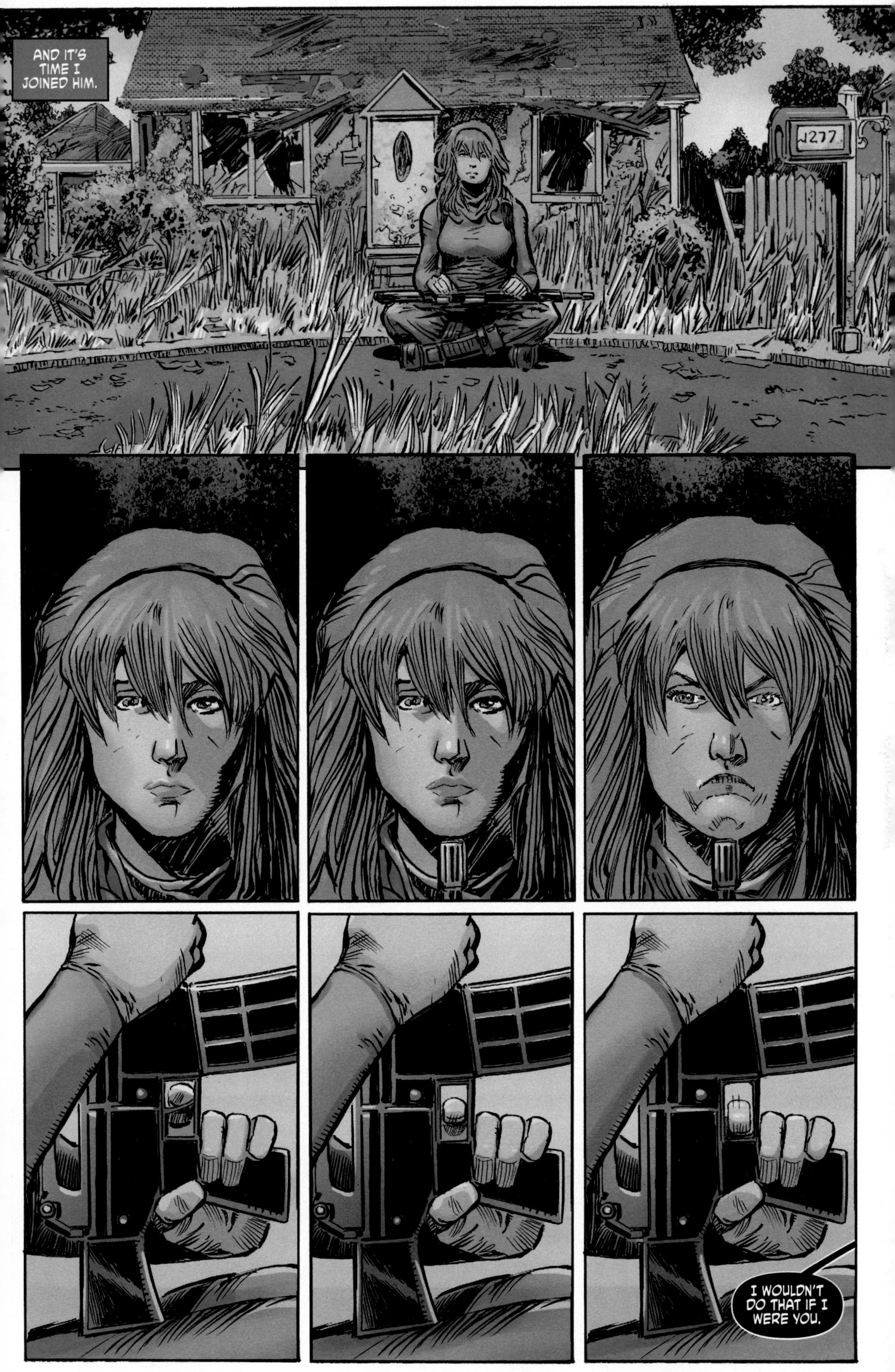
AND IT'S TIME I JOINED HIM.
1277
I WOULDN'T DO THAT IF I WERE YOU.

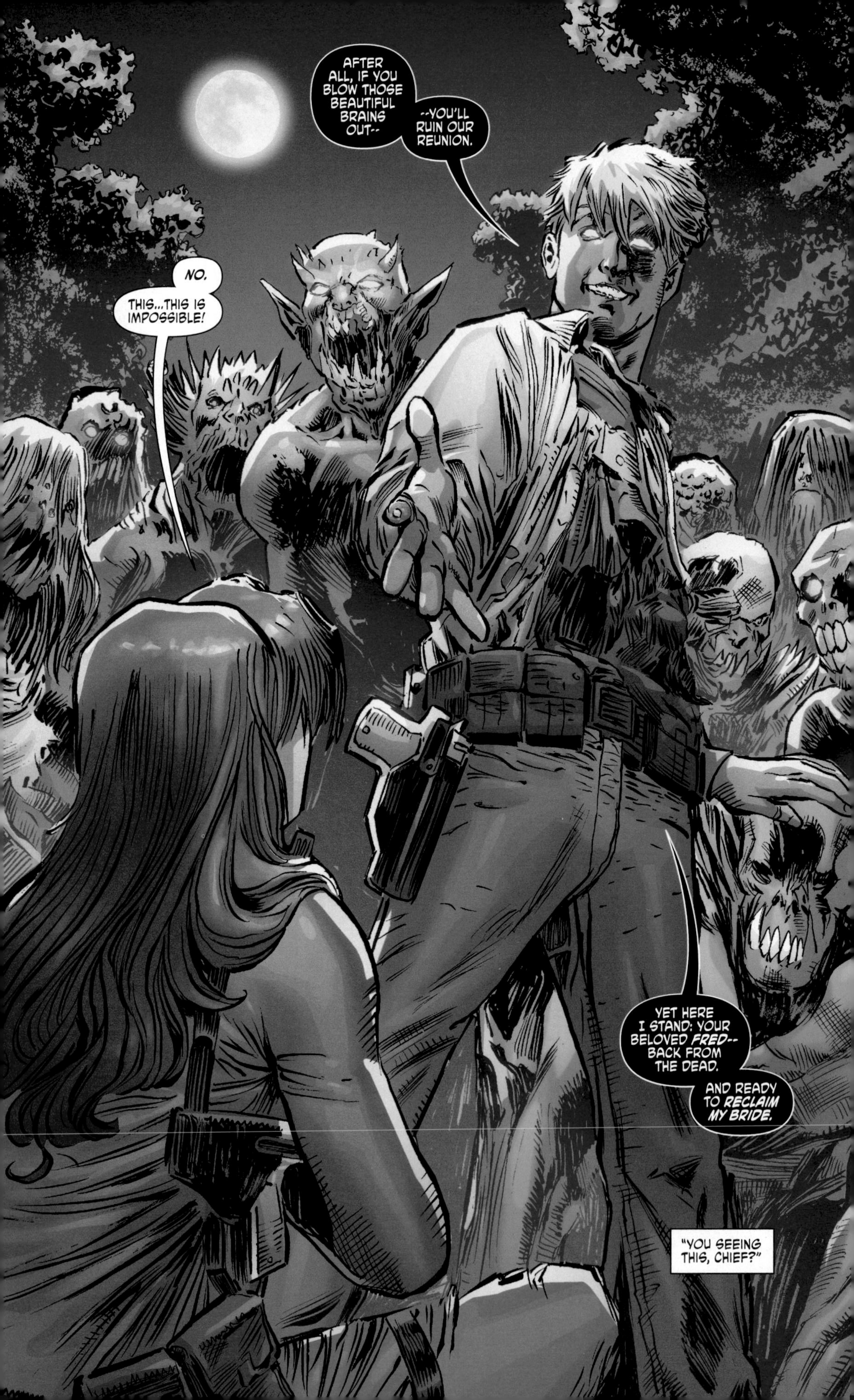
AFTER ALL, IF YOU BLOW THOSE BEAUTIFUL BRAINS OUT--
--YOU'LL RUIN OUR REUNION.
NO.
THIS...THIS IS IMPOSSIBLE!
YET HERE I STAND: YOUR BELOVED FRED-- BACK FROM THE DEAD.
AND READY TO RECLAIM MY BRIDE.
"YOU SEEING THIS, CHIEF?"

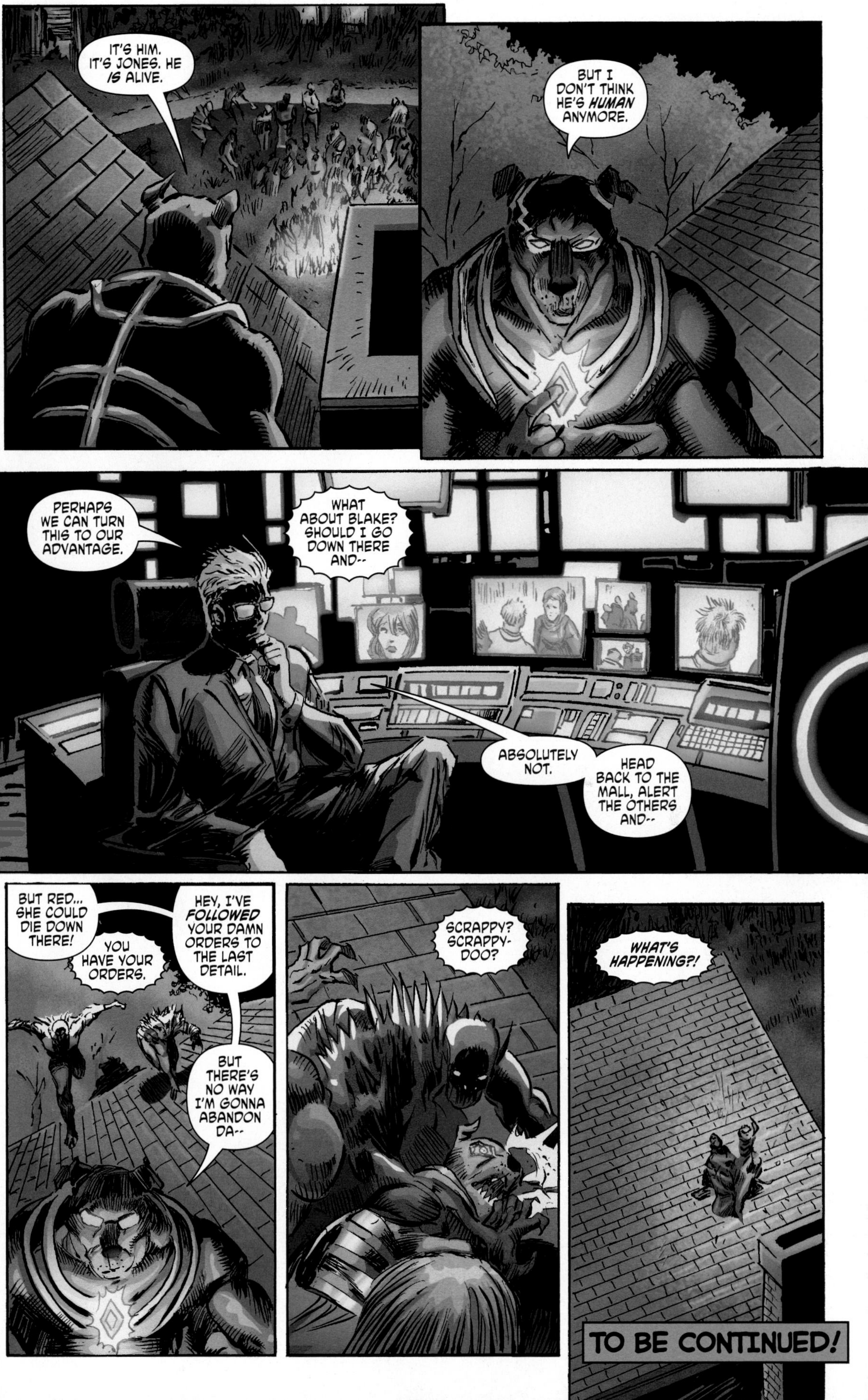
IT'S HIM. IT'S JONES. HE *IS* ALIVE.
BUT I DON'T THINK HE'S *HUMAN* ANYMORE.
PERHAPS WE CAN TURN THIS TO OUR ADVANTAGE.
WHAT ABOUT BLAKE? SHOULD I GO DOWN THERE AND--
ABSOLUTELY NOT.
HEAD BACK TO THE MALL, ALERT THE OTHERS AND--
BUT RED... SHE COULD DIE DOWN THERE!
YOU HAVE YOUR ORDERS.
HEY, I'VE *FOLLOWED* YOUR DAMN ORDERS TO THE LAST DETAIL.
BUT THERE'S NO WAY I'M GONNA ABANDON DA--
SCRAPPY? SCRAPPY-DOO?
WHAT'S HAPPENING?!
TO BE CONTINUED!

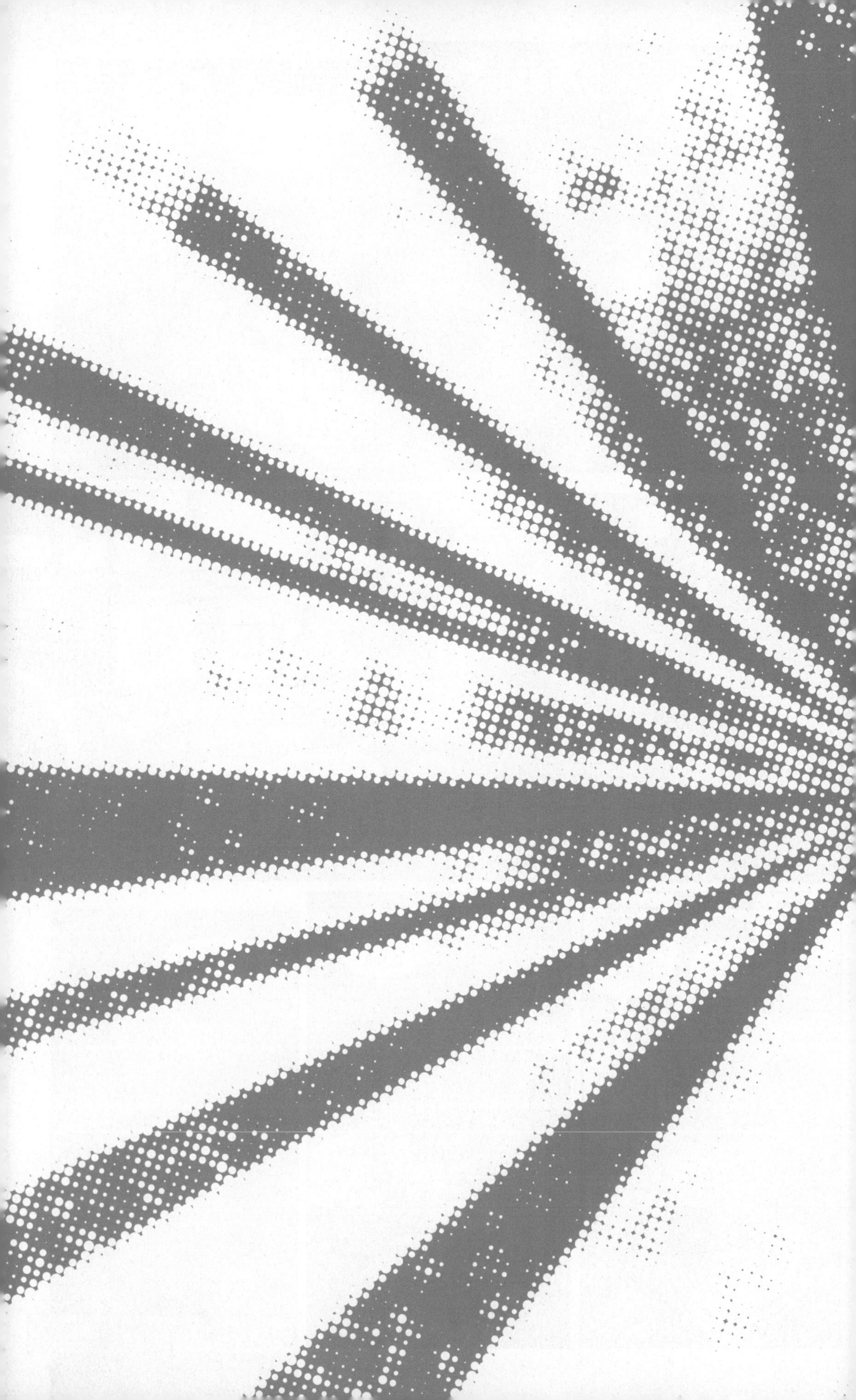

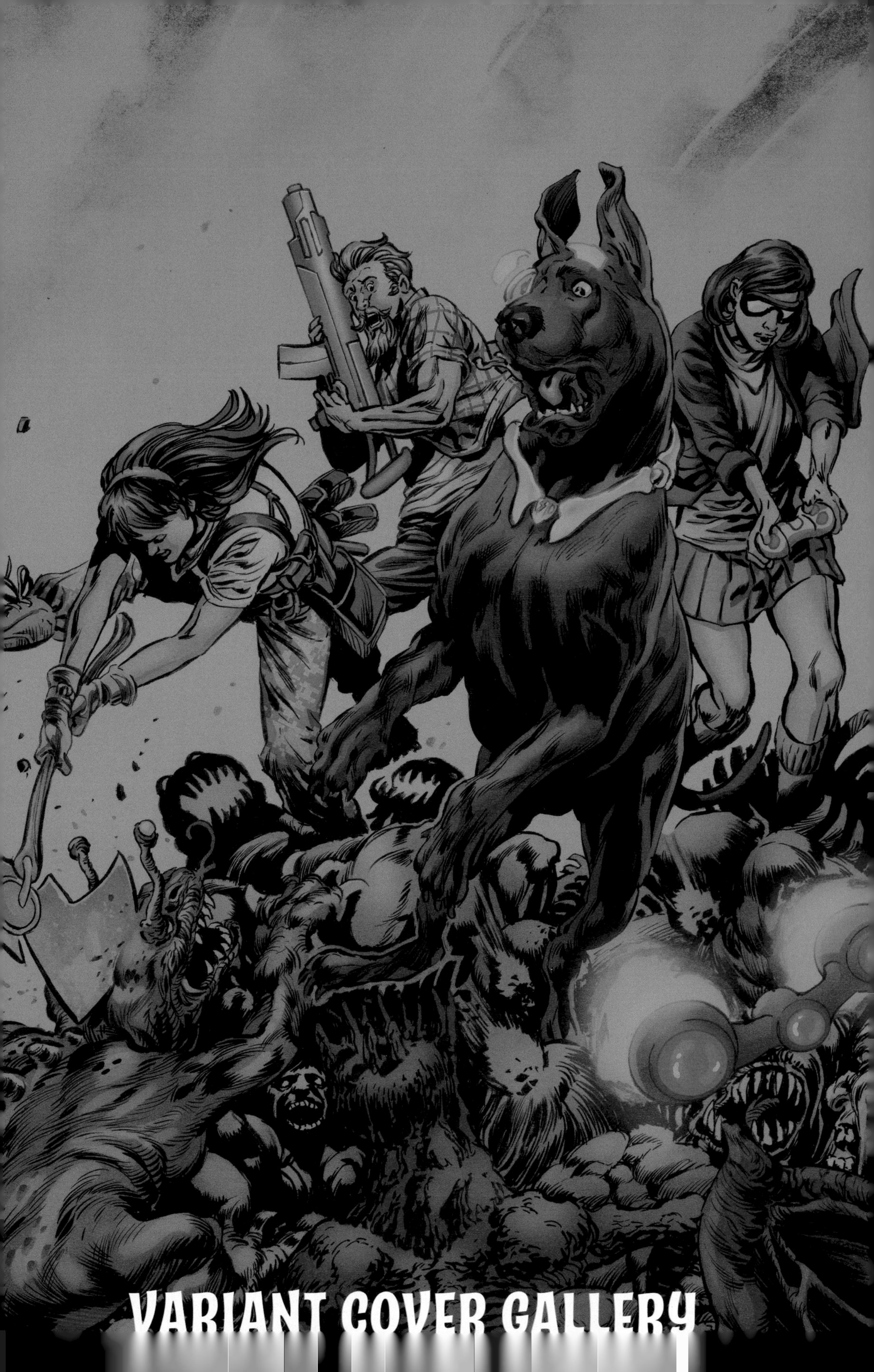

VARIANT COVER GALLERY

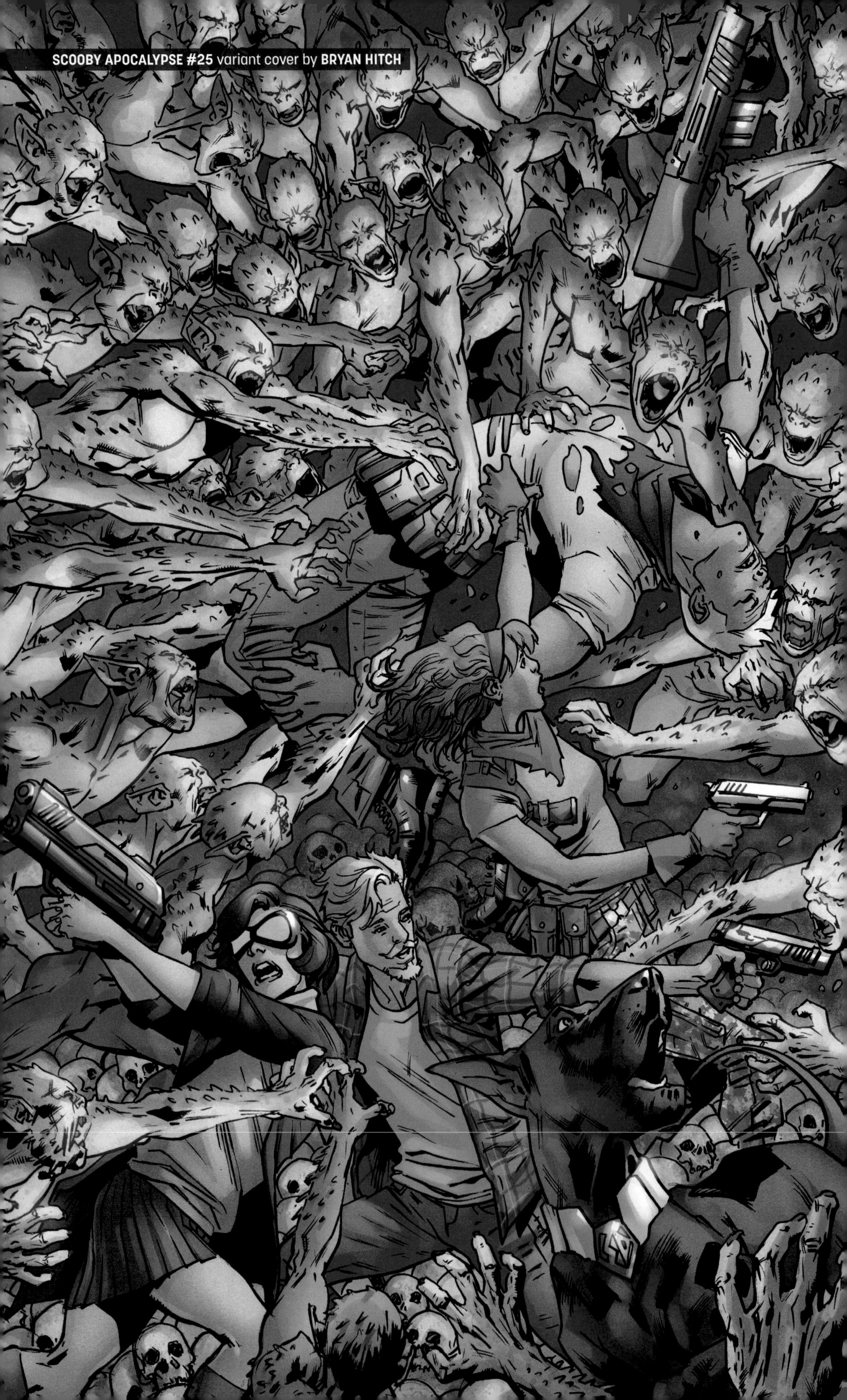

SCOOBY APOCALYPSE #25 variant cover by **BRYAN HITCH**

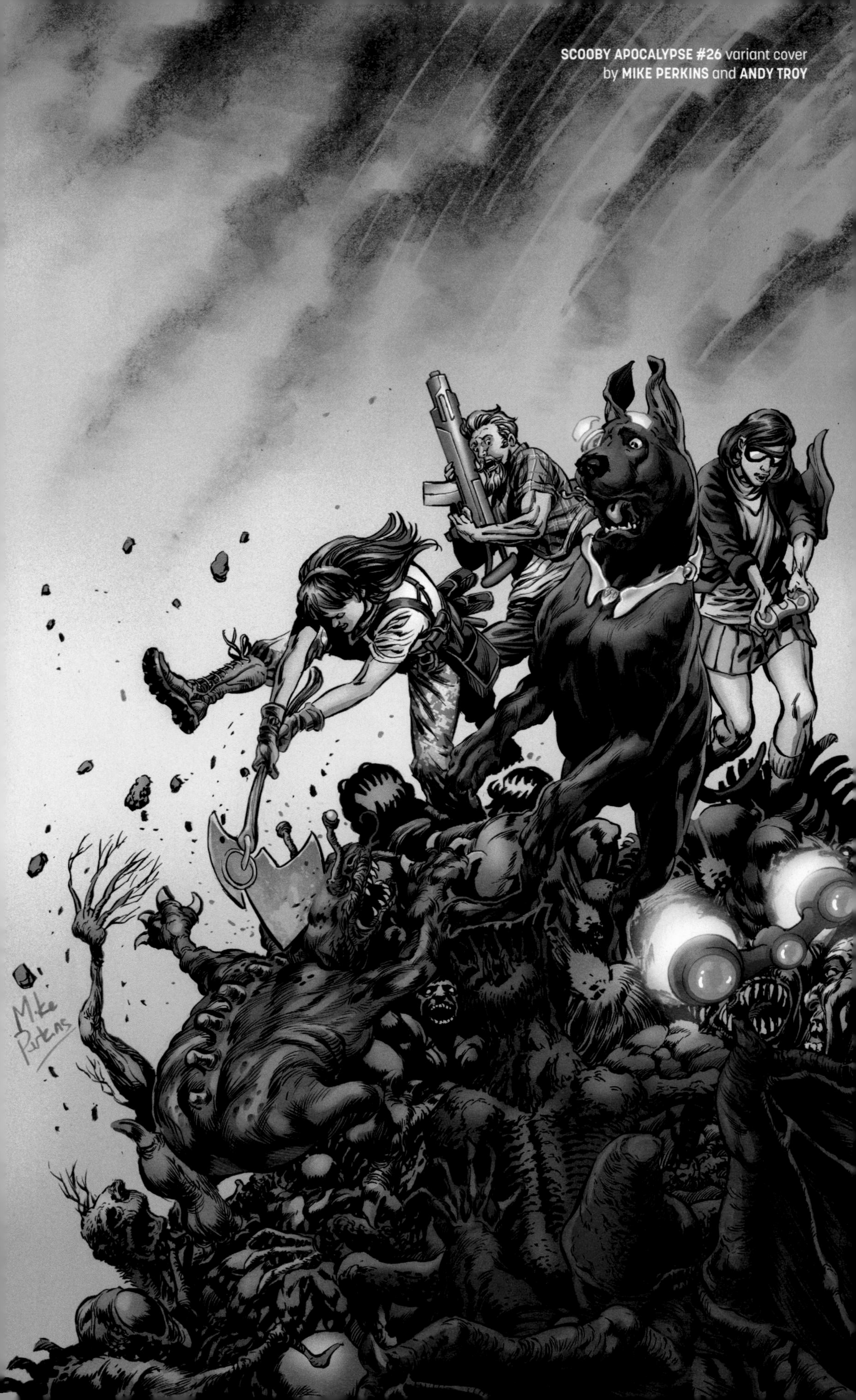
Mike Perkins

SCOOBY APOCALYPSE #26 variant cover
by **MIKE PERKINS** and **ANDY TROY**

SCOOBY APOCALYPSE #27 variant cover by JONBOY MEYERS

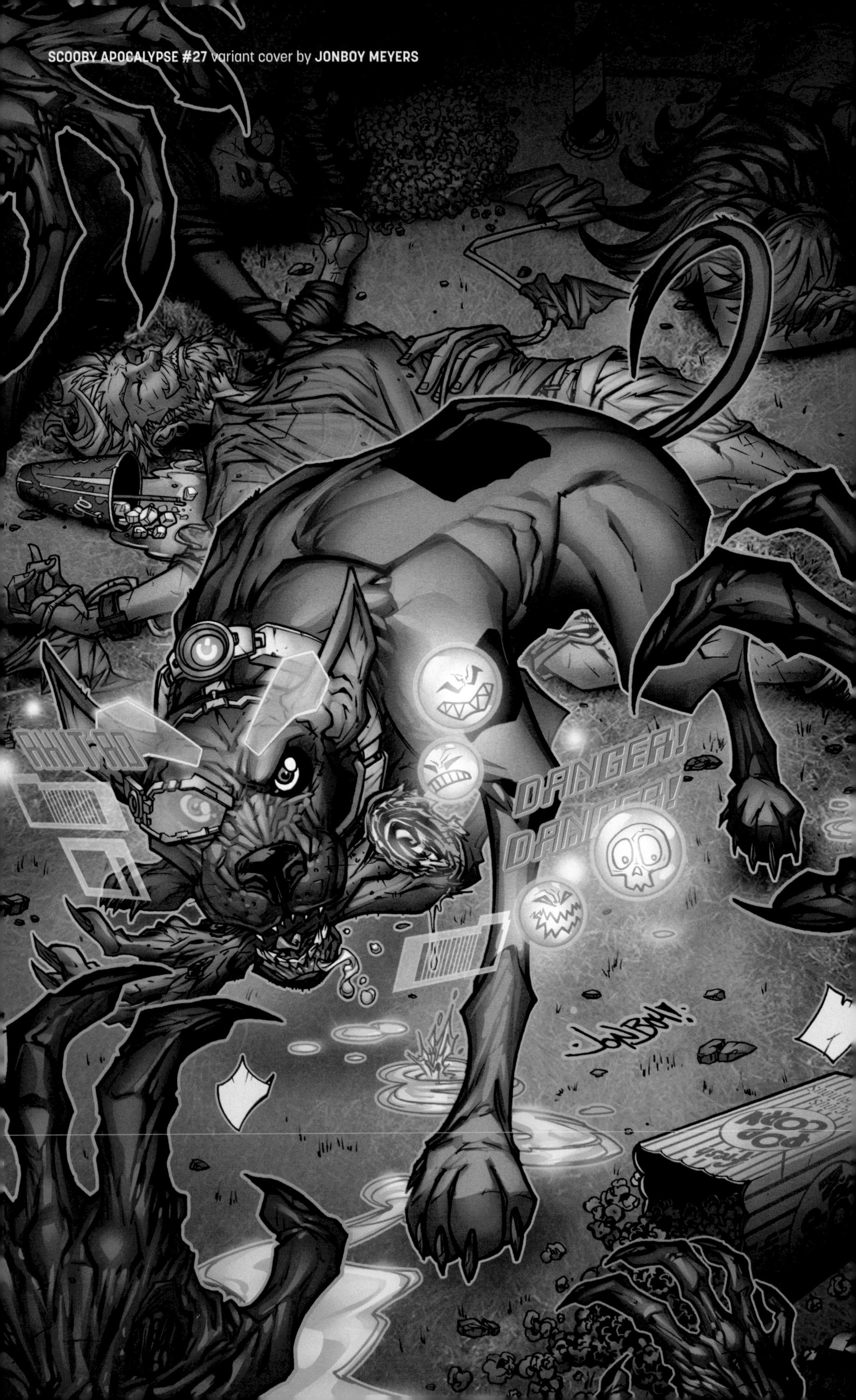
DANGER!
DANGER!

SCOOBY APOCALYPSE #28 variant cover by YASMINE PUTRI

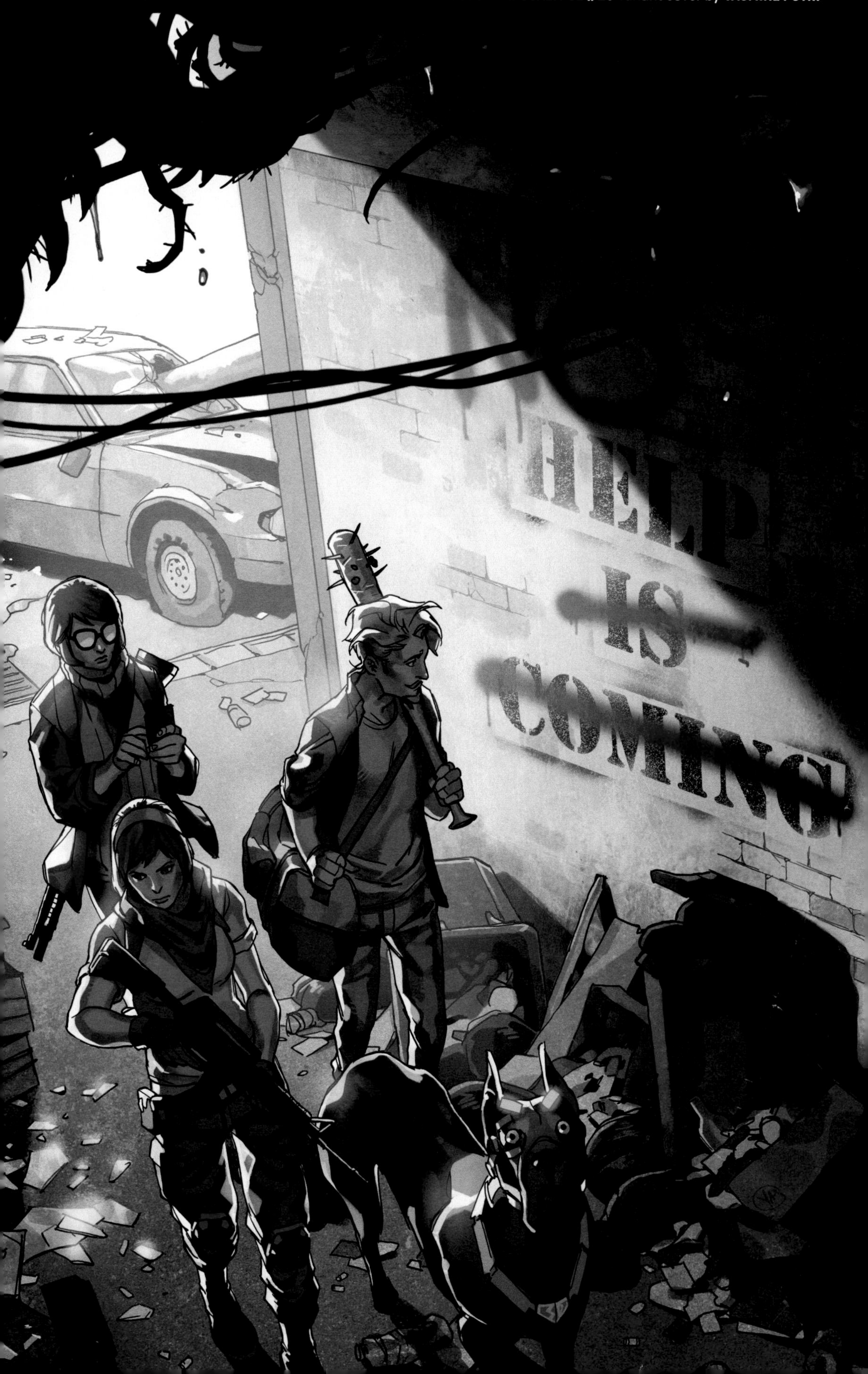
HELP
IS
COMING

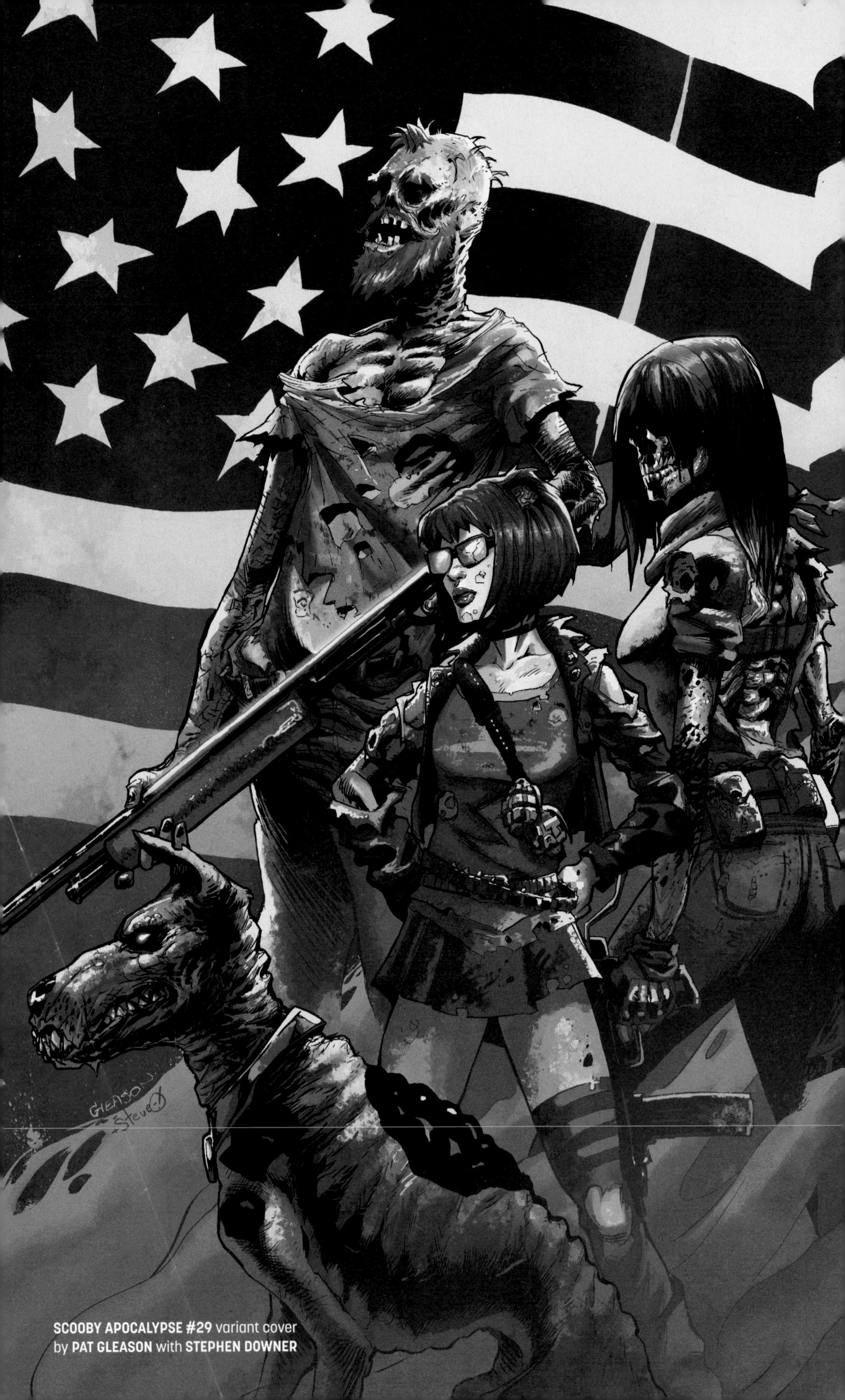

SCOOBY APOCALYPSE #29 variant cover
by **PAT GLEASON** with **STEPHEN DOWNER**

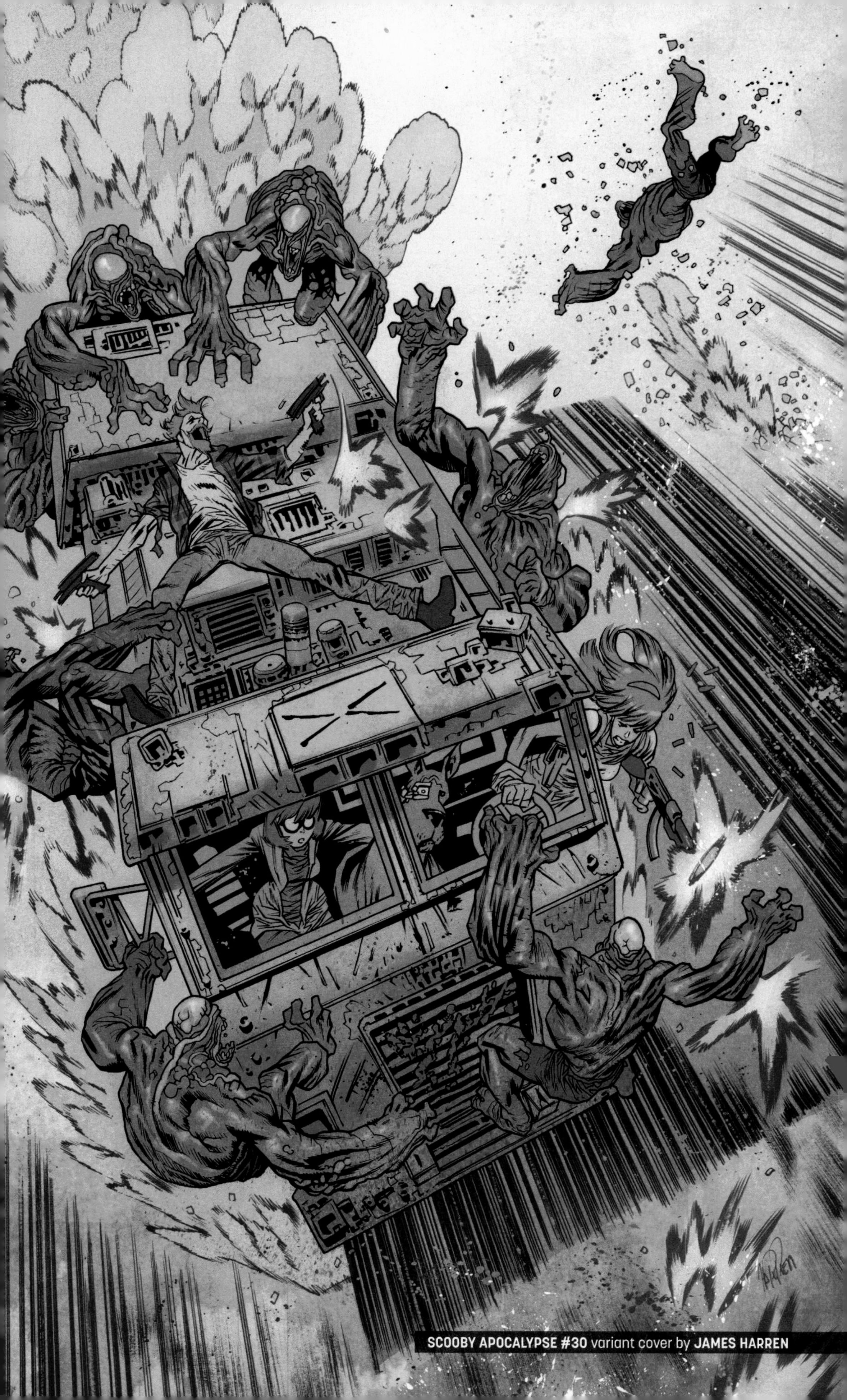

SCOOBY APOCALYPSE #30 variant cover by JAMES HARREN

Pinup by **JUAN FERREYRA**

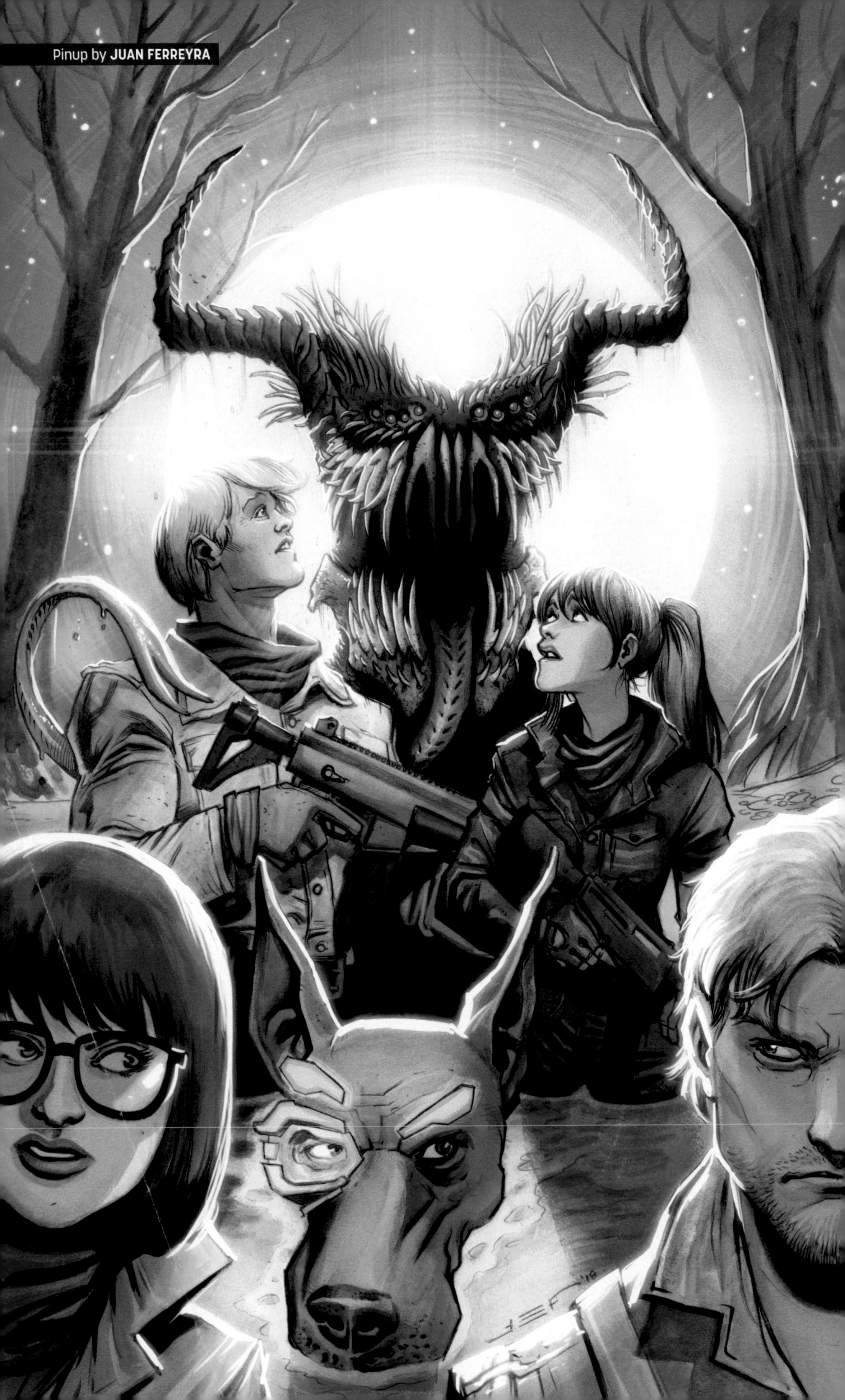

Pinup by **KAARE ANDREWS**

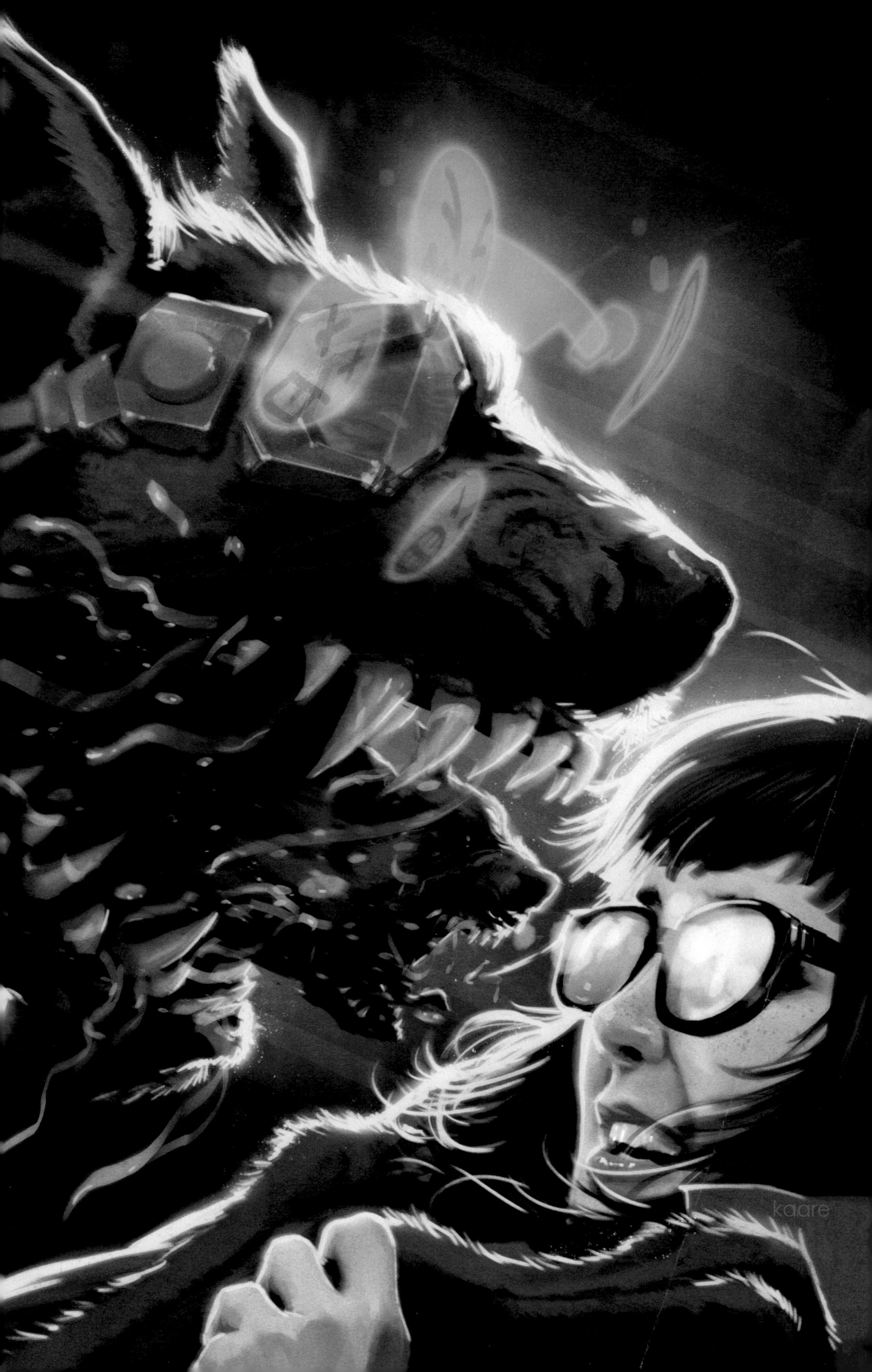
kaare

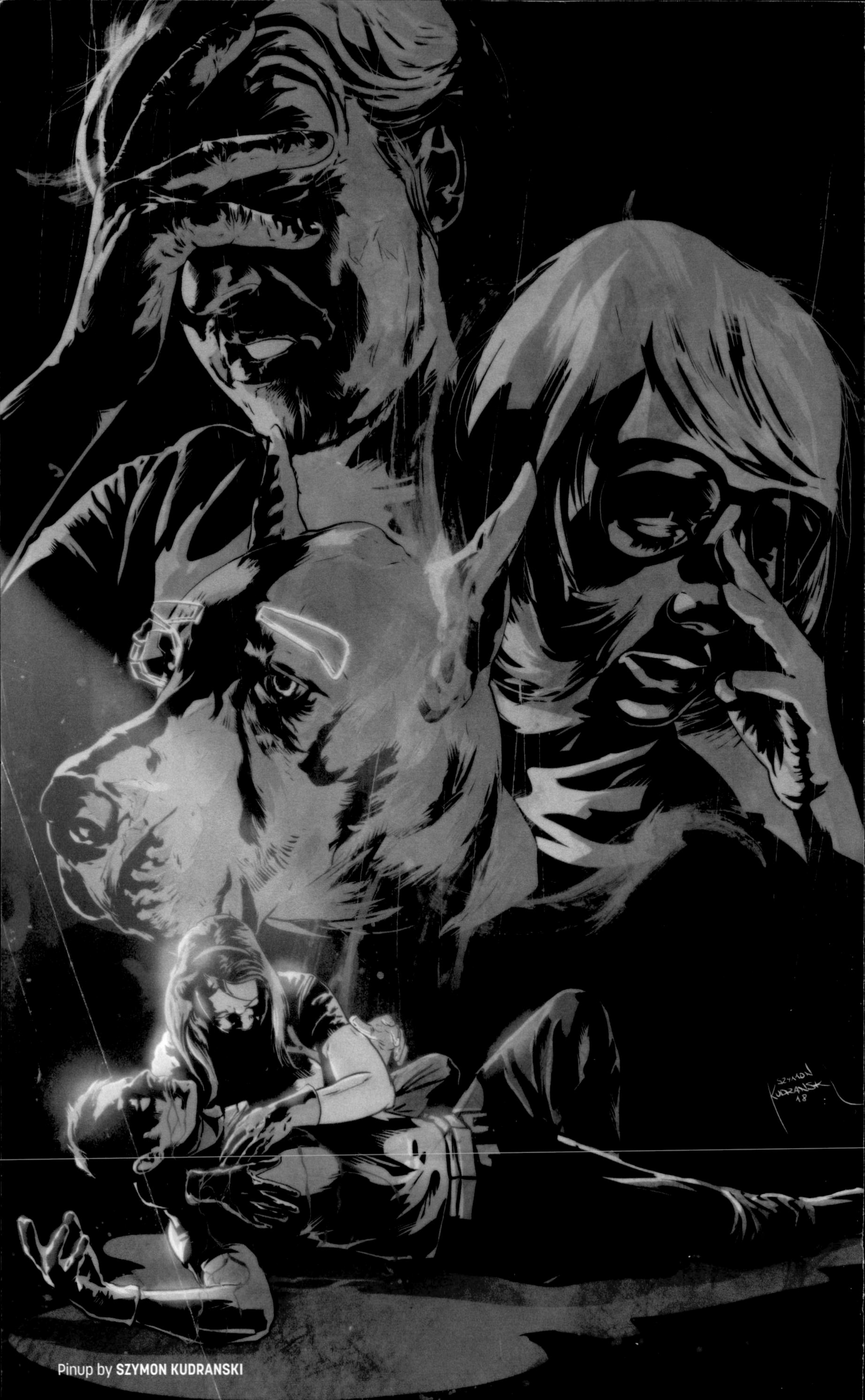
SZYMON KUDRANSKI 18
Pinup by **SZYMON KUDRANSKI**

SCOOBY APOCALYPSE #27 page 8
pencils by **PAT OLLIFFE**, inks by **SCOTT HANNA**

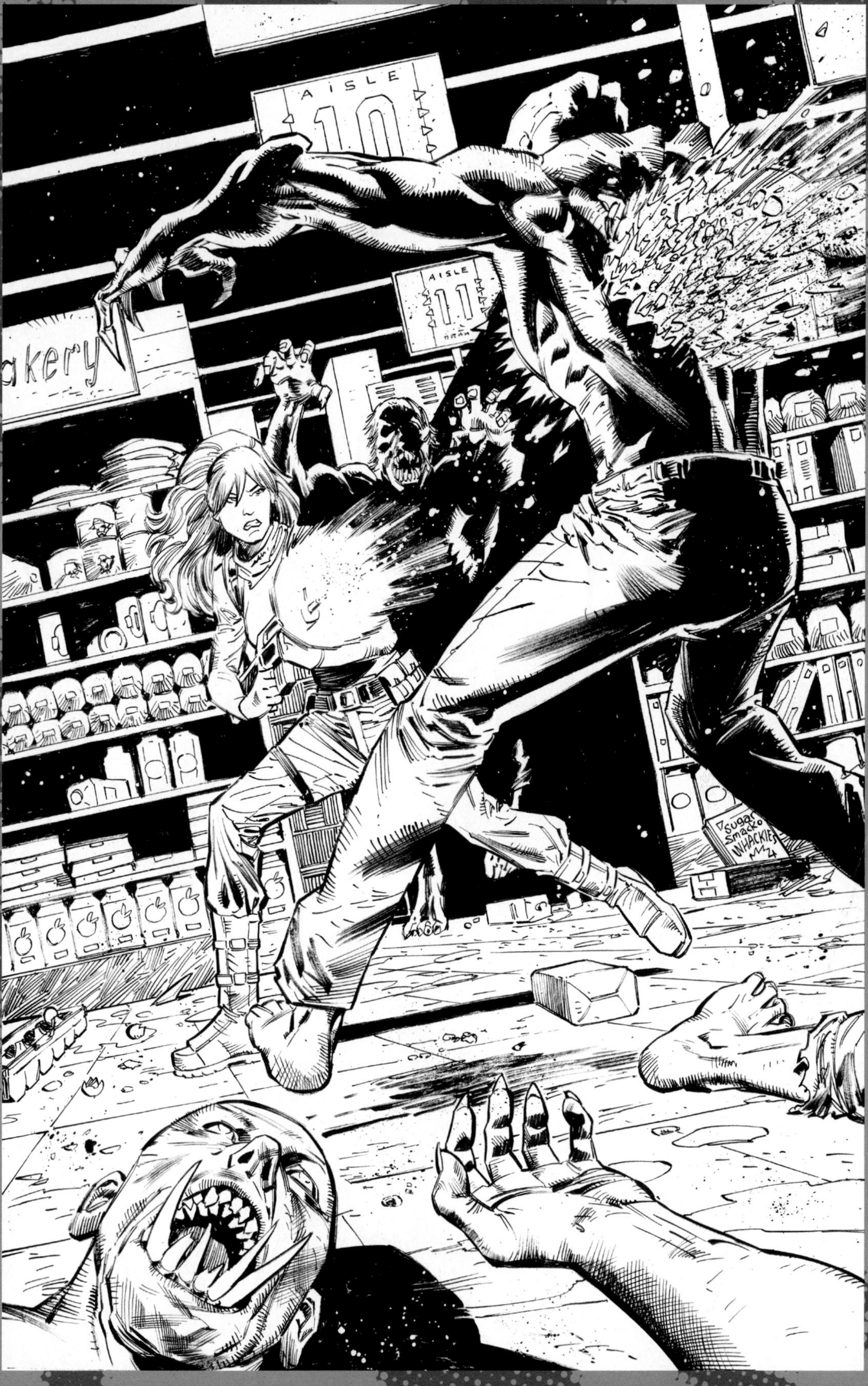
AISLE
10
AISLE
11
akery

SCOOBY APOCALYPSE #30 page 16
pencils by **PAT OLLIFFE**, inks by **TOM PALMER**

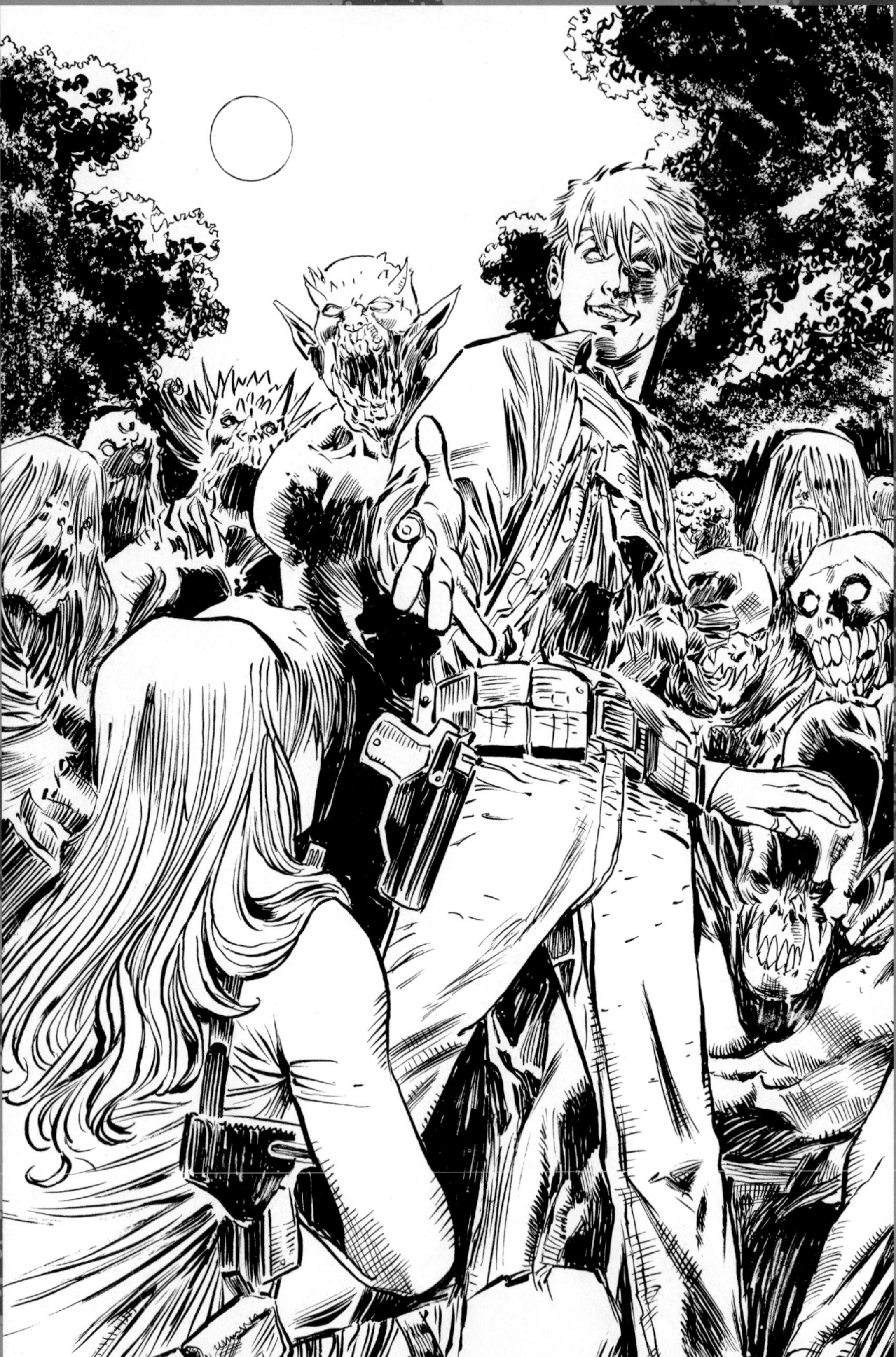